The Power of Words

 ———————————————

Documents in American History

VOLUME I: TO 1877

T. H. Breen, EDITOR

Longman

New York   San Francisco   Boston
London   Toronto   Sydney   Tokyo   Singapore   Madrid
Mexico City   Munich   Paris   Cape Town   Hong Kong   Montreal

Executive Editor: Bruce D. Borland
Developmental Editor: Jeffrey W. Brown
Project Coordination and Text Design: Ruttle, Shaw & Wetherill, Inc.
Cover Designer: Paul Lacy
Cover Illustration: *Mrs. Nancy Lawson*, William Matthew Prior, Shelburne Museum,
Shelburne Vermont; photograph by Ken Burris
Photo Researcher: Leslie Coopersmith
Electronic Production Manager: Angel Gonzalez, Jr.
Manufacturing Manager: Willie Lane
Electronic Page Makeup: Ruttle, Shaw & Wetherill, Inc.
Printer and Binder: R.R. Donnelley & Sons Company
Cover Printer: The Lehigh Press, Inc.

The Power of Words: Documents in American History, Volume I: to 1877

Library of Congress Cataloging-in-Publication Data

The power of words: documents in American history / T. H. Breen,
    editor.
        p.   cm.
    ISBN 0-06-501112-0 (v. 1). — ISBN 0-06-501113-9 (v. 2)
      1. United States—History—Sources.   I. Breen, T. H.
    E173.P83   1996   95-18487
    973—dc20   CIP

98 9 8 7 6 5

Contents

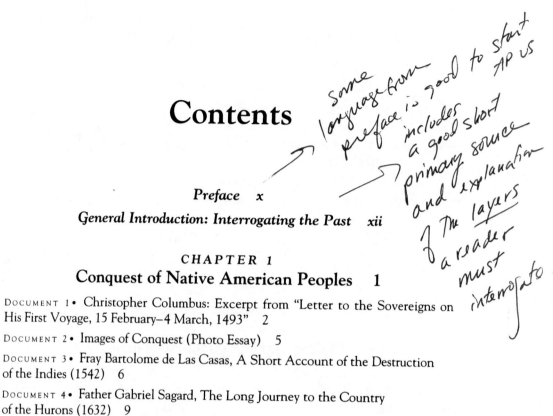

some language from preface is good to start AP US

includes a good short primary source and explanation

The layers a reader must interrogate

CHAPTER 6
Revolution   98

CHAPTER 7
Republican Experiment 126

CHAPTER 8
Politics in the New Nation 153

CHAPTER 9
The Jeffersonian State 182

CHAPTER 10
Early Industrial Transformations   207

CHAPTER 11
Jacksonian Democracy   228

CHAPTER 12
Reforming Society   248

CHAPTER 13
Sectional Crisis   269

CHAPTER 14
The Civil War   291

CHAPTER 15
Reconstruction   309

Preface

The Power of Words is a collection of documents arranged in roughly chronological order from the Conquest of the Americas to the present. The work was designed to supplement major survey texts in American history, but could also stand alone. It invites students and teachers to employ a wide range of primary materials in developing their own interpretations of the past. The selection of documents attempts to strike a balance between social and political history. Each of the thirty units follows a clear pedagogical plan, which moves from the general to the specific, from the political to the personal, and from the public sphere to the private. The presentation of distinct, often conflicting perspectives allows readers to reconstruct the variety of ways that ordinary men and women explained to themselves, their families, and local communities events, movements, and policies over which they had no effective control.

Sections open with an overview of a period. The first document might be a traveler's journal or a major presidential address. These statements set an agenda; they raise issues of broad significance. The reader is then asked to consider the implementation of government or corporate policies. And here the student sees how institutional decisions affect ordinary men and women. The general policies do not work as planned: They create new problems; they spark resistance. The collection captures different voices as they attempt to carve out interpretive space. The various units include the declarations of powerful leaders—the captains of industry or the heads of government agencies, for example. These may explain, justify, or rationalize decisions in which they had a direct interest. The collection also includes the critics—men and women often classified as intellectuals who asked hard questions about subjects such as civil rights, Indian removals, industrial working conditions, and military adventures. The goal is to show the student that the American past is not a story of consensus. Even events that mobilized huge popular support—the American Revolution and World War II, for instance—generated doubts and expectations, opened doors for some, and frustrated others.

The Power of Words presents more than elite explanations of change over time. It also gives ordinary men and women a chance to speak. Each unit shows such people accommodating themselves to changing external conditions, making sense of threats and opportunities, interpreting institutional demands, and resisting what they perceived as unwarranted intrusions into their lives. In the end, the editor wanted to provide the student reader with full appreciation of conflict as well as cooperation and of the pervasive articulation, however subtle, of class, race, and gender as these categories helped mediate larger shaping forces. The collection reconstructs a long, often-disturbing conversation that Americans have had with themselves about the character of the good society. It is a story with winners and losers who, whatever their experiences, all understood—as we must—the power of words.

Many generous and thoughtful people have shaped my understanding of this project. My debt to my colleague and friend James Oakes is great. So too is my obligation to four splendid students who have helped me at every stage of the enterprise. Without David Gellman, Andrew Podolsky, Steven Reich, and Bradley Schrager, the book would have been something less than it is. I thank Bruce Borland for his continuing faith in this work. Betty Slack, Jeffrey Brown, and Jessica Bayne offered creative suggestions, and, as usual, Susan Breen was my most demanding critic. The volumes are dedicated to Russell Maylone, head of Special Collections at the Northwestern University Library. He not only preserves historical documents, but also shares his love and excitement for rare manuscripts with students, who are transformed by the experience.

T. H. Breen

General Introduction: Interrogating the Past

However dramatically technology has transformed the character of modern society, we still derive pleasure and satisfaction from studying the past. College students continue to attend history courses in large numbers. And well they should. Learning about the past helps us to understand how we got to be the way we are. Yet even enthusiastic students face a problem, of which they may only be dimly aware. They seldom have a chance actually to "do history." They usually read books and articles produced by historians who have researched an event and who have brought order to an unruly assemblage of facts. Such people interpret the past for us; they tell us what the past means. If they write clearly and smoothly, we enjoy their narratives, rarely pausing to consider the implications of having an historian stand between us and the past.

As Alice explained to the White Rabbit, the problems gets curiousier and curiouser. Consider, for example, how we acquire a rudimentary knowledge of other academic subjects. Chemistry? Mathematics? Biology? We might think it odd if a college-level course in chemistry assigned only books describing great chemists at work. After a while, someone might inquire about labs, about opportunities to conduct experiments on one's own. We would expect to "do" chemistry, discovering for ourselves why materials react in certain ways. Much the same thing could be said for other academic fields. Mathematicians teach us to solve real problems. Economists show us how to interpret statistical data or manipulate models.

This is not how history is usually taught. College lectures tell us stories about the past or assign books that interpret the flow of events. The facts have already been organized, the meanings highlighted. What is missing is a full appreciation of the research behind these accounts. In this sense, students find themselves studying history without ever learning how to do history. Such an approach puts them at a disadvantage. How do they know whether a narrative that sounds reasonable has, in fact, real merit? They would like to know a little more about the process of "doing history," about interpreting documents, and about the character of the records themselves. Indeed, they might inquire what it means for an historian to interpret the past.

The process starts with words. Ordinary people have always generated accounts of their lives. Government and corporate leaders recorded decisions—often in formal bureaucratic language—and then, if the decisions did not work out quite as they planned, they put forth justifications, defenses, and rationalizations. Over the centuries, foreign visitors have provided insights into the assumptions of American culture. We encounter these words in archives or in collections of printed documents. These are the primary sources of history, the foundation of interpretation. And when we confront the voices of the past, we generally pay close attention to the stories that they have to tell. Depending on the character of the materials, we find the tales from the archives bizarre, interesting, or unsettling. Documents beguile us with claims that their makers have borne witness to a world that we have lost. They seem to provide a direct link between us and a distant past.

What is so easy to forget is that documents themselves—even the most poignant accounts—have a history. Like other artifacts, they are human constructions. Writers prepared them for a purpose, often with a specific audience in mind. Although they may purport to tell a complete story, they offer only perspectives, points of views, and pieces of a larger past. Even their preservation raises troubling questions, for not all documents have had an equal chance of surviving. It is more likely that archives contain the records of powerful institutions and privileged families than of marginal men and women.

The history of one Early American document helps us better to understand these complex interpretive issues. It comes from the earliest period of contact between Native American peoples and European colonists. During the summer of 1642, a Narragansett leader addressed a body of Montauks, living on the eastern end of Long Island. Miantonomi, the Narragansett sachem, wanted the Montauks to join him in resisting whites who had settled Connecticut and Massachusetts Bay.

> . . . for so we are all Indians as the English are, and say brother to one another; so we must be one [people] as they are, otherwise we shall be gone shortly, for you know our fathers had plenty of deer and skins, our plains were full of deer, as also our woods, and of turkies [sic] and our coves full of fish and fowl. But these English having gotten our land, they with scythes cut down the grass, and with axes fell the trees; their cows and horses eat the grass, and their hogs spoil our clam banks and we shall be all starved; therefore it is best for you to do as we, for we are all the Sachems from east to west . . . and we are all resolved to fall upon them all, at one appointed day; and therefore I come to you privately first, because you can persuade the Indians and the Sachem to do what you will . . . and when you see the three fires that will be made forty days hence, in a clear night, then do as we, and the next day fall on and kill men, women, and children, but no cows, for they will serve to eat till our deer be increased again.

What do we make of Miantonomi's fervent appeal to the Indians of southern New England? It certainly rings true. We know from other sources that the settler economy transformed the ecology and, in the process, pushed the Native Americans aside. The Narragansetts seem fully justified in their fears. The speech records a critical moment in the history of the Indians of this region. The future appears bleak, but if the Montauks fail to respond to the "three fires," these desperate peoples will have no future at all.

Before accepting this moving document at face value, we should ask some hard questions. As historians, we begin the process of interrogating the past. First, we might inquire how this information came to be recorded. The Native Americans of seventeenth-century New England had no written language. The printed account of a general Indian uprising against the settlers must owe its existence to a literate European colonist who somehow gained knowledge of the plan. But common sense tells us that the writer probably did not witness the events. Considering the inflammatory content of Miantonomi's speech, the Narragansett sachem would never have allowed a colonist quietly to record the details of conspiracy.

In fact, the story of a planned insurrection—really a warning—can be traced to one of the Montauks who attended the meeting. This man passed the intelligence to Wyandanch, the most powerful Montauk sachem, and it was he who carried the news to Lieutenant Lion Gardiner, an English soldier possessing only primitive knowledge of the local Indian language. Even if Wyandanch had acquired a small English vocabulary, the conversation between the Montauk sachem and Gardiner represented quite a feat of communication. As Gardiner writes, "So he [Wyandanch] came over to me and acquainted me with the manner of the Narragansetts being there with his men, and asked me what I thought of it; and I told him that the Narragansett Sachem was naught to talk with his men secretly in his absence, and I bid him go home, and told him a way he might know all, and then he should come and tell me; and so he did."

We find ourselves trying to unravel a conspiracy within a conspiracy. Since Wyandanch is apparently Gardiner's only source for the Narragansett story, we might inquire whether he was a credible witness. Would he have had any motive for stirring up animosity between Gardiner and the Narragansetts? Might he have had reason to embellish the translation of Miantonomi's oration?

On that matter, there seems no doubt. The Montauk leader had already thrown his lot in with the English colonists. The Long Island Indians were eager to establish regular trade with the Europeans. In an earlier exchange between Gardiner and Wyandanch, the New England soldier noted that the sachem had asked "if we were angry with *all* Indians. I answered No, but only with such as had killed Englishmen. He asked me whether they that lived upon Long-Island might come to trade." Gardiner sensed immediately that he held the upper hand. He observed the Montauks could demonstrate their trustworthiness by capturing and killing Indians currently at war with the whites. "If you have any Indians that have killed English," Gardiner explained, "you must bring their heads also . . . So he [Wyandanch] went away and did as I had said, and sent me five heads."

Wyandanch's manipulation of this affair does not necessarily mean that he fabricated the evidence. Maintonomi may well have appealed to Native American unity. Or perhaps Wyandanch played on Gardiner's deepest fears, a covenant among *all* Indians to drive the white settlers from the continent. By raising the possibility of a general Indian confederation, Wyandanch might have bargained on improving the standing of the Montauks in future negotiations. Or so he may have thought. Although the general insurrection did not take place, the Narragansett got a measure of revenge, sending a huge armada against the Long Island Indians and killing most of the Montauk warriors.

This reconstruction of Miantonomi's impassioned speech tells us how Gardiner first learned of the threat of Indian alliance. But what of the document itself? How did the story of the destruction of preconquest abundance—the deer, turkeys, and clams—come to be recorded? Gardiner did not write his account until 1660, a full eighteen years after the conversation with Wyandanch. By that time

Gardiner was an old man. Two aging veterans of the early wars against the Indians asked him to record his memories of these events. The request took Gardiner by surprise. Before answering his "Loving Friends," he "rummaged and found some old papers then written" [i.e., in the 1640s]. Gardiner confessed that these materials were "a great help to my memory." Whatever materials he employed in preparing his narrative seem to have been lost.

Memory, of course, is a notoriously unreliable source. It is a matter of no little interest, therefore, what Gardiner's frame of mind was at the time of putting pen to paper. Age does not seem to have mellowed the man, at least, not when it came to describing the Native Americans. In 1660 he still believed that they were plotting to kill the whites, and the old soldier thought the New Englanders were too complacent in defending themselves against the Indians. As he declared, "And now I am old, I would fain die a natural death, or like a soldier in the field, with honor, and not to have a sharp stake set in the ground, and thrust into my fundament, and to have my skin flayed off by piece-meal, and cut in pieces and bits, and my flesh roasted and thrust down my throat." Gardiner's vitriolic language does not necessarily mean that we cannot trust his account of the Narragansett sachem's speech, but it does suggest that extreme bias affected anything he had to say about Indians.

Gardiner's "Relation—a twelve-page, almost illegible document—found its way into the possession of several prominent New England families. The Winthrops of Connecticut apparently held the account for almost a century, and then, probably in the 1750s, it passed into the hands of the Trumbulls, a dynasty that produced several governors, revolutionary officers, and local historians. When Governor Jonathan Trumbull died in 1809, his nephew William T. Williams discovered the Gardiner manuscript among Trumbull's private papers. The governor had made a copy of the original document. We have no way of knowing why he went to the trouble of transcribing Gardiner's words, but whatever Trumbull's purpose may have been, Williams dispatched the two manuscripts to the Massachusetts Historical Society.

The organization's publication committee found these materials fascinating. However, there was a problem. The printer contracted to set Gardiner's "Relation" in type could not decipher the soldier's seventeenth-century handwriting. The members of the committee did not do much better, and, finally, in the interest of completing the 1833 volume of the Society's collections, they relied on Trumbull's copy. An editorial explanation appended to Gardiner's narrative states, "The Committee, on account of the difficulty the printer would find in deciphering the original, have followed the orthography of the copy, excepting proper names, where they thought it of more importance to adhere to the ancient orthography."

We have come a long way from the putative meeting between Narragansetts and Montauks in 1642. The path from that gathering to the short document printed in this introduction began with an account supplied to Wyandanch by a loyal supporter who betrayed the conspiracy. A scheming Wyandanch, eager to gain favor with the white settlers, tells Lion Gardiner. The aging Indian fighter does not get around to recording the speech until much later, and, then only to please two old friends who seem no more sympathetic to the Native Americans than does

Gardiner. After a century or more, someone copies the manuscript, and since Gardiner's handwriting defies easy reading, the copy rather than the original becomes the source of the final printed document. In other words, the history of the "Relation" involves oral history, translation from an Indian tongue into English, the fabrication of memory, long preservation under conditions that might have damaged the text, transcription by someone with no direct knowledge of these events, and, finally, publication. Our grasp of a distant reality suddenly seems tenuous. One can almost feel Miantonomi's powerful story of a ravaged physical environment slipping away.

This exercise in detection was not designed to create despair. The reader should know that most documents that they will encounter have not gone through such a tortured history. They seldom involve so many people standing between us and distant events. Rather, the point of interrogating Gardiner's narrative was to encourage skepticism. It is probably the historian's most important mental tool. Before accepting an account as a direct window to the past, the historian must ask hard questions. This is especially true in cases where the sources tell us what we want to hear. At such moments, we must be particularly careful, since it is all too easy to persuade ourselves that agreeable accounts are closer to the "truth" than are stories that we find objectionable. We want to know: Who actually produced the document? What was the man or woman's motive? Who did they think they were addressing? Was the audience a few personal friends or members of a family or did the author intend the words to reach a broader public?

The word "truth" appears in quotation marks as a warning. We may talk of a past reality as if we were really there, as if we had listened to the words of a Narragansett sachem, or an antebellum president, or a slave at the moment of freedom, or an unemployed worker during the Great Depression. But, of course, we were not present. Our only knowledge of these happenings comes through the documents that have somehow survived, and, as the Gardiner story reveals, such sources offer perceptions, partial truths, and self-serving explanations. In this sense, the documents of American history are interpretations of events—stories people in the past have told themselves about life experiences. The search for an objective account is doomed to failure. No one can strip away the biases and assumptions of everyday life. They are unquestioned aspects of human existence.

This apparent limitation on "objectivity" does not deter the skeptical historian. For if the documents, in fact, do record contesting perceptions, different opinions, and interpretations, the historian can weigh the merits of the various accounts. To be sure, most of the time we do not have as much information about the construction of a document as we do for the Gardiner "Relation." But that is not a serious problem. The people who produced interpretations of the past—diaries, letters, newspaper articles, and travelers' reports, for example—adopted rhetorical strategies. They wanted someone to find their stories credible; their goal was persuasion.

And it is precisely here that we must be most suspicious. Throughout American history, certain authors have claimed to "speak for" a group or a people or the members of a certain race. To enhance the credibility of their arguments, they have often drawn on the authority of science, tradition, or public opinion. Thus, a generally liberal figure such as Thomas Jefferson informs us in his *Notes on the State of Virginia* that African Americans are not fully human, at least, not in the way that whites are human, and to lend greater authenticity to the racial argument, he cites the findings of contemporary science. The language of science is employed to trump opposing positions or to cut off debate.

Other American writers—many of them represented in this collection of documents—have claimed authority on the basis of Christian scripture, Western civilization, or simple common sense. In the context of the times in which the author lived such rhetorical devices added greatly to the power of the word. It took courage for ordinary men and women to challenge those who assumed an "objective" voice. The unlettered person is usually reluctant to question the alleged findings of science. During the height of the Cold War, scientists working for the government assured the public that people could survive a nuclear bomb. The dangers of radioactivity, they announced, had been greatly exaggerated. Who could doubt that these experts knew what they were talking about? They spoke for science. With such examples in mind, the skeptical historian should always ask who empowered a particular writer to "speak for" the entire community, especially if that collectivity was the American people.

Wary interpreters of documents quickly develop an ear for silence. Like the famous British detective Sherlock Holmes, they must listen carefully for the dog that did *not* bark in the night. American writers who have presumed to "speak for" the people often left out entire groups. Sometimes it was the Native Americans. On other occasions, it was the African Americans, or women, or industrial workers, or members of new ethnic minorities. Documents of this type do not overtly slander women or blacks or Indians; they just leave them out of the story. They relegate them to silence. Modern readers must restore the missing voices. When national leaders speak of general prosperity, for example, the skeptical historian immediately asks whether the good times were shared by all. When writers celebrate the growth of American democracy, the skeptical historian asks whether anyone has been silenced. Does the concept include the poor? Women? African Americans? Others? And if not, why not? The goal is not to belittle prosperity or democracy—we need a lot more of both—but to understand more fully how these familiar terms evolved over the course of American history.

The reader will encounter another type of document in this collection. These statements might be best characterized as "speaking to" some imagined audience. During Reconstruction, for example, federal officers employed by the Freeman's Bureau lectured the newly liberated slaves about the benefits of wage labor. The captains of late nineteenth-century industry—among them, Andrew Carnegie—informed the members of the working classes about blessings of diligence and responsibility. These performances were designed to persuade the members of other groups of the justice and superiority of the speaker's values. They assume that any reasonable, well-intentioned person would agree with the argument being advanced. Slaves should appreciate the advantages of free labor, even if that system means that African Americans work for their former masters at low wages. The factory workers should see the virtues of hard work and honest ambition, even if most of them spend their days in dangerous, low-paying jobs. The skeptical historian learns to spot self-interested rhetoric and to strip away assumptions about gender and race that usually pass without comment.

In our discussion of the interrogation of documents, we have stressed one aspect of the "power of words." Throughout recorded history, people have employed words to gain dominance, to justify policies, to rationalize decisions that represent the interests of a minority, and to persuade others to accept a specific set of values and to behave in certain ways. But even as we study the texts for such rhetorical practices, we should remember that words possess other powers. They announce freedom. They can call forth nobility and self-sacrifice. They invite scattered strangers to unite in common cause. To classify such performances as "speaking against" makes them seem too defensive—the stuff of resistance rather than liberation. They were both, and sometimes more. Words often simply helped ordinary men and women to make sense out of their lives, to accommodate economic and social change, and to assure themselves that there was more to existence than material reward.

Each chapter in *The Power of Words* brings together different voices. Sometimes the documents address common issues; sometimes they speak at cross-purposes. They challenge the skeptical historian to make sense out of contesting claims and conflicting assumptions. The process of interrogating the past dramatically opens up the story of American history. The process of interrogating the past dramatically broadens our knowledge of the story of American history and, at the same time, deepens our understanding of our own lives and times.

* * * * * *

A word of advice is necessary for students unfamiliar with historical documents, especially texts dating from before the American Revolution. I have not attempted to modernize these sources. Unless the meaning is unclear, I have reproduced the words exactly as they were written. This decision means that I have preserved the texture of words; I remind readers of how hard it was for poorer or semi-literate people in the past to express themselves effectively on paper. Sometimes the spelling will seem odd, and the voices contained in this collection sometimes speak of howses rather than houses, cattell rather than cattle, publique rather than public. Because the standardization of spelling is a relatively modern phenomenon, writers in the early period often spelled the same word several different ways in the same document. The goal here is not to force these men and women to conform to our rules, but to listen carefully to what they had to say about worlds—or more precisely—words we have lost.

1

Perspectives re: meeting & interraction

Conquest of Native American Peoples

N ative Americans of the preconquest period speak today in muted voice. Because Indian peoples living in North America had no writing, we know them only through the interpretation of artifacts—stone tools and weapons, for example—or through the testimony of Europeans whose very presence in the New World forever transformed Native American cultures.

However sympathetic the Europeans may sound to modern readers, they were not prepared fully to comprehend the Indian cultures encountered in America. Their statements should be seen as fragments, as partial descriptions, as stories that visitors told themselves about conquered peoples. We must treat these reports with great care, listening for contradictions, inconsistencies, and projections of European values onto men and women who resisted cultural imperialism. Most of all, we should attend to silences, reminding ourselves of what went unsaid—about racism and violence—in the chronicles of exploration.

Since Christopher Columbus believed he had landed in Asia, he labeled the curious peoples found on the American shore *Indians*. His early descriptions of the native Caribbeans contain contradictions of which he himself may not have been aware. In a 1493 letter to the Spanish sovereigns (Document 1), the admiral observed "of anything they [the native peoples] have, if you ask them for it, they never say no." And to protect the innocent Indians, Columbus forbade the Spanish from giving them "things so worthless as pieces of broken crockery and broken glass." But Columbus remained suspicious, crediting dark rumors as truth. On other Caribbean islands, he insisted, dwelled "people who are regarded . . . as very ferocious and who eat human flesh." The Spanish explorer never reconciled how the children of paradise could also practice cannibalism.

Europeans who stayed home learned about Native American culture through crude, but powerful woodcuts (Document 2). Three early prints show Indian men and women as interpreted by European artists. Like printed reports, the pictures are highly partisan accounts of a strange New World, depicting Native Americans as simple inhabitants of Eden, as terrifying cannibals, and as victims of European greed. Many ordinary Europeans who later traveled to America as soldiers and settlers formed opinions of Indian life from sources like these.

Fray Bartolome de Las Casas invites us (Document 3) to consider moral issues already hotly contested in the mid-sixteenth century. The outspoken Dominican friar criticized European treatment of the Indians, and he published a passionate account of the conquest that undermined heroic, self-serving narratives of exploration then circulating in Spain.

As early Europeans quickly discovered, the act of describing Indian cultures raised unsettling questions about their own customs. Confrontation with strangers sparked comparisons. Father Gabriel Sagard (Document 4), a French missionary in seventeenth-century Canada, stressed similarities between Huron games and those played "in our parts." The role of women in Indian societies, however, baffled the inquisitive Frenchman. The annual report for 1657–1658 filed by the Jesuits living in Canada (Document 5) reads like modern anthropology. Their observations of Native American practices challenged European assumptions of cultural superiority. The Jesuit relations reveal that Indians found many Europeans habits ridiculous and were not shy about expressing their views.

In a graphic account written in 1524 (Document 6), Giovanni de Verrazzano reminds us that "official" reports are not windows into a "real" past, but imaginative, Eurocentric tales of failed communication between Indians and explorers. Perhaps Verrazzano's sailors had heard stories of Native American cannibalism or seen woodcuts depicting Indian families devouring human bodies. Whatever the case, when one Frenchman accidentally washed up on shore, other Europeans assumed that their colleague would soon be served for dinner. The Indians confirmed their worst fears, carrying the young man to a large open fire. In fact, as the French soon discovered, the Native Americans were drying and warming a boy who had nearly drowned and, with "the greatest kindness, they accompanied him to the sea. . . . and stood watching until he was in the boat." These European documents capture impressions—some favorable, some critical—but for the Indians, the cultural conversation was largely one-sided. Regardless of the rhetoric the Europeans employed, the Native Americans experienced conquest.

DOCUMENT 1

Christopher Columbus, Excerpt from "Letter to the Sovereigns on His First Voyage, 15 February–4 March 1493"

This document is the first printed account of the New World. This famous letter captures Columbus's sense of wonder and excitement as he attempts to describe what he believes to be an Asian frontier but which in fact were Caribbean islands. The letter went through sixteen editions before 1500 and perhaps, more than any other single document from the early period of exploration, sparked European dreams of glory and gold.

❦   ❦

.... The people of this island [Hispaniola] and of all the other islands which I have found and seen, or have not seen, all go naked, men and women, as their mothers bore them, except that some women cover one place only with the leaf of a plant or with a net of cotton which they make for that purpose. They have no iron or steel or weapons, nor are they capable of using them, although they are well-built people of handsome stature, because they are wondrous timid. They have no other arms than arms of canes, [cut] when they are in seed time, to the end of which they fix a sharp little stick; and they dare not make use of these, for oftentimes it has happened that I have sent ashore two or three men to some town to have speech, and people without number have come out to them, as soon as they saw them coming, they fled; even a father would not stay for his son; and this was not because wrong has been done to anyone; on the contrary, at every point where I have been and have been able to have speech, I have given them of all that I had, such as cloth and many other things, without receiving anything for it; but they are like that, timid beyond cure. It is true that after they have been reassured and have lost this fear, they are so artless and so free with all they possess, that no one would believe it without having seen it. Of anything they have, if you ask them for it, they never say no; rather they invite the person to share it, and show as much love as if they were giving their hearts; and whether the thing be of value or of small price, at once they are content with whatever little thing of whatever kind may be given to them. I forbade that they should be given things so worthless as pieces of broken crockery and broken glass, and lace points, although when they were able to get them, they thought they had the best jewel in the world; thus it was learned that a sailor for a lace point received gold to the weight of two and a half *castellanos*, and others much more for other things which were worth much less; yea, for new *blancas*, for them they would give all that they had, although it might be two or three castellanos' weight of gold or an arroba or two of spun cotton; they even took pieces of the broken hoops of the wine casks and, like animals, gave what they had, so that it seemed to me to be wrong and I forbade it, and I gave them a thousand good, pleasing things which I had brought, in order that they might be fond of us, and furthermore might become Christians and be inclined to the love and service of Their Highnesses and of the whole Castilian nation, and try to help us and to give us of the things which they have in abundance and which are necessary to us. And they know neither sect nor idolatry, with the exception that all believe that the source of all power and goodness is in the sky, and they believe very firmly that I, with these ships and people, came from the sky, and in this belief they everywhere received me, after they had overcome their fear. And this does not result from their being ignorant (for they are of a very keen intelligence and men who navigate all those seas, so that it is wondrous the good account they give of everything), but because they have never seen people clothed or ships like ours.

And as soon as I arrived in the Indies, in the first island which I found, I took by force some of them in order that they might learn [Castilian] and give me information of what they had in those parts; it so worked out that they soon understood us, and we them, either by speech or signs, and they have been very serviceable. I still have them with me, and they are still of the opinion that I come from the sky, in spite of all the intercourse which they have had with me, and they were the first to announce this wherever I went, and the others went running from house to house and the neighboring towns with loud cries of, "Come! Come! See the people from the sky!" They all came, men and women alike, as soon as they had confidence in us, so that not one, big or little, remained behind, and all brought something to eat and drink, which they gave with marvelous love. In all the islands they have very many *canoas* like rowing *fustes,[small boats]* some bigger and some smaller, and some are bigger than a *fusta* of eighteen benches. They are not so beamy, because they are made of a single log, but a *fusta* could not keep up with them by rowing, since they make incredible speed, and in these they navigate all those islands, which are innumerable, and carry their merchandise. Some of these canoes I have seen with 70 and 80 men on board, each with his oar.

In all these islands, I saw no great diversity in the appearance of the people or in their manners and language, but they all understand one another, which is a very singular thing, on account of which I hope that Their Highnesses will determine upon their conversion to our holy faith, towards which they are much inclined.

I have already said how I went 107 leagues in a straight line from west to east along the coast of Juana, and as a result of that voyage I can say that this island is larger than England and Scotland together; for, beyond these 107 leagues, there remain to the westward two provinces where I have not been, one of which they call Avan [Havana] and there the people are born with tails. Those provinces cannot have a length of less than 50 or 60 leagues, as I could understand from those Indians whom I retain and who know all the islands know how to behave themselves.

In all these islands, it appears, all the men are content with one woman, but to their *Maioral*, or king, they give up to twenty. It appears to me that the women work more than the men. I have been unable to learn whether they hold private property, but it appeared true to me that all took a share in anything that one had, especially in victuals.

In these islands I have so far found no human monstrosities, as many expected, on the contrary, among all these people good looks are esteemed, nor are they Negroes, as in Guinea, but with flowing hair, and they are not born where there is excessive force in the solar rays; it is true that the sun there

has great strength, although it is distant from the Equator 26 degrees. In these islands, where there are high mountains, the cold this winter was severe, but they endure it through habit and with the help of food which they eat with many and excessively hot spices. Thus I have neither found monsters nor had report of any, except in an island [Dominica] which is the second at the entrance to the Indies, which is inhabited by a people who are regarded in all the islands as very ferocious and who eat human flesh; they have many canoes with which they range all the islands of India and pillage and take as much as they can; they are no more malformed than the others, except that they have the custom of wearing their hair long like women, and they use bows and arrows of the same stems of cane with a little piece of wood at the tip for want of iron, which they have not. They are ferocious toward these other people, who are exceedingly great cowards, but I make no more account of them than of the rest. These are those who have intercourse with the women of *Matremonio*, [Martinique] which is the first island met on the way from Spain to the Indies, in which there is not one man. These women use no feminine exercises, but bows and arrows of cane, like the abovesaid; and they arm and cover themselves with plates of copper, of which they have plenty. In another island which they assure me is larger than His*panola*, the people have no hair. In this there is countless gold, and from it and from the other islands I bring with me *Indios* as evidence.

Done on board the caravel off the Canary Islands, on the fifteenth of February, year 1493.

At your service.

The Admiral.

DOCUMENT 2

Images of Conquest

"The Arrival of the Spaniards in Mexico," Bernardo de Sahagun (ca. 1570). This drawing depicts a peaceful landing of Europeans, showing also the bounty of the New World available for the taking.

A German woodcut from the 1500s illustrates an early European conception of native culture. Nearly naked, these natives were as exotic to the Europeans as the Europeans were to them.

"The Cruelty of the Conquerors," Theodore de Bry (1598). Here, what Las Casas called the "Destruction of the Indies" is represented: wholesale devastation of Indian communities in conflict with European designs in the New World.

DOCUMENT 3

Fray Bartolome de Las Casas, A Short Account of the Destruction of the Indies (1542)

Las Casas, a Dominican friar, became the earliest and most vocal opponent of the activities of the Spanish crown and its conquistadors in the New World. Writing only twenty years after European conquest in New Spain, Las Casas lashed out at the regime of disease, brutality and forced labor Spaniards had brought upon the Indians. His account takes the form of an open letter to Prince Philip of Spain and attempts to document atrocities. Shocked by the genocidal abuses he witnessed in America, Las Casas insisted that the Indians must be considered human and therefore afforded basic rights and religious guidance. In the passage that follows, Las Casas recounts one of the famous tales of the New World, that of Cortès and the defeat of Montezuma, but his bitter tone contrasts with the usual heroic accounts of the scene.

❦   ❧

New Spain was discovered in 1517 and, at the time, great atrocities were committed against the indigenous people of the region and some were killed by members of the expedition. In 1518 the so-called Christians set about stealing from the people and murdering them on the pretence of settling the area. And from that year until this—and it is now 1542—the great iniquities and injustices, the outrageous acts of violence and the bloody tyranny of these Christians have steadily escalated, the perpetrators having lost all fear of God, all love of their sovereign, and all sense of self-respect. Even now, in September 1542, the atrocities get worse by the day, it being the case, as we have said, that the infernal brutality and utter inhumanity of the acts committed have readily increased as time has gone on. . . .

Among other massacres was one which took place in Cholula, a great city of some thirty thousand inhabitants. When all the dignitaries of the city and the region came out to welcomew the Spaniards with all due pomp and ceremony, the priests to the fore and the high priest at the head of the procession, and they proceeded to escort them into the city and lodge them in the houses of the lord and the leading citizens, the Spaniards decided that the moment had come to organize a massacre (or 'punishment' as they themselves express such things) in order to inspire fear and terror in all the people of the territory. This was, indeed, the pattern they followed in all the lands they invaded: to stage a bloody massacre of the most public possible kind in order to terrorize those meek and gentle peoples. What they did was the following. They requested the local lord to send for all the nobles and leading citizens of the city and of all the surrounding communities subject to it and, as soon as they arrived and entered the building to begin talks with the Spanish commander, they were seized without anyone outside getting wind of what was afoot. Part of the original request was that they should bring with them five or six thousand native bearers and these were mustered in the courtyards when and as they arrived. One could not watch these poor wretches getting ready to carry the Spaniards' packs without taking pity on them, stark naked as they were with only their modesty hidden from view, each with a kind of little net on his shoulders in which he carried his own modest store of provisions. They all got down on their haunches and waited patiently like sheep. Once they were all safely inside the courtyard, together with a number of others who were also there at the time, armed guards took up positions covering the exits and Spanish soldiers unsheathed their swords and grasped their lances and proceeded to slaughter these poor innocents. Not a single soul escaped.

From Cholula they made their way to Mexico City. On their journey, they were showered with thousands of gifts from the great king Montezuma who also sent some of his men to stage entertainments and banquets for them on the way. When they reached the Great Causeway which runs for some two leagues right up to the city itself, they were greeted by Montezuma's own brother and many local dignitaries bearing valuable gifts of gold, silver and apparel from the great lord.

Yet that same day, or so I am reliably informed by a number of eye-witnesses, the Spaniards seized the great king unawares by means of a trick and held him under armed guard of eighty soldiers, eventually putting him in irons. But, leaving aside all of this, although much passed of consequence and one could dwell upon it at length, I should like to relate just one incident contrived by these tyrants. It happened that the Spanish commander [Cortès] had occasion to go to the sea-port to deal with one of his captains who was planning an attack on him and he left another of his henchmen, with a hundred or so men at his command, to guard King Montezuma while he was away. The garrison decided to stage a show of strength and thereby boost the fear they inspired in the people of this kingdom, a classic Spanish tactic in these campaigns, as we have had occasion to remark before. All the local citizens, great and small, as well as all the members of the court, were wholly taken up with entertaining their imprisoned lord. To this end, they organized fiestas, some of which involved staging traditional dances every afternoon and evening in squares and residential quarters throughout the city. These dances are called in the local language *mitotes* (those typical of the islands being known as *areitos*); and since these dances are the principal form of public entertainment and enjoyment among the people, they deck themselves out in all their best finery. And the entertainments were organized with close attention to rank and station, the noblest of the citizens dancing nearest the building where their lord was being held. Close by this building, then, danced over two thousand youths of quality, the flower of the nobility of Montezuma's whole empire. Thither the Spanish captain made his way, accompanied by a platoon of his men, under pretence of wanting to watch the spectacle but in fact carrying orders to attack the revellers at a prearranged time, further platoons with identical orders having been dispatched to the other squares where entertainments were being staged. The nobles were totally absorbed in what they were doing and had no thought for their own safety when the soldiers drew their swords and shouting: "For Saint James, and at 'em, men! proceeded to slice open the lithe and naked bodies of the dancers and to spill their noble blood. Not one dancer was left alive, and the same story was repeated in the other squares throughout the city. This series of events caused horror, anguish and bitterness throughout the land; the whole nation was plunged into mourning and, until the end of time, or at least as long as a few of these people survive, they will not cease to tell and re-tell, in their *areitos* and dances, just as we do at home in Spain with our ballads, this sad story of a massacre which wiped out their entire nobility, beloved and respected by them for generations and generations.

It should be recalled that the pretext upon which the Spanish invaded each of these provinces and proceeded to massacre the people and destroy their lands—lands which teemed with people and should surely have been a joy and a delight to any true Christian—was purely and simply that they were making good the claim of the Spanish Crown to the territories in question. At no stage had any order been issued entitling them to massacre the people or to enslave them. Yet, whenever the natives did not

drop everything and rush to recognize publicly the truth of the irrational and illogical claims that were made, and whenever they did not immediately place themselves completely at the mercy of the iniquitous and cruel and bestial individuals who were making such claims, they were dubbed outlaws and held to be in rebellion against His Majesty. This, indeed, was the tenor of the letters that were sent back to the Spanish court, and everybody involved in the administration of the New World was blind to the simple truth enshrined in the first principles of law and government that nobody who is not a subject of a civil power in the first place can be deemed in law to be in rebellion against that power. Any reasonable person who knows anything of God, of rights and of civil law can imagine for himself what the likely reaction would be of any people living peaceably within their own frontiers, unaware that they owe allegiance to anyone save their natural lords, were a stranger suddenly to issue a demand along the following lines: 'You shall henceforth obey a foreign king, whom you have never seen nor ever heard of and, if you do not, we will cut you to pieces'—especially when they discover that these strangers are indeed quite prepared to carry out this threat to the letter. Even more shocking is the fact that when the local people do obey such commands they are harshly treated as common slaves, put to hard labour and subjected to all manner of abuse and to agonizing torments that ensure a slower and more painful death than would summary execution. Indeed, for them, the end result is the same: they, their wives and their children all perish and the whole of their nation is wiped from the face of the earth. And so blinded by ambition and driven by greed are the devils who advocate such treatment of these people that they cannot see that, when their victoms come to obey under duress this foreign overlord and publicly recognize his authority over them, simply because of their fear of what will happen to them if they do not, such a recognition of suzerainty has no standing in law whatever, any such prerogative obtained by menaces from any people anywhere in the world being invalid. In practice, the only rights these perfidious crusaders have earned which can be upheld in human, divine, or natural law are the right to eternal damnation and the right to answer for the offences and the harm they have done the Spanish Crown by utterly ruining every one of these kingdoms and (as far as it is within their power) invalidating all claims the Spanish Crown may have to the territories of the New World. These, then, are the true services they have performed and continue to perform for their sovereign in this part of the world.

DOCUMENT 4

Father Gabriel Sagard, The Long Journey to the Country of the Hurons (1632)

Father Sagard, a Recollect missionary from France, met the Hurons of Canada dressed in traditional grey robe and cord belt. Like other members of his religious order, he had shaved the top of his head. The local Native Americans must have found his customs as strange as he did theirs. In this document Sagard considers gender roles among the Indians and the training of young people.

The occupation of the young boys and girls

The usual and daily practice of the young boys is none other than drawing the bow and shooting the arrow, making it rise and glide in a straight line a little higher than the ground. They play a game with curved sticks, making them slide over the snow and hit a ball of light wood, just as is done in our parts; they learn to throw the prong with which they spear fish, and practise other little sports and exercises, and then they put in an appearance at the lodge at meal-times, or else when they feel hungry. But if a mother asks her son to go for water or wood or do some similar household service, he will reply to her that this is a girl's work and will do none of it. If sometimes we got them to perform similar services it was on condition that they should always have ac-

cess to our lodge, or for some pin, feather, or other little thing for adorning themselves, and this satisfied them very well, and us also, as a return for the small and petty services rendered us.

There were, however, some mischievous boys who delighted in cutting the cord that held up our door after the manner of the country, so as to make it fall when one opened it, and then afterwards they would deny it absolutely or take to flight. Moreover they never admit their faults or tricks, being great liars, except when they have no fear of being blamed or reproached for them, for though they are savages and incapable of receiving correction they are at the same time very proud and covetous of honour, and do not like to be thought mischievous or naughty, although they may be so.

We had made a beginning of teaching them their letters, but as they are all for freedom and only want to play and give themselves a good time, as I said, they forgot in three days what we had taken four to teach, for lack of perserverance and for neglect of coming back to us at the hours appointed them; and if they told us that they had been prevented because of a game, they were clear. Besides, it was not yet advisable to be severe with them or reprove them otherwise than gently, and we could only in a complaisant manner urge them to be thorough in gaining knowledge which would be such an advantage to them and bring them satisfaction in time to come.

Just as the little boys have their special training and teach one another to shoot with the bow as soon as they begin to walk, so also the little girls, whenever they begin to put one foot in front of the other, have a little stick put into their hands to train them and teach them early to pound corn, and when they are grown somewhat they also play various little games with their companions, and in the course of these small frolics they are trained quietly to perform trifling and petty household duties, sometimes also to do the evil that they see going on before their eyes, and this makes them worthless for the most part when grown up, and with few exceptions worse even than the boys, boasting often of the wickedness which should make them blush. They vie with one another as to which shall have the most lovers, and if the mother finds none for herself she freely offers her daughter and the daughter offers herself, and the husband also sometimes offers his wife, if she be willing, for some small and trifling present; and there are procurers and wicked people in the towns and villages who apply themselves to no other occupation than that of offering and bringing some of these creatures to the men who desire them. I give praises to our Lord that the women received our reproofs in quite good part, and

finally begin to practise modesty and show some shame at their dissoluteness, no longer venturing, except very rarely, to make use of improper language in our presence; and they were full of admiration and approval of the propriety of the girls in France of whom we told them. This gave us hopes of great amendment and alteration of their mode of living in a short time, if the Frenchmen who came up with us, most of them, had not told them the contrary, in order always to be able, like beasts, to enjoy their sensual pleasures to the full, in which they wallowed, even keeping together groups of these bad girls in several places, so that those who should have seconded us in teaching and being a good example to these people were the very ones who went about destroying and obstructing the good that we were building up for the salvation of the tribes and for the advancement of the glory of God. There were, however, some good men, virtuous and of good life, with whom we were well content and from whom we received spiritual encouragement, just as, on the contrary, we were scandalized by those other brutal, godless, and sensual men who hindered the conversion and amendment of these poor folk.

One of the Frenchmen had been trading among a nation towards the north, about a hundred leagues from us, getting copper from a mine. He told us on his return that he had seen several girls there with the end of their nose cut off, according to the custom of their country (quite the opposite and reverse from that of the Hurons), for having made a breach in their chastity; and he assured us also that he had seen these savages offer some form of prayer before taking their meals. This made Father Nicholas and me greatly long to go there, if necessity had not forced us to return to the province of Canada, and from there to France.

DOCUMENT 5

Relation of What Occurred Most Remarkable in the Missions of the Fathers of the Society of Jesus in New France in the Years 1657 and 1658

For the Jesuits in seventeenth-century Canada, interpretation of Native American customs became a comparative project. The Frenchmen made fun of certain Indian assumptions, but to their credit, they also appreciated how the Native Americans perceived odd European behavior such as blowing the nose in a clean piece of linen cloth. In this remarkable document the Jesuit author comes close to defining culture from a relativistic perspective; beauty—and a lot more—was in the eye of the beholder.

Of the difference between the manners and customs of the French, or the Europeans, and those of the savages

I know not whether I am mistaken, but I would be willing to say that the organs of our senses resemble, in some respects, primary matter, which, having neither beauty nor deformity in itself, yet composes the most beautiful or the most ugly things, according to the forms given it by the Agents. The temperament of our senses,—whencesoever it comes, whether from our birth or from our habits,—gives to them inclination or aversion, love or hate, for the objects presented to them. From this source, as I believe, arises the great difference that exists between the senses of the Savages and those of the French, or of the Europeans; for you would say, in many instances, that what is sugar to the one people is wormwood to the other. Let us begin with the sense of smell.

There are found, in these regions of America, animals to which the French have given the name of musk-Rats, because in truth they resemble the rats of France,—except that they are much larger,—and smell of musk in the Spring. The

French are very fond of this odor; the Savages dislike it as if it were a stench. They anoint themselves, and smear their heads and faces with oils and grease that smell to us like carrion. It is their musk, their orangeade, and their benzoin [tree gum extract]. The rose, the pink, the clove, the nutmeg, and similar odors, which are agreeable to us, are insipid to them; and tobacco, which causes nausea to those unaccustomed to smell it, constitutes one of their chief delights.

Concerning the sense of hearing, although the Savages take much pleasure in singing, a concert of music sounds to them like a confusion of voices, and a roulade like a bird's twittering. I admit that the warbling of birds is not disagreeable to them; but their own songs, which are so heavy and dismal as to give us ideas of night, seem to them as beautiful as the blush of dawn. They sing amid dangers, in torments, and at the approach of death; while the French usually preserve a deep silence on all such occasions. Salt, which seasons all viands eaten in Europe, renders them bitter to the Savage taste. Their smoked meat, which to us is almost soot, is very savory to them. Intercommunication causes the palates of some Frenchmen to adapt themselves to smoked flesh, and those of some Savages to salted food. It is true that, up to the present moment, I have never seen a Savage that did not abhor Dutch cheese, radishes, spices, mustard, and similar condiments. I remember in this connection, the following incident. A Savage chanced to be at table with some French people when mustard was served, and his curiosity to taste of every dish, without knowing its nature, made him dip his spoon into this condiment. Taking a tolerably good dose, he thrust it into his mouth before any one had told him how it was usually eaten. God knows whether he furnished merriment for all the company. It is a Savage's glory to be a hearty eater, as it is that of many a European to be a lusty drinker; and this good fellow, wishing to show the strength of his courage, strove to keep his countenance. His tears, however, betrayed him, although he set his teeth and compressed his lips to the utmost; until at last the little maintenance of appearances and facial control that he possessed escaped him, and he was left highly astonished at the strength of that "yellow porridge," as he called it. Finally, he was instructed how mustard was to be eaten; but he never put the lesson into practice, being content with that first experience for the rest of his days. Sauces, condiments, dressings, which are the delight of epicures, would here make a little hell for the Savage's gullet.

Although they have a tenderer and more delicate skin than the French,—if one accept the evidence of the lancet and the hand of the Surgeon, who ascribes this delicacy to the oil and grease with which they anoint and rub themselves,—yet those good people have none of our Europeans' softness and delicacy. They find sleep sweeter upon the earth for a bed, with a pillow of wood, than do many upon down. It is a fact that habit causes the sense of touch to rebel against too great softness, finding its pleasure and satisfaction in things harder and rougher. I have known Fathers who could not take their sleep on a bed, because they had become accustomed to sleep like the Savages. If they were given, on returning from their Missions, a pallet or mattress, they were obliged, until they had regained their former

habits, to pass a portion of the night upon the paved floor of the room, in order to sleep for a little while more at their ease. In short, the Savages go almost half naked during the Winter, while the French dress as warmly as they can.

Concerning the sense of sight, it is quite certain that, in general, it is more perfect among the Savages than among the French, as is proved by experience nearly every day. If any object is to be descried, the French do not trust their own eyes so much as those of the Savages. The latter all have black eyes, and smaller than other people's. I would readily believe that the superiority enjoyed by them over us, in this particular, is due to their not drinking wine or eating salt, spices, or other things capable of drying up the humors of the eye and impairing its tone. However it may be regarding the excellence of their eyesight, it must be admitted that it often finds beauty where ours sees only ugliness. Those who say that the beauty of a face consists in the symmetry of its parts and in the whiteness and vermilion covering it, must retract one-half of their definition if they would not offend the Africans, the Americans, and many Asiatics. But let us take up the details of this subject.

In France, to make a face more beautiful, it is cleansed of oil and washed as carefully as possible. The Savages, on the contrary, anoint and grease it as much as they can, thinking it more pleasing the more shiny it is with their grease or oil. To make oneself hideous in Europe, one daubs himself with black, yellow, and blue; and that is the very thing that makes a Savage handsome and of very pleasing appearance. When one of them wishes to pay a visit or attend some feast or dance, he has his face painted in various colors by some woman or girl; for that is one of their arts, as it was of old among the Jews. After he has been well bedaubed, he is looked upon as a handsome man, whereas in Europe he would be taken for a demon.

In France, large eyes, and lips rather compressed than open, are beautiful. In Africa, small eyes, the blackest complexion, and hanging, recurved lips make a beautiful face. In Canadas, black eyes and a large face, after the style of the ancient Caesars, bear off the prize for beauty and grace. In Europe, the whitest teeth are the most beautiful. The Moors and Savages surpass us in this attraction, having teeth whiter than ivory. In some parts of Oriental India, those who eat the Betel-nut have red teeth; and this color constitutes a part of their glory.

In France, hair that is a little blond, well washed with soap and cleansed of oil, carefully arranged and curled, is the most beautiful. Negroes like it short, black, and very crisp. The Savages wish it long, stiff, black, and all lustrous with grease. A curly head is as ugly to them as it is beautiful in France. . . .

The beard is held to add grace and adornment to man, but this opinion is not everywhere received. In that new world, a beard is the greatest disfigurement that a face can have. The peoples of those countries call the Europeans "bearded," as a gross insult. Some time ago a Savage, looking into a Frechman's fce with most extraordinary attention and in profound silence, suddenly exclaimed, after considering him a long time, "Oh, the bearded man! Oh, how ugly he is!" They have such dread of this disfigurement that, if some hair is inclined to grow on the chins, they pluck it out immediately, to rid themselves of what is beautiful to us, but ugly to them.

Ladies in Europe take pleasure in having their hair well dressed, and it is indecorous for them to appear bare-headed, and with hair flying in disorder. This is one of the charms of Canadian women; they commonly go bare-headed, and consider themselves very pretty when their hair has a bright gloss and is very stiff with grease. They wear it loose on each side, but gather it up behind into a little mass which they adorn with small beads of their porcelain. . . .

We cut our nails; the Savages let theirs grow. If you accuse them of uncouthness, you will be condemned by whole peoples of Oriental India, who foster the utmost possible growth of their nails as a mark of their nobility—wishing to indicate thereby that their fingers, encumbered by these natural superfluities, are not fitted for work.

In France, men and women have their clothes made rather tight-fitting, in order to impart a lighter appearance, the girls especially priding themselves on their slenderness. In Canadas, every one dressed so as to look large, both men and women wearing robes which they gird in two places, below the navel and above the stomach, tucking up their ample robes and letting the fold hang down. Thus, they have a great sack, as it were, around the body, in which they stow away a thousand things. Here mothers put their children, to fondle them and keep them warm.

The longer a Lady's dress, the more graceful it is; but Savage women would make fun of a dress that came down much below the knees. Their work compels them to follow this fashion. . . .

Politeness and propriety have taught us to carry handkerchiefs. In this manner the Savages charge us with filthiness—because, they say, we place what is unclean in a fine white piece of linen, and put it away in our pockets as something very precious, while they throw it upon the ground. Hence it happened that, when a Savage one day saw a Frenchman fold up his handkerchief after wiping his nose, he said to him laughingly, "If thou likest that filth, give me thy handkerchief and I will soon fill it." I do not profess to observe much order in this medley; it comes from my pen as the items occur to my mind.

DOCUMENT 6

Giovanni da Verrazzano, "Letter to King Francis I" *(1624)*

Giovanni da Verrazzano, an Italian navigator employed by a French monarch, sailed the eastern shore of North America in 1624 from the Carolinas to Maine. Like other European explorers, Verrazzano seemed as much interested in what Native Americans thought of the "white" visitors as he did in the Indians themselves. The text raises profound questions about the ability of the two peoples to communicate. Although Verrazzano placed great faith in sign language, he always seemed to hear from the Indians precisely what he wanted to hear.

In another xxv days we sailed more than four hundred leagues, where there appeared a new land which had never been seen before by any man, either ancient or modern. At first it appeared to be rather low-lying; having approached to within a quarter of a league, we realized that it was inhabited, for huge fires had been built on the seashore. We saw that the land stretched southward, and coasted along it in search of some port where we might anchor the ship and investigate the nature of the land, but in fifty leagues we found no harbor or place where we could stop with the ship. Seeing that the land continued to the south, we decided to turn and skirt it toward the north, where we found the land we had sighted earlier. So we anchored off the coast and sent the small boat in to land. We had seen many people coming to the seashore, but they fled when they saw us approaching; several times they stopped and turned around to look at us in great wonderment. We reassured them with various signs, and some of them came up, showing great delight at seeing us and marveling at our clothes, appearance, and our whiteness; they showed us by various signs where we could most easily secure the boat, and offered us some of their food. We were on land, and I shall now tell Your Majesty briefly what we were able to learn of their life and customs.

They go completely naked except that around their loins they wear skins of small animals like martens, with a narrow belt of grass around the body, to which they tie various tails of other animals, which hang down to the knees; the rest of the body is bare, and so is the head. Some of them wear garlands of birds' feathers. They are dark in color, not unlike the Ethiopians, with thick black hair, not very long, tied back beyind the head like a small tail. As for the physique of these men, they are well proportioned, of medium height, a little taller than we are. They have broad chests, strong arms, and the legs and other parts of the body are well composed. There is nothing else, except that they tend to be rather broad in the face: but not all, for we saw many with angular faces. They have big black eyes, and an attentive and open look. They are not very strong, but they have a sharp cunning, and are agile and swift runners. From what we could tell from observation, in the last two respects they resemble the Orientals, particularly those from the farthest Sinarian regions. We could not learn the details of the life and customs of these people because of the short time we spent on land, due to the fact that there were few men, and the ship was anchored on the high seas. Not far from these people, we found others on the shore whose way of life we think is similar.

We saw many people on the beach making various friendly signs, and beckoning us ashore, and there I saw a magnificent deed, as Your Majesty will hear. We sent one of our young sailors swimming ashore to take the people some trinkets, such as little bells, mirrors, and other trifles, and when he came without four fathoms of them, he threw them the goods and tried to turn back, but he was so tossed about by the waves that he was carried up onto the beach half dead. Seeing this, the native people immediately ran up; they took him by the head, the legs, and arms and carried him some distance away. Whereupon the youth, realizing he was being carried away like this, was seized with terror, and began to utter loud cries. They answered him in their language to show him he should not be afraid. Then they placed him on the ground in the sun, at the foot of a small hill, and made gestures of great admiration, looking at the whiteness of his flesh and examining him from head to foot. They took off his shirt and shoes and hose, leaving him naked, then made a huge fire next to him, placing him near the heat. When the sailors in the boat saw this, they were filled with terror, as always when something new occurs, and thought the people wanted to roast him for food. After remaining with them for a while, he regained his strength, and showed them by signs that he wanted to return to the ship. With the greatest kindness, they accompanied him to the sea, holding him close and embracing him; and then to reassure him, they withdrew to a high hill and stood watching him until he was in the boat. The youth learned the following about these people: they are dark in color like the other [tribes], their skin is very glossy, they are of medium height, their faces are more clear-cut, their body and other limbs much more delicate and much less powerful, but they are more quick-witted. He saw nothing else.

We reached another land xv leagues from the island, where we found an excellent harbor; before entering it, we saw about xx boats full of people who came around the ship uttering various cries of wonderment. They did not come nearer than fifty paces, but stopped to look at the structure of our ship, our persons, and our clothes; then all together they raised a loud cry which meant that they were joyful. We reassured them somewhat by imitating their gestures, and they came near enough for us to throw them a few little bells and mirrors and many trinkets, which they took and looked at, laughing, and then they confidently came on board ship. Among them were two kings, who were as beautiful of stature and build as I can possibly describe. The first was about xxxx years old, the other a young man of xxiiii, and they were dressed thus: the older man had on his naked body a stag skin, skillfully worked like damask with various embroideries; the head was bare, the hair tied back with various bands, and around the neck hung a wide chain decorated with many different-colored stones. The young man was dressed in almost the same way. These people are the most beautiful and have the most civil customs that we have found on this voyage. They are taller than we are; they are a bronze color, some tending more toward whiteness, others to a tawny color; the face is clear-cut; the hair is long and black, and they take great pains to decorate it; the eyes are black and alert, and their manner is sweet and gentle, very like the manner of the ancients. I shall not speak to Your Majesty of the other parts of the body, since they have all the proportions belonging to any well-built man. Their women are just as shapely and beautiful; very gracious, of attractive manner and pleasant appearance; their customs and behavior follow womanly custom as far as befits human nature; they go nude except for a stag skin embroidered like the men's, and some wear rich lynx skins on their arms; their bare heads are decorated with various ornaments made of braids of their own hair which hang down over their breasts on either side. Some have other hair arrangements such as the women of Egypt and Syria wear, and these women are older and have been joined in wedlock. Both men and women have various trinkets hanging from their ears as the Orientals do; and we saw that they had many sheets of worked copper which they prize more than gold. They do not value gold because of its color; they think it the most worthless of all, and rate blue and red above all other colors. The things we gave them that they prized the most were little bells, blue crystals, and other trinkets to put in the ear or around the neck. They did not appreciate cloth of silk and gold, nor even of any other kind, nor did they care to have them; the same was true for metals like steel and iron, for many times when we showed them some of our arms, they did not admire them, nor ask for them, but merely examined the workmanship. They did the same with mirrors; they would look at them quickly, and then refuse them, laughing. They are very generous and give away all they have. We made great friends with them and one day before we entered the harbor with the ship, when we were lying at anchor one league out to sea because of unfavorable weather, they came out to the ship with a great number of their boats; they had painted and decorated their faces with various colors, showing us that it was a sign of happiness. They brought us some of their food, and showed us by signs where we should anchor in the port for the ship's safety, and then accompanied us all the way until we dropped anchor. We stayed there for xv days, taking advantage of the place to refresh ourselves. Every day the people came to see us on the ship, bringing their womenfolk. They are very careful with them, for when they come aboard and stay a long time, they make the women wait in the boats; and however many entreaties we made or offers of various gifts, we could not persuade them to let the women come on board ship. One of the two kings often came with the queen and many attendants for the pleasure of seeing us, and at first they always stopped on a piece of ground about two hundred paces away from us, and sent a boat to warn us of their arrival, saying they wanted to come and see the ship: they did this as a kind of precaution. And once they had a reply from us, they came immediately, and watched us for a while; but when they heard the irksome clamor of the crowd of sailors, they sent the queen and her maidens in a light little boat to wait on a small island about a quarter of a league from us. The king

remained a long while, discussing by signs and gestures various fanciful notions, looking at the ship's equipment, and asking especially about its uses; he imitated our manners, tasted our food, and then courteously took his leave of us. Sometimes when our men stayed on a small island near the ship for two or three days for their various needs, as is the custom of sailors, he would come with seven or eight of his attendants, watch our operations, and often ask us if we wanted to stay there any length of time, offering us all his help. Then he would shoot his bow and run and perform various games with his men to give us pleasure.

They live a long time, and rarely fall sick; if they are wounded, they cure themselves with fire without medicine; their end comes with old age. We consider them very compassionate and charitable toward their relatives, for they make great lamentations in time of adversity, recalling in their grief all their past happiness. At the end of their life, the relatives perform together the Sicilian lament, which is mingled with singing and lasts a long time. This is all that we could learn of them. . . .

We did not land there because the weather was favorable and helped us in sailing along the coast: we think it resembles the other. The shore ran eastward. At a distance of fifty leagues, keeping more to the north, we found high country full of very dense forests, composed of pines, cypresses, and similar trees which grow in cold regions. The people were quite different from the others, for while the previous ones had been courteous in manner, these were full of crudity and vices, and were so barbarous that we could never make any communication with them, however many signs we made to them. They were clothed in skins of bear, lynx, sea-wolf and other animals. As far as we could judge from several visits to their houses, we think they live on game, fish, and several fruits which are a species of root which the earth produces itself. They have no pulse, and we saw no sign of cultivation, nor would the land be suitable for producing any fruit or grain on account of its sterility. If we wanted to trade with them for some of their things, they would come to the seashore on some rocks where the breakers were most violent, while we remained in the little boat, and they sent us what they wanted to give on a rope, continually shouting to us not to approach the land; they gave us the barter quickly, and would take in exchange only knives, hooks for fishing, and sharp metal. We found no courtesy in them, and when we had nothing more to exchange and left them, the men made all the signs of scorn and shame that any brute creature would make. Against their wishes, we penetrated two or three leagues inland with xxv armed men, and when we disembarked on the shore, they shot at us with their bows and uttered loud cries before fleeing into the woods.

To Leonardo Tedaldi or to Thomaso Sartini, merchants in Lyons. To be forwarded to Bonacorso Ruscellay.

Study Questions

1. Did the European explorers and missionaries confront the Native Americans with an open mind? Why, for example, was Columbus so concerned about finding "human monstrosities"?

2. How exactly did Native Americans and Europeans manage to communicate? We note the Europeans claimed to have learned about complex abstractions such as color preference and attitudes toward private property. Could one learn such things through sign language?

3. Does Las Casas provide a more reliable picture of Native American cultures simply because he criticized Spanish cruelty and oppression? Considering that each European report is in some manner biased and self-serving, how can we claim to know anything about early Indian cultures?

2

An English New World

The rulers of early modern England envied Spain's successes in the New World. They too dreamed of golden treasure. But for most of the sixteenth century, England lacked the resources required to compete effectively in the race for empire, and while Spain was busy consolidating its position in Mexico and Peru, the English concentrated on highly divisive matters closer to home. Henry VIII (1509–1547) aggressively supported the Protestant Reformation, and until England had settled its internal religious disputes, it was unable to defend its tenuous claims in North America.

While later English monarchs encouraged their subjects to colonize the New World, they never supplied these entrepreneurs with the state's full financial backing. Wealthy noblemen and private stock companies tried as best they could to raise the substantial funds needed to sustain American settlement. Each group advanced its own plan. Some envisioned bases from which English ships could plunder the Spanish treasure fleet; others hoped to find gold and silver, a short water route to China, or, at the very least, commodities that could be sold for huge profits on the European market.

Whatever the character of the enterprise, English adventurers faced a common problem, persuading ordinary men and women to move to the new world. It was not an easy task. Since no sane person wanted to die in poverty in America, the organizers of the various colonial ventures tried to persuade them that across the Atlantic lay a virtual paradise. Of course, the harsh realities of life in the earliest English settlements deflated such self-serving rhetoric. The documents in this section expose the tensions between inflated expectations and actual experience, between corporate ambitions and private disappointment.

The earliest English subjects to visit North America remain shrouded in mystery. Anonymous fishermen working out of Bristol and other western English ports may have landed in Nova Scotia and Newfoundland soon after Columbus reached the Caribbean. John Cabot, who received "letters patent"—in effect, a royal grant—from Henry VII in 1496 (Document 1), completed his first transatlantic voyage in 1497. Although nothing came of Cabot's efforts, his adventure served as the basis for England's later claims to a share of the New World.

Nearly a century later, Sir Walter Ralegh tried again. In 1584 he dispatched two captains to the coast of present-day North Carolina. Ralegh named the region

Virginia, in honor of his patron Elizabeth, the Virgin Queen. Although he managed to raise funds through a subscription (Document 2), his enterprise suffered extraordinary bad luck. An initial group of settlers arrived in 1585, christening the colony "Roanoke," and after only a few months in America, the hapless colonists received a surprise visit from Sir Francis Drake. While he was there "a great storm arose," and all the settlers insisted on escaping "this paradise of the world" for the security of England (Document 3).

English settlers established the first permanent colonies early in the seventeenth century. While these people probably learned something from earlier failures, they still endured great hardship. The Reverend John Higginson, an employee of the Massachusetts Bay Company, tried valiantly to mask the difficulties of American settlement. In an exaggerated essay (Document 4), he praised the virtues of everyday life in New England. Among other things, Higginson did not have much time to enjoy them. Like so many other English colonists, the reverend succumbed to a fever.

Thomas Dudley presents a powerful counter-discourse. Conditions in early Massachusetts Bay appalled this tough-minded Puritan leader, and in a detailed letter to an English patron, he tried to correct false reports of the joys of living in America. Dudley complained that others—perhaps Higginson—had written "somewhat hyperbolically of many things here." In a letter that he knew would be widely circulated throughout the English countryside, Dudley insisted on using "open and plain dealing, lest other men should fall short of their expectations when they come hither, as we to our great prejudice did."

The archives also contain the complaints of ordinary settlers, people who experienced crushing disappointment when the New World failed to fulfill the promise of the propaganda. It was a story destined to be repeated throughout American history. The same month that Dudley dispatched his letter to the Countess of London, the son of William Pond wrote to his parents in England describing conditions in Massachusetts Bay (Document 6). The country, he wrote pathetically, "is not as we did expect it."

DOCUMENT 1

"Letters Patent Granted to John Cabot and His Sons" (1496)

Eager to prevent other European states from seizing all the newly discovered lands across the Atlantic, England's Henry VII granted John Cabot, an experienced Venician navigator, the right to explore and claim territory in his name. Nothing much came of Cabot's efforts; he certainly did not encounter "towns, castles, [and] cities" during his visit to the North Atlantic coast. However disappointed the king may have been, Cabot's voyages served as a legal justification for England's later colonizing activities.

The First Letters Patent Granted to John Cabot and His Sons, 5 March 1496

For John Cabot and his Sons

The King, to all to whom, etc. Greeting: Be it known and made manifest that we have given and granted as by these presents we give and grant, for us and our heirs, to our well-beloved John Cabot, citizen of Venice, and to Lewis, Sebastian and Sancio, sons of the said John, and to the heirs and deputies of them, and of any one of them, full and free authority, faculty and power to sail to all parts, regions and coasts of the eastern, western and northern sea, under our banners, flags and ensigns, with five ships or vessels of whatsoever burden and quality they may be, and with so many and with such mariners and men as they may wish to take with them in the said ships, at their own proper costs and charges, to find, discover and investigate whatsoever islands, countries, regions or provinces of heathens and infidels, in whatsoever part of the world placed, which before this time were unknown to all Christians. We have also granted to them and to any of them, and to the heirs and deputies of them and any one of them, and have given licence to set up our aforesaid banners and ensigns in any town, city, castle, island or mainland whatsoever, newly found by them. And that the before-mentioned John and his sons or their heirs and deputies may conquer, occupy and possess whatsoever such towns, castles, cities and islands by them thus discovered that they may be able to conquer, occupy and possess, as our vassals and governors lieutenants and deputies therein, acquiring for us the dominion, title and jurisdiction of the same towns, castles, cities, islands and mainlands so discovered; in such a way nevertheless that of all the

fruits, profits, emoluments, commodities, gains and revenues accruing from this voyage, the said John and sons and their heirs and deputies shall be bounden and under obligation for every their voyage, as often as they shall arrive at our port of Bristol, at which they are bound and holden only to arrive, all necessary charges and expenses incurred by them having been deducted, to pay to us, either in goods or money, the fifth part of the whole capital gained, we giving and granting to them and to their heirs and deputies, that they shall be free and exempt from all payment of customs on all and singular the goods and merchandise that they may bring back with them from those places thus newly discovered.

And further we have given and granted to them and to their heirs and deputies, that all mainlands, islands, towns, cities, castles and other places whatsoever discovered by them, however numerous they may happen to be, may not be frequented or visited by any other subjects of ours whatsoever without the licence of the aforesaid John and his sons and of their deputies, on pain of the loss as well of the ships or vessels daring to sail to these places discovered, as of all goods whatsoever. Willing and strictly commanding all singular our subjects as well by land as by sea, that they shall render good assistance to the aforesaid John and his sons and deputies, and that they shall give them all their favour and help as well in fitting out the ships or vessels as in buying stores and provisions with their money and in providing the other things which they must take with them on the said voyage.

In witness whereof, etc.

Witness ourself at Westminster on the fifth day of March.

By the King himself, etc.

DOCUMENT 2

"An Attempt to Raise Subscriptions in Exeter" (1586)

Before launching an American colony, Sir Walter Ralegh had to raise substantial funds. No single person, no matter how wealthy, could possibly have covered the entire cost of settlement. But the Merchant Adventurers of Exeter, a professional guild, had already invested in another enterprise, and these hard-nosed businessmen informed Ralegh that they would not advance new money "until they see that voyage ended or some success thereof."

16 January 1586.

An Attempt to Raise Subscriptions in Exeter

16 Jan., 1585. 'At this Courte [of the Merchant Adventurers] there were certaine Articles brought in. . . . touchinge a pretended voiage to Wyngandacoia and a noate of the marchantable and other commodities there founde, which beinge published and reade, *our* deputie did move the Companie to be venturers that waie. Wherevnto the Companie did answere That forasmuche as they were adventurers already with *Master* Audrian Gilberte [Adrian Gilbert] in a voyage into China they will not aduenture anie more in anie suche voiages vntil they see that voiage ended or some success thereof.'

DOCUMENT 3

Richard Hakluyt, "The 1586 Voyages" (1589)

Although Richard Hakluyt never visited America, he kept alive the English dreams of empire by publicizing explorers' accounts of the New World. For Hakluyt, colonization served as an index of national pride; it was a means of demonstrating to rival Catholic nations that a Protestant state could successfully compete for American treasure. He interviewed sailors, collecting their reports in a massive piece of propaganda entitled *The Principall Navigations, Voyages, and Discoveries of the English Nation.* In this section, Hakluyt tried to explain what had gone wrong at Roanoke, "this paradise of the worlde."

The third voyage made by a Ship, sent in the yeere 1586. to the reliefe of the Colonie planted in Virginia, at the sole charges of Sir Walter Raleigh.

In the yeere of our Lord, 1586. sir Walter Raleigh at his owne charge prepared a ship of 100. tunnes, fraighted with all maner of things in most plentiful maner for the supplie and relief of his Colonie then remaining in Virginia: but before they set saile from England, it was after Easter, so that our Colonie halfe dispaired of the comming of any supplie, wherefore euery man prepared for himselfe, determining resolutely to spend the residue of their life time in that countrey, and for the better performance of this their determination, they sowed, planted, and set such things as were necessarie for their reliefe in so plentifull a manner, as might have suffised them two yeeres without any further labor: thus trusting to their owne haruest they passed the summer till the tenth of Iune, at which time their corne which they had sowed was within one fortnight of reaping.

But then it happened, that Sir Frauncis Drake in his prosperous returne from the sacking of [Spanish settlements at] Saint Domingo, Cartagena, and Saint Augustines determined in his way homewarde to visit his countrymen the English Colonie then remayning in Virginia: so passing along coastes of Florida, the fell with the partes, where our English Colony inhabited, and hauing espyed some of that company, there he ankered, and went alande where he conferred with them of their state and welfare, and howe things had past with them: they aunswered him that they liued all, but hitherto in some scarsitie, and as yet coulde here of no supplye out of England: therefore they requested him that he would leaue with them some two or three shippes, that if in some reasonable time they heard not out of England, they might return themselues: which hee agreed to.

Some were then writing their letters to send into England, and some others making reportes of the accidents of their trauels each to other, some on lande, some on boord, a great storme arose, and droue the most of their fleete from their ankers to Sea, in which shippes, at that instant were the chiefest of the English Colony: the rest on land perceiuing this, hasted to those three sayles which were appointed to be left there, and for feare they should be left behinde, left all thinges so confusedly, as if they had bene chased from thence by a mightie armie, and no doubt so they were, for the hande of God came vpon them for the crueltie, and outrages committed by some of them against the natiue inhabitantes of that Countrie.

Immediatly after the departing of our English Colonie out of this paradise of the worlde, the shippe aboue mentioned sent and set forth at the charges of Sir Walter Ralegh, and his direction, arriued, who after some time spent in seeking our Colony vp in the Countrie, and not finding them, returned with all the aforesayd prouision into England.

About fourteene or fifteene daies after the departure of the aforesayd shippe, Sir Richard Grindfeld [Grenville] Generall of Virginia, accompanied awith three shippes well appointed for the same voyage arriued there, who not finding the aforesayd ship according to his expectation, nor hearing any newes of our English Colony, there seated, and left by him, Anno 1585, him selfe trauailing vp into diuers places of the Countrey, as well to see if he could here any newes of the Colony left there by him the yere before, vnder the charge of Master Lane his deputie, as also to discouer some places of the Countrie: but after some time spent therein not hearing any newes of them, and finding the place which they inhabited desolate, yet unwilling to loose the possession of the Countrie, which Englishmen had so long helde: after good deliberation he determined to leaue some men behinde to retaine possession of the Country: whereupon he landed 15. men in the Ile of Roanoake furnished plentifully with all maner of prouision for two yeeres, and so departed for England.

Not long after he fell with the Isles of Acores, on some of which Ilandes he landed, and spoyled the Townes of all such thinges as were worth cariage, where also he tooke diuers Spanyardes: with these, and many other exploytes done by him in this voyage, as well outwarde as homeward, he returned into England.

DOCUMENT 4

The Reverend John Higginson, "New-England's Plantation" (1630)

The Reverend John Higginson, an employee of the Massachusetts Bay Company, traveled to the New World with high expectations. Nothing he encountered there seems to have disappointed him. In a report certified as "the truth," the minister described New England as a Garden of Eden, a place where everyone could experience excellent health, great prosperity and perpetual happiness. As other documents in this section suggest, ordinary men and women were completely taken in by Higginson's promise of the good life in America.

New-Englands Plantation

I will indeauour to shew you what *New-England* is . . . and truly indeauour by Gods help to report nothing but the naked truth, and that both to tell you of the discommodities as well as of the commodities, though as the idle Prouerbe is, *Trauellers may lye by autoritie,* and so may of my selfe as once *Nehemiah* did in another case: *Shall such a Man as I lye?* No verily: It becommeth not a Preacher of Truth to be a Writer of Falshod in any degree: and therefore I haue partly seene with mine owne Eyes, and partly heard and inquired from the mouths of verie honest and religious persons, who by liuing in the Countrey a good space of time haue had experience and knowledge of the state thereof, and whose testimonies I doe beleeue as my selfe.

First therefore of the Earth of *New-England* and all the appertenances thereof: It is a Land of diuers and sundry sorts all about *Massachusetts* Bay, and at *Charles* Riuer is as fat blacke Earth as can be seene anywhere: and in other places you haue a clay soyle, in other grauell, in other sandy, as it is all about our Plantation at *Salem,* for so our Towne is now named, *Psal. 76.2.*

The forme of the Earth here in the superficies of it is neither too flat in the plainnesse, nor too high in Hils, but partakes of both in a mediocritie, and fit for Pasture, or for Plow or meddow ground, as Men please to employ it: though all the Countrey bee as it were a thicke Wood for the generall, yet in diuers places there is much ground cleared by the *Indians,* and especially about the Plantation: and I am told that about three miles from vs a Man may stand on a little hilly place and see diuers thousands of acres of ground as good as need to be, and not a Tree in the same. It is thought here is good Clay to make Bricke and Tyles and Earthen-Pot as need to be. At this instant we are setting a Bricke-Kill on worke to make Brickes and Tiles for the building of our Houses. For Stone, here is plentie of Slates at the Ile of Slate in *Massachusetts* Bay, and Lime-stone, Free-stone, and Smooth-stone, and Iron-stone, and Marble-stone also in such store, that he haue great Rocks of it, and a Harbour hard by. Our Plantation is from thence called Marble-harbour.

Of Minerals there hath yet beene but little triall made, yet we are not without great hope of being furnished in that Soyle.

The fertilitie of the Soyle is to be admired at, as appeareth in the aboundance of Grasse that groweth euerie where boh verie thicke, verie long, and verie high in diuers places: but it groweth verie wildly with a great stalke and a broad and ranker blade, because it neuer had been eaten with Cattle, nor mowed with a Sythe, and seldome trampled on by foot. It is scarce to be beleeued how our Kine and Goats, Horses and Hogges, doe thriue and prosper here and like well of this Countrey.

In our Plantation we haue already a quart of Milke for a penny: but the aboundant encrease of Corne proues this Countrey to bee a wonderment. Thirtie, fortie, fiftie, sixtie are ordinaire here: yet *Iosephs* encrease in *AEgypt* is out-stript here with vs. Out planters hope to haue more then a hundred fould this yere: and all this while I am within compasse; what will you say of two hundred fould and vpwards? It is almost incredible what great gaine some of our England Planters haue had by our Indian Corne. Credible persons haue assured me, and the partie himselfe auouched the truth of it to me, that of the setting of 13 Gallons of Corne hee hath had encrease of it 52 Hogsheads, euery Hogshead holding seuen Bushels of *London* measure, and euery Bushell was by him sold and trusted to the *Indians* for so much Beauer as was worth 18 shillings; and so of this 13 Gallons of Corne which was worth 6 shillings 8 pence, he made about 327 pounds of it the yeere following, as by reckoning will appeare: where you may see how God blessed husbandry in this Land. There is not such greate and plentifull eares of Corne I suppose any where else to bee found but in this Country: because also of varietie of colours, as red, blew and yellow, etc. and of one Corne there springeth foure or fiue hundred. I haue sent you many Eares of diuers colours that you might see the truth of it.

Little Children here by setting of Corne may earne much more than their owne maintenance.

They haue tryed our *English* Corne at new *Plimmouth* Plantation, so that all our seuerall Graines will grow here verie well, and haue a fitting Soyle for their nature.

Our Gouerner hath store of greene Pease growing in his Garden as good as euer I eat in *England*.

This Countrey aboundeth naturally with store of Rootes of great varietie and good to eat. Our Turnips, Parsnips and Carrots are here both bigger and sweeter then is ordinarily to bee found in *England*. Here are store of Pumpions, Cowcombers, and other things of that nature which I know not. Also

diuers excellent Pot-herbs grow abundantly among the Grasse, as Strawberrie leaues in all places of the Countrey, and plentie of Strawberries in their time, and Penyroyall, Wintersauerie Sorrell, Brookelime, Liuerwort, Caruell and Watercresses, also Leekes and Onions are ordinarie, and diuers Physicall Herbs. Here are also aboundance of other sweet Hearbs delightfull to the smell, whose names we know not, etc, and plentie of single Damaske Roses verie sweete; and two kinds of Herbes that beare two kinds of Flowers very sweet, which they say, are as good to make Cordage or Cloath as any Hempe or Flaxe we haue.

Excellent Vines are here vp and downe in the Woodes. Our Gouernour hath already planted a Vineyard with great hope of encrease.

Also, Mulberries, Plums, Raspberries, Corrance, Chestnuts, Filberds, Walnuts, Smalnuts, Hurtleberies and Hawes of Whitehorne neere as good as our Cherries in *England*, they grow in plentie here.

For Wood there is no better in the World I thinke, here being foure sorts of Oke differing both in the Leafe, Timber and Colour, all excellent good. There is also good Ash, Elme, Willow, Birch, Bewech, Saxafras, Iuniper Cipres, cedar, Spruce, Pines and Firre that will yeeld abundance of Turopentine, Pitch, Tarre, Masts and other materials for building both of Ships and Houses. Also here are store of Sumacke Trees, they are good for dying and tanning of Leather, likewise such Trees yeeld a precious Gem called Wine Beniamen, that they say is excellent for perfumes. Also here be diuers Roots and Berries wherewith the *Indians* dye excellent holding colours that no raine nor washing can alter. Also, wee haue materials to make Sope-Ashes and Salt-Peter in aboundance.

For Beasts there are some Beares, and they say some Lyons also; for they haue been seen at Cape Anne. Also here are seuerall sorts of Deere, some whereof bring three or foure young ones at once, which is not ordinarie in *England*. Also Wolues, Foxes, Beauers, Otters, Martins, great wild Cats, and a great Beast called a Molke [moose] as bigge as an Oxe. I haue seen the Skins of all these Beasts since I same to this Plantation excepting Lyons. Also here are great store of Squerrls, some greater, and some smaller and lesser: there are some of the lesser sort, they tell men, that by a certain Skill will fly from Tree to Tree though they stand farre distant.

Of the Aire of New-England with the temper and Creatures in it

The Tempers of the Aire of *New-England* is one speciall thing that commends this place. Experience doth manifest that there is hardly a more healthfull place to be found in the World that agreeth better with our English bodyes. Many that haue beene weake and sickly in old *England,* by comming hither haue been thoroughly healed and growne healthfull strong. For here is an extraordinarie cleere and dry Aire that is of a most healing nature to all such as are of a Cold, Melancholy, Flegmatick, Rheumatick temper of Body. None can more truely speake hereof by their own experience then my selfe. My Friends that knew me can well tell how verie sickly I haue bin and continually in Physick, being much troubled with a tormenting paine through an extraordinarie weaknesse of my Stomacke, and abundance of Melancholicke humors; but since I came hither on this Voyage, I thanke God, I haue had perfect health, and freed from paine and vomiting, hauing a Stomacke to digest the hardest and coursest fare, who before could not eat finest meat; and whereas my Stomacke could onely digest and didt require such drinke as was both strong and stale, now I ca and doe often times drink *New-England* water verie well; and I that haue not gone without a Cap for many yeeres together, neither durst leaue off the same, haue now cast away my Cap, and doe weare none at all in the day time: and whereas beforetime I cloathed my selfe with double cloathes and thicke Wastcoates to keepe me warme, euen in the Summer time, I doe now goe as thin clad as any, onely wearing a light Stuffe Cassocke vpon my Shirt, and Stuffe Breeches of one thicknesse without Linings. Besides I haue one of my Children that was formerly most lamentably handled with sore breaking out of both his hands and feet of the Kings- Euill, but since

he came hither hee is very well ouer [*sic*] he was, and there is hoep of perfect recouerie shortly euen by the very wholesomnesse of the Aire, altering, digesting and drying vup the cold and crude humous [*sic*] of the Body: and therefore I thinke it is a wise course for al cold complections to come to take Physick in *New-England:* for a sup of *New-Englands* Aire is better than a whole draught of old *Englands* Ale.

In the Summer time in the midst of *Iuly* and *August,* it is a good deale hotter than in old *England:* and in Winter, *Ianuary* and *February* are much colder as they say: but the Spring and Autumne are of a middle temper.

Fowles of the Aire are plentifull here, and of all sorts as we haue in *England* as farre as I can learne, and a great many of strange Fowles which wee know not. Whilst I was writing these things, one of our Men brought home an Eagle which hee had killed in the Wood: they say they are good meate. Also here are many kinds of excellent Hawkes, both Sea Hawkes and Land Hawkes: and my selfe walking in the Woods with another in company, sprung a Partridge so bigge that through the heauinesse of his Body could fly but a little way: they that haue killed them, say they are as bigge as our Hens. Here are likewise aboundance of Turkies often killed in the Woods, farre greater then our English Turkies, and exceeding fat, sweet and fleshy, for here they haue aboundance of feeding all the yeere long, as Strawberries, in Summer al places are full of them, and all manner of Berries and Fruits. In the Winter time I haue seene Flockes of Pidgeons, and haue eaten of them: they doe fly from Tree to Tree as other Birds doe, which our Pidgeons will not doe in *England:* they are of all colours as ours are, but their wings and tayles are far longer and therefore it is likely they fly swifter to escape the terrible Hawkes in this Country. In Winter time this Country doth abound with wild Geese, wild Duckes, and other Sea Fowle, that a great part of winter the Planters haue eaten nothing but roastmeate of diuers Fowles which they haue killed. . . .

Thus of *New-Englands* commodities, now I will tell you of some discommodities that are here to be found.

First, in the Summer season for these three months, *Iune, Iuly*, and *August*, we are troubled much with little Flyes called Musketoes, being the same they are troubled with in *Lincolneshiere* and the Fens: and they are nothing but Gnats, which except they bee smoked out of their houses are troublesome in the night season.

Secondly, in the Winter season for two months space, the earth is commonly couered with Snow, which is accompanied with sharp biting Frosts, something more sharpe then is in old *England*, and therefore are forced to make great Fires.

Thirdly, the Countrey being very full of Woods, and Wilderness, doth also much abound with Snakes and Serpents of strange colours, and huge greatnesse: yea there are some Serpents called Rattle-snakes, that haue Rattles in their Tailes, that will not fly from a man as others will, but will flye vpon him and sting him so mortally, that hee will dye within a quarter of an houre after, except the parttie [sic] stinged haue about him some of the root of an Herbe called Snakeweed to bit on, and then hee shall receiue no harme: but yet seldome falles it out that any hurt is done by these. About three yeares since, an *Indian* was stung to death by one of them, but wee heard of none since that time.

Fourthly and lastly, Here wants as it were good company of honest Christians to bring with them Horses, Kine and Sheepe to make vse of this fruitfull Land: great pitty it is to see so much good ground for Corne and for Grasse as any is vnder the Heauens, to ly altogether vnoccupied, when so many honest Men and their Families in old *England* through the populousnesse thereof, do make very hard shift to liue one by the other.

Now, thus you know what *New-England* is, as also with the commodities and discommodities thereof: now I will shew you a little of the Inhabitants thereof, and their gouernment.

For their Gouerners they haue Kings, which they call *Saggamores*, some greater, and some lesser, according to the number of their Subiects.

The greatest *Saggamores* about vs can not make aboue three hundred Men, and other lesse *Sagg-amores* haue not aboue fifteen Subiects, and others neere about us but two.

Their Subiects aboue twelue yeeres since were swept away by a great and grieuous Plague that was amongst them, so that there are verie few left to inhabite the Country.

The *Indians* are not able to make vse of the one fourth part of the Land, neither haue they any setled places, as Townes to dwell in, nor any ground as they challenge for their owne possession, but change their habitation from place to place.

For their Statures, they are a tall and strong limmed People, their colours are tawny, they goe naked, saue only they are in part couered with Beasts Skins on one of their shoulders, and weare something before their Priuities: their Haire is generally blacke, and cut before like our Gentelewomen, and one locke longer then the rest, much like to our Gentelmen, which fashion I thinke came from hence into *England*.

For their weapons, they haue Bowes and Arrowes, some of them headed with Bone, and some with Brasse: I haue sent you some of them for an example.

The Men for the most part liue idely, they doe nothing but hunt and fish: their wiues set their Corne and doe all their other worke. They haue little Household stuffe, as a kettle, and some other Vessels like Trayes, Spoones, Dishes and Baskets.

Their Houses are verie little and homely, being made with small Poles pricked into the ground, and so bended and fastned at the tops, and on the sides they are matted with Boughes and couered on the Roofe with Sedge and old Mats, and for their beds that they take their rest on, they haue a Mat.

They doe generally professe to like well of our comming and planting here; partly because there is aboundance of ground that they cannot possesse nor make vse of, and partly because our being heere will bee a meanes both of relief to them when they want, and also a defence from their Enemies, wherewith (I say) bfore [sic] this Plantation began, they were often indangered.

For their Religion, they doe worship two Gods, a good God and an euill God: the good God they call *Tantum*, and their euill God whom they feare will doe them hurt, they call *Squantum*.

For their dealing with vs, we neither feare them nor trust them, for fourtie of our Musketeeres will driue fiue hundred of them out of the Field. We vse them kindly, they will come into our Houses sometimes by halfe a douzen or halfe a score at a time when we are at victuals, but will aske or take nothing but what we giue them.

We purpose to learne their language as soone as we can, which will be a meanes to do them good.

DOCUMENT 5

Thomas Dudley, "Letter to the Right Honourable, My Very Good Lady, the Lady Bridget, Countess of Lincoln" (1631)

Before departing for America, Thomas Dudley had held a responsible position under the Earl of Lincoln. Like his employer, Dudley became a Puritan. Because of his strength of character, the members of the Massachusetts Bay Company elected Dudley the colony's first deputy governor. In this letter he informs the Countess of Lincoln of the suffering that the settlers have endured, and while his perceptions of the New World obviously differ from those of the Reverend Higginson, Dudley envisions a successful colony peopled by god-fearing men and women.

Madam,

Your letters (which are not common nor cheap) following me hither into *New England*, and bringing with them renewed testimonies of the accustomed favours you honoured me with in the *old*, have drawn from me this narrative retribution, which (in respect of your proper interest in some persons of great note amongst us) was the thankfullest present I had to send over the seas. . . .

> Your Honour's
> Old
> Thankful Servant,
> THOMAS DUDLEY.

Boston in *New England*,
[March 12, 1631]

For the satisfaction of your Honour, and some friends, and for the use of such as shall hereafter intend to increase our plantation in *New England*, I have . . . thought fit to commit to memory our present condition, and see what hath befallen us since our arrival here; which I will do shortly, after my usual manner, and must do rudely, having yet no table, nor other room to write in, than by the fireside upon my knee, in this sharp winter; to which my family must have leave to resort, though they break good manners, and make me sometimes forget what I would say, and say what I would not.

Touching the plantacon which wee here have begun, it fell out thus:—About the yeare 1627, some friends beeing togeather in Lincolnshire, fell into some discourse about New England, and the plantinge of the gospell there; and after some deliberation wee imparted our reasons by lres [letters] and messages to some in London and the west country, where it was likewise deliberately thought uppon, and at length with often negotiation soe ripened that in the year 1628, wee procured a patent from his Matie for our planing betweene the Matachusets Bay and Charles River on the south and the River of Merimack on the North; and 3 miles on eyther side of those Rivers and Bay; as allso for the government of thos who did or should inhabit wth. in that compass.

Wee came to such resolution that in April, 1630, wee sett saile from old England with 4 good shipps. And in May following, 8 more followed; 2 haveing gone before in February and March, and 2 more following in June and August, besides another set out by a private merchant. Theis 17 shipps arrived all safe in New England for the increase of the plantacon here this yeare 1630—but make a long, a troublesome and costly voyage, beeing all windbound long in England, and hindred with contrary winds, after they sett saile and soe scattered wth. mists and tempests that few of them arrived together. Our 4 shipps which sett out in Aprill arrived here in June and July, where wee found the Colony in a sadd and unexpected condition, above 80 of them beeing dead the winter before, and many of those alive, weake and sicke; all the corne and bread amongst them all, hardly sufficient to feed upon a fortnight, insomuch that the remainder of the 180 servents wee had the two yeares before sent over, cominge to us for victualls to sustaine them, wee found ourselves wholly unable to feed them by reason that the provisions shipped for them were taken out of the shipp they were put in, and they who were trusted to shipp them in another, failed us, and left them behind; whereupon necessity enforced us to our extreme loss to give them all libertie, who had cost us about 16 or 20 £. a person furnishing and sending over. But bearing theis things as wee might, wee be-

ganne to consult of the place of our sitting downe; for Salem, where wee landed, pleased us not.

Wee were forced . . . and for our present shelter to plant dispersedly, some at Charles Towne which standeth on the North side of the mouth of Charles river; some on the south side thereof, which place wee named Boston; (as wee intended to have done the place wee first resolved on) some of us upon Mistick, which wee named Meadford; some of us westwards on Charles river, 4 miles from Charles Towne, which place wee named Watertowne; others of us 2 miles from Boston, in a place wee named Rocksbury; others upon the river of Sawgus betweene Salem and Charles Towne; and the western men 4 miles South from Boston, at a place wee named Dorchester. This dispersion troubled some of us, but helpe it wee could not; wanting ability to remoove to any place fitt to build a Towne upon, and the time too short to deliberate any longer, least the winter should surprize us before wee had builded our houses. The best counsel wee could find out was, to build a fort to retire to, in some convenient place, if an enemy pressed thereunto, after wee should have fortified ourselves against the injuries of wett and cold. So ceasing to consult further for that time, they who had health to labour fell to building, wherein many were interrupted with sicknes and many dyed weekely, yea almost dayley. . . . Insomuch that the shipps beeing now upon their returne, some for England, some for Ireland, there was, as I take it not much less than an hundred (some thing many more) partly out of dislike of our government which restrained and punished their excesses, and partly through fear of famine, not seeing other meanes than by their labour to feed themselves, which returned back againe. And glad were wee so to bee rid of them. Others also afterwards heareing of men of their owne disposition, which were planted at Pascataway, went from us to them, whereby though our numbers were lessened, yet wee accounted ourselves nothing weakened by their removeall. . . .

The shipps beeinge gone, victuals wastinge, and mortality increasinge, wee held diverse fasts in our severall congregations, but the Lord would not yet

A Declaration for the certaine time of dravving the great ftanding Lottery.

Excitement about the New World reached ordinary English people who never intended to migrate. An advertisement for a lottery designed to raise money for the Virginia Company captures the commercial character of colonization.

bee depricated; for about the beginning of September, dyed Mr. *Gager*, a right godly man, a skilful chirurgeon, and one of the deacons of our congregation; and Mr. *Higginson*, one of the ministers of Salem, a zealous and a profitable preacher;—this of a consumption, that of a feaver, and on the 30th of September, dyed Mr. *Johnson* another of the 5 undertakers (the Lady *Arrabella*, his wife, being dead a month before.) This gentleman was a prime man amongst us, haveing the best estate of any, zealous for religion and greatest furtherer of this plantation. He made a most godly end, dying willingly, professing his life better spent in promoting this plantacon than it would have beene any other way. He left to us a loss greater than the most conceived. . . .and of the people who came over with us, from the time of their setting saile from England in Aprill, 1630, untill December followinge, there dyed by estimacon about 200 at the least—Soe lowe hath the Lord brought us! Well, yet they who survived were not discouraged, but bearing God's corrections with humilitye and trusting in his mercies. . . .

I should before have mentioned how both the English and Indian corne beeinge at tenne shillings a strike, and beaver beeinge valued a. 6 shilling a pound, wee made laws to restraine the selling of corne to the Indians, and to leave the price of beaver at libertie, which was presently sold for tenne and 20 shillings a pound. I should alsoe have remembered how the halfe of our cowes and almost all our mares and goats, sent us out of England dyed at sea in their passage hither, and that those intended to be sent us out of Ireland were not sent at all; all which togeather with the loss of our six months building, occasioned by our intended removeall to a Towne to bee fortified weakened our estates, especially the estates of the undertakers, who were 3 or 4000£. engaged in the joynt stock, which was now not above soe many hundreds; yet many of us laboured to beare it as comfortably as wee could, rememberinge the end of our comeinge hether and knowinge the power of God who canne support and raise us againe, and useth to bring his servants lowe that the meeke may bee made glorious by deliverance. Psal. 112. . . .

But now haveing some leasure to discourse of the motives for other men's comeinge to this place, or their abstaininge from it, after my breif manner I say this;—That if any come hether to plant for worldly ends that canne live well at home, he committs an errour, of which he will soone repent him. But if for spirituall, and that noe particular obstacle hinder his removeall, hee may find here what may well content him vizt: materialls to build, fewell to burne, ground to plant, seas and rivers to fish in, a pure ayer to breathe in, good water to drinke, till wine or beare canne be made; which, togeather with the cowees, hoggs and goates brought hether allready, may suffice for food; for as for foule and venison, they are dainties here as well as in England. For cloaths and bedding, they must bringe them wth. them, till time and industry produce them here. In a word, wee yett enjoy little to be envyed, but endure much to be pittyed in the siknes and mortallitye of our people. And I do the more willingly use this open and plaine dealinge, least other men should fall short of their expectacons when they come hetehr, as wee to our great prejudice did, by meanes of letters sent us from hence into England, wherein honest man out of a desire to draw over others to them, wrote somewhat hyperbolically of many things here. If any godly men, out of religious ends, will come over to helpe us in the good worke wee are about, I think they cannot dispose of themselves nor of their estates more to God's glory, and the furtherance of their owne reckoninge; but they must not bee of the poorer sort yett, for diverse years; for wee have found by experience that they have hindred, not furthered the worke—And for profaine and deboshed persons, their oversight in comeinge

hether is wondered at, where they shall find nothing to content them. If there bee any endued with grace and furnished with meanes to feed themselves and theirs for 18 months, and to build and plant, lett them come over into our Macedonia and helpe us, and not spend themselves and their estates in a less profittable employment; for others I conceive they are not yet fitted for this busines.

Touching the discouragements which the sicknes and mortality which every first year hath seized upon us. . . . may give to such who have cast any thoughts this way (of which mortality it may bee said of us allmost as of the Egiptians, that there is not an house where there is not one dead, and in some howses many) the naturall causes seem to bee in the want of warm lodginge, and good dyet, to which Englishmen are habittuated at home; and in the suddain increase of heate which they endure that are landed here in somer, the salt meates at sea haveinge prepared their bodyes thereto, for those onely 2 last yeares dyed of feavers who landed in June and July; as those of plymouth who landed in the winter dyed of the scirvy, as did our poorer sort, whose howses and bedding kept them not sufficiently warm, nor their dyet sufficiently in heart. . . .

Amongst those who dyed about the end of this Jannuary, there was a girle of 11 years old, the daugher of one *John Ruggles* of whose family and kindred dyed so many, that for some reason it was matter of observacon amongst us; who in the time of her sicknes expressed to the minister and to those about her, soe much faith and assurance of salvation, as is rarely found in any of that age, which I thought not unworthy here to committ to memory; and if any taxe mee for wastinge paper with recordinge theis small matters, such may consider that little mothers bring fourth little children, small common wealths;—matters of small moment, the reading whereof yett is not to be despised by the judicious, because small things in the beginning of naturall or politique bodyes are as remarkable as greater in bodyes full growne.

DOCUMENT 6

Pond, Letter to His Parents (1631)

L ike the Countess of Lincoln (see Document 5), William Pond and his wife in England received a letter describing life in Massachusetts in March 1631. But their letter came not from the deputy governor but from their son, whose first name is not known. Like many settlers to New England, the younger Pond traveled with his own wife and children. Pond acquainted his parents with the harshness of emigrant life: scarce food supplies, disease and death, and danger from Indians. Pond believed the colonists would survive only "if we may have supplies every year from old England, otherwise we can not subsist."

[March 15, 1631.]

To my lovinge father William Ponde, at Etherston in Suffolcke give theis

Most loveinge & kinde Father & Mother,—My humble deutye remembreid unto you, trusteinge in God you are in good hellthe, & I pray remembr̄ love unto my brother Joseife. . . . I knowe, lovinge father & do confese that I wase an undeuteyefull cheilld unto you when I liveied withe you & by you, for the wiche I am muche sorrowful & greveid for it, trusteinge in God that he will geide me that I will never offend you so aney more & I truste in God that you will forgive me for it. My wreightein unto you is to lete you understand what a cuntrey theis New Eingland is whar we live. Her ar but fewoe Eingeines [Indians], a great parte of them deyeid theis winture, it was thought it wase of the plage. Thay ar a craftey peple & thaye will cusson [cozen] & cheat, & thay ar a suttell peple, & whareas we ded expect gret stor of bever her is littell or non to be had. . . .Thay are proper men & clenjointeide men & maney of them go nacked with a skein abought thare loines, but now sume of them get Eingellishemenes parell; & the cuntrey is verie rockey & heilley & sume champine ground & the soile is verie flete, & her is sume good ground & marshe ground, but her is no Myckellmes. Springe cattell threive well here, but thay give small stor of mylck. The best cattell for proffeit is sweines & a good sweine is her at 5ᵗ preise, a goose is worthe 2ᵗ a good one gote. Her is teimbur good store & ackornes good stor, and her is good stor of feishe ife we had botes to goo for & leynes to serv to feishein. Her are good stor of weield foule, but thay are hard to come bye. It is hardur to get a shoot then it is in ould Eingland & peple her ar subjecte to deisesese, for her have deyeid of the scurveye & of the burninge fever neye too hundreid & ode; beside as maney leyethe lame . . . & proviseyones ar her at a wondurfull rat. Wheat mell [meal] is xiiijˢ a bushell, & pese xˢ, & mault xˢ, & Einder seid wheat is xvˢ & thare other wheat is xˢ. Buttr xiiᵈ a pound & chese is 8ᵈ a pound, & all kind of speyseis verie der & allmoste non to be got. If theis ship had but thanckes be to God for sendinge of it in.[1] I reseyvied from the shipe a hogseite of mell, & the Governor tellethe me of a hundreid waight of chese the wiche I have reseyveid parte of it. I humblie thancke you for it. I ded expecte too coues, the wiche I had non, nor I do not arnestly deseyer that you shoold send me aney, becauese the cuntrey is not so as we ded expecte it. Therefor, lovinge father, I wolld intret you that wou woolld send me a ferckeine of buttr & a hogseit of mault onground, for we dreinck notheinge but wall-tre. . . . For the fraute, if you of youer love will send them I will paye the fraute, for her is notheinge to be gote witheought we had cumemodeytes to go up to the Este partes amonckest the Eingeines to truck, for her whare we live her is no bever. Her is no clothe to be had to mack no parell, & shoes are at 5ˢ a payer for me, & that clothe that is woorthe 2ˢ 8ᵈ a yard is woorthe her 5ˢ. So I pray, father, send me fouer or five yardes of clothe to mack us sume parell, & lovinge father, thoue I be far distante from you yet I pray you remembure me as youer cheield, & we do not know how longe we may subseiste, for we can not live her witheought provyseyones from ould Eingland. Therefore, I pray do not put away youer shope stufe, for I theinck that in the eind, if I live it, it must be my leveinge, for we do not know how longe theis plantatyon will stand, for sume of the magnautes that ded uphould it have turned off thare men & have givene it overe. Beseides, God hath tacken away the chefeiste stud in the land, Mʳ Johnson & the ladye Arabella his wife, wiche wase the cheifeste man of estate in the land & one that woold a don moste good.²

Her cam over xxv passeingares & thare came backe agayn fouer skore & od parsones, & as maney more wolld a cume if thay had whare withe all to bringe them hom, for her ar maney that cam over the laste yere wiche wase woorthe too hundreid poundes afore thay cam ought of ould Eingland that betwine theis & Myckellmes [September], wille be hardly worthe xxxʳ. So her we may live if we have suppleyes everey yere from ould Eingland, otherweyse we can not subseiset. I may, as I will, worek hard, sete an ackorne of Eindey wheat, & if we do not set it withe fishe & that will coste xxˢ, if we set it witheought fishe they shall have but a por crope. So father, I pray, consedre of my cause, for her will be but a verey por beinge, no beinge witheought, lovinge father, youer helpe withe provisseyones from ould Eingland. I had thought to a cam home in theis sheipe, for my provisseyones were allmoste all spente, but that I humbley thanck you for youer gret love &kindnes in seindinge me sume provissyones, or elles I sholld & myne a bine halef faminyshed, but now I will, if it plese God that I have my hellthe, I will plant what corne I can, & if provisseyones be not cheper betwein theis & Myckellmes & that I do no her from you what I wase beste to do, I purpose to cume hom at Myckellmes.

From Walltmtowne [Watertown] in New England the 15 of Marche, 1630 [1631].

We ware wondurfule seick as we cam at sea, withe the small poxe. No man thought that I & my leittell cheilld woolld a liveid. My boye is lame & my gurell too, & thar deyeid in the sheip that I cam in xiiij persones.

Study Questions

1. Why, after reports of the problems at Roanoke had been published, did the New England colonists seem so ill-prepared for the demands of daily life in the New World?

2. How can you explain the different perceptions of New England presented in the writings of Higginson, Dudley, and Pond?

3. Pond was clearly having a very difficult time surviving in New England. If he just needed food and clothes for his family, why did he appeal to his distant father and not to someone living in Massachusetts?

❦   ❧

❧ 3 ❧

Puritan Commonwealth

During the early decades of the seventeenth century, English people of various classes and backgrounds came to a similar conclusion. The state-supported Church of England desperately required reform. Their enemies called them Puritans, and as the movement gained force the reformers took the cause to Parliament. Charles I (1625–1649) detested pushy reformers, and to counter their growing influence in church and state, he decided not only to rule England without the assistance of an elected Parliament but also to elevate church officials who hated Puritanism.

Advocates of religious reform believed God would chastise the nation for its failure to purify the church. To avoid that punishment, Puritans fled England by the thousands, trusting that the Lord would "provide a shelter and a hiding place for us and ours." During the so-called Great Migration of the 1630s more than 10,000 Puritans left for America, and in this sanctuary they dedicated themselves to achieving the religious and political reforms that had eluded them in England.

These emigrants have not fared well in history books. Later generations have blamed the Puritans for almost everything they dislike in contemporary society. The founders of New England, we learn, hated sex, strong drink, and good times. They dressed in somber clothing and, worst of all, spent their days persecuting neighbors for petty faults. Few of these accusations of this sort have a basis in fact. It is best to avoid such stereotypes and confront the Puritans directly, as people who had made a very hard decision to move to the New World and once there faced the daunting task of remodeling English society.

The documents presented in this chapter explore the difficult issues confronting the Puritans in America. They understood that human society contains the seeds of conflict. The problem was finding a means to bring order out of diversity, to unite individuals into cohesive communities. In the name of reform, New England Puritans struggled to find answers. John Winthrop, the first governor of Massachusetts Bay, drew up a plan for a new godly society while the settlers were still at sea. In his speech aboard the *Arbella* (Document 1), Winthrop urged the colonists to bring the spirit of Christian "love" to their daily affairs and to remember that God had formed a special covenant with the people of New England. If they purified the church in the wilderness, the Lord would preserve them from danger.

The covenant model pervaded all aspects of public life in seventeenth-century Massachusetts. New England towns were not loose collections of people who happened to settle land in a certain area. The first settlers of Springfield, for example, entered into a formal agreement (Document 2) stating exactly how godly families— "rich and poore"—might live in peace and prosperity.

The key element in Puritan thought was voluntarism. The founders of the Bay Colony learned—as the leaders of some modern societies have not—that genuine communities cannot be based on force. Violence may yield temporary obedience, but it never promotes effective cohesion. *The Laws and Liberties* (Document 3), a sophisticated code of law written in 1648, insisted that ordinary people—those who had elected representatives to the colonial legislature—fully understand the rules governing their society. Adult male citizens took oaths as "freemen" (Document 4), and it is not surprising that a commonwealth stressing voluntarism should have allowed a much larger percentage of its population to vote than did England. In 1636 the Reverend John Cotton had to teach an English nobleman about the democratization of New England politics (Document 5), a difficult task he handled with admirable diplomacy. The goal was to establish a proper balance between liberty and authority. That was precisely the point Winthrop made in a lecture to the colonial assembly in 1645 (Document 6).

Ordinary Puritans came to New England primarily for religious reasons. In Congregational churches established in each community, men and women wrestled with their own sinful condition. After reading Scripture and listening to educated ministers, some people experienced the stirrings of grace, a wonderful sense that they might be among the Lord's "elect." For many settlers, making a statement of faith before their neighbors was the high point of their lives. The Reverend Thomas Shepard, the Congregational minister for Cambridge, recorded the confessions of Goodwife Stevenson and Abram Arrington, the town blacksmith (Document 7). Anne Bradstreet, Thomas Dudley's daughter (see chapter 2), expressed her faith in lyric poetry, powerfully placing a woman's everyday concerns in divine perspective (Document 8).

DOCUMENT 1

John Winthrop, "A Modell of Christian Charity" (1630)

John Winthrop (1588–1649) had been a modestly successful lawyer in England. The decision to move to the New World revealed his brilliant capacity for leadership, and no one thought more deeply about the Puritan mission to America. In this document Governor Winthrop explained how diverse individuals might form a cohesive, godly society. This was no utopian exercise. Winthrop believed that a covenanted people could substitute Christian love for self-interest.

❦ ❦

Christian Charitie

A Modell Hereof

God Almightie in his most holy and wise providence hath soe disposed of the Condicion of mankinde, as in all times some must be rich some poore, some highe and eminent in power and dignitie; others meane and in subieccion.

The Reason Hereof

1. Reas: *First,* to hold conformity with the rest of his workes, being delighted to shewe forthe the glory of his wisdome in the variety and differance of the Creatures and the glory of his power, in ordering all these differences for the preservacion and good of the whole, and the glory of his greatnes that as it is the glory of princes to haue many officers, soe this great King will haue many Stewards counting himselfe more honoured in dispenceing his guifts to man by man, then if hee did it by his owne immediate hand.

2. Reas: *Secondly,* That he might haue the more occasion to manifest the worke of his Spirit: first, vpon the wicked in moderateing and restraineing them: soe that the riche and mighty should not eate vvp the poore, nor the poore, and dispised rise vpp against theire superiours, and shake off theire yoake; 2ly in the regenerate in exercising his graces in them, as in the greate ones, theire loue mercy, gentlenes, temperance etc., in the poore and inferiour sorte, theire faithe patience, obedience etc:

3. Reas: Thirdly, That every man might haue need of other, and from hence they might be all knitt more nearly together in the Bond of brotherly afeccion: from hence it appeares plainely that noe man is made more honourable then another or more wealthy etc., out of any perticuler and singular respect to himselfe but for the glory of his Creator and the Common good of the Creature, Man. . . .

The diffinition which the Scripture giues vs of loue is this Loue is the bond of perfection. First, it is a bond, or ligament, 2ly, it makes the worke perfect. There is noe body but consistes of partes and that which knitts these partes together giues the body its perfection, because it makes eache parte soe contiguous to other as thereby they doe mutually participate with eache other, both in strengthe and infirmity in pleasure and paine, to instance in the most perfect of all bodies, Christ and his church make one body: the severall partes of this body considered apart before they were vnited were as disproportionate and as much disordering as soe many contrary quallities or elements but when christ comes and by his spirit and loue knitts all these partes to himselfe and each to other, it is become the most perfect and best proportioned boldly in the world. . . .

For patterns wee haue that first of our Saviour whoe out of his good will in obedence to his father, becomeing a parte of this body, and being knitt with it in the bond of loue, found such a natiue sensiblenes of our infirmities and sorrowes as hee willingly yeilded himselfe to deathe to ease the infirmities of the rest of his body and soe heale theire sorrowes: from the like Sympathy of partes did the Apostles and many thousands of the Saintes lay downe theire liues for Christ againe, the like wee may see in the members of this body among themselues. . . .

Wee shall finde in the histories of the churche in all ages the sweete Sympathie of affeccions which was in the members of this body one towards another, theire chearfulnes in serueing and suffering together how liberall they were without repineing harbourers without grudgeing and helpfull without reproacheing and all from hence they had feruent loue amongst them which onely make[s] the practise of mercy constant and easie.

The next consideracion is how this loue comes to be wrought; Adam in his first estate was a perfect modell of mankinde in all theire generacions, and in him this loue was perfected in regard of the habit, but Adam Rent in himselfe from his Creator, rent all his posterity allsoe one from another, whence it comes that every man is borne with this principle in him, to loue and seeke himselfe onely and thus a man continueth till Christ comes and takes possession of the soule, and infuseth another principle loue to God and our brother. And this latter haueing continuall supply from Christ, as the head and roote by which hee is vnited get the predominence in the soule, soe by little and little expells the former 1 John 4. 7. loue cometh of god and every one that loueth is borne of god, soe that this loue is the fruite of the new birthe, and none can haue it but the new Creature. . . .

Thus it is betweene the members of Christ, each discernes by the worke of the spirit his owne Image and resemblance in another, and therefore cannot but loue him as he loues himselfe: Now when the soule which is of a sociable nature finds any thing like to it selfe, it is like Adam when Eue was brought to him, shee must haue it one with herselfe this is fleshe of my fleshe (saith shee) and bone of my bone shee conceiues a greate delighte in it, therefore shee desires nearenes and familiarity with it: shee hath a greate propensity to doe it good and receiues such content in it, as feareing the miscarriage of her beloued sheet bestowes it in the inmost closett of her heart, shee will not endure that it shall want any good which shee can giue it, if by occasion shee be withdrawne from the Company of it, shee is still lookeing towardes the place where shee left her beloued, if shee heare it groane shee is with it presently, if shee finde it sadd and disconsolate shee sighes and mournes with it, shee hath noe such ioy, as to see her beloued merry and thriueing, if shee see it wronged, shee cannot beare it without passion, shee setts noe boundes of her affeccions, nor hath any thought of reward, shee findes recompence enoughe in the exercise of her loue towardes it. . . .

It rests now to make some applicacion of this discourse by the present designe which gaue the occasion by writeing of it.

1. For the persons, wee are a Company professing our selues fellow members of Christ, In which respect onely though wee were absent from eache other many miles, and had our imploymentes as farre distant, yet wee ought to account our selues knitt together by this bond of loue, and liue in the exercise of it, if wee would haue comforte of our being in Christ. . . .

2ly. for the worke wee haue in hand, it is by a mutuall consent through a speciall overruleing providence, and a more than an ordinary approbation of the Churches of Christ to seeke out a place of Cohabitation and Consorteshipp vnder a due forme of Government both ciuill and ecclesiasticall. In such cases as this the care of the publique must oversway all private repsects, by which not onely conscience, but meare Ciuill pollicy doth binde vs; for it is a true rule that perticuler estates cannott subsist in the ruine of the publique.

3ly. The end is to improue our liues to doe more seruice to the Lord the comforte and encrease of the body of christe whereof wee are members that our selues and posterity may be the better preserued from the Common corrupcions of this euill world to serue the Lord and worke out our Salvacion vnder the power and purity of his holy Ordinances.

4ly for the meanes whereby this must bee effected, they are 2fold, a Conformity with the worke and end wee aime at, these wee see are extraordinary, therefore wee must not content our selues with vsuall ordinary meanes whatsoever wee did or ought to haue done when wee liued in England, the same must wee doe and more alsoe where wee goe: That which the most in theire Churches maineteine as a truthe in professional onely, wee must bring into familiar and constant practise, as in this duty of loue wee must loue brotherly without dissimulation, wee must loue one another with a pure heart feruently wee must beare one anothers burthens, wee must not looke onely on our owne things, but allsoe on the things of our brethren, neither must wee think that the lord will beare with such faileings at our hands as hee dothe from those among whome wee haue liued. . . .

Thus stands the cause between God and vs, wee are entered into Covenant with him for this worke, wee haue taken out a Commission, the Lord hath giuen vs leaue to drawe our owne Articles wee haue herevpon besought him of favour and blessing: Now if the Lord shall please to heare vs, and bring vs in peace to the place wee desire, then hath hee ratified this Covenant and sealed our Commission, [and] will expect a strickt performance of the Articles contained in it, but if wee shall neglect the observacion of these Articles which are the ends wee haue propounded, and dissembling with our God, shall fall to embrace this present world and prosecute our carnall intencions, seekeing great things for our selues and our posterity, the Lord will surely breake out in wrathe against vs be revenged of such a periured people and make vs knowe the price of the breache of such a Covenant.

Now the onely way to avoyde this shipwracke and to provide for our posterity is to followe the Counsell of Micah, to doe Justly, to loue mercy, to talke humbly with our God, for this end, wee must be knitt together in this worke as one man, wee must entertaine each other in brotherly Affeccion, wee must be willing to abridge our selues of our superfluities, for the supply of others necessities, wee must vphold a familiar Commerce together in all meekeness, gentlenes, patience and liberallity, wee must delight in eache other, make others Condicions our owne reioyce together, mourne together, labour, and suffer together, allwayes haueing before our eyes our Commission and Community in the worke, our Community as members of the same body, soe shall wee keepe the unitie of the spirit in the bond of peace, the Lord will be our God and delight to dwell among vs, as his owne people and will commaund a blessing vpon vs in all our wayes, soe that wee shall see much more of his wisdome power goodnes and truthe then formerly wee haue beene

acquainted with, wee shall finde that the God of Israell is among vs, when tenn of vs shall be able to resist a thousand of our enemies, when hee shall make vs a prayse and glory, that men shall say of succeeding plantacions: the lord make it like that of New England: for wee must Consider that wee shall be as a Citty vpon a Hill, the eies of oll people are vppon vs; soe that if wee shall deale falsely withour god in this worke wee haue vndertaken and soe cause him to withdrawe his present help from vs, wee shall be made a story and a by-word through the world, wee shall open the mouthes of enemies to speake euill of the wayes of god and all professours for Gods sake; wee shall shame the faces of many of gods worthy seruants, and cause theire prayers to be turned into Cursses vpon vs till wee be consumed out of the good land whether wee are goeing: And to shutt vpp this discourse with that exhortacion of Moses that faithfull seruant of the Lord in his last farewell to Israel Deut. 30. Beloued there is now sett before vs life, and good, deathe and euill in that wee are Commaunded this day to loue the Lord our God, and the loue one another to walke in his wayes and to keepe his Commaundements and his Ordinance, and his lawes, and the Articles of our Covenant with him that wee may liue and be multiplyed, and that the Lord our God may blesse vs in the land whether wee goe to possesse it: But if our heartes shall turne away soe that wee will not obey, but shall be seduced and worshipp other Gods our pleasures, and proffitts, and serue them; it is propounded vnto vs this day, wee shall surely perishe out of the good Land whether wee passe over this vast Sea to possesse it;

Therefore lett vs choose life,
that wee, and our Seede,
may liue; by obeyeing his
voyce, and cleaueing to him,
for hee is our life, and
our prosperity.

DOCUMENT 2

Springfield, Massachusetts "Articles of Agreement" (1636)

W inthrop and most people who participated in the "Great Migration" settled in small communities in eastern Massachusetts. A few ventured further west, however, and in 1636 a group led by William Pynchon, a wealthy Puritan merchant, founded Springfield on the Connecticut River. The first settlers not only distributed town lands but also accepted a procedure that awarded Pynchon and other prominent figures in this covenanted village more acreage than poorer men received.

Article of Agreement

May the 14th 1636

Wee whose names are underwritten beinge by Gods Providence ingaged togeather to make a Plantation at and over agaynst Agaam [Agawam] upon Conecticot, doe mutually agree to certayn articles and orders to be observed and kept by us and by our successors, except wee and every of us for our selves and in our own persons shall thinke meete uppon better reasons to alter our present resolutions:

1ly. Wee intend by Gods grace as soone as wee can with all convenient speede to procure some Godly and faithfull minister with whome we purpose to joyne in Church Covenant to walk in all the ways of Christ:

2ly. Wee intend that our towne shall be composed of fourty familys or if wee thinke meete after to alter our purpose yet not to exceed the number of fifty familys, rich and poore.

3ly. That every inhabitant shall have a convenient proportion for a house lott as wee shall see meete for every ones quality and estate.

4ly. That every one that hath a howse lott shall have a proportion of the Cow pasture to the North of Ende brooke lyinge Northward from the towne: and alsoe that every one shall have a share Hassokey Marsh over and agaynst his lott if it bee to be

had, and every one to have his proportionable share of all the woodland.

5ly. That every one shall have a share of the meddowe or plantinge ground over agaynst them as nigh as may be on the Agaam side.

6ly. That the long Meddowe called Masacksick lyinge in the way to Dorchester shall be distributed to every man as we shall thinke meete except we shall find other conveniency for some of theyr milch cattayle and other cattayle alsoe.

7ly. That meddowe and pasture calles Nayas toward Patuckett on the side of Agaam lyinge about fower miles above in the river shall be distributed [six lines missing in manuscript] as above sayd in the former order and this was altered with consent before the hands were set to it.

8ly. That all rates [taxes] that shall arise upon the Towne shall be layed upon Lands according to every ones proportion aker for aker of howse lotts and aker for aker of meddowe both alike on this side and both alike on the other side and for farms that shall lyé further off a less proportion as we shall after agree: except we shall see meete to remitte one halfe of the rate from land to other estate.

9ly. That whereas Mr. William Pynchon, Jeheu Burr and Henry Smith have constantly continued to prosecute this plantation when others fell off for feare of the difficultys, and continued to prosecure the same at greate charges and at a greate personall adventure: therefore it is mutually agreed that fourty acres of meddowe lyinge on the South of End-brook under a hill side, shall belong to the said partyes free from all charges for every: that is to say twenty acres to Mr. Pynchon and his heyrs & assigns for ever; and ten Acres to Jeheu Burr, and ten acres to Henry Smith and to theyr heyrs and assigns for ever: which said 40 acres is not disposed to them as any alotments of towne lands but they are to have theyr accommodations in all other places not with standinge.

10ly. That wheras a howse was built at a common charge which cost 6 :and alsoe the Indians demaund a greate some [sum] to buye theyr right in the said lands and alsoe 2 greate shallops [ships] which was requisite for the first plantinge: the value of which engagements is to be borne by inhabitant at theyr first entrance as they shall be rated by us, till the said disbursements shall be satisfyed: or else in case the said howse and boats be not soe satisfyed for, then soe much meddowe to be sett out about the said hose as may countervayle the said extraordinary charge.

11ly. It is agreed to that no man except Mr. William Pynchon shall have above 10 acres for his house lott:

12ly. [Cancelled] It is alsoe agreed that if any man sell any tymber out of his lott in any common ground, if he let it ly above three months before he works it out, it shall be lawfull for any other man to take it that hath present use of it:

13ly. Wheras there are two Cowe pastures the one lyinge toward Dorchester, and the other North-ward from End brooke It is agreed that both these pasturs shall not be fed at once, but that the towne shall be ordered by us in the disposinge of for tyms and seasons till it be lotted out and fenced in severally.

May 16th, 1636

14. It is agreed that after this day we shall observe this rule about devidinge of plantinge ground and meddowe in all plantinge ground to regard chiefly persons who are most apt to use such ground: and in all meddowe and pasture to regard chiefly Cattell and estate, because estate is like to be improved in cattell, and such ground is aptest for theyr use: and yet we agree that noe person that is master of a lott though he have noe cattayle shall have less than three acres of mowinge ground: and none that have cowes Steeres or yeare olds shall have under two akers apiece and all horses not less than fower akers and this order in devidinge meddowe by cattell to take place the last of March next: soe that all cattayle that then appear, and all estate that shall then truly appeare at 20 a Cowe shall have this proportion in the meddows on the Agawam side, and in the longe meddowe Mascksick, and in the other longe meddowe called Nayas, and in the pasture at the North end of the Towne called End-brooke.

15. It is ordered that for the disposings of the Hassaky Marsh and the grantinge of home lotts these five men undernamed or theyr deputys are appointed to have full power, namely Mr. Pynchon, Mr. Michell, Jehue Burr, William Blake, Henry Smith. . . .

DOCUMENT 3
The Lawes and Liberties of Massachusets (1648)

*T*he *Lawes and Liberties* represent a striking legal innovation. The legislature of Massachusetts produced the first alphabetized code of law published in the English language. The listing attempted to balance the needs of a growing commercial colony and a commonwealth founded on reformed religion. The preamble explains how the code evolved, with leaders of church and state contributing ideas, although the final statement probably did not satisfy all participants, it established a certain rule of law and guaranteed due process.

To Our Beloved Brethren and Neighbours

the Inhabitants of the Massachusetts, the Governour, Assistants and Deputies assembled in the Generall Court of tht Jurisdiction wish grace and peace in our Lord Jesus Christ

So soon as God had set up Politicall Government among his people Israel hee gave them a body of laws for judgement both in civil and criminal causes. These were brief and fundamental principles, yet withall so full and comprehensive as out of them clear deductions were to be drawne to all particular cases in future times. For a Common-wealth without lawes is like a ship without rigging and steeredge. Nor is it sufficient to have principles and fundamentalls, but these are to be drawn out into so many of their deductions as the time and condition of that people may have use of. And it is very unsafe & injurious to the body of the people to put them to learn their duty and libertie from generall rules, nor is it enough to have lawes except they be also just. Therefore among other priviledges which the Lord bestowed upon his peculiar people, these he calls them specially to consider of, that God was neerer to them and their lawes were more righteous than other nations. God was sayd to be amongst them or neer to them because of his Ordnances established by himselfe, and their lawes righteous because himselfe was their Law-giver: yet in the comparison are implyed two things, first that other nations had something of Gods presence amongst them. Secondly that there was also somewhat of equitie in their lawes, for it pleased the Father (upon the

Covenant of Redemption with his Son) to restore so much of his Image to lost man as whereby all nations are disposed to worship God, and to advance righteousness: which appears in that of the Apostle *Rom.*

1.21 They knew God &c: and in the *2.14. They did by nature the things conteined in the law of God.* But the nations corrupting his Ordinances (both of Religion, and Justice) God withdrew his presence from them proportionably whereby they were given up to abominable lusts *Rom. 2.21* Whereas if they had walked according to that light & law of nature they might have been preserved from such moral evils and might have enjoyed a common blessing in all their natural and civil Ordinance: now, if it might have been so with the nations who were so much strangers to the Covenant of Grace, what advantage have they who have interest in this Covenant, and may injoy the special presence of god in the puritie and native simplicitie of all his Ordinances by which he is so neer to his owne people. This hath been no small priveledge, and advantage to us in New-England that our Churches, and civil State have been planted, and growne up (like two twinnes) together like that of Israel in the wilderness by which we were put in minde (and had opportunities put into our hands) not only to gather our Churches, and set up the Ordinances of Christ Jesus in them according to the Apostolick patterne by such light as the Lord graciously afforded us: but also withall to frame our civil Politie, and lawes according to the rules of his most holy word whereby each do help and strengthen other (the Churches the civil Authoritie, and the civil Authoritie the

John Freake, a successful Boston merchant, is shown here with his wife and child. Note how lavishly these Puritans dressed. Both Massachusetts Bay and Connecticut passed sumptuary laws—statutes limiting the wearing of fine apparel to the wealthy and prominent. The laws were meant to distinguish between people who were genuinely wealthy and people who dressed beyond their social status.

Churches) and so both prosper the better without such emulation, and contention for priviledges or priority as have proved the misery (if not ruine) of both in some other places.

l. . . . We have not published it [the code] as a perfect body of laws sufficient to carry on the Government established for future times, nor could it be expected that we should promise such a thing. For if no disparagement to the wisedome of that High Court of Parliament in england that in four hundred years they could not so compile their lawes, and regulate proceedings in Courts of justice &c: but that they had still new work to do of the same kinde almost every Parliament: there can be no just cause to blame a poor Colonie (being unfurnished of Lawyers and Statesmen) that in eighteen years hath produced no more, nor better rules for a good, and setled Government then this book holds forth: nor

have you (our Brethren and Neighbours) any cause, whether you look back upon our Native Country, or take your observation by other States, & Common wealths in Europe to complaine of such as you have imployed in this service; for the time which hath been spent in making lawes, and repealing and altering them so often, nor of the charge which the Country hath been put to for those occasions, the Civilian gives you a atrisfactorie reason of such continuall alterations, additions, &c:

These Lawes which were made successively in divers former years, we have reduced under severall heads in an alphabeticall method, that so they might the more readilye be found, & that the diverse lawes concerning one matter being placed together the scope and intent of the whole and every one of them might be more easily apprehended: we must confesse we have not been so exact in placing every law under its most proper title as we might, and would have been: the reason was our hasty indeavour to satisfie your longing expectation, and frequent complaints for want of such a volume to be published in print: wherin (upon every occasiona) you might readily see the rule which you ought to walke by. And in this (we hope) you will finde satisfaction, by the help of the references under the severall heads, and the Table which we have added in the end. For such lawes and orders as are not of generall concernment we have not put them into this booke, but they remain still in force, and are to be seen in the booke of the Records of the Court, but all generall laws not heer inserted nor mentioned to be still of force are to be accounted repealed.

You have called us from among the rest of our Brethren and given us power to make these lawes: we must now call upon you to see them executed: remembering that old & true proverb, *The execution of the law is the life of the law.* If one sort of you *viz:* non-Freemen should object that you had no hand in calling us to this worke, and therefore think yorselvs not bound to obedience &c. Wee answer that a subsequent, or implicit consent is of like force in this case, as an expresse precedent power: for in putting your persons and estates into the protection and way of subsistance held forth and exercised within this Jurisdiction, you doe tacitly submit to this Government and to all the wholesome lawes thereof, and so is the common repute in all nations. . . .

If any one of you meet with some law that seemes not to tend to your particular benefit, you must consider that lawes are made with respect to the whole people, and not to each particular person: and obedience to them must be yielded with respect to the common welfare, not to thy private advantage, and as thou yieldest obedience to the law for the common good, but to thy disadvantage: so another must observe some other law for thy good, though to his own damage; thus must we be content to bear anothers burden and to fulfill the Law of Christ.

That distinction which is put between the Lawes of God and the lawes of men, becomes a snare to many as it is mis-applyed in the ordering of their obedience to civil Authoritie; for whcn the Authoritie is of God and that in way of an Ordinance *Rom.13.1* and when the administration of it is according to deductions, and rules gathered from the word of God, and the clear light of nature in civil nations, surely there is no humane law that tendeth to common good (according to those principles) but the same is mediately a law of God, and that in way of an Ordinance which all are to submit unto and that for conscience take.

By order of the Generall Court

DOCUMENT 4

"The Oath of a Freeman" (1634)

The founders of Massachusetts Bay redefined the nature of citizenship. In England adult males who owned a stipulated amount of property were allowed to vote in local elections. But the Puritans insisted that voters should be members of a church, and colonial authorities accepted no man as a "freeman" unless he had already joined a Congregational church. While this requirement seems quite restrictive, the majority of the adult males who migrated to Massachusetts Bay during the 1630s qualified for suffrage.

The Oath of a Freeman

I, A.B., being, by Gods providence, an inhabitant & freeman within the jurisdiction of this commonweal, doe freely acknowledge my selfe to be subject to the government thereof, & threfore doe heere sweare, by the greate & dreadfull name of the everliving God, that I will be true & faithfull to the same, & will accordingly yielde assistance & support thereunto, with my person and estate, as in equity I am bound, & will also truely indevaor to mainetaine & persevere all the libertyes and priveledges thereof, submitting my selfe to the wholesome lawes and orders made & established by the same; and fur-

ther, that I will not plott nor practise any evill aginst it, nor consent to any that shall soe doe, but will timely discover & reveale the same to lawfull authority nowe here established, for the speedy preventing thereof. Moreover, I doe solemnly bynde my selfe, in the sight of God, that when I shall be called to give my voice touching any matter of this state, wherein freemen are to deale, I will give my vote & suffrage, as I shall judge in myne owne conscience may best conduce and tend to the publique weale of the body, without respect of persons, or favor of any man. Soe help me God, in the Lord Jesus Christ.

DOCUMENT 5

Copy of a Letter from John Cotton to Lord Say and Seal in the Year 1636

Lord Say and Seal was one of the most powerful Puritans remaining in England. The nobleman let it be known that he might move to the New World, and since he enjoyed such prominence, American Puritans enthusiastically encouraged him to do so. But there was a problem. Lord Say and Seal expressed doubts about the relationship between church and state in Massachusetts Bay. What was the justification, he asked, for insisting that high civil officers be church members? Did not the election of magistrates indicate that the colony had become too democratic? It fell to the Reverend John Cotton, Boston's leading Congregational minister, to provide an honest response without thereby discouraging an influential English aristocrat.

Copy of a Letter from Mr. Cotton to Lord Say and Seal in the Year 1636

Right honourable,

Your Lordships advertisement touching the civill state of this colony, as they doe breath forth your singular wisdome, and faithfulness, and tender care of the peace, so wee have noe reason to misinterprite, or undervalue your Lordships eyther directions, or intentions therein. I know noe man under heaven (I speake in Gods feare without flattery) whose counsell I should rather depend upon, for the wise adminsitration of a civill state according to God, than upon your Lordship. . . .

God hath so framed the state of church government and ordinances, that they may be compatible to any common-wealth, though never so much disordered is his frame. But yet when a commonwealth hath liberty to mould his owne frame I conceyve the scripture hath given full direction for the right ordering of the same. . . . It is better that the commonwealth be fashioned to the setting forth of Gods house, which is his church: than to accommodate the church frame to the civill state. Democracy, I do not conceyve that ever God did ordeyne as a fitt government eyther for church or commonwealth. If the people be governors, who shall be governed? As for monarchy, and aristocracy, they are both of them clearly approved, and directed in scripture, yet so as referreth the soveraigntie to himselfe, and setteth up Theocracy in both, as the best forme of government in the commonwealth, as well as in the church.

The law, which your Lordship instanceth in that none shall be chosen to magistracy among us but a church member was made and enacted before I cam into the country; but I have hitherto wanted sufficient light to plead against it. 1st. The rule that directeth the choice of supreame governors, is of like equity and weight in all magistrates, that one of their brethren (not a stranger) should be set over them. . . . Deut. 17. 15. and Jethroes counsell to Moses was approved of God, that the judges, and officers to be set over the people, should be men fearing God, Exod. 18. 21. and Solomon maketh it the

joy of a commonwealth, when the righteous are in authority, and then mourning when the wicked rule, Prov. 29. 21. Jab 34. 30. Your Lordship's feare, that this will bring in papal excommunication, is just, and pious: but let your Lordship be pleased againe to consider whether the consequence be necessary. . . . Non-membership may be a just cause of non-admission to the place of magistracy, but yet, ejection out of this membership will not be a just cause of ejecting him out of his magistracy. A godly woman, being to make choice of a husband, may justly refuse a man that is eyther cast out of church fellowship, or is not yet receyved into it, but yet, when shee is once given to him, shee may not reject him then, for such defect. Mr. Humfrey was chosen for an assistant (as I heare) before the colony came over hither: and, though he be not as yet ioyned into church fellowship (by reason of the unsetlednes of the congregation where he liveth) yet the commonwealth doe still continue his magistracy to him, as knowing he waiteth for oppertunity of enjoying church fellowship shortly.

When your Lordship doubteth, that this co[u]rse will draw all things under the determination of the church, (seeing the church is to determine who shall be members, and none but a member may have to doe in the government of a commonwealth) be pleased to pray you) to conceyve, that magistrates are neyther chosen to office in the church, nor doe governe by directions from the church, but by civil lawes and those enacted in generall corts, and executed in corts of justice, by the governors and assistants. In all which, the church (as the church hath nothing to doe: onely, it prepareth fitt instruments both to rule, and to choose rulers, which is no ambition in the church, nor dishonor to the commonwealth, the apostle, on the contrary, thought it a great dishonor and reporach to the church of Christ, if it were not able to yield able judges to heare and determine all causes amongst their brethren, 1 Corin 1. to 5. which place alone seemeth to me fully to decide the question: for it plainely holdeth forth this argument: It is a shame to the church to want able judges of civill matters and an audacious act in any church member voluntarily to go for judgment, otherwhere than before the saints then it will be noe arrogance nor folly in church members, nor prejudice to the commonwealth, if voluntarily they never choose any civil judges, but from amongst the saints, such as church members are called to be.

But your Lordship doubteth, that if such a rule were necessary, then the church estate and the best ordered commonwealth in the world were not compatible. But let not our Lordship so conceyve. For, the church submitteth itselfe to all the lawes and ordinances of men, in what commonwealth soever they come to dwell. But it is one thing, to submit unto what they have noe calling to reform: another thing, voluntarily to ordeyne a forme of government, which to the best discerning of many of us (for I speake not of myselfe) is expressly contrary to rule. Nor neede your Lordship feare (which yet I speake with submission to your Lordships between judgment) that this corse will lay such a foundation, as nothing but a mere democracy can be built upon it. . . . Yet the government is not a democracy, if it be administered, not by the people, but by the governors, whether one (for then it is a monarchy, though elective), or by many, for then (as you know) it is aristocracy. In which respect it is, that church-government is justly denyed. . . to be demo-cratical, though the people choose their owne officers and leaders.

Nor neede wee feare, that this course will, in time, cast the commonwealth into distractions, and popular confusions. For (under correction) these three things doe not undermine, but doe mutually and strongly mainteyne one another (even thouse three which wee principally aime at) authority in magistrates, liberty in people, purity in the church. Purity, preserved in the church, will preserve well ordered liberty in the people, and both of them establish well-balanced authority in the magistrates. God is the author of all these three, and neyther is himselfe the God of confusion, nor are his wayes the wayes of confusion, but of peace. . . .

Now the Lord Jesus Christ (the prince of peace) keepe and bless your Lordship, and dispose of all your times and talents to his best advantage: and let the covenant of his grace and peace rest upon your honourable family and posterity throughout all generations.

Thus, humbly craving pardon for my boldnesse and length, I take leave and rest,

Your Honours to serve in Christ Jesus,

J. C.

DOCUMENT 6

John Winthrop, "Little Speech" (1645)

Members of the lower house of the Massachusetts legislature complained that elected officials like Winthrop often acted without clear authority. After a series of minor confrontations, they attempted a radical solution—impeachment. The specific charges related to a dispute in Hingham, and a group of angry townsmen accused Winthrop of infringing "their liberties." A formal trial in 1645 fully acquitted the aging leader, but before the legislature adjourned, Winthrop insisted on delivering a "little speech," a concise restatement of Puritan political theory. As he reminded the lower house, an official might be elected by the people, but he derived his authority from God. By resisting a godly magistrate, the critics had debased true liberty, behaving "worse than brute beasts."

I suppose something may be expected from me, upon this charge that is befallen me, which moves me to speak now to you; yet I intend not to intermeddle in the proceedings of the court, or with any of the persons concerned therein. Only I bless God, that I see an issue of this troublesome business. I also acknowledge the justice of the court, and, for mine own part, I am well satisfied, I was publicly charged, and I am publicly and legally acquitted, which is all I did expect or desire. And though this be sufficient for my justification before me, yet not so before the God, who hath seen so much amiss in my dispensations (and even in this affair) as calls me to be humble. For to be publicly and criminally charged in this court, is matter of humiliation, (and I desire to make a right use of it,) notwithstanding I be thus acquitted.

I am unwilling to stay you from your urgent affairs, yet give me leave (upon this special occasion) to speak a little more to this assembly. It may be of some good use, to inform and rectify the judgments of some of the people, and may prevent such distempers as have arisen amongst us. The great questions that have troubled the country, are about the authority of the magistrates and the liberty of the people. It is yourselves who have called us to this office, and being called by you, we have our authority from God, in way of an ordinance, such as hath the image of God eminently stamped upon it, the contempt and violation whereof hath been vindicated with examples of divine vengeance. I entreat you to consider, that when you choose magistrates, you take them from among yourselves, men subject to like passions as you are. Therefore when you see infirmities in us, and not be severe censurers of the failings of your magistrates, when you have continual experience of the like infirmities in yourselves and others. We account him a good servant, who breaks not his covenant. The covenant between you and us is

the oath you have taken of us, which is to this purpose, that we shall govern you and judge your causes by the rules of God's laws and our own, according to our best skill. When you agree with a workman to build you a ship or house, etc., he undertakes as well for his skill as for his faithfulness, for it is his profession, and you pay him for both. But when you call one to be a magistrate, he doth not profess nor undertake to have sufficient skill for that office, nor can you furnish him with gifts, etc., therefore you must run the hazard of his skill and ability. But if he fail in faithfulness, which by his oath he is bound unto, that he must answer for. If it fall out that the case be clear to common apprehension, and the rule clear also, if he transgress here, the error is not in the skill, but in the evil of the will: it must be required of him. But if the case be doubtful, or the rule doubtful, to men of such understanding and parts as your magistrates are, if your magistrates should err here, yourselves must bear it.

For the other point concerning liberty, I observe a great mistake in the country about that. There is a twofold liberty, natural (I mean as our nature is now corrupt) and civil or federal. The first is common to man with beasts and other creatures. By this, man, as he stands in relation to man simply, hath liberty to do what he lists; it is a liberty to evil as well as to good. This liberty is incompatible and inconsistent with authority, and cannot endure the least restraint of the most just authority. The exercise and maintaining of this liberty makes men grow more evil, and in time to be worse than brute beasts. This is that great enemy of truth and peace, that wild beast, which all the ordinances of God are bent against, to restrain and subdue it.

The other kind of liberty I call civil or federal, it may also be termed moral, in reference to the covenant between God and man, in the moral law, and the political covenants and constitutions, amongst men themselves. This liberty is the proper end and object of authority, and cannot subsist without it; and it is a liberty to that only which is good, just, and honest. This liberty you are to stand for, with the hazard (not only of your goods, but) of your lives, if need be. Whatsoever crosseth this, is not authority, but a distemper thereof. This liberty is maintained and exercised in a way of subjection to authority; it is of the same kind of liberty where-with Christ hath made us free. The woman's own choice makes such a man her husband; yet being so chosen, he is her lord, and she is to be subject to him, yet in a way of liberty, not of bondage; and a true wife accounts her subjection her honor and freedom, and would not think her condition safe and free, but in her subjection to her husband's authority. Such is the liberty of the church under the authority of Christ, her king and husband; his yoke is so easy and sweet to her as a bride's ornaments; and if through frowardness or wantonness, etc., she shake it off, at any time, she is at no rest in her spirit, until she take it up again; and whether her lord smiles upon her, and embraceth her in his arms,

or whether he frowns, or rebukes, or smites her, she apprehends the sweetness of his love in all, and is refreshed, supported, and instructed by every such dispensation of his authority over her. On the other side, you know who they are that complain of this yoke and say, let us break their bands, etc., we will not have this man to rulew over us. Even so, brethren, it will be between you and your magistrates. If you stand for your natural corrupt liberties, and will do what is good in your own eyes, you will not endure the least weight of authority, but will murmur, and oppose, and be always striving to shake off that yoke; but if you will be satisfied to enjoy such civil and lawful liberties, such as Christ allows you, then will you quietly and cheerfully submit unto that authority which is set over you, in all the administrations of it, for your good. Wherein, if we fail at any time, we hope we shall be willing (by God's assistance) to hearken to good advice from any of you, or in any other way of God; so shall your liberties be preserved, in upholding the honor and power of authority amongst you.

DOCUMENT 7

Confessions of Faith Presented by Jane Stephenson and Abram Arrington, Recorded by the Reverend Thomas Shepard, Cambridge (1648–1649)

Both Goodwife Jane Stevenson and Abram Arrington offered accounts of their conversion experiences before the Reverend Thomas Shepard's congregation in 1648 and 1649. Jane Stevenson migrated to the New World with her husband and daughter, and in America bore seven additional children. Her husband, a shoemaker, had already become a member of the local church and in 1643 had taken the freeman's oath. Jane Stevenson's confession apparently impressed Shepard's congregation, for she was immediately accepted into full membership. Not so Abram Arrington. His confession failed to persuade the "saints," and he had to wait until 1663 before joining his wife as a member of the Cambridge church.

❧ ❧

Goodwife Stevenson

When the Lord was pleased to convince me of sin, it was by affliction, the plague being in the place; I [was] in the midst of wrath of God, and some whom I have been in company with, within 24 hours laid in grave, and yet the Lord spared me, and I knew not but I might be next at grave by reason of my sins. And I had sinned against God and disobeyed parents, and hence I thought God would visit me, and I was unfit to live and [would] die by my sins, and hence prayed God would spare me. The Lord afflicted me among the rest, yet the Lord gave my my life and spared me. And hence I had a greater desire to hear the word. And hence sin no more lest a worse befall thee—that came to me. And a godly man asked me how I walked now, and I told him I desired to know more of God, and he asked me what I thought of my prayers: would they carry me to heaven, and Lord accept of them[?] I said so. And he told me that then every prayer was abomination, and he might damn me for them, so long as I rested upon anything I did. And I asked him what I should do; if ever he did me good, it must be for his name sake and out of his grace, and hence I saw my own unworthiness more. And hence having way made to New England, I desired God would glorify himself by my coming. And here I met with difficulties and trials and fell to great discontent. And when I heard [on] the Sabbath what God would bring on discontented creatures and how the Israelites did so, and then, though they had their desire, it was with a curse, and this made me fear. And the Lord departed from me, and my sins were so great against such deliverance as I did enjoy. And the Lord brought that scripture, All you that are weary, I will give you rest and Though sins as crimson yet Lord would make them as wool. And I heard Mr. S[hepard] that Christ would come in flaming fire, etc and hence desired the Lord that I might know him. And hearing Mr. S[hepard] that the Lord would search for secret sins, vain thoughts, and I desired the Lord to set his fear in my heart. And that place in Scripture, I have chosen you, that they who will not lay down father and life is not worthy,

I have oft thought whether I should ever do so unless Lord gave me strength. And Mr.S[hepard] showing how ready we were to content ourselves with things of this life.

Asked where Christ was a spirit. At right hand was all righteous.

Abram Arrington

The first time Lord did me any good was what [sic] a friend, a godly man, brother Isaac, being at work togetgher, he spake to me how it stood with me about my estate and asked me whether God gave me a heart to seek him. So I told him I had little mind or heart that way. And he then said it was high time to look to it, for now was a fair season. And his words affected me, and he took much pains in his family. Ecclesiastes 12: Remember Creator. He pressed it upon me as my duty now in my youth to seek after God. And coming to hearing word [of the] Lord out of John 14, penultimate, The Price of the world comes, [which] showed that Satan did assault Christ at time of his departure, when [he] found no sin [in Christ], and hence terror to all wicked men, the Lord will find something in them. And I was affected with this sermon, and he let me see that there was that sin in my heart for which the Lord might justly condemn and cast me out of sight. But going on in use of [m]eans, another man, Mr. Newman [preached on] If gospel be hid, 'tis to them that be lost and I saw I was lost and under wrath. And going on, Look to things which are eternal and I saw I minded nothing but sin and my own pleasure and lusts. And hearing another [preach on] God be merciful to me a sinner he saw nothing but sin and misery and hence cried out to God for mercy but yet thought mercy did not belong to me, had not made it such a misery, yet 6 Hosea, If [ye] follow on to know the Lord, ye shall know him. And thus the Lord spake by Mr. Shepard concerning sight and sense of sin, that it must be an intolerable burden to make it restless to seek after Christ. And hence I thought I wanting this, I was not fit for mercy. But that scripture, Lord came to seek that which is lost, which did somewhat encourage me to seek after

God still. And so by Mr. Mather [preaching] John 6:37, All given shall come to him, use of exhortaton to come to Christ unless prove yourselves repro-

bates, Lord's desire was. And hence I was encouraged to seek after himself. Lord let me see my desires were after him and to seek him.

DOCUMENT 8

Anne Bradstreet, "Some Verses Upon the Burning of Our House, July 10th, 1666"

Anne (Dudley) Bradstreet migrated to New England in 1630. Only sixteen years old, she was already married to Simon Bradstreet, a man later elected governor of Massachusetts Bay. She was a devout Puritan, a devoted wife and mother, and a gifted poet. Anne Bradstreet translated her love for family and observations of daily life in North Andover into lyric expressions of religious faith. As her deeply moving poem on the destruction of her home by fire reveals, she never doubted—in the words of John Donne—that "All comes from God's hand."

Here Follows Some Versus Upon the Burning of our House, July 10th, 1666 Copyed out of a Loose paper

In silent night when rest I took,
For sorrow neer I did not look,
I waken'd was with thundring nois
And Piteous shrieks of dreadfull voice.
That fearfull sound of fire and fire,
Let no man know is my Desire.

I, starting up, the light did spye,
And to my God my heart did cry
To strengthen me in my Distresse
And not to leave me succorlesse.
Then coming out beheld a space,
The flame consume my dwelling place.

And, when I could no longer look,
I blest his Name that gave and took,
That layd my goods now in the dust:
Yea so it was, and so 'twas just.
It was his own: it was not mine;
Far be it that I should repine.

* * *

Here stood that trunk, and there that chest;
There lay the store I counted best:
My pleasant things in ashes lye,
And them behold no more shall I.
Under thy roof no quest shall sitt,
Nor at thy Table eat a bitt.
No pleasant tale shall 'ere be told,
Nor things recounted done of old.
No Candle 'ere shall shine in Thee,
Nor bridegroom's voice 'ere heard shall bee.
In silence ever shalt thou lye;
Adieu, Adieu; All's vanity.

* * *

A Prise so vast as is unknown.
Yet, by his Gift, is made thine own.
Ther's wealth enough, I need no more;
Farewell my Pelf, farewell my Store.
The world no longer let me Love,
My hope and Treasure lyes Above.

Study Questions

1. Do you think that John Winthrop or people who shared his political persuasion would have been surprised or disappointed that many New Englanders did not live according to the principles of "Christian charity"?

2. Did Puritan political thought allow for meaningful dissent?

3. How did religion affect social and political institutions in early New England?

4. What does it mean for a society to declare that "wee shall be as a Citty upon a Hill, the eies of all people are uppon us"?

❧ 4 ❧

Life and Labor in the Plantation Colonies

arly Virginia always generated expectations it could not possibly fulfill. English promoters such as Richard Hakluyt promised rich rewards for anyone possessing the courage and capital to underwrite colonial settlement. But avarice was not the whole story. English nationalism fed ambition, and during the first decade of the seventeenth century, people talked excitedly about breaking Spain's monopoly of the treasure flowing from the New World. In 1606 a group of London investors formed the Virginia Company, a private enterprise designed to turn colonization into profits and in the process bring greater glory to England. They persuaded James I to grant a charter authorizing the establishment of plantations in Virginia. Within only a few months, the company had dispatched ships and settlers to America.

Virginia mocked the eager investors. As Captain John Smith explained in his *Generall Historie* (Document 1), the enterprise got off to a disastrous start. The company poured people into the settlement. Some were gentlemen with no experience in managing complex affairs, and when the colony failed to yield instant returns, they lost interest. Others were ordinary men and women sent to Jamestown as company employees. Whatever hopes they may have entertained, they encountered hideous conditions. Inadequate food, rampant disease, and hostile Indians killed most of the first migrants, and near anarchy in Virginia forced the company to institute martial law (Document 2).

A "stinking weed" saved the colony. Native Americans had long known about tobacco, but commercial development required a European market. As smoking became an English habit, the price of tobacco took off. Settlers who had so recently despaired of Virginia's future rushed to cultivate the new export. Tobacco was hardly an adequate substitute for gold and silver, but it was sufficient to rekindle dreams of wealth. People such as John Pory (Document 3) announced that Virginia had at last turned the corner. He was wrong. Thousands of settlers died during the early 1620s. In fact, the company's mismanagement had become such a scandal that in 1625 the king annulled its charter, transforming Virginia into a royal colony.

All the settlement needed for economic success was workers. John Hammond (Document 4) recruited English men and women to the Chesapeake with familiar guarantees of prosperity. Migrants flooded into the area, most coming as indentured servants (Document 5). Established planters invested their capital in these laborers, trusting that a worker who lived to the end of the contract would more than repay the initial outlay in the form of tobacco. The system bred cruelty and misunderstanding. Young single migrants anticipated a better life in the New World. What greeted them on the tobacco plantations was hard labor, crass exploitation, and sexual deprivation. Not surprisingly, colonial law favored the masters, and for the servants every misstep added extra time to the indenture. If workers managed to achieve freedom—and mortality rates remained high for most of the century—they often found themselves in poverty and still working for their former masters. African Americans joined the white servants in the tobacco fields, but unlike their coworkers, the blacks were generally defined as slaves.

The lives of most seventeenth-century Virginians remain obscure. Literacy rates were low, and many records that might have provided fuller insight into this community have not survived. A few statements exist, however, and in the case of Richard Frethorne's gripping letter to his parents in 1623 (Document 6), they bear witness to terrible and needless suffering. Sometimes private discontent bred collective protest. Workers deserted their masters, running away in groups that included both whites and blacks. Others threatened more violent resistance. In 1661 Isaac Friend, an outspoken servant, organized angry laborers in York County (Document 7), declaring he would "get Armes & he would be the first & have them cry as they went along, 'who would be for Liberty, and free from bondage,' & that there would be enough come to them & they would either be free or die for it." The issue that finally drove Friend over the top was lack of food.

The great planters who ruled Virginia feared their own laborers. During the course of the seventeenth century, the colony experienced several coups against hated governors, several servant risings, and one full-scale civil war known as Bacon's Rebellion (1676). Exploitation of the workers led directly to political instability. Governors simply could not count on the loyalty of the lower classes in an emergency. When a Dutch expeditionary force threatened to invade Virginia in 1673 (Document 8), for example, gentry leaders worried that a body of poor freemen, dejected indentured servants, and African American slaves would support the Dutch.

DOCUMENT 1

Captain John Smith, *The Generall Historie of Virginia* (1631)

Captain John Smith impressed contemporaries—especially pretentious gentlemen to whom he did not defer—as a shameless self-promoter. Smith's humble origins in England may have affected his dealings with social superiors, making him seem at once brash and defensive. But Smith's genuine talents, are not in doubt. He was a courageous soldier, a prolific writer, and a gifted manager. Like most people who sailed for Virginia in 1607, Smith anticipated marvelous returns. Reality quickly dashed such expectations. The managers of the Virginia Company, the colony's original sponsors, demanded immediate profits, and in their haste they failed to provide the first adventurers with necessary supplies. As a result, they died in America of disease, Indian attack, and starvation. Some succumbed to profound depression. Smith chronicled these difficult years, noting repeatedly that chronic greed and poor planning had transferred an imagined paradise into a death trap.

It might well be thought, a Countrie so faire (as Virginia is) and a people so tractable, would long ere this have beene quietly possessed, to the satisfaction of the adventurers, & the eternizing of the memory of those that effected it. But because all the world doe see a defailement [failure]; this following Treatise shall give satisfaction to all indifferent Readers, how the business hath bin carried: where no doubt they will easily understand and answer to their question, how it came to passe there was no better speed and success in those proceedings. . . .

It was the Spanyards good hap to happen in those parts where were infinite numbers of people, who had manured the ground with that providence, it affoorded victuals at all times. And time had brought them to that perfection, they had the use of gold and silver, and the most of such commodities as those Countries affoorded: so that what the Spanyard got was chiefly the spoyle and pillage of those Countrey people, and not the labours of their owne hands. But had those fruitfull Countries beene as salavage [savage], as barbarous, as ill people, as little

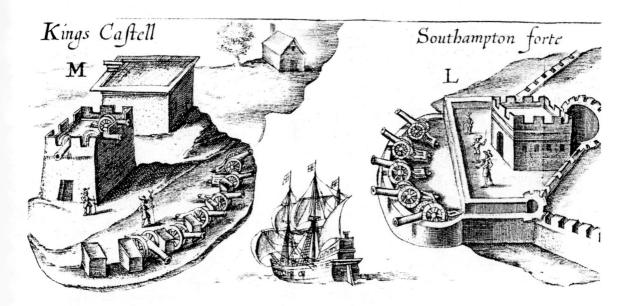

A sketch, allegedly by Captain John Smith (ca. 1625), showing early seventeenth-century fortification. For people of Smith's background and training the New World represented a military challenge.

planted, laboured, and manured, as Virginia: their proper labours it is likely would have produced as small profit as ours. . . .

But we chanced in a Land even as God made it, where we found onely an idle, improvident, scattered people, ignorant of the knowledge of gold or silver, or any commodities, and carelesse of anything but from hand to mouth, except ba[u]bles of no worth; nothing to incourage us, but what accidentally we found Nature affoorded. Which ere we could bring to recompence our paines, defray our charges, and satisfie our Adventurers; we were [expected] to discover the Countrey, subdue the people, bring them to be tractable, civill, and industrious, and teach them trades, that the fruits of their labours might make us some recompence, or plant such Colonies of our owne, that must first make provision how to live of themselves, ere they can bring to perfection the commodities for England, as the West Indies for Spaine, if it be rightly managed. . . .

[Captain Smith describes the state of the colony when he assumed the presidency of Virginia in 1608.]

When the Ships departed, all the provision of the Store. . . . was so rotten with the last Summer's raine, and eaten with Rats and Wormes, as the Hogges would scarcely eate it. . . .so that we found nothing done, but our victuals spent, and the most part of our tools, and a good part of our Armes conveyed to the Savages. But now casting up the Store, and finding sufficient till the next harvest, the feare of starving was abandoned, and the company divided into tens, fifteens, or as the businesse required; six hours each day was spent in worke, the rest in Pastime and merry exercises, but the untowardnesse of the greatest number caused the President [i.e., Smith] to advise as followeth.

Countrymen, the long experience of our late miseries, I hope is sufficient to persuade everyone to a present correction of himselfe, and thinke not that either my pains, nor the Adventurers' [those who had purchased shares in the Virginia Company] purses, will ever maintaine you in idleness and sloath. I speake not this to you all, for divers of you I know deserve both honour and reward, better than

is yet here to be had: but the greater part must be more industrious, or starve, however, you have been tollerated by [the local authorities who preceded Smith]. . . . You see now that power resteth wholly in my selfe: you must obey this now for a Law, that he that will not worke shall not eate (except by sicknesse he be disabled:) for the labours or thirtie or fortie honest and industrious men shall not be consumed to maintaine an hundred and fiftie idel loyterers. And though you presume the authoritie here is but a shadow, and that I dare not touch the lives of any but my owne must answer [for] it: the Letters patents shall each weeke be read to you, whose Contents will tell you the contrary. I would wish you therefore without contempt seeke to observe these orders set downe, for there are now no more Counsellers to protect you, nor curbe my endevours. Therefore he that offendeth, let him assuredly expect his due punishment. . . .

[In 1609 a severe accident forced Smith to return to England. He provides an assessment of the colony's resources at the moment of his departure.]

Leaving us [the Virginia colonists] thus with three ships, seaven boats, commodities readie to trade, the harvest newly gathered, ten weeks provision in the store, foure hundred nintie and od[d] persons, twentie-foure Pieces of Ordnance, three hundred Muskets, Snaphances, and Firelockes, Shot, Powder, and Match sufficient. . . .the Savages, their language and habitations well knowne to an hundred well trayned and expert Souldiers; Nets for fishing; Tooles of all sorts to worke; apparell to supply our wants; six Mares and a Horse; five or sixe hundred Swine; as many Hennes and Chickens; some Goats; some sheepe; what was brought or bred there remained. . . .

Besides Jamestowne that was strongly Pallizadoed, containing some fiftie or sixtie houses, he [Smith] left five or six other several Forts and Plantations: though they were not so sumptuous as our successors expected, they were better than they provided any for us. All this time we had but one Carpenter in the Countrey, and three others that could doe little, but desired to be learners: two Blacksmiths; two saylers, & those we write [label] labourers were for most part footmen, and such as they that were Adventurers brought to attend them, that never did not what a dayes worke was, except the Dutchmen and Poles, and some dozen other[s]. For all the rest were poore Gentlement, Tradesmen, Servingmen, libertines, and such like, ten times more fit to spoyle a Commonwealth, than either begin one, or but helpe to maintaine one. For when neither the feare of God, nor the law, nor shame, nor displeasure of their friends could rule them [in England], there is small hope ever to bring one in twentie of them ever to be good [in Virginia]. Notwithstanding, I confess divers amongst them had better mindes and grew much more industrious than was expected: yet ten good workemen would have done more substantial worke in a day, than ten of them in a weeke. . . .

[Drawing on materials supplied to him in England, Smith recounts how the Virginians behaved during the months immediately following his departure.]

The day before Captaine Smith returned for England with the ships, Captain Davis arrived in a small Pinace [a small sailing vessel], with some sixteene proper men more: To these were added a company from Jamestowne, under the command of Captaine John Sickelmore alias Ratliffe, to inhabit Point Comfort. Captaine Martin and Captain West, having lost their boats and nere half their men among the Savages, were returned to Jamestowne; for the Savages no sooner understood Smith was gone, but they all revolted, and did spoile and murther [murder] all they incountered. Now wee were all constrained to live onely on that Smith had onely for his owne Companie, for the rest had consumed their proportions, and now they had twentie Presidents with all their appurtenances: Master Piercie our new President, was so sicke hee could neither goe nor stand. But ere all was consumed, Captaine West and Captain Sickelmore, each with a small ship and thirtie or fortie men well appointed, sought aboard to trade. Sickelmore upon the confidence of Powhatan [leader of the local Native Americans],

with about thirtie others as carelesse as himselfe, were all slaine. . . . Powhatan still as he found meanes, cut off their Boats, denied them trade, so that Captaine West set saile for England. Now we found the losse of Captain Smith, yea his greatest maligners could now curse his losse: as for corne, provision, and contributions from the Savages, we had nothing but mortall wounds, with clubs and arrowes; as for our Hogs, Hens, Goats, Sheepe, Horse, or what lived, our commanders, officers & Savages daily consumed them, some small proportions sometimes we tasted, till all was devoured; then swords, armes, pieces, or anything, wee traded with the Savages, whose cruell fingers were so oft inbrewed in our blouds, that what by their crueltie, our Governour's indiscretion, and the losse of our ships, of five hundred [people] within six moneths after Captaine Smith's departure, there remained not past sixtie men, women and children, most miserable and poore creatures; and those were preserved for the most part, by roots, herbes, acornes, walnuts, berries, now and then a little fish: they that had startch in these extremities, made no small use of it; yea, even the very skinnes of our horses. Nay, so great was our famine, that a Savage we slew, and buried, the poorer sort tooke him up againe and eat him, and so did divers one another boiled and stewed with roots and herbs: And one amongst the rest did kill his wife, powdered her, and had eaten part of her before it was knowne, for which hee was executed, as hee well deserved; now whether shee was better roasted, boiled or carbonadoes [broiled], I know not, but of such a dish as powdered wife I never heard of. This was that time, which still to this day we called the starving time; it were too vile to say, and scarce to be beleeved, what we endured: but the occasion [of it] was our owne, for want of providence, industrie and government, and not the barrennesse and defect of the Countrie, as is generally supposed. . . . had wee beene even in Paradice itselfe with these Governours, it would not have beene much better with us.

DOCUMENT 2

Lawes Divine, Morall and Martiall, Etc., Compiled by William Strachey (1612)

With conditions in the colony spinning out of control, the directors of the Virginia Company in London became desperate. Their investment in America had produced no profits, and those people still alive in the New World—some independent planters, other tenants working for the company—were drifting into anarchy. To save Virginia, the company dispatched two seasoned military veterans to America, instructing them to institute harsh discipline. Sir Thomas Gates and Sir Thomas Dale placed the entire population under martial law, an extreme remedy that calmed those who feared "the utter subversion and ruine of the Colony." Whatever the justification, everyone knew that civilians in England would never have tolerated such an autocratic code of law. William Strachey, a highly educated gentleman who had emigrated to Virginia, edited the document for publication.

Articles, Lawes, and Orders, Divine, Politique, and Martiall for the Colony in Virginea: first established by Sir Thomas Gates Knight, Lieutenant Generall, the 24th of May 1610. exemplified and approved by the Right Honourable Sir Thomas West Knight, Lord Lawair, Lord Governour and Captaine Generall the 12th of June 1610. Againe exemplified and enlarged by Sir Thomas Dale Knight, Marshall, and Deputie Governour, the 22nd of June. 1611.

Whereas his Majestie like himselfe a most zealous Prince hath in his owne Realmes a principall care of true Religion, and reverence to God, and hath alwaies strictly commaunded his Generals and Governours, with all his forces wheresoever, to let their waies be like his ends, for the glorie of God.

And forasmuch as no good service can be performed, or warre well managed, where militarie discipline is not observed, and militarie discipline cannot be kept, where the rules or chiefe parts thereof, be not certainely set downe, and generally knowne, I have (with the advise and counsell of Sir *Thomas Gates* Knight, Lieutenant Generall) adhered unto the lawes divine, and orders politique, and martiall of his Lordship (the same exemplified) an addition of such others, as I have found either the necessitie of the present State of the Colonie to require, or the infancie, and weaknesse of the body thereof, as yet able to digest, and doe now publish them to all persons in the Colonie, that they may as well take knowledge of the Lawes themselves, as of the penaltie and punishment, which without partialitie shall be inflicted upon the breakers of the same.

1 First since we owe our highest and supreme duty, our greatest, and all our allegeance to him, from whom all power and authoritie is derived, and flowes as from the first, and onely fountaine, and being especiall souldiers emprest in this sacred cause, we must alone expect our successe from him, who is onely the blesser of all good attempts, the King of kings, the commaunder of commaunders, and Lord of Hostes, I do strictly commaund and charge all Captaines and Officers, of what qualitie or nature soever, whether commanders in the field, or in towne, or townes, forts, or fortresses, to have a care that the Almightie God bee duly and daily served, and that they call upon their people to heare Sermons, as that also they diligently frequent Morning

and Evening praier themselves by their owne exemplar and daily life, and dutie herein, encouraging others thereunto, and that such, who shall often and wilfully absent themselves, be duly punished according to the martiall law in that case provided.

2 That no man speake impiously or maliciously, against the holy and blessed Trinitie, or any of the three persons, that is to say, against God the Father, God the Son, and God the holy Ghost, or against the knowne Articles of the Christian faith, upon paine of death. . . .

4 No man shall use any traiterous words against his Majesties Person, or royall authority upon paine of death.

5 No man shall speake any word, or do any act, which may tend to the derision, or despight [defiance] of Gods holy word upon paine of death: Nor shall any man unworthily demeane himselfe unto any Preacher, or Minister of the same, but generally hold them in all reverent regard, and dutiful intreatie, [treatment] otherwise he the offender shall openly be whipt three times, and ask publike forgivenesse in the assembly of the congregation three several Saboth daies.

6 Everie man and woman duly twice a day upon the first towling of the Bell shall upon the working daies repaire unto the Church, to hear divine Service upon pain of losing his or her dayes allowance for the first omission, for the second to be whipt, and for the third to be condemned to the Gallies for six Moneths. Likewise no man or woman shall dare to violate or breake the Sabboth by any gaming, publique, or private abroad, or at home, but duly sanctifie and observe the same, both himselfe and his familie, by preparing themselves at home with private prayer, that they may be the better fitted for the publique, according to the commandements of God, and the orders of our Church, as also every man and woman shall repaire in the morning to the divine service, and Sermons preached upon the Saboth day, and in the afternoon to divine service, and Catechising, upon paine, for the first fault to lose their provision, and allowance for the whole weeke following, for the second to lose the said al-

lowance, and also to be whipt, and for the third to suffer death. . . .

7 No man shal commit the horrible, and detestable sins of Sodomie upon pain of death; and he or she that can be lawfully convict of Adultery shall be punished with death. No man shall ravish or force any woman, maid or Indian, or other, upon pain of death, and know the that he or shee, that shall commit fornication, and evident proofe made thereof, for their first fault shall be whipt, for their second they shall be whipt, and for the third they shall be whipt three times a weeke for one month, and aske publique forgivenesse in the Assembly of the Congregation. . . .

8 Hee that shall take an oath untruly, or beare false witnesse in any cause, or against any man whatsoever, shall be punished with death.

9 No manner of person whatsoever, shall dare to detract, slander, calumniate, or utter unseemely, and unfitting speeches, either against his Majesties Honourable Councell for this Colony, resident in England, or against the Committees, Assistants unto the said Councell, or against the zealous indeavors, and intentions of the whole body of Adventurers for this pious and Christian Plantation, or against any publique booke, or bookes, which by their mature advise, and grave wisdomes, shall be thought fit, to be set foorth and publisht, for the advancement of the good of this Colony, and the felicity thereof, upon paine for the first time so offending, to bee whipt three severall times, and upon his knees to acknowledge his offence and to aske forgivenesse upon the Saboth day in the assembly of the congregation, and for the second time so offending to be condemned to the Galley for three years, and for the third time so offending to be punished with death. . . .

10 He that shall conspire any thing against the person of the Lord Governour, and Captaine Generall, against the Lieutenant Generall, or against the Marshall, or against any publike service commaunded by them, for the dignitie, and advancement of the good of the Colony, shall be punished with death: and he that shall have knowledge of any

such pretended act of disloyalty or treason, and shall not reveale the same unto his Captain, or unto the Governour of that fort or towne wherein he is, within the space of one houre, shall for the conceal-ing of the same after that time, be not onely held an accessary, but alike culpable as the principall traitor or conspirer, and for the same likewise he shall suffer death.

DOCUMENT 3

John Pory, "A Letter" (1619)

O nly a few years earlier, many people living in Jamestown as well as London had written off the entire settlement as a failure. And yet, in this remarkable letter, the secretary of the colony contemplates bringing the "Colony to perfection." As John Pory explains, Virginians had stumbled upon the treasure promised by the propagandists so long ago. English courtiers had taken up smoking, creating a new market for the leaf, and the eager colonists rushed to satisfy the demand. One Virginian described the sudden transformation of the settlement: "the market-place, and the streets, and all other spare places [are] planted with Tobacco." So long as the weed sold well in England, the colonists made good money. But notice that Pory does not claim that tobacco is the source of affluence. Rather, "Our principall wealth. . . .consisteth in servants." One person could cultivate only so much tobacco. If that person controlled the labor of other people—if he owned them—then the profits multiplied. The discovery of a lucrative cash crop encouraged powerful Virginians to exploit the poor and the vulnerable, whites as well as blacks.

John Pory. A Letter to "The Right Honble and My Singular Good Lorde

September 30, 1619

. . . As touching the quality of this country, three thinges there bee, which in fewe yeares may bring this Colony to perfection; the English plough, Vineyards, & Cattle. For the first, there be many grounds here cleared by the Indians to our handes, which being muche worne out, will beare no more of their corne, which requireth an extraordinary deale of sappe & substance to nourish it: but of our graine of all sortes it will beare great abundance. We have had this yeare a plentiful cropp of English wheat, tho the last haruest 1618. was onely shed upon the stubble, and so selfe-sowne, without any other manurance. In July last so soon as we had reaped this self-sowen wheate, we sett Indian corne upon the same ground, which is come up in great abundance; and so by this meanes we are to enjoye two crops in one year from off one & the same fielde. The greatest labour we haue yet bestowed upon English wheate, hath bene, upon newe broken up groundes, one ploughing onely & one harrowing, far shorte of the Tilthe used in Christendome, which when we shall haue ability enough to performe we shall produce miracles out of this earthe. Vines here are in suche abundance, as wheresoeuer a man treads, they are ready to embrace his foote. I haue tasted here of a great black grape as big as a Damascin, that hath a true Muscatell-taste; the vine whereof now spending itselfe even to the topps of high trees, if it were reduced into a vineyard, and there domesticated, would yield incomparable fruite. The like or a better taste haue I founde in a lesser sorte of black grapes. White grapes also of great excellency I haue hearde to be in the country; but they are very rare, nor did I euer see or taste of them. For cattle, they do mightily increase here, both kine, hogges, & goates, and are much greater in stature, then the race of them first brought out of England. No lesse are our horses and mares likely to multiply, which proove of a delicate shape, & of as good spirite & metall. All our riches for the present doe consiste in Tobacco, wherein one man by his owne labour hath in one yeare, raised to himselfe to the value of 200 £ sterling; and another by the means of six seruants hath cleared at one crop a thousand pound english.

These be true, yet indeed rare examples, yet possible to be done by others. Our principall wealth (I should haue said) consisteth in seruants: but they are chardgeable to be furnished with armes, apparell, & bedding, and for their transportation, and casuall both at sea, & for their first yeare cõmonly at lande also: but if they escape, they prooue very hardy, and sound able men.

. . . [W]e are not the veriest beggars in the world, our Cowe-keeper here of James citty on Sundayes goes acowtered [attired] all in freshe flaming silkes and a wife of one that in England had professed the black arte not of a scholler but of a collier of Croydon, weares her rough beuer hat with a faire perle hattband, and a silken suite. . . .

. . . All possible happines I wishe to your lordship, and to my most honoured lady; and though remote in place, yet neare in affection, doe reste

Your lordship euer most humbly at your lordship cõmaunde

Jo: Pory

James citty in Virginia Sept. 30, 1619.

DOCUMENT 4

John Hammond, Leah and Rachell, or the Two Fruitfull Sisters of Virginia and Mary-land (1656)

Despite having lived in the Chesapeake for twenty-one years, John Hammond was an obscure figure. While visiting England, he produced this glowing account of Virginia and Maryland. It was obviously designed to recruit new settlers. Hammond knew that convincing the English would be no easy task. Even the poorest people in London seem to have heard disparaging reports about "the Two Fruitfull Sisters." Professing objectivity, Hammon admitted past mistakes but, like so many promotional writers, he promised a new beginning. Men and women would find prosperity in the Chesapeake; the work was not too demanding, the climate temperate. The supply of gullible people in England remained ample, and in the words of Governor William Berkeley, they flocked to Virginia in "hope of bettering their condition in a Growing Country."

It is the glory of every Nation to enlarge themselves, to encourage their own forraign attempts, and to be able to have of their own, within their own territories, as many several commodities as they can attain to, that so others may rather be beholding to them, then they to others; and to this purpose have Encouragements, Priviledges and been given to any Discoveries or Adventurers into remote Colonies, by all politique Common Wealths in the world.

But alas, we Englishmen (in all things else famous, and to other Countries terrible) do not onely faile in this, but vilifie, scandalize and cry down such parts of the unknown world, as have been found out, setled and made flourishing, by the charge, hazzard and diligence of their own brethren, as if because removed from us, we either account them people of another world or enemies.

This is too truly made good in the odiums and cruell slanders cast on those two famous Countries of *Virginia* and *Mary-land*, whereby those Countries, not onely are many times at a stand, but are in danger to moulder away, and come in time to nothing; nor is there any thing but the fertility and natural gratefulnesse of them, left a remedy to prevent it. . . .

I will not over extoll the places, as if they were rather Paradices than earthly habitations; but truly let ye know, what they are, and how the people there live. Which when impartially viewed, will undoubtedly clear up those Foggy Mists, that hath to their own ruine blinded and kept off many from going thither, whose miseries and misfortunes by staying in *England* are much to be lamented, and much to be pittied. . . .

The Country is reported to be an unhealthy place, a nest of Rogues, whores, desolate and rooking persons; a place of intolerable labour, bad usage and hard Diet, &c.

To Answer these several calumnies, I shall first shew what it was? next, what it is?

At the first settling and many years after, it deserved most of those aspersions (nor were they then aspersions but truths) it was not settled at the publique charge; but when found out, challenged, and maintained by Adventurers, whose avarice and inhumanity, brought in these inconveniences, which to this day brands *Virginia*.

Then were Jayls emptied, youth seduced, infamous women drilled in, the provisions all brought out of *England*, and that embezzelled by the Trustees (for they durst neither hunt fowl, nor Fish, for fear of the *Indian*, which they stood in awe of, their labour was almost perpetuall, their allowance of victual small, few or no cattle, no use of horses nor oxen to draw or carry, (which labours men supplyed themselves) all which caused a mortality; no civil courts of justice but under a Marshal law. . . .

The Country is now very full of sober, modest persons, both men and women, and many that truly fear God and follow that perfect rule of our blessed Saviour, to do as they would be done by; and of such a happy inclination is the Country, that many who in *England* have been lewd and idle, there in emulation of imitation (for example moves more than precept) of the industry of those they finde there, not onely grow ashamed of their former courses, but abhor to hear of them, and in small time wipe off those stains they have formerly been tainted with. . . .

I can confidently affirm, that since my being in *England*, which is not yet four moneths, I have been an eye and ear witnesse of more deceits and villanies (and such as modesty forbids me to utter) then I either ever saw or heard mention made of in *Virginia*, in my one and twenty years aboad in those parts.

And therefore those that shall blemish *Virginia* any more, do but like the Dog bark against the

Moon, until they be blind and weary; and *Virginia* is now in that secure growing condition, that like the Moon so barked at, she will passe on her course, maugre [despite] all detractors, and a few years will bring it to that glorious hapinesse, that many of her calumniators, will intercede to procure admittance thither, when it will be hard to be attained to; for in small time, little land will be to be taken up; and after a while none at all; and as the Mulberry Trees grows up, which are by every one planted, Tobacco will be laid by, and we shall wholy fall to making of Silk (a Sample of 4001. hath already been sent for *England,* and approved of) which will require little labour; and therefore shall have little use of Servants; besides, Children increase and thrive so well there, that they themselves will sufficiently supply the defect of Servants: And in small time become a Nation of themselves sufficient to people the Country: And this good policy is there used; As the Children there born grow to maturity, and capable (as they are generally very capable and apt) they are still preferred and put into authority, and carry themselves therein civilly and discretly; and few there are but are able to give some Portions with their daughters, more or lesse, according to their abilities; so that many comming out of *England* have raised themselves good fortunes there merely by matching with Maidens born in the Country.

And therefore I cannot but admire, and indeed much pitty the dull stupidity of people necessitated in *England,* who rather than they will remove themselves, live here a base, slavish, penurious life; as if there were a necessity to live and to live so, choosing rather then they will forsake *England* to stuff *New-Gate, Bridewell,* and other Jayles [jails] with their carkessies, nay cleave to Tyburne it selfe; and so bring confusion to their souls horror and infamine to their kindred or posteritie, others itch out their wearisome lives in reliance of other mens charities, an uncertaine and unmanly expectation; some more abhorring such courses betake themselve to almost perpetuall and restlesse toyle and druggeries out of which (whilst their strength lasteth) they (observing hard diets, earlie and late houres)

make hard shift to subsist from hand to mouth, until age or sicknesse takes them off from labour and directs them the way to beggerie, and such indeed are to be pittied, relieved and provided for.

I have seriously considered when I have (passing the strets) heard the several Cryes, and noting the commodities, and the worth of them they have carried and cryed up and down; how possibly a livelihood could be exacted out of them, as to cry Matches, Smal-coal, Blacking, Pen and Ink, Thredlaces, and a hundred more such kinde of trifling merchandizes; then looking on the nastinesse of their linnen habits and bodies: I conclude if gain sufficient could be raised out of them for subsistance; yet their manner of living was degenerate and base; and their condition to be far below the meanest servant in *Virginia.*

The other day, I saw a man heavily loaden with a burden of Faggots [sticks] on his back, crying, Dry Faggots, Dry Faggots; he travailed much ground, bawled frequently, and sweat with his burthen: but I saw none buy any, neer three houres I followed him, in which time he rested, I entered into discourse with him, offered him drink, which he thankfully accepted of (as desirous to learn the mistery of his trade) I enquired what he got by each burden when sold? he answered me three pence: I further asked him what he usually got a day? he replyed, some dayes nothing some dayes six pence; some time more, but seldom; me thought it was a pittifull life, and I admired how he could live on it; And yet it were dangerous to advise these wretches to better their conditions by travaile, for fear of the cry of, a spirit, a spirit.

The Country is not only plentifull but pleasant and profitable, pleasant in regard of the brightnesse of the weather, the many delightfull rivers, on which the inhabitants are settled (every man almost living in sight of a lovely river) the abundance of game, the extraordinary good neighbour-hood and loving conversation they have one with the other.

Pleasant in their building, which although for most part they are but one story besides the loft, and built of wood, yet contrived so delightfull, that your ordinary houses in England are not so handsome, for usually the rooms are large, daubed and whitelimed, glazed and flowered, and if not glazed windows, shutters which are made very pritty and convenient.

Pleasant in observing their stocks and flockes of Cattle, Hoggs, and Poultry, grazing, whisking and skipping in their sights, pleasant in having all things of their own, growing or breeding without drawing the peny to send for this and that, without which, in England they cannot be supplyed.

The manner of living and trading there is thus, each man almost lives a free-holder, nothing but the value of 12. d. a year to be paid as rent, for every 50. Acrees of land; firing cost nothing every man plants his own corne and neede take no care for bread: if any thing he bought, it is for commodity, exchanged presently, or for a day, payment is usuall made but once a year, and for that Bill taken (for accounts are not pleadable.)

In summer when fresh meat will not keep (seeing every man kils of his own, and quantities are inconvenient, they lend from one to another, such portions of flesh as they can spare, which is repaied again when the borrower kils his.

If any fall sick, and cannot compasse to follow his crope which if not followed, will soon be lost, the adjoyning neighbour, will either voluntarily or upon a request joyn together, and work in it by spels, untill the honour recovers, and that gratis, so that no man by sicknesse loose any part of his years worke.

Let any travell, it is without charge, and at every house is entertainment as in a hostery, and with it hearty welcome are stranger entertained.

In a word, *Virginia* wants not good victual, wants not good dispositions, and as God hath freely bestowed it, they as freely impart with it, yet are there as wel bad natures as good.

The profit of the country is either by their labour, their stockes, or their trades.

By their labours is produced corne and Tobacco, and all other growing provisions, and this Tobacco however now low-rated, yet a good maintenance may be had out of it, (for they have nothing of necessity but cloathing to purchasse) or can this mean price of Tobacco long hold, for these reasons, First that in England it is prohibited, next that they attained of late those sorts equall with the best Spanish, Thirdly that the sickenesse in Holland is decreasing, which hath been a great obstruction to the sail of Tobacco.

And lastly, that as the mulbery tree grows up, tobacco will be neglected and silke, flax, two staple commodities generally fallen upon.

On the increase of cattle and hoggs, much advantage is made, by selling biefe, porke, and bacon, and butter &c. either to shipping, or to send to the Barbadoes, and other Islands, and he is a very poor man that hath not sometimes provision to put off.

By trading with Indians for Skine, Beaver, Furres and other commodities oftentimes good profits are raised; The Indians are in absolute subjection to the English, so that they both pay tribute to them and receive all their severall king from them, and as one dies they repaire to the English for a successor, so that none neede doubt it a place of securitie.

Several ways of advancement there are and imployments both for the learned and laborer, recreation for the gentry, traffique for the adventurer, congregations for the ministrie (and oh that God would stir, up the hearts of more to go over, such as would teach good doctrine, and not paddle in faction, or state matters; they could not want maintenance, they would find an assisting, an imbracing, a conforming people.)

It is knowne (such preferment hath this Country rewarded the industrious with) that some from being wool-hoppers and of as mean and meaner imployment in England have there grown great merchants, and attained to the most eminent advancements the Country afforded. If men cannot gaine (by diligence) states in those parts.) I speake not only mine owne opinion, but divers others, and something by experience) it will hardly be done (unless by meere lucke as gamsters thrive, and other accidentals in any other part whatsoever.

Now having briefly set down the present state of *Virginia* not in fiction, but in realitie, I wish the juditious reader to consider what dislike can be had of the Country, or upon what grounds it is so infamously injured, I only therein covet to stop those blackmouthed babblers, that not only have and do abuse so noble a plantation, but abuse Gods great blessing in adding to England so flourishing a branch, in perswading many souls, rather to follow desparate and miserable courses in England, then to ingage in so honourable an undertaking as to travile and inhabit there; but to those I shall (if admonition will not worke on their recreant spirits) only say. Let him that is *filthie be filthie still*.

DOCUMENT 5

Legal Constraints on Indentured Servants and Slaves

During the mid-seventeenth century, thousands of young English people emigrated to Virginia and Maryland as indentured servants. Most were unmarried and in their late teens. In exchange for the cost of transportation to the New World and maintenance while in service, they formally agreed with an American master to work for a set number of years. Length of indenture depended on age. At the conclusion of the contract, usually five to seven years, the servant was freed. Most of these people grew tobacco, and while they labored as servants, colonial law tightly regulated their behavior.

Because indentured workers were completely dependent on their masters, and because masters often took advantage of their power over the workers, the system generated serious abuse. Young women were particularly vulnerable. Since the members of the Virginia legislature were themselves large landowners, they had little incentive to protect these people. The masters wanted a secure return on their human investment. The servants apparently expected better treatment than they in fact received, and at mid-century one person reported that servants "not finding what was promised, their courage abates, and their minds being dejected, their work is according." Over time, an ever larger percentage of the unfree labor force in the Chesapeake colonies came from Africa; unlike the poor whites, these men and women were forced into permanent bondage.

Records of the Maryland Provincial Court, 1660: Two indenture agreements

Richard Smyth Came this day the 19th of December 1660 and demands the ensuing Indentures to be recorded among the Records of the Prouinciall Court, in regard hee is to send them to Virginia vizt

This Indenture made the Eight day of August in the yeare of our Lord one thowsand Six hundred ffifty and Nyne Betweene Richard Smyth of Potomocke in the Iland of Virginea in the parts beyond the Seas Planter on th one parte, And Thomas Allison son of Thomas Allison of Gaston in the County of Lancaster husbandman on thother parte. Witnesseth that the said Thomas Allison doth Covenant promise and grant to and with the said Richard Smyth his Executors and Assignes by these presents from the day of the date hereof untill his first and next arrivall in the Iland of Virginea aforesaid, and after for and during the tearme of Seven yeares to serue, in such service and imployment as he the said Richard Smyth, or his Assignes shall there imploy him according to the Custome of the Countrey in the like kind, In consideration whereof the said Thomas Smyth doth hereby covenant and grant to and with the said Thomas Allison to pay for. . . . and lodging with other necessaries during the said terme, and at the end of the said tearme to pay the said Thomas Allison two suites of Apparrell, three Barrells of good marchantable Corne and fifty acres of land. In wittnes whereof the said parties to these present Indentures haue interchangeably sett their hands and Seales the day and yeare aboue-said Signed Richard Smyth

Sealed and deliuered in presence of vs Andrew A Dickinson his marke, George fflouke his marke X Locus Sigilli X

This Indenture made the 24th day of August in the yeare of our Lord 1659 betweene Richard Smyth of Virginia Planter of the one parte And Margarett Williams of Bristoll Spinster of the other parte, Wittnesseth that the said Margarett doth hereby Covenant promise and grantg to and with the said Richard his Executors & Assignes from the day of the date hereof, untill her first and next arrivall at Virginea, and after for and during the tearme of ffower yeares to serue in such service and imployment as the said Richard or his Assigners shall there imploy her, according to the Custome of the Countrey in the like kind. In Consideration whereof the said Master doth hereby Covenant and grant to and with the said Servant to pay for her passing, and to find and allow her meate, drinke, apparrell and lodging with other Necessaries during the said tearme, And at the end of the said tearme to pay vnto her One Ax one Howe, double Apparrell fifty acres of land one yeares provision according to the Custome of the Countrey. In wittnes whereof the parties abouenamed to these Indentures haue inter-

changeably sett their hands and Seales the day and yeare aboue written

Sealed & dd in pesence of Geo.   Md worth Hawkins   The marke of Margarett Williams

Laws of Virginia: Control of Servants and Slaves, 1661–1680

Against secrett marriage

WHEREAS much losse and detriment doth arise to diverse masters of ffamilyes by the secrett marriage of servants, the said servants through that occasion neglecting their works and often perloyning their masters goods and provisions, *Bee it therefore enacted* that noe minister either publish the banns or celebrate the contract of marriage between any servants unles he have from both their masters a certificate that it is done with their consent, and the minister doing otherwise shalbe fined ten thousand pounds of tobacco, and the said servants both man and woman that shall by any indirect meanes procure themselves to be marryed without consent of his and her master, shall for such their offence each of them serve their respective masters one whole yeare after their tyme of service by indenture is expired, and if any person being free shall clandestinely marry with a servant as aforesaid, hee or shee soe marrying shall pay to the master of the servant fifteen hudnred pounds of tobacco or a yeares service, and the servant soe being marryed shall abide with his or her master, the time by indenture or custome and a yeare after as aforesaid.

Against ffornication

FOR restraint of the ffilthy sin of ffornication, *Be it enacted* that what may or woman soever shall commit ffornication, he and she soe offending, upon proofe thereof by confession or evidence shall pay each of them five hundred pounds of tobacco fine, (a) to the use of the parish or parishes they dwell in, and be bound to their good behavior, and be imprisoned untill they find security to be bound with them, and if they or either of them committing ffornication as aforesaid be servants then the master of such servant soe offending shall pay the said ffive hundred pounds of tobacco as aforesaid to the use of the parish aforesaid, for which the said servant shall serve half a yeare after the time by indenture or custome is expired; and if the master shall refuse to pay the ffine then the servant to be whipped; and if it happen a bastard child to be gotten in such ffornication then the woman if a servant in regard of the losse and trouble her master doth sustaine by her haveing a bastard shall serve two yeares after her time by indenture is expired or pay two thousand pounds of tobacco to her master besides the ffine or punishment for committing the offence and the reputed ffather to put in security to keep the child and save the parish harmelesse.

Run-aways

WHEREAS there are diverse loytering runaways in this country who very often absent themselves from their masters service and sometimes in a long time cannot be found, that losse of the time and the charge in the seeking them often exceeding the value of their labor: *Bee it therefore enacted* that all runaways that shall absent themselves from their said masters service, shalbe lyable to make satisfaction by service after the times by custome or indenture is expired (vizt.) double their times of service soe neglected, and if the time of their running away was in the crop or the charge of recovering them extraordinary the court shall lymitt a longer time of service proportionable to the damage the master shall make appeare he hath susteyned, and because the adjudging the time they should serve is often referred untill the time by indenture is expired, when the proofe of what is due is very uncertaine, *it is enacted* that the master of any runaway that intends to take the benefitt of this act, shall as soone as he hath recovered him carry him to the next commissioner and there declare and prove the time of his absence, and the charge he hath bin at in his recovery, which commissioner thereupon shall grant his certificate, and the court on that certificate passe judgment for the time he shall serve for his absence; and in case any English servant shall run away in

company of any negroes who are incapable of making satisfaction by addition of a time, *it is enacted* that the English soe running away in the company with them shall at the time of service to their owne masters expired, serve the masters of the said negroes for their absence soe long as they should have done by this act if they had not beene slaves, every christian in company serving his proportion; and if the negroes be lost or dye in such time of their being run away, the christian servants in company with them shall be proportion among them, either pay fower thousand five hundred pounds of tobacco and caske or fower yeares service for every negroe soe lost or dead.

Cruelty of masters prohibited

WHEREAS the barbarous usuage of some servants by cruell masters bring soe much scandall and infamy to the country in generall, that people who would willingly adventure themselves hither, are through feare thereof diverted, and by that meanes the supplies of particular men and the well seating his majesties country very much obstructed. *Be it therefore enacted that every master shall provide for his servants compotent dyett, clothing and lodging, and that he shall not exceed the bounds of moderation in correct them beyond the meritt of their offences; and that it shalbe lawfull for any servant giving notice to their masters (haveing just cause of complaint against them) for harsh and bad usage, or else for want of dyett or convenient necessaries to repaire to the next commissioner to make his or their complaint, and if the said commissioner shall find by just proofes that the said servants cause of complaint is just the said commissioner is hereby required to give order for the warning of such master to the next country court where the matter in difference shalbe determined, and the servant have remedy for his grievances.*

Against unruly servants

WHEREAS the audatious unrulines of many stubborne and incorrigible servants resisting their masters and overseers have brought many mischiefs and losses to diverse inhabitants of this country, *Be it enacted and ordayned* that the servant that shall lay violent hands on his or her master, mistress or overseer, and be convicted thereof by confession or evidence of his fellow servants or otherwise before any court in this country, the same court is hereby required and authorized to order such servant or servants to serve his or her said master or mistris or their assignes one yeare after his or her time by custome indenture or law is expired. . . .

Women servants gott with child by their masters after their time expired to be sold by the Churchwardens for two yeares for the good of the parish.

WHEREAS by act of Assembly every woman servant haveing a bastard is to serve two yeares, and late experiente shew that some dissolute masters have gotten their maides with child, and yet claime the benefitt of their service, and on the contrary if a woman gott with child by her master should be freed from that service it might probably induce such loose persons to lay all their bastards to their masters; *it is therefore thought fitt and accordingly enacted, and be it enacted henceforward* that each woman servant gott with child by her master shall after her time by indenture or custome is expired be by the churchwardens of the parish where she lived when she was brought to bed of such bastard, sold for two yeares, and the tobacco to be imployed by the vestry for the use of the parish.

Negro womens children to serve according to the condition of the mother

WHEREAS some doubts have arrisen whether children got by any Englishman upon a negro woman should be slave or ffree, *Be it therefore enacted and declared by this present grand assembly,* that all children borne in this country shalbe held bond or free only according to the condition of the mother, *And* that if any christian shall commit ffornication with a negro man or woman, hee or shee soe offending shall pay double the ffines imposed by the former act.

An act for preventing Negro Insurrections

WHEREAS the frequent meeting of considerable numbers of negroe slaves under pretence of feasts and burialls is judged of dangerous consequence; for prevention whereof for the future, *Bee it enacted by the kings most excellent majestie by and with the consent of the generall assembly, and it is hereby enacted by the authority aforesaid,* that from and after the publication of this law, it shall not be lawfull for any negroe or other slave to carry or arme himselfe with any club, staffe, gunn, sword or any other weapon of defence or offence, nor to goe or depart from of his masters ground without a certificate from his master, mistris or overseer, and such permission not to be granted but upon perticuler and necessary occasions; and every negroe or slave soe offending not haveing a certificate as aforesaid shalbe sent to the next constable, who is hereby enjoyned and required to give the said negroe twenty lashes on his bare back well layd on, and soe sent home to his said master, mistris or overseer. *And it is further enacted by the authority aforesaid* that if any negroe or other slave shall presume to lift up his hand in opposition against any christian, shall for every such offence, upon due proofe made therof by the oath of the party before a magistrate, have and receive thirty lashes on his bare back well laid on. *And it is hereby further enacted by the authority aforesaid* that if any negroe or other slave shall absent himself from this masters service and lye hid and lurking in obscure places, comitting injuries to the inhabitants, and shall resist any person or persons that shalby any lawfull authority be imployed to apprehend and take the said negroe, that then in case of such resistance, it shalbe lawfull for such person or persons to kill the said negroe or slave soe lying out and resisting, and that this law be once every six months published at the respective county courts and parish churchers within this colony.

DOCUMENT 6

Richard Frethorne, "Letter to His Father and Mother" *(1623)*

Richard Frethorne was an ordinary indentured servant. Why he decided to emigrate to Virginia is not known. Whatever his private reasons may have been, Frethorne's life in the New World was a nightmare. The work was very hard, the food terrible. The only persons with whom he could share his fear and suffering were his parents, who lived in England. Frethorne grew tobacco on a private plantation called Martyn's Hundred. As he explains, many of the young servant's coworkers died when Powhatan attacked the Virginia settlements in 1622. In the face of such extreme danger, Frethorne was now allowed to retreat from the exposed plantation. His own hope was that his parents—probably people of modest estate—would redeem his contract and let him escape a colony where "there is nothing to be gotten. . . .but sickness, and death, except that one [has] money to lay out in some thinges for profit."

Richard Frethorne. Letter to his Father and Mother: March 20, April 2 and 3, 1623

Loveing and kind father and mother my most humble duty remembered to you hoping in God of your good health,. . . . this is to let you vnderstand that I your Child am in a most heavie Case by reasons of the nature of the Country is such that it Causeth much sicknes, as the scurvie and the bloody flux, and divers other diseases, which maketh the bodie very poore, and Weake, and when wee are sicke there is nothing to Comfort us; for since I came out of the ship, I never had anie thing but pease, and loblollie (that is water gruell) as for deare or venison I never saw anie since I came into this land, ther is indeed some foule, but Wee are not allowed to goe, and get it, but must Worke hard both earelie, and late for a messe of water gruell, and a mouthfull of bread, and beef, a mouthfull of bread for a pennie loafe must serve for 4 men which is most pitiful if you did knowe as much as I, when

people crie out day, and night, Oh that they were in England without their lymbes and would not care to loose anie lymbe to bee in England againe, yea though they beg from doore to doore, for wee live in feare of the Enimy every hour, yet wee haue had a Combate with them on the Sunday . . . and wee tooke two alive, and make slaves of them, but it was by pollicie, for wee are in great danger, for our Plantaçon is very weake, by reason of the death, and sicknes, of our Companie.

There came some for other men yet to lyve with vs, of which ther is but one alive, and our Leiftenant is dead, and his ffather, and his brother, and there was some 5 or 6 of the laste yeares 20 of which there is but 3 left, so that wee are faine to get other men to plant with us, and yet wee are but 32 to fight against 3000 if they should Come, and the nighest helpe that Wee have is ten miles of us, and when the rogues overcame this place last, they slew 80 Persons, how then shall wee doe for wee lye even in their teeth, they easilie take us but that God is merciful. . . . I haue nothing to Comfort me, nor ther is nothing to be gotten here but sicknes, and death, except that one had money to lay out in some thinges for profit; But I haue nothing at all, no not a shirt to my backe, but two Ragges nor no Clothes, but one poore suite, nor but one paire of shooes, but one paire of stockins, but one Capp, but two bande, my Cloke is stollen by one of my owne fellowes, and to his dying hower would not tell mee what he did with it but some of my fellows saw him have butter and beef out of a ship, which my Cloke I doubt paid for, so that I have not a penny, nor a a penny Worth to helpe me to either spice, or sugar, or strong Waters, without the which one cannot live here, for as strong beare in England doth fatten and strengthen them so water here doth wash and weaken theis here, onelie keepe life and soule togeather. but I am not halfe a quarter so strong as I ws in England, and all is for want of victuals, for I doe protest vnto you, that I haue eaten more in day at home than I haue allowed me here for a Weeke. you haue given more than my dayes allowance to a beggar at the doore . . . [A friend] much marvailed that you would send me a servaunt to the Companie, he saith I had beene better knockd on the head, and Indeede so I fyne it now to my greate greife and miserie, and saith, that if you love me you will redeeme me suddenlie, for which I doe Intreate and begg, and if you cannot get the marchaunt to redeeme me for some litle money then for God's sake get a gathering or intreat some good folks to lay out some little Sum of moneye, in meale, and

Cheese and butter, and beef, anie eating meate will yeald great profit, oile and vyniger is verie good, but father ther is greate losse in leakinge, but for God's sake send beef and Cheese and butter or the more of one sort and none of another, but if you send Cheese it must bee very old Cheese, and at the Chesmongers you may buy good Cheese for twopence farthing or halfepenny that will be liked verie well, but if you send Cheese you must haue a Care how you packe it in barrells, and you must put Coopers Chips betweene every Cheese, or else the heat of the hold will rott them . . .

[I] begg the profit to redeeme me, and if I die before it Come I have intreated Goodman Jackson to send you the worth of it, who hath promised he will; If you send you must direct your letters to Goodman Jackson, at James Towne a Gunsmith . . . good father, doe not forget me, but haue mercy and pittye my miserable Case. I know if you did but see me you would weepe to see me, for I haue but one suite, but it is a strange one, it is very well guarded, wherefore for God's sake pittie me, I pray you to remember my loue my love to all my freinds, and kindred, I hope all my Brothers and Sisters are in good health, and as for my part I have set downe my resolution that certainelie Wilbe, that is, that the Answeare of this letter wilbee life or death to me, therefore good father send as soone as you can . . .

Richard Ffethorne
Martyns Hundred.

DOCUMENT 7

"A Mutiny Of the Servants" (1661)

The major planters desperately needed indentured servants to cultivate tobacco, Virginia's only profitable export. The masters hoped that the indentured workers would quietly go about their business, and the laborers seem to have largely adjusted to the demands of life in the New World. But a few servants found conditions unbearable. Grumbling about inadequate food or broken promises sparked conspiracies. The planters came to fear their own workers, and rumors of servant plots always received immediate attention. In 1670 the leading planters of three Virginia counties told royal officials of "the horror yet remaining amongst us of the barbarous designe of those villaines in September 1663 who attempted at once the subversion of our Religion, Lawes, libertyes, rights and priviledges." It is doubtful that Isaac Friend and his followers entertained such revolutionary designs. Like most marginal workers in the seventeenth-century Virginia, they simply demanded decent food and humane treatment.

A Mutiny of the Servants

January the 24th, 1661

The examination of Thomas Collins taken before Major Thomas Beale, 6th January 1661, says That being at the house of Major James Goodwin amongst the servants, they were there talking of their hard usage, and that they had nothing but corn and water, and were not kept according to the Law of the Country as one Isaac, now called captain general, said for they ought to have meat 3 times a week, and had not, and therefore it was fit that they should join in a petition to send for England to the king to have it redressed. To which William Cheshire answered that they should not find a trusty friend to deliver unless it was such an one as old George, for he had been a servant in the country, and knew the country. Then the said Isaac said that they would get a mattr of forty of them together, and get Arms and he would be the first and have them cry as they went along, "Who would be for Liberty and free from bondage," and that there would enough come to them and they would go through the country and kill those that made any opposition, and that they would either be free or die for it, to which Will Cheshire answered he would be one, and that he believed all the rest of their house

would do the like; and also one of Mr. Hughes' servants (which of them he remembered not being there) said that he would be one with all his heart, when they would go about it. And he further saith that he hath heard the said Isaac speak to this effect severall times, and that on Saturday last he being sent unto Jonothan Parkes of an Errand, and then going into Major Goodwin's Quarter, and asking the servants if John Clarke was not within when these words was related, the said Isaac said these words, I did say so and do say so still (meaning as is above related), and what then, they can do nothing at me for it.

The mark of
Thomas T. Collins

Taken this 6th of January, 1661, before me Thomas Beale, Jurat in Cor. January, 1661

The examination of Isaac Friend, taken as aforesaid, Saith that he doth acknowledge that these words affirmed by Thomas Collins above written to be by him spoken, he says that it is probable that he might speak such words when they were all together, and that if the said Thomas Collins do swear it, it is in vain for him to deny it, but he doth not remember that he did say so, and if he did say so he never did go about it, nor intended to go about it, and further saith that he were present when William Clutton being in Major Goodwin's Quarter told Major Beale amongst the rest of Major Goodwin's servants that servants ought to have pone [corn bread] and hominy [boiled grain] and meat wice a week.

Isaac Friend

Taken before me this 6th of January, 1661, thomas Beale. Sworn 23rd, 1661

The examination of William Barton before Major Thomas Beale the sixth day of January, 1661. Saith that he hath heard William Clutton oft to say that when he the said William Clutton was a servant he would have meat three times a week, or else he used to keep a clash and that he commonly had it so and if that when he was at work in the woods if they sent him bread and cheese if he thought it too little, he would send it back again, and that the last year of his service was harder than any of the other. And further saith that he heard that the said Clutton should say that the reason that he would not be Mr. Beale's overseer was because he could not have meat for them 3 times a week and as many cows for milk as he himself though good, and that wheresoever he lived the servants should have meat 3 times a week.

Mark of
Will N. Barton

The examination of George White, taken as aforesaid, Saith that he hath heard William clutton say that it was the custom of the country for servants to have meat 3 times a week, and that the reason why he broke off with Major Beale was because he could not have meat for the servants 3 times a week.

The examination of john Parke taken the 6th day of January, 1661, before major Thomas Beale saith that Major Beale being at the house of Major Goodwin where the said examinant is overseer, and the said examinant acquainting the said Major Beale with the refractoriness of the said servants, the said Major Beale going to the quarter and demanding of the servants there of the reason of such their refractoriness, and telling them that the said John Parkes had the command of them and was as their master, and that they ought and must obey him, at which the said servants being very well satisfied till William Clutton came and told Major Beale upon some discourse betwixt them that servants ought by the custom of the country to have meat 3 times a week, which he, speaking in the hearing of the said servants, was an occasion of setting them to further discontent and murmuring amongst them till Major Beale pacified them.

The Mark of
John J. Parkes

DOCUMENT 8

Letter from Governor William Berkeley and Other Members of the Council to the King and Privy Council (1673)

During the seventeenth century, England fought several wars against its powerful commercial rival, Holland. Like the English, the Dutch had developed an excellent navy, and on at least one occasion, Dutch ships attacked the English tobacco fleet anchored in Virginia waters. Governor Berkeley anticipated a general invasion, but because of the restlessness of the colony's labor force—poor freeman, white indentured servants, and African American slaves—he feared that the defense of Virginia might trigger large-scale rebellion against the established government. As Berkeley complained on another occasion, it was almost impossible to control a population "where six parts of seven at least are Poor, Indebted, Discontented and Armed." Berkeley's letter in 1673 reminds us that the peculiar structure of the Chesapeake labor force profoundly affected every aspect of this society.

The Dutch Burn the Tobacco Fleet, July 1673: The Problem of Defending Virginia Against Attack

To the Kings Most Excellent Majestie and the Lords of Your

Majesties most Honorable Privy Councell

The Govenor and Councell of his Majesties Collony of Virginia

In all Humility Present

That on Fryday the 11th of this Instant July (which was foure Dayes before the Fleet was ordered to Saile from hence) To our very great Griefe and Damage, arrived on our Coast Foure Saile of Holland Men of Warr from above thirty to Fourty foure Gunns Under the Command of Jacob Bincke. That upon their first Arrivall on Fryday they were discovered by our Centinalls on the Coasts, and [Sundry?] advice Given to Capt. Gardner and Capt. Corterell, who Commanded your Majesties Shipps here, Who presently Commanded Severall Masters of the abler Merchants Shipps in James River on Board, and order'd them to Cleare their Shipps for fight, and Press'd as many men as they thought fitt out of the Weaker Shipps. . . .

Two and twenty of our Shipps Stood upp James River and the Rest went under the Fort at Nansemond, Where the Enemy looked on them five Dayes but Attempted them not; Five of those which stood upp James River Comeing on Ground, They Sent upp three of their Smallest Shipps to them And Gott of[f] one, and burnt the other foure, the rest Getting above the Fort at James Towne were

Safe; And here wee expect it will be Objected that had not Soe long A Time bene given for the Departure of our Fleet this Misfortune had bin Avoided; To Which wee humbly Offer this answer That Capt. Cotrterell arriveing here neere the 20th of June and representing to us Some Dayes after (in presence of all the Masters) that for want of Wood and water and other necessaries, he could not be ready before the 15th of July, was the Reason for the appointing that Day; Next the Masters of the Yorke Shipps were not ready till then, and the Enemy was within our Capes before the most Considerable Shipps of Maryland came to us besides Five Saile in Rappahannocke not Ready and two upp the Bay which in all two and twenty Saile, A Number Too Considerable to be left behind by your Majesties Convoy; This May it please your Majestie and your most Honorable Councell being the true State of our Misfortune in the present losse of Eleaven Shipps and Goods (wherein the Inhabitants of James River bore A very Great Share) Wee thought it our Duty, for the Better Vindication of our Selves from Such Injuries as the Mallice of Some may indeavor to fix on us, by Misrepresenting us and our indeavors to your Majestie and most Honorable Councell, to Sett forth in this our Declaration, the true State and Condition of this Country in Generall and our particular disadvantages and disabilities to entertaine A Warr at the time of this Invasion, And therefore doe most humbly beseech your Majesty and your most Honorable Councell to Consider tha though all that Land which now bares the name of Virginia be Reduced to little more than sixty Miles in breadth towards the Sea, Yet that Small tract is intersected by Soe many Vast Rivers as makes more Miles to Defend, then wee have men of trust to Defend them, For by our neerest computation Wee leave at our backs as Many Servants (besides Negroes as their are freemen to defend the Shoars and all our Frontiers, [against] the Indians) Both which gives men fearfull apprehensions of the dainger they leave their Estates and Families in, Whilest they are drawne from their houses to defend the Borders, Of which number alsoe at least one third are Single freemen (whose labour Will hardly maintaine them) or men much in debt, both which Wee may reasonably expect upon any Small advantage the Enemy may gaine upon us, wo[u]ld revolt to them in hopes of bettering their Condition by Shareing the Plunder of the Countrey With them, Nor can wee Keepe any number of Soldiers long together in A Place for Want of Provissions, For the aire being hott and Moist wee could never yett find the way of keeping any Sort of Corne A Yeare from Being eaten out by Vermine Which hinders our haveing Publique Magazines of Provisions necessary for Such occations, and our men (though their has bin Great Care taken in Exercizing them) haveing for Many yeares bene unacquainted with dainger. wee cannot with much Confidence rely on their Courage against an Enemy better practiced in the Hazards of Warr; But may it please your most Sacred Majestie and your most Honorable Councell, Their were many more difficultries from this last attempt, for diseases this Winter before haveing destroyed at least fifty thousand Cattell and their Owners to preserve them haveing given them almost all their Corne Brought Soe great A Scarcety of Provision amongst us as men Could not have bene keept long together, and the Enemies Arrivall being in A time when all mens Cropps both of tobacco and corne lay hardest upon their hands (being much in the weeds by reason for the great Raine which fell Sometime before) It Troubled them much to be drawne away from their Worke (though for their Common defense) Yett notwithstanding these and many more disadvantages they appeared Soe ready in Every place that the Enemy descended not on the Land though they wanted water to great Extremety, The losse then being wholy on the Shipps and Loading (Except some fugative Servants who escapeing our dilligence gott to them and were Carryed away) Our industry for their defense wee humbly hope will appeare in this that their was not A Shipp lost which run not on Ground before She gott within the protection of one or other of our Forts, Nor did Your Majesties Shipps or any of the Merchant men want any Assistance wee could possibly helpe them too, Though in this alsoe their lay very great difficulty, For In these times of warr, the Merchant gives our Inhabitants Soe very little for their labour as will not Cloath them and their Famelies, which disasorts them as they rather rejoyce at their loss, then Shew any desire to defend them nor would they have bene brought to appeare for them by any other Motive then the affection they have to the Gentleness and Justice of the Government they have Soe long lived under, Yet though wee have Certainly done our utmost for them to our very great expense and hazard of our Cropps Wee expect A Complaint against us for not haveing A FFort at Point Comfort, which Some Suppose wo[u]ld have prevented all this losse, though the Considerable part of it happened farr off in the Bay beyond the reach of any Gunn. . . .

Your Majesties Most Loyall and Obedient Subject and Servants

William Berkeley	Henry Chicheley
Edward Digges	Thomas Ludwell
Nathaniel Bacon	Augustine Warner
Henry Corbin	Daniel Parke
Thomas Ballard	Nicholas Spencer

Study Questions

1. Compare the early history of Virginia to that of Puritan New England. What was the basis of community in the two regions?

2. Considering this colony's disastrous start, why were so many new servants willing to take a chance on Virginia?

3. What might the history of early Virginia have been like had the settlers not discovered a lucrative market for tobacco?

4. Was the cultivation of tobacco responsible for the institution of slavery?

5

Anglo-American Empire of the Eighteenth Century

etween 1690 and 1776 Britain's mainland American colonies experienced a profound transformation. The earliest settlements broke with the dominant English culture and society. The first Puritan migrants, for example, dreamed of creating a "city on a hill," a religious model designed to reform the homeland. Catholics in Maryland and Quakers in Pennsylvania also invited people to participate in societies that looked nothing like those they would have known in Europe. And the plantation colonies unleashed exploitative forces that encouraged the spread of institutions like slavery that contemporary English would never have condoned—at least, not within their own country.

During the eighteenth century the British Empire reabsorbed these scattered American experiments. Some historians describe the process as "recolonization." It is a useful term, for England did, in fact, intervene more aggressively in American affairs. The shift did not result primarily from coherent government policy. Rather, as trade between the colonies and England expanded, the Americans were increasingly exposed to an alluring cosmopolitan culture. After the civil wars of the previous century, the English achieved remarkable political stability, and the nation's celebrated "balanced constitution" guaranteed that Parliament would never again allow despotic kings to trample the traditional laws and liberties of the land. England's growing influence meant that wherever Americans lived, they had to confront the demands of empire.

Members of the colonial ruling class tried as well as they could to emulate British culture. They were certainly not scheming to achieve independence. In that sense the eighteenth-century American gentry should be compared to the provincial elites of Scotland and Ireland. As William Eddis, a British gentleman traveling through Maryland in 1770, discovered (Document 1), wealthy Americans evinced a high degree of cultural refinement. They seemed almost English. Colonial status always made Americans a little uneasy, as if they suspected that polite London society saw them as country bumpkins. William Byrd, a successful Virginia planter, tried to have it both ways. He begged acceptance by an English nobleman while at the same

"Southeast View of Boston in 1743" by William Burgis. The painting of this busy commercial center draws attention to phenomenal population growth in British America during the eighteenth century. Within 70 years, the population increased nearly tenfold, from roughly 250,000 in 1700 to 2,150,000 in 1770.

time singing the praises of provincial Virginia (Document 2).

Even ordinary Americans understood that decisions made in England—about war and commerce, for example—profoundly influenced life in the colonies. In 1747 the Reverend Hull Abbot, a Congregational minister in Massachusetts, explained what the suppression of a Catholic rebellion in Scotland meant to New England (Document 3). Abbot and his contemporaries no longer spoke of a "city on a hill." They found themselves reacting to external events. The minister gave unreserved loyalty to George II, defender of Protestant interests against Catholic aggression. Abbot's immediate concern was the French in Canada, and on several occasions during the eighteenth century Americans joined British troops in the battle to control North America. By their own lights, the colonists performed well. Two statements written during the Seven Years' War (1756–1763) reveal different perspectives on imperial combat (Document 4). A flood of imported manufactured goods—what Samuel Adams called the "Baubles of Britain"—introduced Americans to more fluid social relationships. One outspoken colonial traveler in Maryland (Document 5) insisted that anyone who dressed in the latest fashions or drank tea should be treated as a proper gentleman.

Benjamin Franklin understood this vibrant imperial society as well as any individual. Rising from humble origins in Massachusetts, he became a wealthy printer in Philadelphia. He not only entered polite society, but championed the new science associated with the Enlightenment. Franklin's experiments brought him fame in England. He tried to establish provincial institutions (Document 6) in which reasonable men like himself could exchange ideas and work to better society.

For most Americans, however, the Great Awakening eclipsed the Enlightenment. The Reverend George Whitefield, a charismatic English preacher, sparked a huge evangelical movement that swept through the colonial population, bringing men and women of all backgrounds to the "new birth." Whitefield's outspoken supporter, the Reverend Gilbert Tennent, urged people to judge for themselves whether established ministers were really sincere Christians (Document 7). Tennent informed colonists that if the ministers failed, the people should seek out itinerants. This seemed an invitation to religious anarchy, and one shaken opponent of the new evangelical faith, Charles Woodmason, condemned the social disorder generated by itineracy (Document 8). But a simple Connecticut farmer, Nathan Cole, probably came closer than Woodmason to understanding the powerful religious forces transforming American society.

DOCUMENT 1

William Eddis, Letters from America (1770)

William Eddis (1738 2–1825), a young Englishman, spent eight years in Annapolis on the eve of the American Revolution. As a minor officeholder in the Maryland goverment, he had an opportunity to meet wealthy planters and their families. Unlike many contemporary visitors from England, Eddis felt comfortable in provincial society. He had a sharp eye for fashion, and he thought Americans adopted new consumer fads almost as quickly as did the British. While he enjoyed the company of the local gentry, Eddis recognized a strong egalitarian current in white society. "An idea of equality," he observed, ". . . . seems generally to prevail and the inferior order of people pay but little external respect to those who occupy superior stations."

Annapolis, January 15, 1770

Colonel Fitzhugh, a gentleman of considerable propperty and a member of the [Maryland] council, early in December engaged the governor, with a circle of select friends, to pass a few days during the Christmas vacation at his seat in Calvert County, about seventy miles distant from Annapolis. Having the honor to be included in the party, I embarked on the twenty-second with the colonel on board a schooner which he had fitted up for occasional excursions; and considering the season of the year, we had a pleasant run to the place of our destination, which is delightfully situated within view of the Cheasapeake, on the fertile banks of the river Patuxent.

Rousby Hall, which is the name of my friend's hospitable mansion, is as well known to the weary indigent traveler as to the affluent guest. In a country where hospitality is the distinguishing feature, the benevolent owner has established a preeminence which places his character in an exalted point of view.

The governor, on account of some particular engagements, did not quit Annapolis till the twenty-sixth; and on the thirtieth I accompanied Colonel Fitzhugh to the habitation of a gentleman, about twenty miles distant, where by appointment we met His Excellency with a numerous party who had assembled to bid him welcome. All the good things of a plentiful country decorated the table of our munificent host; the wines were excellent and various; and cheerful blazing fires, with enlivening conversation, exhilarated the spirits, and rendered us totally regardless of the rigor of an American winter. On the ensuing day, the whole company proceeded to Rousby Hall, where we continued, in the full enjoyment of genuine hospitality, till the third instant; and it was with the utmost reluctance we were then permitted to take our departure.

Since we quitted Colonel Fitzhugh, we have visited most of the principal families in Calvert, St. Mary's, Charles, Prince George's, and Anne Arundel Counties, and were everywhere received with the most obliging proofs of regard and attention. From the severity of the weather we occasionally encountered some hardships and inconveniences, but we were amply compensated at the end of every stage by excellent accommodations and sumptuous fare. Notwithstanding the dreary season, the eye was gratified with many picturesque and noble objects: we traveled a considerable way on the banks of the great river Potomac, which separates Maryland from Virginia; and though this country is greatly inferior in its present state to the highly cultivated parts of South Britain, yet on the whole it is well settled; the generality of the plantations are disposed with the utmost regularity, and in very many of the habitations we found elegance as well as comfort.

We passed an agreeable evening with a family nearly opposite to Alexandria in Virginia; and, had the weather been moderate, intended to have crossed the river on a visit to Major [George] Washington, who, as you may recollect, particulary distinguished himself in the transactions of the late war [Seven Years War]; this gentleman has a pleasant seat on the banks of the Potomac, in the vicinity of the above town, which is named Mount Vernon, where he resides in full possession of universal love and esteem.

Yesterday we returned safe to Annapolis, greatly satisfied with our expedition.

February 20

On Saturday last our little city appeared in all its splendor. It was the anniversary of the [Lord Baltimore's] birth. The governor gave a grand entertainment on the occasion to a numerous party; the company brought with them every disposition to render each other happy; and the festivity concluded with cards and dancing, which engaged the attention of their respective votaries till an early hour.

I am persuaded there is not a town in England of the same size as Annapolis which can boast a greater number of fashionable and handsome women; and were I not satisfied to the contrary, I should suppose that the majority of our belles possessed every advantage of a long and familiar intercourse with the manners and habits of your great metropolis.

I am told that beauty in this country is not of long duration: it is also asserted that in general the men do not possess such good stamina as the natives of Great Britain. Though every way equal in genius and enterprise, they are supposed less able to support fatigue, and to encounter the hardships of laborious employments.

During the winter there are assemblies every fortnight; the room for dancing is large; the construction elegant; and the whole illuminated to great advantage. At each extremity are apartments for the card tables, where select companies enjoy the circulation of the party-colored gentry without having their attention diverted by the sound of fiddles and the evolutions of youthful performers.

About Christmas an intense frost set in, which has continued till a few days since with unremitting severity. Our principal rivers for several weeks have been passable for carriages heavily laden; and in particular situations, innumerable skaters have exhibited on the glassy surface their feats of dexterity.

It is certainly extraordinary that in a latitude nearly parallel with Gilbraltar the inhabitants should experience, for a considerable duration, a degree of cold to which the northern extremities of the British Islands have never been accustomed; this, I am informed, proceeds entirely from local circumstances; the winds, prevalent in winter, blowing over those immense lakes situated to the westward of this and some neighboring provinces, impregnate the air with frigid particles that make us sensible of an inclemency equal to that experienced by the shivering Laplander.

In this country a heavy snow generally precedes the frost, during the continuance of which the atmosphere is beautifully serene, without any of those pernicious fogs so prevalent in your humid climate.

Notwithstanding the extensive forests that abound throughout this vast continent, fuel is an expensive article in all the considerable towns: provisions are in general cheap, but the price of labor is high, from which circumstance firing is comparatively dead, even on the most economical plan. I am, however, persuaded that by prudent management a respectable appearance may be supported in Maryland on terms infinitely more reasonable than in most parts of the mother country; and that greater opportunities are afforded to the industrious and enterprising to lay the foundation of a comfortable provision for a succeeding generation.

Annapolis, June 8, 1770

Though we are yet far behind the mother country with respect to cultivation and improvements, yet, in a comparative view Maryland may boast considerable advantages. The inhabitants are enterprising and industrious; commerce and agriculture are encouraged; and every circumstance clearly evinces that this colony is making a rapid progress to wealth, power, and population.

Provisions of every kind are excellent and plentiful; and the Chesapeake, with our numerous rivers, affords a surprising variety of excellent fish. Poultry and wild fowl abound amongst the humble cottagers; and beef, mutton, pork, and other provisions are at least equal to the production of the best British markets.

Deer a few years since were very numerous in the interior settlements; but from the unfair methods adopted by the hunters their numbers are exceedingly diminished. These people, whose only motive was to procure the hide of the animal, were dexterous, during the winter season, in tracing their path through the snow; and from the animal's incapacity to exert speed under such circumstances, great multitudes of them were annually slaughtered and their carcasses left in the woods. This practice, however, has been thought worthy the attention of the legislature, and an act of assembly has taken place, laying severe penalties on "persons detected in pursuing or destroying deer, within a limited term": and it is probable the apprehension of punishment may very greatly restrain if not totally eradicate an evil founded on cruelty and rapacity.

In England, almost every county is distinguished by a peculiar dialect; even different habits and different modes of thinking evidently discriminate inhabitants, whose local situation is not far remote; but in Maryland and throughout the adjacent provinces, it is worthy of observation that a striking similarity of speech universally prevails; and it is strictly true that the pronunciation of the generality of the people has an accuracy and elegance that cannot fail of gratifying the most judicious ear.

The colonists are composed of adventurers, not only from every district of Great Britain and Ireland, but from almost every other European government where the principles of liberty and commerce have operated with spirit and efficacy. Is it not, therefore, reasonable to suppose that the English language must be greatly corrupted by such a strange intermixture of various nations? The reverse is, however, true. The language of the immediate descendants of such a promiscuous ancestry is perfectly uniform and unadulterated; nor has it borrowed any provincial or national accent from its British or foreign parentage.

For my part, I confess myself totally at a loss to account for the apparent difference between the colonists and persons under equal circumstances of education and fortune resident in the mother country. This uniformity of language prevails not only on the coast, where Europeans form a considerable mass of the people, but likewise in the interior parts, where population has made but slow advances, and where opportunities seldom occur to derive any great advantages from an intercourse with intelligent strangers. . . .

DOCUMENT 2

William Byrd II to John Boyle, Baron Boyle of Broghill (1731)

When William Byrd wrote this letter to an English friend, he had achieved almost everything a colonial gentleman could desire. After inheriting considerable property from his father, Byrd became a leading political figure in Virginia, a major planter, and a respected writer. However much he claimed to love his impressive James River plantation called Westover, Byrd spent almost half his adult life in London, as the tone of the letter indicates—a blend of extreme deference to the English nobleman and pride in the tranquil beauty of Virginia—Byrd felt the simultaneous pull of two cultures. His romantic depiction of life as a colonial patriarch fails to mention the slaves that made Westover possible. In another letter Byrd complained that blacks "blow up the pride and ruin the industry of our white people, who seeing a rank of poor creatures below them, detest work for fear it should make them look like slaves."

Virginia, the 15 of June, 1731

I lament the poor colonels loss of so many facultys, tho lameness can be no great misfortune to a man who would never use his leggs when he had them, he may still have the benefit of a gocart within doors, and a chair without. We all know it *is* not age that has demolished our worthey friend in this cruel manner, I rather think it is the scurvy, arising from high feeding and no exercize; tho' perhaps he may be obliged to the intrigues he used to bost of, with those ladies of distinction, who were so fond of his sweet person, that they have left him some tokens to remember them by, which as he is a man of honour, he will keep for their sakes as long as he lives, even at the expence of the loss of all his limbs.

Among all our polite acquaintance you make no mention of that great patriot Archibald Hutcheson Esqr. The last tydings I heard of him were that he was a fourth time married, the poor man is so lost in wedlock that I have never heard one sylable from him since. . . .

But to encourage your Lordship to come over in proper person, and not run the hazard of being ill represented, I beg leave to present you with a short sketch of the country. In the first place it lies in much the same latitude with Italy, Greece, Sicily, Asia-minor, Syria, Persia and all other fine clymates of the world, and what still more recommends our situation, it differs but a very few degrees from that of Paradise. The sun that imparts life, growth and motion to the animal and vegetable world, looks upon us every day in the year. Our summers are warm enough to ripen a great variety of fine fruit, and our winters clear enough to make our cold delightfull. Heaven pours out its horn of plenty upon us, and furnishes us even to luxury. We live in all the innocence of the patriarchs, under our vines and our fig-trees, surrounded with our flocks and our herds. We enjoy our moderate possessions in great security both from publick and private robbers. We are all of one religion, and of one party in politicks, so there can be no doubt of our being good neighbours. There are no people more hospitable to strangers, and to *one* another. The merchants in England take care that none of us grow very rich,

and the felicity of the clymate hinders us from being very poor so we have the happiness of being exactly in that state Agur prayed for. "Give me neither poverty nor riches, feed me with food convenient for me: least I be full, and deny thee and say, Who is the Lord! or least I be poor and steal, and take the name of my God in vain." We have no beggars but for places, which for want of favorites, court mistresses, and first ministers are never sold. If a country like this can tempt your Lordship to leave the gaitys of London, I wish you would take the government of it into your hands and make a good natured people thereby very happy.

I am, my Lord, your Lordships most obedient servant Wm. Byrd.

DOCUMENT 3

Hull Abbot, The Duty of God's People to Pray for the Peace of Jerusalem (1746)

The Reverend Hull Abbot (1702–1774) graduated from Harvard College in 1720 and served for many years as the Congregational minister for Charleston, Massachusetts. Although Abbot never distinguished himself as a scholar, he managed to keep his parishioners happy, a notable achievement during a period of bitter religious controversy. Abbot's sermon helped the people of his community interpret distant events, in this case an unsuccessful rebellion in Scotland aimed at overthrowing George II. The leader of the Scottish rising was Prince Charles, the Stuart pretender to the British crown who enjoyed French support and sympathized with the Catholic faith. Like other Americans, Abbot expressed fierce loyalty for George, the Protestant monarch who spent a lifetime fighting Catholic France and who had come to symbolize commercial prosperity and constitutional rule throughout the British empire.

❧   ❧

HE.   Hull Abbot Sermon:#

The Duty of God's People (1746)
Evans #5724

Psalm cxxii. 6,7

Pray for the Peace of Jerusalem——

Peace be within thy Walls, and Prosperity

within thy Palaces

I Doubt not, my Brethren, but upon hearing the Words, that have been read, your Thoughts had immediate Recourse to the sad Occasion, in Providence, which makes the Consideration of them peculiarly *seasonable*, and the Duty mentioned in them *necessary* to be performed by us all; viz. the melancholy Circumstances of our Nation, by Reason of the *horrid Rebellion* of many of His MAJESTY'S subjects, against the Crown and Dignity of our rightful Sovereign King GEORGE, and the Protestant Succession in his Royal Family, in Favour of a *popish Pretender*; whereby the Nation is thrown into a great Ferment, and they are call'd to Arms in all the Parts of it, by the Will of GOD, to suppress the same: that so the King's Rebel-Subjects may be scatter'd, *and made to lick the Dust*, and *be cloathed with Shame* and Confusion, while on his Royal Head the Crown does steadily Flourish; and that His popish Enemies abroad, of *France & Spain &c.* who have *intended Evil against Him*, and *imagined this mischievous Device*, and made such great Preparations for the Execution of it, may be entirely disappointed and not able to perform it; and that they may be brought down and fall together, while His MAJESTY and His loyal Subjects, arise and stand upright; as thro' the signal Favour of divine Providence, has been the Case, when such wicked Attempts, against the Protestant Establishment have been heretofore made in our Nation, which we should speak of to the Glory of GOD's Name, and should *now* be a Foundation of Hope and Trust in Him.

And this not only shews that the Consideration of these Words is seasonable at this Time; but also the *Necessity* of our serious Performance of the Duty therein enjoyed upon the People of GOD in such a Case, *viz*. That of *Prayer*, earnest and unceasing Prayer and Supplications unto GOD, the everblessed and glorious JEHOVAH, with whom is infinite Wisdom and everlesting Strength; who rules in the Kingdom of Men, and has the Hearts of all in his Hands; and who stilleth the Noise of the Seas, the Noise of their Waves, and the Tumult of the People by a *Word;* And who only can restore and settle Peace and Quietness within the *Walls* of our Nation, and continue and increase Prosperity within the *Palaces* of it, and in the Royal House of His Servant the KING: and this, to the Security of the Civil and Religious Liberties of the People, and to the Tranquility and Happiness of our Nation, with all its Dependencies, to all Generations. . . .

I. *We may consider several Things supposed and implied in the Words, as a Foundaiton for the Duty required.* . . .

It implies. . . . [that God's professing people] may want Peace *at home*, and be embroil'd in Civil Wars within their Walls; that there may be intestine Jarrs, Divisions, and Animosities, and even Acts of Hostilityt committed among a People of the same Nation, one against another; and this, either raised among themselves, by Reason of differing Sentiments, &c. and by discontented and factious Spirits; or excited and fomented by their Enemies abroad, who are often instrumental, of bringing about such unnatural Ferments, that they may have an Advantage and Opportunity against them. This Kind of War is the most dangerous of any, and of the most pernicious Tendency and Consequence, as sad Experience has taught the *English* Nation; and this not only as it destroys Peace and Union, and brings on the most cruel *Discord among Brethren*, and shocks that very Foundations in Church and State; but also as hereby they become expos'd to their Enemies, and are made an easy Prey to them. . . . Whereas when they are heartily united in Interest and Affection at Home; when they are like *Jerusalem as a well compacted City*, and enjoy Peace and Tranquility within their own Walls, and among themselves,

This eighteenth-century overmantle (oil on wood) shows the Potter family with their slave. In the northern colonies, many slaves typically worked as house and body servants.

they are not so likely to be disturbed with any foreign Invasions; or if they should, will be ready with one Heart and Hand, vigorously to defend themselves against a common Enemy . . .

What remains now is the *Applicaiton* of the Discourse, and that with some special Reference to the melancholy Circumstances of our Nation with Regard to the *present, unnatural* REBELLION in *Scotland.* . . . in Favour of a *Popish Pretender,* and with a Design to bring in *Popery* and *Slavery,* and an arbitrary cruel Government into our Nation, which if it should obtain (but I humbly hope in GOD it never will) will not abide there confin'd in the Walls and Palaces of our Mother-Kingdom, but will extend its baneful Influences, to the remotest Provinces, and even to us in this Land, who derive therefrom. . . .

Wherefore, Let us all now, from what has been offer'd, be exhorted and persuaded, to unite together as one, in a serious Consideration of the sad State of our Nation, and in our humble, sincere, earnest and importune Prayers for GOD's Mercy to his Servant the KING upon the Throne, and to all in AUTHORITY in Church and State, and to all his Subjects over whom he has placed him: Particu-

larly, that Peace may be restored and establish'd *within their Walls, and Prosperity in their Palaces;* more especially, that GOD *would prepare Mercy and Truth to preserve the King,* and deliver him from the hurtful Sword and give Salvation to him. And that he would give him his Judgments, and his Righteousness to the King's Sons, and to all his royal Issue, and the Protestant Succession in His illustrious House may abide before GOD forever, and that He would continually preserve a Lamp to his annointed, and would always clothe his Enemies with Shame, and cause the Crown to flourish on his Royal Head, and in his Posterity to the latest Generations. And I am persuaded, my Brethren, you will readily obey the Exhortation, considering your Loyalty to the Crown, your Attachment to the Protestant Succession in the illustrious House of *Hanover,* and your Abhorrence of the Superstitions and idolatries of the *Popish Religion:* And this I suppose may be said of the Inhabitants of *New-England* universally, where the KING has as Loyal Subjects, and as faithful a People, as any in all his Dominions. . . .

Especially should we at such a Time, employ our Minds upon *that,* brought about by King WILLIAM, our glorious Deliverer, by the Will of GOD, and at the Desire of the Nationl the Father of his Country and the Patron of Liberty, whose Name is as Ointment pured forth, and I trust will be so to every true Englishman and Protestant to the latest Posterity. . . .

Thus as a tender Father [William III], he left behind him a glorious Legacy, or rather an *Inheritance* most precious and invaluable: He could not satisfy himself to deliver one Generation only from Idolatry and Slavery, but did his Part to perpetuate the Mercy, and to transmit our Religion and Laws safe to all succeeding Generations. And in this happy Settlement the Laws of the Nation have particularly establish'd the Line of Succession in the Protestant House of *Hanover*, a Fair Branch proceeding from the ancient Royal-Stock, of which is his present sacred MAJESTY, our lawful and rightful Sovereign. Oh! with what humble Adoration and exalted Praise should we recollect those Mercies? and the Wisdom and Goodness of Providence, in uniting the Hearts of his People, to provide such Acts for the Preservation and Continuance of their invaluable Liberties and Privileges! saying, *The Lord hath done great Things for us, whereof we are glad.* Psal. 126.3.

We must also to shew our Sincerity therein, and the Sense that we have of the Greatness of the Mercises, make earnest Prayers to GOD for the Continuance of them, and that he would engage his Power and Providence for the Defence of our Laws, and for the Preservation of the Protestant Succession agreeable thereto; and that he would do so especially at this Time. For we see alas! that we have Enemies both at Home and Abroad, that would, if possible, raze it to the Foundation of it, and again entangle our Necks in the Yoke of Bondage, from which GOD by his mighty Arm had made us free.

We should therefore pray to GOD in particular for the Preservation of his Majesty's Royal Person, Crown and Dignity (whose Government has been so mild and gracious) and that from all secret Attempts and open Violence: And that the Methods he is taking in his Dominions, may be prosper'd by his good Providence, for the effectual Suppressing of the unnatural Insurrection among his own Subjects; and that his Enemies may be together scatter'd and counfounded. . . . And that the Hearts of the People may be more strongly than ever united to his MAJESTY; and fill'd with greater Abhorrence of all Attempts to bring in *Popery and an Arbitrary Government*, to the utter Destruction of our happy Privileges, Religious and Civil, which we enjoy, and which are our Glory. And we have Reason to be thankful to GOD, for the Prospect of it, in the present happy Accord between the King and his Parliament, and almost all his Protestant Loyal Subjects, by the Accounts that we have from Home.

DOCUMENT 4

Provincial Accounts of the War for Empire

Throughout the century Americans were drawn into Britain's conflict with France. Contrary to what some historians have claimed, the colonists made a substantial contribution—in terms of men and supplies—to the ongoing effort to conquer Canada. It is estimated that during the Seven Years War (1756–1763) in Massachusetts alone at least 30 percent of all men aged between sixteen and twenty-nine served in the provincial army. John Winslow, a distinguished military veteran from Marshfield, led the Massachusetts forces in 1755. As a Provincial officer he ranked lower than the lowest British officer, a practice that irritated Americans like Winslow and George Washington, and tensions between Redcoats and colonists flared up when the British condescended to their American allies. Joseph Nicholas, also from Massachusetts, was an ordinary Provincial soldier. He participated in some disastrous actions against the French fortress at Ticonderoga, New York in 1758. His diary provides insight into how religion shaped Nicholas's interpretation of major imperial events.

John Winslow (Nova Scotia) to Henry Fox, Secretary of War in London (1755)

And only Congratulate your Honr on the Success of his Majesty's Arms in this Province which Seams to be Intierly Given up by the French and the Indians by them Deserted in the Transaction of these affairs. I apprehend the Americans have had their Equal Share of Duty with the regulars and all Sides Seams to be Aiming at doing their Best for the Service, and the acquisition of the Quiate Possession of Nova Scotia to his Majesty's Seams to be Compleated, and that with the Loss of three Men only Kild and Divers wounded.

Flater my Self that the Cheerful and Ready Disposition Shown by the New England men in this and Every other Ocation that offers wherin they have had oppertunity to Distinguish their zeal in Distroying the Enemys of Briton will meet with ye Royal approbation and that Even my Endeavors for his Majesty's Service May obtain your Smiles. and this I have to Say that I am the oldest officer in the Kings pay & the only remaining Captain of the late Cartherginia Expedition in New England and for Many years have been in the Service. Some times of the Crown and Sometimes of the Province.

your Honr. will Pardon this Freedom which is Drawn from Me by his Excellency our Colo being from his Regiment on his Majesty's Service to the Westward and no one but my Self Left to Speak for the Regiment am with the Greatest regards your Honrs. Most obedient & Most Humble Servt.

To the Honble Henry Fox Secretary at war and at the war office

JOHN WINSLOW
Westminster.

Excerpts from the Diary of Joseph Nicholas, Massachusetts Soldier (1758)

March the 27th, 1758. I'listed [in his] majesty's service against Canada, and myself to do a turn this year for Captain Belknap's two sons, *viz.,* Samuel Howard and Jeremiah Belknap. . . .

Our enemies fired upon our men and cut them down like grass. The fire continued exceeding hot, and one regiment was drawn up after another. In about an hour, orders came for Colonel Bagley's regiment to march up directly. We marched up a small space and then orders came to halt. Several of the soldiers went up without order and was killed, and several wounded. Our captain took care to keep us back from going forward, and keep our ground good, so our company fell not a prey as many of other companies did. The engagement lasted from . . . [ten o'clock] till just as the sun set; then we carried off some of our wounded men, and I am apt to think many was left to the mercy of the enemy.

. . . news came that the enemy was coming to fall upon us. Oh, the confusion that we was in at that time; for we was a poor situation for an enemy to attack us, being joined to a point of land, and the batteaux lay joining to one another fifteen deep from land. The cry of "Enemy" made our people cry out and make sad lamentations. We made the best of our way off, and received not hurt. . . .

The spirits of our men seem to fail. I doubt [i.e., "I fear"] we are losing our [*illeg.*] courage that in years past we had the credit of. It is a common saying that money makes the man to go; and I make no doubt if, in case our natures was refreshed with diet agreeable to what we are used to, our strength and courage would come to us like an armed man—I would be understood, in a natural cause.

Our people seems to be in a confused posture and our men are very much discouraged and beat out with their late hardship. 'Twas observed that in the late actions our men behaved bravely, not the least daunted when ordered to battle. But oh, our unhappiness and misfortune that we have sustained! May God of his infinite mercy and grace grant that our men may humble themselves before our Maker and repent of our sins, so that God would remember mercy and give success to our army; so that we may not return to our friends with shame as they have heretofore done. Observed our men refrain somewhat from profaneness and observe many reading in their books.

[T]he battle is not to the strong nor the race to the swift, but victory undoubtedly comes from the Lord. It appeared to me when we went to Ticonderoga we boasted too much of our numbers, how we were able to drive Canada. As for Ticonderoga,

that would be nothing in our hands. But alas! how was our designs blasted! Instead of driving Canada, we were not able to rout our enemies fropm their first stronghold, but retreated back from them who was much inferior in numbers, with the loss of my brave Lord Howe and a great number of brave officers and soldiers. Some affirm we had upwards of eighteen hundred killed, wounded, and missing. Then to make our case more deplorable, in a few days after we arrived from Ticonderoga we sustained two great losses by the enemy, who by waylaying our stores killed and took about one hundred persons and much spoil to our great [be]musement and discouragement. But it seems in the midst of our disappointment God had remembered mercy for us; in the late battle [i.e., Rogers's 8 August encounter with the French] we he had.

Oh, that God would enable us to sing of mercy in the midst of judgment, discouragement, and disappointment! Out people have been very much disheartened here at the lake occasioned by our great disappointment*. . . . Oh, that God would enable us to rejoice at our heart and return him sincere praise for such a great favor!

*July 8th at Ticonderoga; when we expected to take their fortress with ease. But God who is wise ordered it otherwise and we returned with shame and as it were with astonishment.

DOCUMENT 5

Alexander Hamilton, Itinerarium: Being a Narrative of a Journey (*1744*)

Dr. Alexander Hamilton (1712–1756)—no relation to the famous secretary of the Treasury—emigrated to Annapolis, Maryland, from Scotland. Although he built up a fine medical practice, he aspired to be more than a colonial physician. Like William Byrd and Benjamin Franklin, he exposed Americans to the cosmopolitan culture of Great Britain, and he organized a private group in Annapolis, the "Tuesday Club," modeled on the famous clubs of eighteenth-century London and Edinburgh.

After an illness in 1743, Hamilton took a long therapeutic trip to New England accompanied by his slave Dromo. In a journal published as the *Itinerarium* Hamilton poked fun at the pretensions of various Americans he had encountered, especially those like William Morison, an ambitious man who insisted that anyone able to afford the new British imports deserved to be called a gentleman.

Pennsylvania—Newcastle

Tuesday, June 5th.—I took horse a little after five in the morning, and after a solitary ride thro' stony, unequal road, where the country people stared at me like sheep when I inquired of them the way, I arrived at Newcastle, upon Delaware, at nine o'clock in the morning and baited my horses at one Curtis's, at the sign of the Indian King, a good house of entertainment.

This town stands upon stony ground, just upon the water, there being from thence a large prospect eastward, towards the Bay of Delaware and the Province of the Jerseys. The houses are chiefly brick, built after the Dutch model, the town having been originally founded and inhabited by the Dutch, when it belonged to New York government. It consists chiefly of one great street, which makes an elbow at right angles. A great many of the houses are old and crazy. There are in the town two public buildings; viz., a court-house and church.

At Curtis's I met company going to Philadelphia, and was pleased at it, being myself an utter stranger to the roads. This company consisted of three men,—Thomas Howard, Timothy Smith, and William Morison. I treated them with some lemon punch, and desired the favour of their company. They readily granted my request, and stayed some time for me, til I had eat breakfast.

Smith, in his coat and hat, had the appearance of a Quaker, but his discourse was purged of *thee's* and *thou's*, tho' his delivery seemed to be solemn and slow-paced.

Howard was a talkative man, abounding with words and profuse in compliments, which were generally blunt, and came out in an awkward manner.

He bestowed much panegyrick upon his own behaviour and conduct.

Morison (who, I understood, had been at the Land Office in Annapolis, inquiring about a title he had to some land in Maryland) was a very rough-spun, forward, clownish blade, much addicted to swearing, at the same time desirous to pass for a gentleman, notwithstanding which ambition, the conscientiousness of his natural boorishness obliged him frequently to frame ill-timed apologies for his misbehaviour, which he termed frankness and freeness. It was often,—"Damn me, gentlemen, excuse me; I am a plain, honest fellow; all is right down plain-dealing, by God." He was much affronted with the landlady at Curtis's, who, seeing him in a greasy jacket and breeches, and a dirty worsted cap, and withal a heavy, forward, clownish air and behaviour, I suppose took him for some ploughman or carman, and so presented him with some scraps of cold veal for breakfast, he having declared that he could not drink "your damned washy tea." As soon as he saw his mess, he swore,—"Damn him, if it wa'n't out of respect to the gentlemen in company" (meaning me) "he would throw her cold scraps out at the window and break her table all to pieces, should it cost him 100 pounds for damages." Then, taking off his worsted nightcap, he pulled a linen one out of his pocket, and clapping it upon his head,—"Now," says he, "I'm upon the borders of Pennsylvania and must look like a gentleman; t' other was good enough for Maryland, and damn my blood, if ever I come into that rascally Province again if I don't procure a leather jacket, that I may be in a trim to box the saucy Jacks there and not run the hazard of tearing my coat." This showed, by the bye, that he paid more regard to his coat than his person, a remark-

The Plantation, an idealized portrait of an early eighteenth-century Maryland estate by an unknown artist, shows the outbuildings—the mill, the warehouses, and the slave quarters—leading up to the main house.

able instance of modesty and self-denyal. He then made a transition to politicks, and damned the late Sir Robert Walpole for a rascal.

We asked him his reasons for cursing Sir Robert Walpole—[Prime Minister of England], but he would give us no other but this,—that he was certainly informed by some very good gentlemen who understood the thing right well, that the said Sir R—— was a damned rogue, and at the conclusion of each rodomontade he told us that tho' he seemed to be but a plain, homely fellow, yet he would have us know that he was able to afford better than many that went finer; he had good linen in his bags, a pair of silver buckles, silver clasps, and gold sleeve buttons, two Holland shirts and some neat nightcaps, and that his little woman at home drank tea twice a day, and he himself lived very well and expected to live better. . . .

The chief topic of conversation among these three Pennsylvanian dons upon the road, was the insignificancy of the neighbouring Province of Maryland when compared to that of Pennsylvania. They laid out all the advantages of the latter which their bungling judgment could suggest, and displayed all the imperfections and disadvantages of the first.

They enlarged upon the immorality, drunkenness, rudeness, and immoderate swearing, so much practised in Maryland, and added that no such vices were to be found in Pennsylvania. I heard this and contradicted it not, because I knew that the first part of the proposition was pretty true.

DOCUMENT 6

Benjamin Franklin, "A Proposal for Promoting Useful Knowledge Among the British Plantations in America" (1743)

A mong his many accomplishments, Benjamin Franklin wrote an autobiography that quickly became a classic of American literature. The work chronicles his rise from a poor boy in Boston to one of the cosmopolitan leaders of Philadelphia. By the time Franklin circulated "A Proposal," he had secured his own material well-being and turned his attentions increasingly to improving provincial society. He appreciated that mid-eighteenth century Americans had moved beyond the "Drudgery of Settling New Colonies" and were prepared to establish proper intellectual institutions. What the scattered colonists needed most, Franklin insisted, was a means of exchanging useful information, especially on scientific topics, and his response was the creation of the American Philosophical Society. Franklin was trying to include provincial thinkers in a larger imperial world; for him the key to social improvement was more rapid communication.

A Proposal for Promoting Useful Knowledge among the British Plantations in America

Philadelphia, May 14, 1743

The English are possess'd of a long Tract of Continent, from Nova Scotia to Georgia, extending North and South thro' different Climates, having different Soils, producing different Plants, Mines and Minerals, and capable of different Improvements, Manufactures, & c.

The first Drudgery of Settling new Colonies, which confines the Attention of People to mere Necessaries, is now pretty well over; and there are many in every Province in Circumstances that set them at Ease, and afford Leisure to cultivate the finer Arts, and improve the common Stock of Knowledge. To such of these who are Men of Speculation, many Hints must from time to time arise, many Observations occur, which if well-examined,

pursued and improved, might produce Discoveries to the Advantage of some or all of the British Plantations, or to the Benefit of Mankind in general.

But as from the Extent of the Country such Persons are widely separated, and seldom can see and converse or be acquainted with each other, so that many useful Particulars remain uncommunicated, die with the Discoverers, and are lost to Mankind; it is, to remedy this Inconvenience for the future, proposed,

That One Society be formed of Virtuosi or ingenious Men residing in the several Colonies, to be called *The American Philosophical Society;* who are to maintain a constant Correspondence.

That Philadelphia being the City nearest the Centre of the Continent-Colonies, communicating with all of them northward and southward by Post, and with all the islands by Sea, and having the Advantage of a good growing Library, be the Centre of the Society.

That at Philadelphia there be always at least seven Members, viz. a Physician, a Botanist, a

American statesman, scientist, and author, Benjamin Franklin greatly admired eighteenth-century British culture. After Parliament began taxing the colonists without representation, he reluctantly joined the patriot cause, helping to draft the Declaration of Independence.

Mathematician, a Chemist, a Mechanician, a Geographer, and a general Natural Philosopher, besides a President, Treasurer and Secretary.

That these Members meet once a Month, or oftner, at their own Expence, to communicate to each other their Observations, Experiments, &c. to receive, read and consider such Letters, Communications, or Queries as shall be sent from distant Members; to direct the Dispersing of Copies of such Communications as are valuable, to other distant Members, in order to procure their Sentiments thereupon, &c.

That the Subjects of the Correspondence be, All new-discovered Plants, Herbs, Trees, Roots, &c. trheir Virtues, Uses, &c. Methods of Propagating them, and making such as are useful, but particular to some Plantations, more general. Improvements of vegetable Juices, as Cyders, Wines, & c. New Methods of Curing or Preventing Diseases. All new-discovered Fossils in different Countries, as Mines, Minerals, Quarries, &c. New and useful Improvements in any Branch of Mathematics. New Discoveries in Chemistry, such as Improvements in Distillation, Brewing, Assaying of Ores, &c. New Mechanical Inventions for saving Labour, as Mills, Carriages, &c. and for Raising and Conveying of Water, Draining of Meadows, &c. All new Arts, Trades, Manufactures, &c. that may be proposed or thought of. Surveys, Maps and Charts of particular Parts of the Sea-coasts, or Inland Countries; Course and Junction of Rivers and great Roads, Situation of Lakes and Mountains, Nature of the Soil and Productions, &c. New Methods of Improving the Breed of useful Animals, Introducing other Sorts from foreign Countries. New Improvements in Planting, Gardening, Clearing Land, &c. And all philosophical Experiments that let Light into the Nature of Things, tend to increase the Power of Man over Matter, and multiply the Conveniences or Pleasures of Life.

That a Correspondence already begun by some intended Members, shall be kept up by this Society with the Royal Society of London, and with the Dublin Society.

That every Member shall have Abstracts sent him Quarterly of every Thing valuable communicated to the Society's Secretary at Philadelphia; free of all Charge except the Yearly Payment hereafter mentioned.

That by Permission of the Postmaster-General, such Communications pass between the Secretary of the Society and the Members, Postage-free.

That for defraying the Expence of such Experiments as the Society shall judge proper to cause to be made, and other contingent Charges for the common Good, every Member send a Piece of Eight *per Annum* to the Treasurer, at Philadelphia, to form a Common Stock, to be disburs'd by Order of the President with the Consent of the Majority of the Members that can conveniently be consulted thereupon, to such Persons and Places where and by whom the Experiments are to be made, and otherwise as there shall be Occasion; of which Disbvursements an exact Account shall be kept, and communicated yearly to every Member.

That at the first Meetings of the Members at Philadelphia, such Rules be formed for Regulating their Meetings and Transactions for the General Benefit, as shall be convenient and necessary; to be afterwards changed and improv'd as there shall be Occasion, wherein due Regard is to be had to the Advice of distant Members.

That at the End of every Year, Collections be made and printed, of such Experiments, Discoveries, Improvements, &c. as may be thought of publick Advantage: And that every Member have a Copy sent him.

That the Business and Duty of the Secretary be, To receive all Letters intended for the Society, and lay them before the President and Members at their Meetings; to abstract, correct and methodize such Papers, &c. as require it, and as he shall be directed to do by the President, after they have been considered, debated and digested in the Society; to enter Copies thereof in the Society's Books, and make out Copies for distant Members; to answer their Letters by Direction of the President, and keep Records of all material Transactions of the Society, &c.

Benjamin Franklin, the Writer of this Proposal, offers himself to serve the Society as their Secretary, 'till they shall be provided with one more capable.

DOCUMENT 7

Gilbert Tennent, *The Danger of an Unconverted Ministry (1741)*

When George Whitefield, the great British itinerant, launched his second and most important American crusade in 1740, few people outside the Mid-Atlantic colonies had heard of the Reverend Gilbert Tennent. He sympathized with evangelical Christianity, but it required Whitefield's triumph to persuade Tennent to take word of the "new birth" to people living in other parts of America. Whitefield urged Tennent to promote the Great Awakening in Boston "in order to blow up the divine fire lately kindled there." Although Tennent's preaching style angered traditional Christian ministers, he enjoyed notable success. His *Danger of an Uncoverted Ministry* contains a radical invitation to ordinary people to judge for themselves whether their own ministers had been saved.

MARK VI. 34.

And Jesus, when he came out, saw much People and was moved with Compassion towards them, because they were as Sheep not having a Shepherd.

As a faithful Ministry is a great Ornament, Blessing and Comfort, to the Church of GOD; even the Feet of such Messengers are beautiful: So on the contrary, an ungodly Ministry is a great Curse and

Judgment: These Caterpillars labour to devour every green Thing. . . .

My *Brethren*, We should mourn over those, that are destitute of faithful Ministers, and sympathize with them. Our Bowels should be moved with the most compassionate Tenderness, over those dear fainting Souls, that are *as Sheep having no Shepherd;* and that after the Example of our blessed LORD.

Dear Sirs! we should also most *earnestly pray* for them, that the compassionate Saviour may preserve them, by his *mighty* Power, thro' Faith unto Salvation; support their sinking Spirits, under the *melancholy Uneasinesses of a dead Ministry;* sanctify and sweeten to them the *dry* Morsels they get under such blind Men, when they have none better to repair to.

And more especially, *my Brethren*, we should pray to the LORD of the Harvest, to send forth faithful Labourers into his Harvest; seeing that the Harvest truly is plenteous, but the Labourers are few. And O Sirs! how humble, believing, and importunate should we be in this Petition! O! let us follow the LORD, Day and Night, with Cries, Tears, Pleadings and Groanings upon this Account! For God knows there is great *Necessity* of it. *O! thou Fountain of Mercy, and Father of Pity, pour forth upon thy poor Children a Spirit of Prayer, for the Obtaining this important Mercy! Help, help, O Eternal GOD and Father, for Christ's sake!*

And indeed, *my Brethren*, we should join our Endeavours to our *Prayers.* 'The most likely Method to stock the Church with a faithful *Ministry*, in the present Situation of Things, the publick Academies being so much corrupted and abused generally, is, To encourage private Schools, or Seminaries of Learning, which are under the Care of skilful and experienced Christians; in which those only should be admitted, who upon strict Examination, have in the Judgment of a reasonable *Charity*, the plain Evidences of experimental Religion. Pious and experienced Youths, who have a good natural Capacity, and great Desires after the Ministerial Work, from good Motives, might be sought for, and found up and down in the *Country*, and put to Private Schools of the Prophets; especially in such Places, where the Publick ones are not. This Method, in my

Opinion, has a *noble Tendency*, to build up the Church of God. And those who have any Love to Christ, or Desire after the Coming of his Kingdom, should be *ready*, according to their Ability, to give somewhat, from time to time, for the Support of such poor Youths, who have nothing of their own. And truly, Brethren, this *Charity* to the Souls of Men, is the most noble kind of *Charity*-O! if the Love of God be in you, it will constrain you to do something, to promote so noble and necessary a Work. It looks Hypocrite-like to go no further, when other Things are required, than *cheap Prayer.* Don't think it much, if the Pharisees should be offended at such a Proposal; these subtle selfish Hypocrites are wont to be scar'd about their Credit, and their Kingdom; and truly they are both little worth, for all the Bustle they make about them. If they could help it, they wo'dn't let one faithful Man come into the Ministry; and therefore their Opposition is an encouraging Sign. Let all the Followers of the Lamb stand up and act for GOD against all Opposers: Who is upon GOD's Side? who? . . .

2. From what has been said, we may learn, That such who are contented under a *dead Ministry*, have not in them the Temper of that Saviour they profess. It's an awful Sign, that they are as blind as Moles, and as dead as Stones, without any spiritual Taste and Relish. And alas! isn't this the Case of Multitudes? If they can get one, that has the Name of a Minister, with a Band, and a black Coat or Gown to carry on a *Sabbath-days* among them, although never so coldly, and *insuccessfully;* if he is free from gross Crimes in Practice, and takes good Care to keep a due Distance from their Consciences, and is never troubled about his Insuccessfulness; O! think the poor Fools, that is a fine Man indeed; our Minister is a prudent charitable Man, he is not always harping upon Terror, and sounding Damnation in our Ears, like some rash-headed Preachers, who by their uncharitable Methods, are ready to put poor People out of their Wits, or to run them into Despair; O! how terrible a Thing is that Dispair! Ay, our Minister, honest Man, gives us good Caution against it. Poor silly Souls consider *seriously* these Passages, of the Prophet, *Jeremiah* 5. 30, 31. . . .

4. If the Ministry of natural Men be as it has been represented; Then it is both lawful and expedient to go from them to hear Godly Persons; yea, it's so far from being sinful to do this, that one who lives under a pious Minister of lesser Gifts, after having honestly endeavour'd to get Benefit by his Ministry, and yet gets little or none, but doth find real Benefit and more Benefit elsewhere; I say, he may *lawfully* go, and that *frequently*, where he gets most Good to his precious Soul, after regular Application to the Pastor where he lives, for his Consent, and proposing the Reasons thereof: when this is done in the Spirit of Love and Meekness, without Contempt of any as also without rash *Anger* or vain *Curiosity*. . . .

To trust the Care of our Souls to those who have little or no Care for their own, to those who are both unskilful and unfaithful, is contrary to the common Practice of considerate Mankind, relating to the Affairs of their Bodies and Estates; and would signify, that we set light by our Souls, and did not care what became of them. For if the Blind lead the Blind, will they not both fall into the Ditch? . . .

If it be opposed to the preceding Reasonings, That such an Opinion and Practice would be apt to cause Heats and Contentions among People;

I answer, That the aforesaid Practice, accompanied with Love, Meekness, and Humility, is not the proper *Cause* of those Divisions, but the *Occasion* only, or the Cause by Accident, and not by itself. If a Person exercising Modesty and Love in his Carriage to his Minister and Neighbours, thro' Uprightness of Heart, designing nothing but his own greater Good, repairs there frequently where he attains it; is this any reasonable Cause of Anger? will any be offended with him because he loves his Soul, and seeks the greater Good thereof, and is not like a senseless Stone, without Choice, Sense, and Taste? Pray must we leave off every Duty, that is the Occasion of Contention or Division? Then we must quit powerful Religion altogether. For *he that will live godly in Christ Jesus, shall suffer Persecution.* And particularly we must carefully avoid faithful Preaching: For that is won't to occasion Disturbances and Divisions, especially when accompanied with divine Power. 1 Thess. 1. 5, 6. *Our Gospel came not unto you in Word only, but in Power:* And then it is added, That they *received the Word in much Affliction.* And the Apostle *Paul* informs us, 1 Cor. 16. 9. That a great Door and effectual was open'd unto him, and that their were many Adversaries. Blessed *Paul* was accounted a common Disturber of the Peace, as well as *Elijah* long before him: And yet he left not off Preaching for all that. Yea, our blessed LORD informs us, That he came not to send Peace on Earth, but rather a Sword, Variance, Fire, and Division, and that even among Relations. *Mat.* 10. 34, 35, 36. *Luke* 12. 49, 51, 52, 53. As also, That while the strong Men armed keeps the House, all the Goods are in Peace. It is true the Power of the Gospel is not the proper Cause of those Divisions, but the innocent Occasion only: No; the proper Cause of sinful Division, is that Enmity against God, and Holiness, which is in the Hearts of natural Men, of every Order; being stirred up by the Devil, and their own proud and selfish Lusts. And very often natural Men, who are the proper Causes of the Divisions aforesaid, are won't to deal with God's Servants as *Potiphar's* Wife did by *Joseph*; they lay all the Blame of their own Wickedness at their Doors, and make a loud Cry!

Such as confine Opposition and Division, as following upon living Godliness and successful Preaching, to the first Ages of Christianity; it is much to be fear'd neither know themselves, nor the Gospel of Christ. For surely the nature of true Religion, as well as of Men and Devils, is the same in every Age.

Is not the visible Church composed of Persons of the most contrary Characters? While some are sincere Servants of God, are not many Servants of Satan, under a religious Mask? and have not these a fixed Enmity against the other? How is it then possible, that a Harmony should subsist between such, till their Nature be changed? Can Light dwell with Darkness?

Undoubtedly it is a great Duty, to avoid giving just Cause of Offence to any; and it is also highly necessary, that pious Souls should maintain Union and Harmony among themselves; notwithstanding of their different Opinions in lesser Things. And no doubt this is the Drift of the many Exhortations which we have to peace and Unity in Scripture.

Surely, it cannot be reasonably suppos'd, that we are exhorted, to a Unity in any Thing that is wicked, or inconsistent with the Good, or greater Good of our poor Souls: For that would be like the Unity of the Devils, a Legion of which dwelt peaceably in one Man: Or like the Unity of *Ahab's* false Prophets; all these four Hundred Daubers were very peaceable and much united, and all harped on the pleasing String: Ay, they were moderate Men, and had the Majority on their Side. . . .

Because that the Apostle, in the aforesaid Place, reproves an excessive Love to, or Admiration of particular Ministers, accompanied with a sinful Contention, Slighting and Disdaining of others, who are truly godly, and with Sect-making: To say that from hence it necessarily follows, That we must make no Difference in our Choice, or in the Degrees of our Esteem of different Ministers, according to their Different Gifts and Graces; is an Argument of as great Force, as to say, Because Gluttony & Drunkenness are forbidden, therefore we must neither eat nor drink, or make any Choice in Drinks or Victuals, let our Constitution be what it will.

Surely the very Nature of Christian Love inclines those that are possessed of it, to love others chiefly for their Goodness, and therefore in Proportion thereto. Now, seeing the Inference in the Objection is secretly built upon this Supposition, That we should love all good Men alike; it strikes at the Foundation of that Love to the Brethren, which is laid down in Scripture, as a Mark of true Christianity, 1 *Joh.* 5. and so is carnal, with a Witness.

Again it may be objected, That the aforesaid Practice tends to grieve our Parish-Minister, and to break Congregations in Pieces.

I answer, If our Parish-Minister be grieved at our greater Good, or prefers his Credit before it; then he has good Cause to grieve over his own Rottenness, and Hypocrisie. And as for Breaking of Congregations to Pieces, upon the Account of People's Going from Place to Place, to hear the Word, with a View to get greater Good; that spiritual Blindness and Death, that so generally prevails, will put this out of Danger. It is but a very few, that have got any spiritual Relish; the most will venture their Souls with any Formalist, and be well satisfied with the sapless Discourses of such dead Drones. . . .

I would conclude my present Meditations upon this Subject, by Exhorting

All those who enjoy a faithful Ministry, to a speedy and sincere Improvement of so rare and valuable a Privilege; lest by, their foolish Ingratitude the Righteous GOD be provok'd, to remove the Means they enjoy, or his Blessing from them, and so at last to expose them in another State to Enduring and greater Miseries. For surely, these Sins which are committed against great Light and Mercy, are more presumptuous, ungrateful, and inexcusable; there is in them a greater Contempt of GOD's Authority, and Slight of his Mercy; those Evils do awfully violate the Conscience, and declare a Love to Sin as Sin; such Transgressors do rush upon the Bosses of GOD's Buckler, they court Destruction without a Covering, and embrace their own Ruin with open Arms. And therefore according to the Nature of Justice, which proportions Sinners Pains, according to the Number and Heinousness of their Crimes, and the Declaration of Divine Truth, you must expect an enflamed Damnation: Surely, it shall be more tolerable for *Sodom* and *Gomorrah*, in the Day of the LORD, than for you, except ye repent.

And let gracious Souls be exhorted, to express the most tender Pity over such as have none but Pharisee-Teachers; and that in the Manner before described: To which let the Example of the LORD in the Text before us, be an inducing and effectual Incitement; as well as the gracious and immense Rewards, which follow upon so generous and noble a Charity, in this and the next State.

And let those who live under the Ministry of dead Men, whether they have got the Form of Religion or not, repair to the Living, where they may be edified. Let who will, oppose . . . .

But tho' your Neighbours growl against you, and reproach you for doing your Duty, in seeking your Souls Good; bear their unjust Censures with Christian Meekness, and persevere; as knowing that Suffering is the Lot of Christ's Followers and that spiritual Benefits do infinitely overbalance all temporal difficulties.

And O! that vacant Congregations would take due care in the Choice of their Ministers! Here indeed they should hasten slowly. The Church of *Ephesus* is commended, for Trying them which said they were Apostles, and were not; and for finding them Liars. Hypocrites are against all Knowing of others, and Judging, in order to hide their own Filthiness; like Thieves they flee a Search, because of the stolen Goods. But the more they endeavour to hide, the more they expose their Shame. Does not the spiritual Man judge all Things? Tho' he cannot know the States of subtil Hypocrites infallibly; yet may he not give a near Guess, who are the Sons of *Sceva*, by their Manner of Praying, Preaching, and Living? Many Pharisee-Teachers have got a long fine String of Prayer by Heart, so that they are never at a Loss about it; their Prayers and Preachings are generally of a Length, and both as dead as a Stone, and without all Savour. I beseech you, my dear Brethren, to consider, That there is no Probability

of your getting Good, by the Ministry of Pharisees. For they are no Shepherds (no faithful ones) in Christ's Account. They are as good as none, nay, worse than none, upon some Accounts. For take them first and last, and they generally do more Hurt than Good. They strive to keep better out of the Places where they live; nay, when the Life of Piety comes near their Quarters, they rise up in Arms against it, consult, contrive and combine in their Conclaves against it, as a common Enemy, that discovers and condemns their Craft and Hypocrisie. And with what Art, Rhetorick, and Appearances of Piety, will they varnish their Opposition of Christ's Kingdom? As the Magicians imitated the Works of *Moses*, so do false Apostles, and deceitful Workers, the Apostles of Christ.

I shall conclude this Discourse with the Words of the Apostle *Paul*, 2 Cor. 11. 14. 15.

And no Marvel; for Satan himself is transformed into an Angel of Light: Therefore it is no great Thing if his Ministers also be transformed as the Ministers of Righteousness; whose End shall be according to their Works.

DOCUMENT 8

Charles Woodmason, "Peoples Brains are Turn'd and Bewilder'd" (1768 or 1769)

In 1766 Charles Woodmason abandoned the comforts of Charleston, South Carolina—perhaps the most refined city in provincial America—to become an Anglican itinerant on the Carolina frontier. Woodmason had cause to lament his decision. He traveled over 3000 miles a year through the backcountry. The people he encountered were the children of the Great Awakening. They gave allegiance to scores of different Protestant sects, but regardless whether they called themselves Seventh Day Baptists, Regular Baptists, or Presbyterians, they were all New Lights, in other words, converts to a form of evangelical religion stressing the centrality of the "new birth." The ignorance of frontier Christians frightened and appalled Woodmason, but neither he nor other conservative ministers were able to slow the movement.

❦　❧

Instead of having any fix'd Place of Abode, they [the New Light Clergy] are continually ranging from River to River devouring the fastings [?] of the Land. When one is gone, comes another and another. The wont is, That they don't all agree in one Tune. For one sings this Doctrine, and the next a different— So that Peoples Brains are turn'd and bewilder'd. But You may depend that they'l bring Scripture for all that they assert. As one lately did in Excuse for a Woman who had robbed her Husband to give to Him. He [said] she had a Right to the Money the same as God has to ev'ry thing. And as God bad[e] the Israelites to borrow of the Egyptians with out any Intention of repaying them, so this Woman was equally justifiable. The taking that Money from Him with which He was to pay the Merchant for Goods credited Him, was borrowing from the Egyptians to give to the Israelites. Rare Doctrine this, for benefit of the Merchants. But I observe, that among all these gifted and spiritualized Persons—all their Quotations and Metaphors, are drawn entirely from the O. T. And we never hear one Passage from our Lords Divine Sermon on the Mount. The first Article they begin with is to set the People against their several Ministers be they of whatever denomination. But especially the Established Clergy, against whom they utter all the vile and abominable Speeches, their rank Hearts can devise. Altho' there are not a more regular and Serious Body of Men on this Continent. The Common Prayer is run down— and the several Modes of Administration of Divine Offices. Then they begin with the Neighbourhood. Some are consigned to Damnation, others to Salvation—That is—Such as are Sensible and valuable Persons, Lovers of Peace and Order, and of the Church of England, and whom they are sensible they can make no Impression on—they are Reprobated—But the Giddy, and the Ignorant the Enthusiastic and Superstitious, whom they judge they may draw round them, such as *decreed* to be sav'd—And their Names are wrote in the Lamb's Book of Life— because they read it there. I ask's some of those deluded Persons, thus infatuated, thus impos'd on, How these Persons, and when, and where they read and saw this Book of Gods decrees when at same Time, they could not read the *Psalter* when laid before them?—And what Language it was In? Because A *Dutchman's* Name would certainly be wrote in *Dutch* and as they could not read *Dutch* How could they tell that the Dutchmans Name was there?— The Answer given, was,—That the finger of God pointed it out to them.

Such are the Proceedings of these Men and in this Manner as they beguile poor unthinking, illiterate Creatures. But this Finger that pointed, was the finger of Satan—That this and that Man had a Good Fat Beef, or Porker, to be Kill'd for the next Assembly of the Saints at his House. This the Poor Wretch takes as a favour little imagining that they come to devour that Bacon, which Himself and family must subsist on in the Winter. And its observable That You never hear of any Preachments at Houses that are too Poor to feed Gods Lambs. . . .

I am sorry, very sorry, that I should ever be driven to utter public Invectives against any Man, or Sett of Men whatever, and especially from the Pulpit, a Place dedicated, and sacred to Divine Matters only. But the Insolence and Presumption of these Incendiaries, is intolerable. They oblige me to break thro' all bounds of Decorum. Not content with vilifying the Common Prayer, the Articles, the Canons and Homilies of our Church (which I dare aver not one of these fellows ever saw or read) But they have made open and publick attacks on me in their Several Congregations. One of them lately to shew his Wit, went quibbling and quirking on my Name. He told the Audience there were various Kinds of *Masons* in the World (and so went on) but that I was a Mason who built on rotten foundations and rais'd Buildings only of Straw and Strubble, and daub'd with untemper'd Mortar, and would never make any Strong buildings for Christ of such Carnal Ordinances—and that tho' I was an Wood Mason, He queried if I was a *Good* Mason—but as Wood was a perishable Matter, and serv'd for Fewel, so that I should Perish Everlastingly and serve for fuel to Hell fire.

Here You have the Church of England call'd A Rotten foundation—The Liturgy and Discipline— Chaff and Strubble. The sacraments, Carnal Ordinances, and her Ministers, Children of Hell. Is this to be born in a Civiliz'd State where the Laws establish a Church and Clergy. But its not my Self only that these Wretches thus abuse; They call'd Mr. Turquand A Turkey Cock (because he has a rosy Complexion) and Mr. Richardson (who is a *Pale Man*) The Pale or White Horse or Death, for his People to ride on to Hell. . . .

If I give out to be at such a Place at such a Time, three or four of these fellows [New Lights] are constantly at my Heels—They either get there before me, and hold forth—or after I have finish'd, or the next Day, or for days together. Had I an hundred

Tongues, or as many Pairs of Legs, I could not *singly* oppose such a Numerous Crew. . . .

How is it possible that I can visit the Sick—Or exhort, or reprove, or admonish When the People are told That I am a Jesuit in disguise—To others that I am a Presbyterian—To the Presbyterians—That I am an Independant—To the Independants That I am a Methodist?—This is done, in order to unsettle me where ever I Go—So that I am determin'd to resign my Commission as this next Week to the Board of Church Commissioners.

DOCUMENT 9

Nathan Cole, "Spiritual Travels" (1740)

Nathan Cole was a farmer of about twenty-nine when the extraordinary George Whitefield came to preach in Middletown, Connecticut. Cole had heard about Whitefield's powerful ability to inspire religious convictions, and he "longed to see and hear him." When word reached Cole of Whitefield's arrival, he and his wife rushed to hear him, as fast as their horse could travel. He was not disappointed: Cole reported that "my hearing him preach, gave me a heart wound."

Now it pleased God to send Mr Whitefield into this land; and my hearing of his preaching at Philadelphia, like one of the Old apostles, and many thousands flocking to hear him preach the Gospel; and great numbers were converted to Christ; I felt the Spirit of God drawing me by conviction; I longed to see and hear him, and wished he would come this way. I heard he was come to New York and the Jerseys and great multitudes flocking after him under great concern for their Souls which brought on my Concern more and more hoping soon to see him but next I heard he was at long Island; then at Boston and next at Northampton; then on a Sudden, in the morning about 8 or 9 of the Clock there came a messenger and said Mr

Whitfield preached at Hartford and Weathersfield yesterday and is to preach at Middletown this morning at ten of the Clock, I was in my field at Work, I dropt my tool that I had in my hand and ran home to my wife telling her to make ready quickly to go and hear Mr Whitfield preach at Middletown, then run to my pasture for my horse with all my might; fearing that I should be too late; having my horse I with my wife soon mounted the horse and went forward as fast as I thought the horse could bear, and when my horse got much out of breath I would get down and put my wife on the Saddle and bid her ride as fast as she could and not Stop or Slack for me except I bad her and so I would run untill I was much out of breath; and then mount my horse again, and so I did several times to favour my horse; we improved every moment to get along as if we were fleeing for our lives; all the while fearing we should be too late to hear the Sermon, for we had twelve miles to ride double in little more than an hour and we went round by the upper housen parish and when we came within about half a mile or a mile of the Road that comes down from Hartford weathersfield and Stepny to Middletown; on high land I saw before me a Cloud or fogg rising; I first thought it came from the great River, but as I came nearer the Road, I heard a noise something like a low rumbling thunder and presently found it was the noise of Horses feet coming down the Road and this Cloud was a Cloud of dust made by the Horses feet; it arose some Rods into the [sic] air over the tops of Hills and trees and when I came within about 20 rods of the Road, I could see men and horses Sliping along in the Cloud like shadows and as I drew nearer it seemed like a steady Stream of horses and their riders, scarcely a horse more than his length behind another, all of a lather and foam with sweat, their breath rolling out of their nostrils every Jump; every horse seemed to go with all his might to carry his rider to hear news from heaven for the saving of Souls, it made me tremble to see the Sight, how the world was in a Struggle; I found a Vacance between two horses to Slip in mine and my Wife said law our Cloaths will be all spoiled see how they look, for they were so Covered with dust, that they looked almost all of a Colour Coats, hats, Shirts, and horses. We went down in the Stream but heard no man speak a word all the way for miles but every one pressing forward in great haste and when we got to Middletown old meeting house there was a great Multitude it was said to be 3 or 4000 of people Assembled together; we dismounted and shook of our Dust; and the ministers were then Coming to the meeting house; I turned and looked towards the Great River and saw the ferry boats running swift backward and forward bringing Over loads of people and the Oars Rowed nimble and quick; every thing men horses and boats needed to be Struggling for life; the land and banks over the river look full with people and horses all along the 12 miles I saw no man at work in this field, but all seemed to be gone—When I saw Mr. Whitfield come upon the Scaffold he lookt almost Angelical; a young, Slim, slender youth amid some thousands of people with a bold undaunted Contenance, and my hearing how God was with him every where as he came along it traumatized my mind; and put me into a trembling fear before he began to search for he looked as if he was Cloathed with Authority from the Godl and a sweet sollome solemnity sat upon his brow And my seeing him preach, gave me a heart wound; By Gods blessing: my old foundation was broken up, and I saw that my righteousness would not save me.

Study Questions

1. What did the British Empire have to offer to eighteenth-century Americans?

2. How did the Great Awakening shape the colonists' sense of identity?

3. Could ordinary Americans have accepted Franklin's practical approach to probem solving as well as Tennent's evangelical Christianity?

4. Commerce, religious revivals, and war brought Americans into contact with men and women whom they would not ordinarily have met. What were the social and political implications of this expanded communication within the empire?

❦ ❧

Revolution

One of the many mysteries about the American Revolution is why it occurred precisely when it did. Why did the colonists not declare independence in 1765? Or in 1770? Or, for that matter, in 1780? Colonial Americans would have had difficulty addressing this question. Most did not seriously contemplate breaking with Great Britain until Redcoats attacked militiamen at Lexington and Concord in April 1775. And however loudly they railed against British tyranny, white colonists could not credibly maintain that they were oppressed peasants of the sort encountered in contemporary Europe.

In a celebrated essay, "What Is an American?" (Document 1), J. Hector St. John Crèvecoeur painted a glorious picture of free, prosperous farmers. Benjamin Franklin offered a less romantic assessment of late colonial society. In a brilliant pioneering study of population growth written in 1751 (Document 2), Franklin predicted that if British politicians left well enough alone, Americans would purchase ever-larger quantities of English goods, thus perpetually cementing Anglo-American union.

But, of course, the British did not leave well enough alone. After successfully concluding the Seven Years' War in 1763, Parliament began taxing the Americans. The British claimed they had to retire a huge national debt incurred in fighting the French, but the colonists remained skeptical. Parliament seemed suddenly to be changing the rules of empire. In 1764 a young Massachusetts lawyer, James Otis, attacked the logic of the British position, and in *The Rights of the British Colonies Asserted and Proved* (Document 3), Otis explained as clearly as did any of his contemporaries how Americans defined political rights.

Quite early in the imperial confrontation, the colonists hit upon an innovative method of protest. They organized massive consumer boycotts, and as tensions between England and America grew, their efforts to discourage the purchase of British manufactures became more effective. As an instrument of political protest, the boycott had the capacity to mobilize Americans of all classes and regions, men as well as women, and as the Virginia Nonimportation Resolutions of 1769 (Document 4) reveal, one's consumer habits became an external badge of patriotism. Popular prints (Document 5) powerfully reinforced political arguments advanced in pamphlets and newspaper essays.

Protest against parliamentary taxation sparked passionate rhetoric about impending enslavement and loss of natural rights. As gentry leaders soon discovered, however, the appeal to liberty encouraged broader participation in politics. Ordinary people who once deferred to their social betters now openly voiced their opinions. George Robert Twelves Hewes was such a person. A poor New England shoemaker, he took part in the most provocative act of the period, the destruction of tea in Boston Harbor in 1773 (Document 6). African Americans also responded to the language of liberty, reminding white colonists of the obligation to extend freedom to their slaves. A 1774 petition from "a Grate Number of Blackes" living in Massachusetts (Document 7) pointed out the hypocrisy of attempting to limit freedom to the members of one race. A few colonists observed that women as well as men had political rights. Abigail Adams challenged her husband, John Adams, then a member of the Continental Congress, to "Remember the Ladies." Like other revolutionary leaders, Adams feared such speculation. If women could vote, he noted, then soon all sorts of people would claim the franchise—those without property or of darker skin, for example (Document 8).

Winners dominate the stories we tell ourselves about the past. The losers, the people who supported king and Parliament—the loyalists—seem perversely out of step with the movement of history. That, of course, is the judgment of hindsight. A large percentage of the population did not support independence. These men and women came from all classes and backgrounds, and most suffered for their beliefs. Peter Oliver, a royal officeholder in Massachusetts, never understood the demand for rights and liberties, and, in a history of the revolution written from the loyalist perspective (Document 9), he blamed political disorder on a small band of self-serving conspirators.

When the moment for declaring independence arrived, even its most fervent advocates expressed concern. No one could guarantee victory; anarchy could well destroy the republic. John Adams appreciated the dangers, but in 1776 he was willing to give the American people a chance to demonstrate political virtue (Document 10). And Thomas Jefferson, the man who penned the Declaration of Independence, lamented the collapse of a great colonial empire (Document 11).

DOCUMENT 1

J. Hector St. John Crèvecoeur, "What Is an American?" (1782)

Born in France, Crèvecoeur (1735–1813) as a young man moved from France to Canada, where he served as a lieutenant in the French army during the Seven

Years' War. At the conclusion of hostilities, Crèvecoeur elected to remain in America. After traveling extensively through frontier regions, he settled in New York, becoming a citizen in 1765 and establishing a successful farm. Crèvecoeur observed his new neighbors closely, marveling how men and women from so many different European backgrounds formed prosperous communities in the New World, and in 1782 he published his reflections as *Letters from an American Farmer*. While the Frenchman admired the independent spirit of the colonial yeomen, he did not support the American Revolution. Moreover, unlike many northern farmers, Crèvecoeur owned slaves.

I wish I could be acquainted with the feelings and thoughts which must agitate the heart and present themselves to the mind of an enlightened Englishman, when he first lands on this continent. He must greatly rejoice that he lived at a time to see this fair country discovered and settled; he must necessarily feel a share of national pride, when he views the chain of settlements which embellishes these extended shores. When he says to himself, this is the work of my countryment, who, when convulsed by factions, afflicted by a variety of miseries and wants, restless and impatient, took refuge here. They brought along with them their national genius, to which they principally owe what liberty they enjoy, and what substance they possess. Here he sees the industry of his native country displayed in a new manner, and traces in their works the embryos of all the arts, sciences, and ingenuity which flourish in Europe. Here he beholds fair cities, substantial villages, extensive fields, an immense country filled with decent houses, good roads, orchards, meadows, and bridges, where an hundred years ago all was wild, woody, and uncultivated! What a train of pleasing ideas this fair spectacle must suggest; it is a prospect which must inspire a good citizen with the most heartfelt pleasure. The difficulty consists in the manner of viewing so extensive a scene. He is arrived on a new continent; a modern society offers itself to his contemplation, different from what he had hitherto seen. It is not composed, as in Europe, of great lords who possess everything, and of a herd of people who have nothing. Here are no aristocratical families, no courts, no kings, no bishops, no ecclesiastical dominion, no invisible power giving to a few a very visible one, no great manufacturers employing thousands, no great refinements of luxury. The rich and the poor are not so far removed from each other as they are in Europe. Some few towns excepted, we are all tillers of the earth, from Nova Scotia to West Florida. We are a people of cultivators, scattered over an immense territory, communicating with each other by means of good roads and navigable rivers, united by the silken bands of mild government, all respecting the laws, without dreading their power, because they are equitable. We are all animated with the spirit of an industry which is unfettered and unrestrained, because each person works for himself. If he travels through our rural districts he views not the hostile castle, and the haughty mansion, contrasted with the clay-built hut and miserable cabin, where cattle and men help to keep each other warm, and dwell in meanness, smoke, and indigence. A pleasing uniformity of decent competence appears throughout our habitations. The meanest of our log-houses is a dry and comfortable habitation. Lawyer or merchant are the fairest titles our towns afford; that of a farmer is the only appellation of the rural inhabitants of our country. It must take some time ere he can reconcile himself to our dictionary, which is but short in words of dignity, and names of honour. There, on a Sunday, he sees a congregation of respectable farmers and their wives, all clad in neat homespun, well mounted, or riding in their own humble waggons. There is not among them an esquire, saving the unlettered magistrate. There he sees a parson as simple as his flock, a farmer who does not riot on the labour of others. We have no princes, for whom we toil, starve, and bleed: we are the most perfect society now existing in the world. Here man is free as he ought to be; nor is this pleasing equality so transitory as many others are. Many ages will not see the shores of our great lakes replenished with inland nations, nor the unknown bounds of North America entirely peopled. Who can tell how far it extends? Who can tell the millions of men whom it will feed and contain? For no European foot has as yet travelled half the extent of this mighty continent!

The next wish of this traveller will be to know whence came all these people? They are a mixture of English, Scotch, Irish, French, Dutch, Germans, and Swedes. From this promiscuous breed, that race now called Americans have arisen. The eastern provinces must indeed be excepted, as being the unmixed descendants of Englishmen. I have heard many wish that they had been more intermixed also: for my part, I am no wisher, and think it much better as it has happened. They exhibit a most conspicuous figure in this great and variegated picture; they too enter for a great share in the pleasing perspective displayed in these thirteen provinces. I know it is fashionable to reflect on them, but I respect them for what they have done, for the accuracy and wisdom with which they have settled their territory; for the decency of their manners; for their early love of letters; their ancient college, the first in this hemisphere; for their industry; which to me who am but a farmer, is the criterion of everything. There never was a people, situated as they are, who with so ungrateful a soil have done more in so short a time. Do you think that the monarchical ingredients which are more prevalent in other governments, have purged them from all foul stains? Their histories assert the contrary.

In this great American asylum, the poor of Europe have by some means met together, and in consequence of various causes; to what purpose should they ask one another what countrymen they are? Alas, two thirds of them had no country. Can a wretch who wanders about, who works and starves, whose life is a continual scene of sore affliction or pinching penury; can that man call England or any other kingdom his country? A country that had no bread for him, whose fields procured him no harvest, who met with nothing but the frowns of the rich, the severity of the laws, with jails and punishments; who owned not a single foot of the extensive surface of this planet? No! urged by a variety of motives, here they came. Every thing has tended to regenerate them; new laws, a new mode of living, a new social system; here they are become men: in Europe they were as so many useless plants, wanting vegetative mould, and refreshing showers; they withered, and were mowed down by want, hunger, and war; but now by the power of transplantation, like all other plants they have taken root and flourished! Formerly they were not numbered in any civil lists of their country, except in those of the poor; here they rank as citizens. By what invisible power has this surprising metamorphosis been performed? By that of the laws and that of their industry. The laws, the indulgent laws, protect them as they arrive, stamping on them the symbol of adoption; they receive ample rewards for their labours; these accumulated rewards procure them lands; those lands confer on them the title of freemen, and to that title every benefit is affixed which men can possibly require. This is the great operation daily performed by our laws. From whence proceed these laws? From our government. Whence the government? It is derived from the original genius and strong desire of the people ratified and confirmed by the Crown. This is the great chain which links us all, this is the picture which every province exhibits, Nova Scotia excepted. . . .

What attachment can a poor European emigrant have for a country where he had nothing? The knowledge of the language, the love a few kindred as poor as himself, were the only cords that tied him: his country is now that which gives him land, bread, protection, and consequence: *Ubi panis ibi patria*, is the motto of all emigrants. What then is the American, this new man? He is either an European, or the descendant of an European, hence that strange mixture of blood, which you will find in no other country. I could point out to you a family whose grandfather was an Englishman, whose wife was Dutch, whose son married a French woman, and whose present four sons have now four wives of different nations. *He* is an American, who, leaving behind him all his ancient prejudices and manners, receives new ones from the new mode of life he has embraced, the new government he obeys, and the new rank he holds. He becomes an American by being received in the broad lap of our great *Alma Mater*. Here individuals of all nations are melted into a new race of men, whose labours and posterity will one day cause great changes in the world. Americans are the western pilgrims, who are carrying along with them that great mass of arts, sciences, vigour, and industry which began long since in the east; they will finish the great circle. The Americans were once scattered all over Europe; here they are incorporated into one of the finest systems of population which has ever appeared, and which will hereafter become distinct by the power of the different climates they inhabit. The American ought therefore to love this country much better than that wherein either he or his forefathers were born. Here the rewards of his industry follow with equal steps the progress of his labour; his labour is founded on the basis of nature, *self-interest*; can it want a stronger alllurement? Wives and children, who before in vain demanded of him a morsel of bread, now, fat and frolicsome, gladly help their father to clear those fields whence exuberant crops are to arise to feed and to clothe them all; without any part being claimed, either by a despotic prince, a rich abbot, or a mighty lord. Here religion demands but little of him; a small voluntary salary to the minister and gratitude to God; can he refuse these? The American is a new man, who acts upon new principles; he must therefore entertain new ideas, and form new opinions. From involuntary idleness, service dependence, penury, and useless labour, he has passed to toils of a very different nature, reward by ample subsistance.—This is an American. . . .

DOCUMENT 2

Benjamin Franklin, "Observations Concerning the Increase of Mankind, Peopling of Countries, &c." (1751)

While analyzing the explosive growth of the American population, Franklin came to appreciate the colonists' extraordinary appetite for British manufactured goods. The Americans were not self-sufficient, nor, at mid-century, did they desire to be so. They purchased great quantities of imported goods, especially cloth. Franklin insisted that trade of this sort promoted general prosperity throughout the empire. No reasonable ruler, he argued, would disturb the commercial harmony existing between the colonies and Great Britain; indeed, he envisioned America's full participation in an ever-stronger imperial union, not rebellion. Franklin advocated a society peopled almost exclusively by Anglo-Saxons, and in his "Observations," he disparaged blacks, Indians, and Germans— indeed, anyone who did not come from Britain.

❦ ❦

Europe is generally full settled with Husband-men, Manufacturers, &c. and therefore cannot now much increase in People: America is chiefly occu-pied by Indians, who subsist mostly by Hunting. But as the Hunter, of all Men, requires the greatest Quantity of Land from whence to draw his Subsis-tence, (the Husbandman subsisting on much less, the Gardner on still less, and the Manufacturer re-quiring least of all), The Europeans found America as fully settled as it well could be by Hunters; yet these having large Tracks, were easily prevail'd on to part with Portions of Territory to the new Com-ers, who did not much interfere with the Natives in Hunting, and furnish'd them with many Things they wanted.

Land being thus plenty in America, and so cheap as that a labouring Man, that understands Hus-bandry, can in a short Time save Money enough to purchase a Piece of new Land sufficient for a Planta-tion, whereon he may subsist a Family; such are not afraid to marry; for if they even look far enough for-ward to consider how their Children when grown up are to be provided for, they see that more Land is to be had at Rates equally easy, all Circumstances considered.

Hence Marriages in America are more general, and more generally early, than in Europe. And if it is reckoned there, that there is but one Marriage per Annum among 100 Persons, perhaps we may here reckon two; and if in Europe they have but 4 Births to a Marriage (many of their Marriages being late) we may here reckon 8, of which if one half grow up, and our Marriages are made, reckoning one with an-other at 20 Years of Age, our People must at least be doubled every 20 Years.

But notwithstanding this Increase, so vast is the Territory of North-America, that it will require many Ages to settle it fully; and till it is fully settled, Labour will never be cheap here, where no Man continues long a Labourer for others, but gets a Plantation of his own, no Man continues long a Journeyman to a Trade, but goes among those new Settlers, and sets up for himself, &c. Hence Labour is no cheaper now, in Pennsylvania, than it was 30

Years ago, tho' so many Thousand labouring People have been imported.

The Danger therefore of these Colonies interfer-ing with their Mother Country in Trades that de-pend on Labour, Manufactures, &c. is too remote to require the Attention of Great-Britain.

But in Proportion to the Increase of the Colonies, a vast Demand is growing for British Manufacturers, a glorious Market wholly in the Power of Britain, in which Foreigners cannot interfere, which will in-crease in a short Time even beyond her Power of supplying, tho' her whole Trade should be to her Colonies: Therefore Britain should not too much restrain Manufactures in her Colonies. A wise and good Mother will not do it. To distress, is to weaken, and weakening the Children, weakens the whole Family.

Besides if the Manufactures of Britain (by Reason of the American Demands) should rise too high in Price, Foreigners who can sell cheaper will drive her Merchants out of Foreign Markets; Foreign Manu-facturers will thereby be encouraged and increased, and consequently foreign Nations, perhaps her Ri-vals in Power, grow more populous and more power-ful; while her own Colonies, kept too low, are un-able to assist her, or add to her Strength.

'Tis an ill-grounded Opinion that by the Labour of Slaves, America may possibly vie in Cheapness of Manufactures with Britain. The Labour of Slaves can never be so cheap here as the Labour of working Men is in Britain. Any one may compute it. Interest of Money is in the Colonies from 6 to 10 per Cent. Slaves one with another cost £30 Sterling per Head. Reckon then the Interest of the first Purchase of a Slave, the Insurance or Risque on his Life, his Cloathing and Diet, Expences in his Sickness and Loss of Time, Loss by his Neglect of Business (Ne-glect is natural to the Man who is not to be bene-fited by his own Care or Diligence), Expence of a Driver to keep him at Work, and his Pilfering from Time to Time, almost every Slave being *by Nature* a Thief, and compare the whole Amount with the Wages of a Manufacturer of Iron or Wool in Eng-land, you will see that Labour is much cheaper there than it ever can be by Negroes here. Why then will Americans purchase Slaves? Because Slaves may be kept as long as a Man pleases, or has Occasion for their Labour; while hired Men are continually leaving their Master (often in the midst of his Business,) and setting up for themselves. . . .

There is in short, no Bound to the prolific Nature of Plants or Animals, but what is made by their crowding and interfering with each others Means of Subsistence. Was the Face of the Earth vacant of other Plants, it might be gradually sowed and overspread with one Kind only; as, for Instance, with Fennel; and were it empty of other Inhabitants, it might in a few Ages be replenish'd from one Nation only; as, for Instance, with Englishmen. Thus there are suppos'd to be now upwards of One Million English Souls in North-America, (tho' 'tis thought scarce 80,000 have been brought over Sea) and yet perhaps there is not one the fewer in Britain, but rather many more, on Account of the Employment the Colonies afford to Manufacturers at Home. This Million doubling, suppose but once in 25 Years, will in another Century be more than the People of England, and the greatest Number of Englishmen will be on this Side the Water. What an Accession of Power to the British Empire by Sea as well as Land! What Increase of Trade and Navigation! What Number of Ships and Seamen! We have been here but little more than 100 Years, and yet the Force of our Privateers in the late War, united, was greater, both in Men and Guns, than that of the whole British Navy in Queen Elizabeth's Time. . . .

And since Detachments of English from Britain sent to America, will have their Places at Home so soon supply'd and increase so largely here; why should the Palatine Boors be suffered to swarm into our Settlements, and by herding together establish their Language and Manners to the Exclusion of ours? Why should Pennsylvania, founded by the English, become a Colony of *Aliens*, who will shortly be so numerous as to Germanize us instead of our Anglifying them, and will never adopt our Language or Customs, any more than they can acquire our Complexion.

Which leads me to add one Remark: That the Number of purely white People in the World is proportionably very small. All Africa is black or tawny. Asia chiefly tawny. America (exlusive of the New Comers) wholly so. And in Europe, the Spaniards, Italians, French, Russians and Swedes, are generally of what we call a swarthy Complexion; as are the Germans also, the Saxons only excepted, who with the English, make the principal Body of White People on the Face of the Earth. I could wish their Numbers were increased. And while we are, as I may call it, *Scouring* our Planet, by clearing America of Woods, and so making this Side of our Globe reflect a brighter Light to the Eyes of Inhabitants in Mars or Venus, why should we in the Sight of Superior Beings, darken its People? why increase the Sons of Africa, by Planting them in America, where we have so fair an Opportunity, by excluding all Blacks and Tawneys, of increasing the lovely White and Red? But perhaps I am partial to the Complexion of my Country, for such Kind of Partiality is natural to Mankind.

DOCUMENT 3

James Otis, The Rights of the British Colonies Asserted and Proved (1763)

James Otis (1725–1783) was one of the more radical political figures of his generation. Otis came from a distinguished Massachusetts family, and, after graduating from Harvard College in 1743, he trained as a lawyer. His talents took him in many different directions. Otis was a respected Latin scholar, a popular Boston politician, and a forceful advocate for colonial rights within the British empire. Drawing on the political philosophy of John Locke, a late–seventeenth-century philosopher, and his own religious beliefs, Otis developed a powerful case for equality. He insisted that women and blacks enjoyed the same natural rights as white males. Mental illness undermined a seemingly promising career, and by the 1770s Otis had lost effective contact with the patriot cause.

❧   ❧

It is . . . true in fact and *experience*, as the great, the incomparable *Harrington* has most abundantly demonstrated in his *Oceana* and other divine writings, that empire follows the balance of *property*. 'Tis also certain that *property* in fact generally *confers* power, though the possessor of it may not have much more wit than a mole or a musquash: and this is too often the cause that riches are sought after without the least concern about the right application of them. But is the fault in the riches, or the general law of nature, or the unworthy possessor? It will never follow from all this that government is *rightfully* founded on *property* alone. What shall we say then? Is not government founded on *grace?* No. Nor on *force?* No. Nor on *compact?* Nor *property?* Not altogether on either. Has it *any* solid foundation, any chief cornerstone but what accident, chance, or confusion may lay one moment and destroy the next? I think it has an everlasing foundation in the *unchangeable will of* GOD, the author of nature, whose laws never vary. The same omniscient, omnipotent, infinitely good and gracious Creator of the universe who has been pleased to make it necessary that what we call matter should *gravitate* for the celestial bodies to roll round their axes, dance their orbits, and perform their various revolutions in that beautiful order and concern which we all admire has made it *equally* necessary that from *Adam* and *Eve* to these degenerate days the different sexes should sweetly *attract* each other, form societies of *single* families, of which *larger* bodies and communities are as naturally, mechanically, and necessarily combined as the dew of heaven and the soft distilling rain is collected by the all-enlivening heat of the sun. *Government* is therefore most evidently founded *on the necessities of our nature*. It is by no means an *arbitrary* thing depending merely on *compact* or *human will* for its existence. . . .

The *end* of government being the *good* of mankind points out its great duties: it is above all things to provide for the security, the quiet, and happy enjoyment of life, liberty, and property. There is no one act which a government can have a *right* to make that does not tend to the advancemewnt of the security, tranquillity, and prosperity of the people. If life, liberty, and property could be [11] enjoyed in as great perfection in *solitude* as in *society* there would be no need of government. But the experience of ages has proved that such is the nature of man, a weak, imperfect being, that the valuable ends of life cannot be obtained without the union and assistance of many. Hence 'tis clear that men cannot live apart or independent of each other. In solitude men would perish, and yet they cannot live together without contests. These contests require some arbitrator to determine them. The necessity of a common, indifferent, and impartial judge makes all men seek one, though few find him in the *sovereign power* of their respective states or anywhere else in *subordination* to it. . . .

I know of no human law founded on the law of *nature* to restrain him from separating himself from all the species if he can find it in his heart to leave them, unless it should be said it is against the great law of *self-preservation:* but of this every man will think himself *his own judge*.

The few *hermits* and *misanthropes* that have ever existed show that those states are *unnatural*. If we were to take out from them those who have made great *worldly* gain of their *godly* hermitage and those who have been under the madness of *enthusiasm* or *disappointed* hopes in their *ambitious* projects for the detriment of mankind, perhaps there might not be left ten from *Adam* to this day.

The form of government is by *nature* and by *right* so far left to the *individuals* of each society that they may alter it from a simple democracy or government of all over all to any other form they please. Such alteration may and ought to be made by express compact. But how seldom this right has been asserted, history will abundantly show. For once that it has been fairly settled by compact, *fraud, force,* or *accident* have determined it an hundred times. As the people have gained upon tyrants, these have been obliged to relax *only* till a fairer opportunity has put it in their power to encroach again.

But if every prince since *Nimrod* had been a tyrant, it would not prove a *right* to tyrannize. There can be no prescription old enough to supersede the law of nature and the grant of GOD Almight, who has given to all men a natural right to be *free*, and they have it ordinarily in their power to make themselves so if they please. . . .

In order to form an idea of the natural rights of the colonists, I presume it will be granted that they are men, the common children of the same Creator with their brethren of Great Britain. Nature has placed all such in a state of equality and perfect freedom to act within the bounds of the laws of nature and reason without consulting the will or regarding the humor, the passions, or whims of any other man, unless they are formed into a society or body politic. . . .

The colonists are by the law of nature freeborn, as indeed all men are, white or black. No better reasons can be given for enslaving those of any color than such as Baron Montesquieu has humorously given as the foundation of that cruel slavery exercised over the poor Ethiopians, which threatens one day to reduce both Europe and America to the ignorance and barbarity of the darkest ages. Does it follow that 'tis right to enslave a man because he is black? Will short curled hair like wool instead of Christian hair, as 'tis called by those whose hearts are as hard as the nether millstone, help the argument? Can any logical inference in favor of slavery

be drawn from a flat nose, a long or a short face? Nothing better can be said in favor of a trade that is the most shocking violation of the law of nature, has a direct tendency to diminish the idea of the inestimable value of liberty, and makes every dealer in it a tyrant, from the director of an African company to the petty chapman in needles and pins on the unhappy coast. It is a clear truth that those who every day barter away other men's liberty will soon care little for their own. . . .

The colonists, being men, have a right to be considered as equally entitled to all the rights of nature with the Europeans, and they are not to be restrained in the exercise of any of these rights but for the evident good of the whole community.

By being or becoming members of society they have not renounced their natural liberty in any greater degree than other good citizens, and if 'tis taken from them without their consent they are so far enslaved.

I also lay it down as one of the first principles from whence I intend to deduce the civil rights of the British colonies, that all of them are subject to and dependent on Great Britain, and that therefore as over subordinate governments the Parliament of Great Britain has an undoubted power and lawful authority to make acts for the general good that, by naming them, shall and ought to be equally binding as upon the subjects of Great Britain within the realm. This principle, I presume, will be readily granted on the other side the Atlantic. It has been practised upon for twenty years to my knowledge, in the province of the *Massachusetts Bay;* and I have ever received it that it has been so from the beginning in this and the sister provinces through the continent. . . .

That the colonists, black and white, born here are freeborn British subjects, and entitled to all the essential civil rights of such is a truth not only manifest from the provincial charters, from the principles of the common law, and acts of Parliament, but from the British constitution, which was re-established at the Revolution with a professed design to secure the liberties of all the subjects to all generations. . . .

The liberties of the subject are spoken of as their best birthrights. No one ever dreamed, surely, that these liberties were confined to the realm. At that rate no British subjects in the dominions could, without a manifest contradiction, be declared entitled to all the privileges of subjects born within the realm to all intents and purposes which are rightly given foreigners by Parliament after residing seven years. These expressions of Parliament as well as of the charters must be vain and empty sounds unless we are allowed the essential rights of our fellow subjects in Great Britain.

Now can there be any liberty where property is taken away without consent? Can it with any color of truth, justice, or equity be affirmed that the northern colonies are represented in Parliament? Has this whole continent of near three thousand miles in length, and in which and his other American dominions His Majesty has or very soon will have some millions of as good, loyal, and useful subjects, white and black, as any in the three kingdoms, the election of one member of the House of Commons?

Is there the least difference as to the consent of the colonists whether taxes and impositions are laid on their trade and other property by the crown alone or by the Parliament? As it is agreed on all hands the crown alone cannot impose them, we should be justifiable in refusing to pay them, but must and ought to yield obedience to an act of Parliament, though erroneous, till repealed. I can see no reason to doubt but the imposition of taxes, whether on trade, or on land, or houses, or ships, on real or personal, fixed ort floating property, in the colonies is absolutely irreconcilable with the rights of the colonists as British subjects and as men. I say men, for in a state of nature no man can take my property from me without my consent: if he does, he deprives me of my liberty and makes me a slave. If such a proceeding is a breach of the law of nature, no law of society can make it just. The very act of taxing exercised over those who are not represented appears to me to be depriving them of one of their most essential rights as freemen, and if continued seems to be in effect an entire disfranchisement of every civil right. . . .

We all think ourselves happy under Great Britain. We love, esteem, and reverence our mother country, and adore our King. And could the choice of independency be offered the colonies or subjection to Great Britain upon any terms above absolute slavery, I am convinced they would accept the latter. The ministry in all future generations may rely on it that British America will never prove undutiful till driven to it as the last fatal resort against ministerial oppression, which will make the wisest mad, and the weakest strong. . . .

The sum of my argument is: that civil government is of God; that the administrators of it were originally the whole people; that they might have devolved it on whom they pleased; that this devolution is fiduciary, for the good of the whole; that by the British constitution this devolution is on the King, Lords and Commons, the supreme, sacred and uncontrollable legislative power not only in the realm but through the dominions; that by the abdication, the original compact was broken to pieces; that by the Revolution it was renewed and more firmly established, and the rights and liberties of the subject in all parts of the dominions more fully explained and confirmed; that in consequence of this establishment and the acts of succession and union, His Majesty GEORGE III is rightful King and sovereign, and, with his Parliament, the supreme legislative of Great Britain, France, and Ireland, and the dominions thereto belonging; that this constitution is the most free one and by far the best now existing on earth; that by this constitution every man in the dominions is a free man; that no parts of His Majesty's dominions can be taxed without their consent; that every part has a right to be represented in the supreme or some subordinate legislature; that the refusal of this would seem to be a contradiction in practice to the theory of the constitution; that the colonies are subordinate dominions and are now in such a state as to make it best for the good of the whole that they should not only be continued in the enjoyment of subordinate legislation but be also represented in some proportion to their number and estates in the grand legislature of the nation; that this would firmly unite all parts of the British empire in the greater peace and prosperity, and render it invulnerable and perpetual.

DOCUMENT 4

"Virginia Nonimportation Resolutions" (1769)

During the Stamp Act protests of 1765, Americans organized boycotts of the British manufactured goods. Although these initial efforts enjoyed only mixed success, colonists maintained that a cessation of consumption might force Parliament to back down. After all, commerce held the empire together. Faced with new British taxes in 1767, Americans called for an even stronger enforcement. As a Boston newspaper exclaimed, "SAVE YOUR MONEY AND YOU WILL SAVE YOUR COUNTRY!" Many colonial legislatures endorsed plans similar to that described in the "Virginia Nonimportation Resolutions." The Great Planters promised to boycott a long list of goods that reads like an inventory from a prosperous dry goods store, and, by so doing, they made consumer behavior a public test of a person's commitment to the preservation of colonial rights.

Virginia Nonimportation Resolutions, 1769

Williamsburg
Wednesday, the 17th May, 1769

About 12 o'clock his Excellency the Governor was pleased, by his Messenger, to command the Attendance of the House of Burgesses in the Council Chamber, whereupon, in Obedience to his Lordship's Command, the House, with their Speaker, immediately waited upon his Excellency, when he thought fit to dissolve the General Assembly.

The late Representatives of the People then judging it necessary that some Measures should be taken in their distressed Situation, for preserving the true and essential Interests of the Colony, resolved upon a Meeting for that very salutary Purpose, and therefore immediately, with the greatest Order and Decorum, repaired to the House of Mr. Anthony Hay in this City, where being assembled, it was first proposed, for the more decent and regular Discussion of such Matters as might be taken into Consideration, that a Moderator should be appointed, and, on the Question being put, Peyton Randolph, Esq; late Speaker of the House of Burgesses,

was unanimously elected.

The true State of the Colony being then opened and fully explained, and it being proposed that a regular Association should be formed, a Committee was appointed to prepare the necessary and most proper Regulations for that Purpose, and they were ordered to make their Report to the General Meeting the next Day at 10 o'Clock.

Thursday, May 18

At a farther Meeting, according to Adjournment, the Committee appointed Yesterday, made their Report, which being read, seriously considered, and approved, was signed by a great Number of the principal Gentlemen of the Colony then present, and is as follows:

We his Majesty's most dutiful Subjects, the late Representatives of all the Freeholders of the Colony of *Virginia*, avowing our inviolable and unshaken Fidelity and Loyalty to our most gracious Sovereign, our Affection for all our Fellow Subjects of *Great-Britain*; protesting against every Act or Thing, which may have the most distant Tendency to interrupt, or in any wise disturb his Majesty's Peace, and the good Order of his Government in this

Colony, which we are resolved, at the Risque of our Lives and Fortunes, to maintain and defend; but, at the same Time, being deeply affected with the Grievances and Distresses, with which his Majesty's *American* Subjects are oppressed, and dreading the Evils which threaten the Ruin of ourselves and our Posterity, by reducing us from a free and happy People to a wretched and miserable State of Slavery; and having taken into our most serious Consideration the present State of the Trade of this Colony, and of the *American* Commerce in general, observe with Anxiety, that the Debt due to *Great-Britain* for Goods imported from thence is very great, and that the Means of paying this Debt, in the present Situation of Affairs, are likely to become more and more precarious; that the Difficulties, under which we now labour, are owning to the Restrictions, Prohibitions, and ill advised Regulations, in several late Acts of Parliament of *Great-Britain*, in particular, that the late unconstitutional Act, imposing Duties on Tea, Paper, Glass, &c. for the sole Purpose of raising a Revenue in *America*, is injurious to Property, and destructive to Liberty, hath a necessary Tendency to prevent the Payment of the Debt due from this Colony to *Great-Britain*, and is, of Consequence, ruinous to Trade; that, notwithstanding the many earnest Applications already made, there is little Reason to expect a Redress of those Grievances; Therefore, in Justice to ourselves and our Posterity, as well as to the Traders of *Great Britain* concerned in the *American* Commerce, we, the Subscribers, have voluntarily and unanimously entered into the following Resolutions, in Hopes that our Example will induce the good People of this Colony to be frugal in the Use and Consumption of *British* Manufacturers, and that the Merchants and Manufacturers of *Great-Britain* may, from Motives of Interest, Friendship, and Justice, be engaged to exert themselves to obtain for us a Redress of those Grievances, under which the Trade and Inhabitants of *America* at present labour; We do therefore most earnestly recommend this our Association to the serious Attention of all Gentlemen, Merchants, Traders, and other Inhabitants of this Colony, in Hopes, that they will very readily and cordially accede thereto.

First, It is UNANIMOUSLY agreed on and resolved this 18th Day of *May*, 1769, that the Subscribers, as well by their own Example, as all other legal Ways and Means in their Power, will promote and encourage Industry and Frugality, and discourage all Manner of Luxury and Extravagance.

Secondly, That they will not at any Time hereafter, directly or indirectly import, or cause to be imported, any Manner of Goods, Merchandize, or Manufactures, which are, or shall hereafter be taxed by Act of Parliament, for the Purpose of raising a Revenue in *America* (except Paper, not exceeding Eight Shillings Sterling per Ream, and except such Articles only, as Orders have been already sent for) nor purchase any such after the First Day of *September* next, of any Person whatsoever, but that they will always consider such Taxation, in every Respect, as an absolute Prohibition, and in all future Orders, direct their Correspondents to ship them no Goods whatever, taxed as aforesaid, except as is above excepted.

Thirdly, That the Subscribers will not hereafter, directly or indirectly, import or cause to be imported from *Great-Britain*, or any Part of *Europe* (except such Articles of the Produce or Manufacture of *Ireland* as may be immediately and legally brought from thence, and except also all such Goods as Orders have been already sent for) any of the Goods herein after enumerated, viz. Spirits, Wind, Cyder, Perry, Beer, Ale, Malt, Barley, Pease, Beef, Pork, Fish, Butter, Cheese, Tallow, Candles, Oil, Fruit, Sugar, Pickles, Confectionary, Pewter, Hoes, Axes, Watches, Clocks, Tables, Chairs, Looking Glasses, Carriages, Joiner's and Cabinet Work of all Sorts, Upholstery of all Sorts, Trinkets and Jewellery, Plate and Gold, and Silversmith's Work of all Sorts, Ribbon and Millinery of all Sorts, Lace of all Sorts, *India* Goods of all Sorts, except Spices, Silks of all Sorts, except Sewing Silk, Cambrick, Lawn, Muslin, Gauze, except Boulting Cloths, Callico or Cotton Stuffs of more than Two Shillings per Yard, Linens of more than Two Shillings per Yard, Woollens, Worsted Stuffs of all Sorts of more than One Shilling and Six Pence per Yard, Broad Cloths of all Kinds at more than Three Shillings per Yard, Hats,

Stockings (Plaid and *Irish* Hose excepted) Shoes and Boots, Saddles, and all Manufacturers of Leather and Skins of all Kinds, until the late Acts of Parliament imposing Duties on Tea, Paper, Glass, &c. for the Purpose of raising a Revenue in *America*, are repealed, and that they will not, after the First of *September* next, purchase any of the above enumerated Goods of any Person whatsoever, unless the above mentioned Acts of Parliament are repealed.

Fourthly, That in all Orders, which any of the Subscribers may hereafter send to *Great-Britain*, they shall, and will expressly direct their Correspondents not to ship them any of the before enumerated Goods, until the before mentioned Acts of Parliament are repealed; and if any Goods are shipped to them contrary to the Tenor of this Agreement, they will refuse to take the same, or make themselves chargeable therewith.

Fifthly, That they will not import any Slaves, or purchase any imported, after the First Day of *November* next, until the said Acts of Parliament are repealed.

Sixthly, That they will not import any Wines of any Kind whatever, or purchase the same from any Person whatever, after the First Day of *September* next, except such Wines as are already ordered, until the Acts of Parliament imposing Duties thereon are repealed.

Seventhly, For the better Preservation of the Breed of Sheep, That they will not kill, or suffer to be killed, any Lambs, that shall be yeaned before the First Day of *May*, in any Year, nor dispose of such to any Butcher or other Person, whom they may have Reason to expect, intends to kill the same.

Eightly and Lastly, That these Resolves shall be binding on all and each of the Subscribers, who do hereby each and every Person for himself, upon his Word and Honour, agree that he will strictly and firmly adhere to and abide by every Article in this Agreement, from the Time of his signing the same, for and during the Continuance of the before mentioned Acts of Parliament, or until a general Meeting of the Subscribers, after one Month's public Notice, shall determine otherwise, the second Article of this Agreement still and for ever continuing in full Power and Force.

DOCUMENT 5

Images of Rebellion

Tobacco was an important crop for both economic and political reasons. Here, Virginians force local merchants to sign the Associations of the Williamsburg Convention of 1774 over a hogshead of tobacco. The Associations sought to halt all commerce with Britain until Parliament repealed the Intolerable Acts.

A political cartoon from 1776 uses female figures to personify Britain and the colonies. The stern and stately matron representing Britain attempts to force obedience on the nearly naked native representing the colonies. "America" rebels, arguing for liberty from the confining yoke of Mother England.

THE HORSE AMERICA, *throwing his Master.*

In a popular political cartoon from 1779, America is the spirited and rebellious horse throwing off its confused and back-ward master, Britain.

DOCUMENT 6

George Robert Twelves Hewes, A Retrospect of the Boston Tea-Party (1834)

Born in 1742, George Robert Twelves Hewes, a struggling Boston shoemaker, lived to the age of ninety-eight, a remarkable feat for this period. His longevity—he was one of the last survivors of the Revolution—guaranteed that he became a kind of cult figure for a generation of Americans with no direct memory of the events leading to national independence. But Hewes was more than a survivor. He had been present at some crucial confrontations; he was personally acquainted with leading New England radicals. Hewes witnessed the Boston Massacre of 1770, for example, and knew four of the five men killed. He also participated in the Boston Tea Party in 1773. His remark-ably clear recollections of that event recorded some sixty-one years later gives us the perspective of an ordinary colonist who risked his life for the patriot cause.

On my inquiring of Hewes if he knew who first proposed the project of destroying the tea, to pre-vent its being landed, he replied that he did not; neither did he know who or what number were to volunteer their services for that purpose. But from the significant allusion of some persons in whom I had confidence, together with the knowledge I had of the spirit of those times, I had no doubt but that a sufficient number of associates would accompany me in that enterprise.

The tea destroyed was contained in three ships, laying near each other, at what was called at that time Griffin's wharf, and were surrounded by armed ships of war; the commanders of which had publicly declared, that if the rebels, as they were pleased to style the Bostonians, should not withdraw their op-position to the landing of the tea before a certain day, the 17th day of December, 1773, they should on that day force it on shore, under the cover of their cannon's mouth. On the day preceding the seventeenth, there was a meeting of the citizens of the county of Suffolk, convened at one of the churches in Boston, for the purpose of consulting on what measures might be considered expedient to prevent the landing of the tea, or secure the people from the collection of the duty. At that meeting a committee was appointed to wait on Governor Hutchison, and request him to inform them whether he would take any measures to satisfy the people on the object of the meeting. To the first application of this committee, the governor told them he would give them a definite answer by five o'clock in the af-ternoon. At the hour appointed, the committee again repaired to the governor's house, and on in-quiry found he had gone to his country seat at Mil-ton, a distance of about six miles. When the com-mittee returned and informed the meeting of the absence of the governor, there was a confused mur-mur among the members, and the meeting was im-mediately dissolved, many of them crying out, Let every man do his duty, and be true to his country; and there was a general huzza for Griffin's wharf. It was now evening, and I immediately dressed myself in the costume of an Indian, equipped with a small hatchet, which I and my associates denominated the tomahawk, with wich, and a club, after having painted my face and hands with coal dust in the shop of a blacksmith, I repaired to Griffin's wharf, where the ships lay that contained the tea. When I first appeared in the street, after being thus dis-guised, I fell in with many who were dressed, equipped and painted as I was, and who fell in with me, and marched in order to the place of our desti-nation. When we arrived at the wharf, there were three of our number who assumed an authority to direct our operations, to which we readily submit-ted. They divided us into three parties, for the pur-pose of boarding the three ships which contained the tea at the same time. The name of him who commanded the division to which I was assigned, was Leonard Pitt. The names of the other comman-ders I never knew. We were immediately ordered by the respective commanders to board all the ships at the same time, which we promptly obeyed. The commander of the division to which I belonged, as soon as we were on board the ship, appointed me boatswain, and ordered me to go to the captain and demand of him the keys to the hatches and a dozen candles. I made the demand accordingly, and the captain promptly replied, and delivered the articles; but requested me at the same time to do no damage to the ship or rigging. We then were ordered by our commander to open the hatches, and take out all the chests of tea and throw them overboard, and we immediately proceeded to execute his orders; first cutting and splitting the chests with our tomahawks, so as thoroughly to expose them to the effects of the water. In about three hours from the time we went on board, we had thus broken and thrown overboard every tea chest to be found in the ship; while those in the other ships were disposing of the tea in the same way, at the same time. We were surrounded by British armed ships, but no attempt was made to resist us. We then quietly retired to our several places of residence without having any conversation with each other, or taking any measures to discover who were our associates; nor do I recollect of our having had the knowledge of the name of a single individual concerned in that affair, except that of Leonard Pitt, the commander of my division, who I have mentioned. There appeared to be an understanding that each individual should volunteer his services, keep his own secret, and risk the consequences for himself. No disorder took place during that transaction, and it was observed at that time, that the stillest night ensued that Boston had enjoyed for many months.

During the time we were throwing the tea overboard, there were several attempts made by some of the citizens of Boston and its vicinity, to carry off small quantities of it for their family use. To effect that object, they would watch their opportunity to snatch up a handful from the deck, where it become plentifully scattered, and put it into their pockets. One Captain O'Conner, whom I well knew, came on board for that purpose, and when he supposed he was not noticed, filled his pockets, and also the lining of his coat. But I had detected him, and gave information to the captain of what he was doing. We

were ordered to take him into custody, and just as he was stepping from the vessel, I seized him by the skirt of his coat, and in attempting to pull him back, I tore it off, but springing forward, by a rapid effort, he made his escape. He had however to run a gauntlet through the crowd upon the wharf; each one, as he passed, giving him a kick or a stroke.

The next day we nailed the skirt of his coat, which I had pulled off, to the whipping post in Charlestown, the place of his residence, with a label upon it, commemorative of the occasion which had thus subjected the proprietor to the popular indignation.

Another attempt was made to save a little tea from the ruins of the cargo, by a tall aged man, who wore a large cocked hat and white wig, which was fashionable at that time. He had slightly slipped a little into his pocket, but being detected, they seized him, and taking his hat and wig from his head, threw them, together with the tea, of which they had emptied his pockets, into the water. In consideration of his advanced age, he was permitted to escape, with now and then a slight kick.

The next morning, after we had cleared the ships of the tea, it was discovered that very considerable quantities of it was floating upon the surface of the water; and to prevent the possibility of any of its being saved for us, a number of small boats were manned by sailors and citizens, who rowed them into those parts of the harbour wherever the tea was visible, and by beating it with our oars and paddles, so thoroughly drenched it, as to render its entire destruction inevitable.

DOCUMENT 7

Petition of "A Grate Number of Blackes of the Province" to Governor Thomas Gage and the Members of the Massachusetts General Court (1774)

The rhetoric of natural rights appealed directly to African American slaves. White patriots regularly protested that "taxation without representation" transformed free men into the "slaves " of Parliament. With the exception of James Otis and a few articulate Quakers from the Middle Colonies, they rarely connected their own passionate defence of "rights" with the enslavement of colonial blacks. The slaves knew better, of course, and, using the language of rights and liberty, they petitioned for freedom. On the eve of independence, a group of Boston slaves eloquently reminded white colonists that "we have in common with all other men a natural right to our freedoms."

Your Petitioners apprehend we have in common with all other men a naturel right to our freedoms without Being depriv'd of them by our fellow men as we are a freeborn Pepel and have never forfeited this Blessing by aney compact or agreement whatever. But we were unjustly dragged by the cruel hand of power from our dearest friends and sum of us stolen from the bosoms of our tender Parents and from a Populous Pleasant and plentiful country and Brought hither to be made slaves for Life in a Christian land. Thus we are deprived of every thing that hath a tendency to make life even tolerable, the endearing ties of husband and wife we are strangers to. . . . Our children are also taken from us by force and sent maney miles from us. . . . Thus our Lives are imbittered. . . . There is a great number of us sencear. . . . members of the Church of Christ how can the master and the slave be said to fulfil that command Live in love let Brotherly Love contuner and abound Beare yea one nothers Bordenes. How can the master be said to Beare my Borden when he Beares me down which the. . . . chanes of slavery. . . . Nither can we reap an equal benefet from the laws of the Land which doth not justifi but condemns Slavery or if there had bin aney Law to hold us in Bondage. . . . ther never was aney to inslave our children for life when Born in a free Countrey. We therefore Bage your Excellency and Honours will. . . . cause an act of the legislative to be pessed that we may obtain our Natural right our freedoms and our children be set at lebety at the yeare of twenty one. . . .

DOCUMENT 8

Rights of Women in an Independent Republic

While a delegate to the Continental Congress in Philadelphia, John Adams regularly corresponded with his wife, Abigail, who remained in Braintree, Massachusetts overseeing the family farm and business. Their extraordinary letters spanned an impressive range of political and personal concerns, from wrongs suffered by colonials under the yoke of Parliament to the daily management of a small New England farm. Like the African Americans who petitioned for freedom in 1774, Abigail sensed that the creation of a new republic held unusual opportunities for women. They too had rights; they too were members of civil society. Her thoughtful appeal to her husband and his condescending response reveal the blindness of male founders to the claims of gender. In a letter addressed a few weeks later to provincial lawyer James Sullivan, Adams argued that since it was neither possible nor desirable for everyone to have the right to vote, some—including women—had to be excluded for the common good.

Abigail Adams to John Adams, Braintree, 31 March 1776

I long to hear that you have declared an independancy—and by the way in the new Code of Laws which I suppose it will be necessary for you to make I desire you would Remember the Ladies, and be more generous and favourable to them than your ancestors. Do not put such umlimited power into the hands of the Husbands. Remember all Men would be tyrants if they could. If perticuliar care and attention is not paid to the Laidies we are determined to foment a Rebelion, and will not hold ourselves bound by any Laws in which we have no voice, or Representation.

That your Sex are Naturally Tyrannical is a Truth so thoroughly established as to admit of no dispute, but such of you as wish to be happy willingly give up the harsh title of Master for the more tender and endearing one of Friend. Why then, not put it out of the power of the vicious and the Lawless to use us with cruelty and indignity with impunity. Men of Sense in all Ages abhor those customs which treat us only as the vassals of your Sex. Regard us then as Beings placed by providence under your pro-

tection and in immitation of the Supreem Being make use of that power only for our happiness.

John Adams to Abigail Adams, Philadelphia, 14 April 1776

As to Declarations of Independency, be patient. Read our Privateering Laws, and our Commercial Laws. What signifies a Word.

As to your extraordinary Code of Laws, I cannot but laugh. We have been told that our Struggle has loosened the bands of Government every where. That Children and Apprentices were disobedient—that schools and Colledges were grown turbulent—that Indians slighted their Guardians and Negroes grew insolent to their Masters. But your Letter was the first Intimation that another Tribe more numerous and powerful than all the rest were grown discontented.—This is rather too coarse a Compliment but you are so saucy, I wont blot it out.

Depend upon it, We know better than to repeal our Masculine systems. Altho they are in full Force, you know they are little more than Theory. We dare not exert our Power in its full Latitude. We are obliged to go fair, and softly, and in Practice you know We are the subjects. We have only the Name of Masters, and rather than give up this, which would compleatly subject Us to the Despotism of the Peticoat, I hope General Washington, and all our brave Heroes would fight. I am sure every good Politician would plot, as long as he would against Despotism, Empire, Monarchy, Aristocracy, Oligarchy, or Ochlocracy.—A fine Story indeed. I begin to think the Ministry as deep as they are wicked. After stirring up Tories, Landjobbers, Trimmers, Bigots, Canadians, Indians, Negrows, Hanoverians, Hessians, Russians, Irish Roman Catholicks, Scotch Renegadoes, at last they have stimulated the [illegible in original] to demand new Priviledges and threaten to rebell.

John Adams to John Sullivan, Philadelphia, 26 May 1776

It is certain in Theory, that the only moral Foundation of Government is the Consent of the People. But to what an Extent Shall We carry this Principle? Shall We Say, that every Individual of the Community, old and young, male and female, as well as rich and poor, must consent, expressly to every Act of Legislation? No, you will Say. This is impossible. How then does the Right arise in the Majority to govern the Minority, against their Will? Whence arises the Right of the Men to govern Women, without their Consent? Whence the Right of the old to bind the Young, without theirs.

But let us first Suppose, that the whole Community of every Age, Rank, Sex, and Condition, has a Right to vote. This Community, is assembled—a Motion is made and carried by a Majority of one Voice. The Minority will not agree to this. Whence arises the Right of the Majority to govern, and the Obligation of the Minority to obey? from Necessity, you will Say, because there can be no other Rule, But why exclude Women? You will Say, because their Delicacy renders them unfit for Practice and Experience, in the great Business of Life, and the hardy Enterprizes of War, as well as the arduous Cares of State. Besides, their attention is So much engaged with the necessary Nurture of their Chil-

dren, that Nature has made them fittest for domestic Cares. And Children have not Judgment or Will of their own. True. But will not these Reasons apply to others? Is it not equally true, that Men in general in every Society, who are wholly destitute of Property, and also too little acquainted with public Affairs to form a Right Judgment, and too dependent upon other Men to have a Will of their own? If this is a Fact, if you give to every Man, who has no Property, a Vote, will you not make a fine encouraging Provision for Corruption by your fundamental Law? Such is the Frailty of the human Heart, that very few Men, who have no Property, have any Judgment of their own. They talk and vote as they are directed by Some Man of Property, who has attached their Minds to his Interest.

Upon my Word, sir, I have long thought an Army, a Piece of Clock Work and to be governed only by Principles and Maxims, as fixed as any in Mechanicks, and by all that I have read in the History of Mankind, and in Authors, who have Speculated upon Society and Government, I am much inclined to think, a Government must manage a Society in the Same manner; and that this is Machinery too.

Harrington has Shewn that Power always follows property. This I believe to be as infallible a Maxim, in Politics, as, that Action and Reaction are equal, as in Mechanicks. Nay I believe We may advance one Step farther and affirm that the Ballance of Power in a Society, accompanies the Ballance of Property in Land. The only possible Way then of preserving the Ballance of Power on the side of equal Liberty and public Virtue, is to make the Acquisition of Land easy to every Member of Society: to make a Division of the Land into Small Quantities, So that the Multitude may be possessed of landed Estates. If the Multitude is possessed of the Ballance of real Estate, the Multitude will have the Ballance of Power, and in that Case the Multitude will take Care of the Liberty, Virtue, and Interest of the Multitude in all Acts of Government.

I believe these Principles have been felt, if not understood in the Massachusetts Bay, from the Beginning: And therefore I Should think that Wisdom and Policy would dictate in these Times, to be very cautious of making Alterations. Our people have never been very rigid in Scrutinizing into the Qualifications of Voters, and I presume they will not now begin to be so. But I would not advise them to make any alteration in the Laws, at present, respecting the Qualifications of Voters.

Your Idea, that those Laws, which affect the Lives and personal Liberty of all, or which inflict corporal Punishment, affect those, who are not qualified to vote, as well as those who are, is just. But, So they do Women, as well as Men, Children as well as Adults. What Reason Should there be, for excluding a Man of Twenty years, Eleven Months and twenty-seven days old, from a Vote when you admit one, who is twenty one? The Reason is, you must fix Some Period in Life, when the Understanding and Will of Men in general is fit to be trusted by the Public. Will not the Same Reason justify the State in fixing upon Some certain Quantity of Property, as a Qualification.

The Same Reasoning, which will induce you to admit all Men, who have no Property, to vote, with those who have, for those Laws, which affect the Person will prove that you ought to admit Women and Children: for generally Speaking, Women and Children, have as good Judgment, and as independent Minds as those Men who are wholly destitute of Property: these last being to all Intents and Purposes as much dependent upon others, who will please to feed, cloath, and employ them, as Women are upon their Husbands, or Children on their Parents.

As to your Idea, or proportioning the Votes of Men in Money Matters, to the Property they hold, it is utterly impracticable. There is no possible Way of Ascertaining, at any one Time, how much every Man in a Community, is worth; and if there was, So fluctuating is Trade and Property, that this State of it, would change in half an Hour. The Property of the whole Community, is Shifting every Hour, and no Record can be kept of the Changes.

Society can be governed only by general Rules. Government cannot accommodate itself to every particular Case, as it happens, nor to the Circumstances of particular Persons. It must establish general, comprehensive Regulations for Cases and Persons. The only Question is, which general Rule, will accommodate most Cases and most Persons.

Depend upon it, sir, it is dangerous to open So fruitfull a Source of Controversy and Altercation, as would be opened by attempting to alter the Qualifications of Voters. There will be no End of it. New Claims will arise. Women will demand a Vote. Lads from 12 to 21 will think their Rights not enough attended to, and every Man, who has not a Farthing, will demand an equal Voice with any other in all Acts of State. It tends to confound and destroy all Distinctions, and prostrate all Ranks, to one common Levell. I am &c.

DOCUMENT 9

Peter Oliver, Origin and Progress of the American Rebellion (1781)

Many colonists remained deaf to the public demands for rights. Like other persons who supported royal government in America, Perer Oliver—the chief justice of Massachusetts—despised the social disorder that rebellion had unleashed. He regarded equality as a preposterous and dangerous notion, a concept promoted by irresponsible leaders of church and state. Oliver's stinging critique of the hypocrisy of Boston's patriots provides insight into the minds of those who resisted independence.

❧   ❧

I am now come to the Year 1767, a Year fraught with Occurrences, as extraordinary as 1765, but of a different Texture. Notwithstanding the Warnings that the Colonies had repeatedly givne, of their determined Resolution to throw off the Supremacy of the british Parliament, yet the then Ministry chose to make another Trial of Skill; never adverting to the ill Success of former Attempts. They might have known, that the Contest had reached so great an Heighth, that the Colonists would never descend one Step untill they had first ascended the last Round of the Ladder. ... But the Ministry confiding in their own good Intentions, & placing too much Confidence in the Gratitude of the Colonists to the parent State (which by the Way they did not possess a Spark of, neither is it to be but seldom Expected to find it inhabit any where but in the private Breast, & too seldom there; to the Disgrace of human Nature), they procured a new Act to be passed, laying Duties upon *Tea, Glass, Paper,* & *Painters Colours.* This Act was not more unreasonable than many other Acts which had been submitted to for many years past, & which, even at this Time, they made no Objection to. But the Colonists had succeeded in their first Experiment of Opposition, & their new Allies in Parliament increased their Importance.

As to the *Glass* in particular, the Duty was so trifling, that it would not have enhanced the Price of it to the Purchaser; for there were so many Sellers who aimed at a Market for their Commodities, & the Merchants had so great a Profit upon their Goods, that they could render the Duty of little or no Importance in their Sales; & this was actually the Case. For the Glass, during the Continuance of the Act, was sold at the same Price which it commanded before the Commencement of the Act. The true Reason of Opposition was this. The Inhabitants of the Colonies were a Race of Smugglers. They carried on an extensive Trade with the *Dutch,* not only in *Holland,* but very greatly with the Dutch Settlements in the *West Indies* & at *Surrinam.* Tea was the objective Part of the Act; & an enormous Quantity of it was consumed on the american Continent; so

great, that I have heard a Gentleman of the Custom House in *Boston,* say, that could the Duty be fairly collected, it would amount to £160,000 p. Year, i.e. at 12d p pound. In some of the Colonies, it was notorious that the smuggled Teas were carted through the Streets at Noon Day: whether owing to the Inattention or Connivance of the Custom House Officers, is not difficult to determine.

The Smugglers then, who were the prevailing Part of the Traders in the Capitals of the several Provinces, found it necessary for their Interest, to unite in defeating the Operation of the Act; & *Boston* appeared in the Front of the Battle. Accordingly they beat to Arms, & manœuvred in a new invented Mode. They entred into nonimportation Agreements. A Subscription Paper was handed about, enumerating a great Variety of Articles not to be imported from *England,* which they supposed would muster the Manufacturers in *England* into a national Mob to support their Interests. Among the various prohibited Articles, were *Silks, Velvets, Clocks, Watches, Coaches* & *Chariots;* & it was highly diverting, to see the names & marks, to the Subscription, of Porters & Washing Women. But every mean & dirty Art was used to compass all their bad Designs. One of those who handed about a Subscription Paper being asked, whether it could be imagined that such Tricks would effectuate their Purposes? He replyed "Yes! It would do to scare them in England:" & perhaps there never was a Nation so easy to be affrighted; witness the preceding Repeal of the Stamp Act.

Nonimportation of British Goods

In order to effectuate their Purposes to have this Act repealed also, they formed many Plans of Operation. Associations were convened to prevent the Importation of Goods from *Great Britain,* & to oblige all those who had already sent for them, to reship them after their arrival. This was such an Attack upon the mercantile Interest, that it was necessary to use private evasive Arts to deceive the Vulgar. Accordingly, when the Goods arrived, they were to be in Warehouses, which were to be guarded by a publick Key, at the same Time the Owners of the Stores & Goods had a Key of their Own. This amused the Rabble, whom the Merchants had set to mobbing; & such were the blessed Effects of some of those Merchants Villainy, that Bales & Trucks were disgorged of their Contents & refilled with Shavings, Brickbats, Legs of Bacon & other Things, & shipped for *England*; where some of them were opened on the King's Wharves or Quays, & the Fraud discovered. Many of those Merchants also continued to import the prohibited Goods, in Disguise; of which a bold Printer of *Boston* detected them in his publick Papers; for which they, out of Revenge, in 1768, attempted to murder him; but narrowly escaping with his Life he fled to *England,* as the civil Power of the Country was not sufficient to protect any one who was obnoxious to the Leaders of the Faction.

Another base Art was used. Under Pretence of Œconomy, the Faction undertook to regulate Funerals, that there might be less Demand for English Manufactures. It was true indeed that the Custom of wearing expensive Mourning at Funerals, had, for many Years past, been noticed for Extravagance, & had ruined some Families of moderate Fortune; but there had been no Exertions to prevent it; 'till now, the Demagogues & their Mirmidons had taken the Government into their Hands. But what at another Time would have been deemed œconomical, was at this Time Spite & Malevolence. One Extreme was exchanged for another. A Funeral now seemed more like a Procession to a *May Fair*; and Processions were lengthened, especially by the Ladies, who figured a way, in order to exhibit their Share of Spite, & their Silk Gowns. In short, it was unhumanizing the Mind, by destroying the Solemnity of a funeral Obsequy, & substituting the Gaiety of Parade in its Stead. The vulgar Maxim, *that there is no Inconvenience without a Convenience,* now took place; for whereas, formerly, a Widow, who had been well rid of a bad Companion, could conceal her Joy under a long black Vail, she was now obliged to use what Female Arts she was mistress of, in order to transform her Joy into the Apperance of a more decent Passion, to impose upon the Croud of ·numerous Spectators.

The Faction deluded their Followers with another Scheme to keep up the Ball of Contention, & to sooth their Hopes of Conquest. They plunged into Manufactures; &, like all other Projectors, suffered their Enthusiasm to stop their Ears against the voice of Reason, which warned them of the ill Effects of their Projects. One of their Manufacturers was to have been in *Wool*. They were advis'd against it; & informed, that all the Sheep in the Province of *Massachusetts Bay*, which most abounded in Sheep of any other Province, would not supply the Inhabitants of it with Wool to cloath their Feet; & that the Wool was of such a Staple as not to make a Cloth above 46 p Yard Price; & that this woud always be the Case; for tho' the Soil was equal to the raising a greater Number of Sheep, yet the Severity of the wintry Climate would prevent the Farmers Profit by propagating them under so great a Disadvantage. But if they were determined to increase their Flocks, that they must practise the Method of one of their own Country Men, who said, that upon getting up early in a Morning he found half a dozen of his Sheep lying dead in his Yard, destroyed by the Wolves who had sucked their Blood & made off. He, finding them warm, used the expedient of tying an old & useless Horse, wch. he owned, to a Tree, & skinned him. He then skinned his dead Sheep, & applied their Skins to his Horse, which united well with ye. horse Flesh; & that he ever after sheared annually 40 £ Wool from his Horse. As Mankind are continually improving in the Arts and Sciences, the Factious might have as rationally tried this Experiment as they had tried that which they were now upon; they would have found old Horses enough for their Purpose, as well as another Race of Animals who most justly demerited a flaying for their Brutalities, & would have succeeded as well.

DOCUMENT 10

John Adams to Abigail Adams (July 3,1776)

A dams could barely contain his excitement. He and his colleagues in the Continental Congress had just voted to separate from Great Britain, an act punishable by death should the patriots fail on the field of battle. At this critical moment Adams expressed profound faith in the ability of the American people to meet the challenges of freedom.

Yesterday the greatest Questions was decided, which ever was debated in America, and a greater perhaps, never was or will be decided among Men. A Resolution was passed without one dissenting Colony "that these united Colonies, are, and of right ought to be free and independent States, and as such, they have, and of Right ought to have full Power to make War, conclude Peace, establish Commerce, and to do all the other Acts and Things, which other States may rightfully do." You will see in a few days a Declaration setting forth the Causes, which have impell'd Us to this mighty Revolution, and the Reasons which will justify it, in the Sight of God and Man. A Plan of Confederation will be taken up in a few days.

When I look back to the Year 1761, and recollect the Argument concerning Writs of Assistance, in the Superiour Court, which I have hitherto considered as the Commencement of the Controversy, between Great Britain and America, and run through the whole Period from that Time to this, and recollect the series of political Events, the Chain of Causes and Effects, I am surprized at the Suddenness, as well as Greatness of this Revolution. Britain has been fill'd with Folly, and America with Wisdom, at least this is my Judgment.—Time must determine. It is the Will of Heaven, that the two Countries should be sundered forever. It may be the Will of Heaven that America shall suffer Calamities still more wasting and Distresses yet more dreadfull. If this is to be the Case, it will have this good Effect,

at least: it will inspire Us with many Virtues, which We have not, and correct many Errors, Follies, and Vices, which threaten to disturb, dishonour, and destroy Us.—The Furnace of Affliction produces Refinement, in States as well as Individuals. And the new Governments we are assuming, in every Part, will require a Purification from our Vices, and an Augmentation of our Virtues or they will be no Blessings. The People will have unbounded Power. And the People are extreamly addicted to Corruption and Venality, as well as the Great.—I am not without Apprehensions from this Quarter. But I must submit all my Hopes and Fears, to an overruling Providence, in which, unfashionable as the Faith may be, I firmly believe.

The Delay of this Declaration to this Time, has many great Advantages attending it.—The Hopes of Reconciliation, which were fondly entertained by Multitudes of honest and well meaning tho weak and mistaken People, have been gradually and at last totally extinguished.—Time has been given for the whole People, maturely to consider the great Question of Independence and to ripen their Judgments, dissipate their Fears, and allure their Hopes, by discussing it in News Papers and Pamphletts, by debating it, in Assemblies, Conventions, Committees of Safety and Inspection, in Town and County Meetings, as well as in private Conversations, so that the whole People in every Colony of the 13, have now adopted it, as their own Act.—This will cement the Union, and avoid those Heats and perhaps Convulsions which might have been occasioned, by such a Declaration Six Months ago.

But the Day is past. The Second Day of July 1776 [the day Congress voted for independence], will be the most memorable Epocha, in the History of America.—I am apt to believe that it will be celebrated, by succeeding Generations, as the great anniversary Festival. It ought to be commemorated, as the Day of Deliverance by solemn Acts of Devotion to God Almighty. It ought to be solemnized with Pomp and Parade, with Shews, Games, Sports, Guns, Bells, Bonfires and Illuminations from one End of this Continent to the other from this Time forward forever more.

You will think me transported with Enthusiasm but I am not—I am well aware of the Toil and Blood and Treasure, that it will cost Us to maintain this Declaration, and support and defend these States.—Yet through all the Gloom I can see the Rays of ravishing Light and Glory. I can see that the End is more than worth all the Means. And that Posterity will tryumph in that Days Transaction, even altho We should rue it, which I trust in God We shall not.

DOCUMENT 11

Thomas Jefferson, "Original Rough Draught" of the Declaration of Independence (1776)

Few modern Americans realize that the Declaration of Independence went through several drafts before being formally accepted by Congress. Delegates compressed the original statement, cutting large sections that Jefferson had written in anger and haste. While the alterations produced a clearer, more persuasive document, Jefferson complained that his colleagues in Congress had diluted the force of his rhetoric. Among the passages that they dropped from the final version was Jefferson's painful farewell to empire.

A Declaration of the Representatives of the United States of America, in General Congress assembled.

When in the course of human events it becomes necessary for a people to advance from that subordination in which they have hitherto remained, & to assume among the powers of the earth the equal & independent station to which the laws of nature & of nature's god entitle them, a decent respect to the opinions of mankind requires that they should declare the causes which impel them to the change.

We hold these truths to be sacred & undeniable that all men are created equal & independant, that from that equal creation they derive rights inherent & inalienable, among which are the preservation of life, & liberty, & the pursuit of happiness; that to secure these ends, governments are instituted among men, deriving their just powers from the consent of the governed; that whenever any form of government shall become destructive of these ends, it is the right of the people to alter or to abolish it, & to institute new government, laying its foundation on such principles & organising it's powers in such form, as to them shall seem most likely to effect their safety & happiness. prudence indeed will dictate that governments long established should not be changed for light & transient causes: and accordingly all experience hath shewn that mankind are more disposed to suffer while evils are sufferable, than to right themselves by abolishing the forms to which they are accustomed. but when a long train of abuses & usurpations, begun at a distinguished period, & pursuing invariably the same object, evinces a design to subject them to arbitrary power, it is their right, it is their duty, to throw off such government & to provide new guards for their future security. such has been the patient sufference of these colonies; & such is now the necessity which contrains them to expunge their former systems of government. the history of his present majesty, is a history of unremitting injuries and usurpations, among which no one fact stands single or solitary to contradict the uniform tenor of the rest, all of which have in direct object the establishment of an absolute tyranny over these states. to prove this, let facts be submitted to a candid world, for the truth of which we pledge a faith yet unsullied by falsehood.

he has refused his assent to laws the most wholesome and necessary for the public good:

he has forbidden his governors to pass laws of immediate & pressing importance, unless suspended in their operation till his assent should be obtained; and when so suspended, he has neglected utterly to attend to them.

he has refused to pass other laws for the accommodation of large districts of people unless those people would relinquish the right of representation, a right inestimable to them, & formidable to tyrants alone.

he has dissolved Representative houses repeatedly & continually, for opposing with manly firmness his invasions on the rights of the people:

he has refused for a long space of time to cause others to be elected, whereby the legislative powers, incapable of annihilation, have returned to the people at large for their exercise, the state re-

maining in the mean time exposed to all the dangers of invasion from without, & convulsions within:

he has endeavored to prevent the population of these states; for that purpose obstructing the laws for naturalization of foreigners; refusing to pass others to encourge their migrations hither; & raising the conditions of new appropriations of lands:

he has suffered the administration of justice totally to cease in some of these colonies, refusing his assent to laws for establishing judiciary powers:

he has made our judges dependent on his will alone, for the tenure of their offices, and amount of their salaries:

he has erected a multitude of new offices by a self-assumed power, & sent hither swarms of officers to harrass our people & eat out their substance:

he has kept among us in times of peace standing armies & ships of war:

he has affected to render the military, independant of & superior to the civil power:

he has combined with others to subject us to a jurisdiction foreign to our constitutions and unacknowleged by our laws; giving his assent to their pretended acts of legislation, for quartering large bodies of armed troops among us;

for protecting them by a mock-trial from punishment for any murders they should commit on the inhabitants of these states;

for cutting off our trade with all parts of the world;

for imposing taxes on us without our consent;

for depriving us of the benefits of trial by jury;

for transporting us beyond seas to be tried for pretended offences:

for taking away our charters, & altering fundamentally the forms of our governments;

for suspending our own legislatures & declaring themselves invested with power to legislate for us in all cases whatsoever:

he has abdicated government here, withdrawing his governors, & declaring us out of his allegiance & protection:

he has plundered our seas, ravaged our coasts, burnt our towns & destroyed the lives of our people:

he is at this time transporting large armies of foreign mercenaries to compleat the works of death, desolation & tyranny, already begun with circumstances of cruelty & perfidy unworthy the head of a civilized nation:

he has endeavored to bring on the inhabitants of our frontiers the merciless Indian savages, whose known rule of warfare is an undistinguished destruction of all ages, sexes, & conditions of existence:

he has incited treasonable insurrections in our fellow-subjects, with the allurements of forefeiture & confiscation of our property:

He has waged cruel war against human nature itself, violating it's most sacred rights of life & liberty in the persons of a distant people who never offended him, captivating & carrying them into slavery in another hemisphere, or to incur miserable death in their transportation thither. this piratical warfare, the opprobrium of *infidel* powers, is the warfare of the CHRISTIAN king of Great Britain. determined to keep open a market where MEN should be bought & sold, he has prostituted his negative for suppressing every legislative attempt to prohibit or to restrain this execrable commerce: and that this assemblage of horrors might want no fact of distinguished die, he is now exciting those very people to rise in arms among us, and to purchase that liberty of which *he* has deprived them, by murdering the people upon whom *he* also obtruded them; thus paying off former crimes committed against the *liberties* of one people, with crimes which he urges them to commit against the *lives* of another.

in every stage of these oppressions we have petitioned for redress in the most humble terms; our repeated petitions have been answered by repeated injury. a prince whose character is thus marked by every act which may define a tyrant, is unfit to be the ruler of a people who mean to be free. future ages will scarce believe that the hardiness of one man, adventured within the short comnpass of 12 years only, on so many acts of tyranny without a mask, over a people fostered & fixed in principles of liberty.

Nor have we been wanting in attentions to our British brethren. we have warned them from time to time of attempts by their legislature to extend a jurisdiction over these our states. we have reminded them of the circumstances of our emigration & settlement here, no one of which could warrant so strange a pretension: that these were effected at the expence of our own blood & treasure, unassisted by the wealth or the strength of Great Britain: that in constituting indeed our several forms of government, we had adopted one common king, thereby laying a foundation for perpetual league & amity with them: but that submission to their parliament was no part of our constitution, nor ever in idea, if history may be credited: and we appealed to their native justice & magnanimity, as well as to the ties of our common kindred to disavow these usurpations which were likely to interrupt our correspondence & connection. they too have been deaf to the voice of justice & of consanguinity, & when occasions have been given them, by the regular course of their laws, of removing from their councils the disturbers of our harmony, they have by their free election re-established them in power. at this very time too they are permitting their chief magistrate to send over not only soldiers of our common blood, but Scotch & foreign mercenaries to invade & deluge us in blood. these facts have given the last stab to agonizing affection, and manly spirit bids us to renounce for ever these unfeeling brethren. we must endeavor to forget our former love for them, and to hold them as we hold the rest of mankind, enemies in war, in peace friends. we might have been a free & a great people together; but a communication of grandeur & of freedom it seems is below their dignity. be it so, since they will have it: the road to glory & happiness is open to us to; we will climb it in a separate state, and acquiesce in the necessity which pronounces our everlasting Adieu!

We therefore the representatives of the United States of America in General Congress assembled do, in the name & by authority of the good people of these states, reject and renounce all allegiance & subject to the kings of Great Britain & all others who may hereafter claim by, through, or under them; we utterly dissolve & break off all political connection which may have heretofore subsisted between us & the people or parliament of Great Britain; and finally we do assert and declare these colonies to be free and independent states, and that as free & independent states they shall hereafter have power to levy war, conclude peace, contract alliances, establish commerce, & to do all other acts and things which independent states may of right do. And for the support of this declaration we mutually pledge to each other our lives, our fortunes, & our sacred honour.

Study Questions

1. In what way was James Otis's pamphlet *The Rights of the British Colonies Asserted and Proved* radical?

2. Why did merchants, consumers, and lawmakers join in organizing boycott movements?

3. What might motivate an individual to become a patriot or a loyalist? Why did one-third of the American colonists remain neutral during the Revolution?

4. Who benefited from the "rights argument" espoused by the colonists? Was anyone disadvantaged by it?

7

Republican Experiment

Americans described the first decade of national independence as the best of times and as the worst of times. Revolution seemed to have unleashed pent-up entrepreneurial energies, and ordinary men and women rushed to take advantage of new opportunities. The population grew at a faster rate during the 1780's than at any other period in the country's history, a sure sign that young families were optimistic about the future of the republic.

But even as economic activity throughout the United States quickened, reflective people from all regions worried that revolution had yielded anarchy. Political disorder seemed a symptom of deeper problems. Critics suggested that perhaps ordinary Americans lacked the virtue required to sustain a strong republic. If every person looked out only for his or her own private interests, then who would look out for the good of the nation? In 1786 George Washington asked rhetorically, "Have we fought for this? Was it with these expectations that we launched into a sea of trouble, and have bravely struggled through the most threatening dangers?"

An insightful Frenchman, the Marquis de Chastellux, appreciated the difficulties facing the young republic. He surveyed the condition of the new nation (Document 1) and concluded that it would be hard for a national government to overcome the independence of the separate states. Local history and culture undermined genuine nationalism, and, what was more disheartening, a heritage of racism divided whites and blacks.

About the force of localism, Chastellux was correct. No sooner had the Continental Congress declared independence than popular voices called for new state constitutions (Document 2). They knew just what they wanted. The new governments would look nothing like the old colonial system. The states reduced the authority of governors—two abolishing the office altogether—and expanded the prerogatives of the elected representatives. They also demanded clear, written guarantees of their rights. One of the more radical documents of the period was the Pennsylvania Constitution (Document 3). Almost no one initially advocated a strong federal government, and the first constitution of the United States, called the Articles of Confederation (Document 4), gave states so much individual power that the national government could hardly function. It could not even raise revenues without the vote of nine of the thirteen states, support that local officials jealously withheld.

Leaders like Washington, Madison, and Hamilton watched these developments with growing anxiety. Foreign countries treated the Confederation with contempt; the states behaved as if they were sovereign countries. The most distressing phenomenon was armed rebellion. When a poor Massachusetts farmer, Daniel Shays, organized an attempt to close the courts and seize a federal arsenal, the call for a stronger national government gained broad support. Rural rebellion fulfilled Henry Knox's worse fears about the collapse of authority, and in 1786 he informed Washington that something had to be done (Document 5).

In the spring of 1787 fifty-five delegates representing twelve states met in Philadelphia to salvage the republican experiment. Their labors resulted in the Constitution, a radically innovative document that completely overturned the Articles of Confederation. Since the deliberations were secret, almost no one knew in advance what the convention had done. By late September the news was out. The Constitution authorized a powerful executive branch and a bicameral legislature. In the name of the American people, it diminished the power of the states.

During the fall and winter of 1787 and 1788, state ratifying conventions met throughout the country. The most heated rhetoric appeared in highly partisan newspapers and pamphlets. Those in favor of the new system called themselves federalists; their opponents were antifederalists. Confrontation generated the fullest, most thoughtful discussion of government this country has ever witnessed (Document 6). In the end the Constitution passed, but among other things, the antifederalists persuaded their opponents to produce a Bill of Rights.

Nation-building raised difficult questions about exclusions. Was every adult a citizen simply because he or she happened to live in the United States? The answer, as Jefferson explained (Document 7), was no. He could not imagine black people participating fully in the political life of the nation, and he advanced a theory of scientific racism to justify treating African Americans as lesser beings. And James Wilson, a gifted legal scholar, provided the standard explanation of why women could not become citizens of the republic.(Document 8)

DOCUMENT 1

Marquis de Chastellux, Travels in North America (1786)

Chastellux (1734–1788) came to the United States during the Revolution as an officer in the French Expeditionary Forces and was present at the Battle of Yorktown. He had already achieved acclaim in France as a gifted writer. Indeed,

Chastellux counted Voltaire among his literary friends. During his travels through the new republic, Chastellux kept a journal, recording perceptive observations of the distinct regional cultures that had evolved in the United States.

The Virginians differ essentially from the inhabitants to the north and eastward of the Bay [Chesapeake], not only in the nature of their climate, soil, and agriculture, but also in that indelible character which every nation acquires at the moment of its origin, and which by perpetuating itself from generation to generation, justifies this great principle, that *every thing which is partakes of that which has been*. . . .

The government [of Virginia] may become democratic, as it is at the present moment; but the national character, the very spirit of the government, will always be aristocratic. Nor can this be doubted when one considers that another cause is still operating to produce the same result. I am referring to slavery, not because it is a mark of distinction or special privilege to possess Negroes, but because the sway held over them nourishes vanity and sloth, two vices which accord wonderfully with established prejudices. It will doubtless be asked how these prejudices have been reconciled with the present revolution, founded on such different principles. I shall answer that they have perhaps contributed to it; that while New England revolted through reason and calculation, Virginia revolted through pride. . . .

Thus, States, like individuals, are born with a temperament of their own, the bad effects of which may be corrected by the régime of government and by habits, but which can never be entirely changed. Thus, legislators, like doctors, ought never presume to believe that they can bestow, at will, a particular temperament on bodies politic, but should attempt to understand the temper they already have, while striving to combat the disadvantages and increase the advantages resulting from it. A general glance at the different states of America will serve to substantiate this opinion.

The peoples of New England had no other motive for setting in the New World than to escape from the arbitrary power of their monarchs, who were both the sovereigns of the State and the heads of the Church, and who were at that time exercising the double tyranny of despotism and intolerance. They were not adventurers, they were men who wished to live in peace, and who labored to live. Their doctrine taught equality and enjoined work and industry. The soil, naturally barren, affording but scanty resources, they resorted to fishing and navigation; and at this hour, they are still friends to equality and industry; they are fishermen and navigators.

The states of New York and the Jerseys were settled by necessitous Dutchmen who lacked land in their own country, and who concerned themselves much more with domestic economy than with public government. These people have kept this same spirit: their interests and their efforts are, so to speak, individual; their views are centered on their families, and it is only from necessity that these families form a state. . . .

If you go farther to the south, and cross the Delaware, you will find that the government of Pennsylvania, in its origin, was founded on two very opposite principles; it was a government of property, in itself feudal, or if you will, a patriarchal government, but whose spirit was characterized by the greatest tolerance and the most complete liberty. Penn's family at first formed the vain idea of establishing a sort of Utopia, a perfect government, and then of deriving the greatest possible advantage from their immense property by attracting foreigners from all parts. As a result of this the people of Pennsylvania has no identity of its own, it is mixed and confused, and more attached to individual than to public liberty, more inclined to anarchy than to democracy.

Maryland, subjected at first to proprietary government, and considered only as a private domain, long remained in a state of the most absolute dependence. Now for the first time it deserves being regarded as a state; but this state seems to be taking shape under good auspices. It may become important after the present revolution, because it was nothing before.

There remain the two Carolinas and Georgia, but I am not sufficiently acquainted with these three states to subject them to my observations, which may not be as correct as they appear to me, but which are in any case delicate and require more than a superficial examination. I know only that North Carolina, peopled for the most part by Scotsmen, brought thither by poverty rather than by industry, is a prey to brigandage and to internal dissensions; and that South Carolina, whose only commerce is the export trade, owes its existence to its seaports, especially to the city of Charleston, which rapidly increased and became a commercial town, where foreigners have abounded, as at Marseilles and Amsterdam, so that the manners there are polished and easy, that the inhabitants love pleasure, the arts, and society—and that this country is in general more European than the rest of America.

Now if there be any accuracy in this sketch, let my readers compare the spirit of the states of America with their present government. I ask them to make the comparison at the present moment, twenty years hence, fifty years hence, and I am persuaded that although these governments resemble each other in that they are all democratic, there will always be found the traces of their former character, of that spirit which has presided over the formation of peoples and the establishment of nations.

Virginia will retain its distinctive character longer than the other states; either because prejudices are the more durable, the more absurd and frivolous they are, or because those which injure only a part of the human race are more noticeable than those which affect all mankind. In the present revolution the old families have with pain seen new men occupying distinguished situations in the army and in the magistracy. . . .

. . . But if Reason must blush at beholding such prejudices so strongly established among new peo-

ples, Humanity has still more to suffer from the state of poverty in which a great number of white people live in Virginia. It is in this state, for the first time since I crossed the sea, that I have seen poor people. For, among these rich plantations where the Negro alone is wretched, one often finds miserable huts inhabited by whites, whose wane looks and ragged garments bespeak poverty. At first I found it hard to understand how, in a country where there is still so much land to clear, men who do not refuse to work could remain in misery. . . .

Beneath this class of inhabitants we must place the Negroes, whose situation would be even more lamentable than theirs, . . . On seeing them ill lodged, ill clothed, and often overwhelmed with work, I concluded that their treatment was as rigorous as everywhere else. I was assured, however, that it was extremely mild in comparison to what they experience in the sugar colonies. You do not, indeed, generally hear, as in Santo Domingo and in Jamaica, the sound of whips and the cries of the unhappy wretches whose bodies are being lashed. This is because the people of Virginia are in general milder than the inhabitants of the sugar islands, who consist wholly of avid men, eager to make their fortune and return to Europe. Another reason is that the yield of agriculture in Virginia not being of so great a value, labor is not urged on the Negroes with so much severity. . . .

One cannot conceal the fact that the abolition of slavery in America is an extremely delicate question. The Negroes in Virginia amount to two hundred thousand. They at least equal, if they do not exceed, the number of white men. . . . Sufficient attention has not been paid to the difference between slavery, such as we have kept it in our colonies, and slavery as it was generally established among the ancients. A white slave, in ancient times, had not other cause of humiliation than his present lot; if he was freed, he could mix straightway with free men and become their equal. Hence that emulation among the slaves to obtain their liberty, either as a favor or to purchase it with the fruit of their labor. Two advantages resulted from this: the possibility of enfranchising them without danger, and that ambition generally prevalent among them, which turned to the advantage of morals and of industry. But in the present case, it is not only the slave who is beneath his master; it is the Negro who is beneath the white man. No act of enfranchisement can efface this unfortunate distinction; accordingly the Negroes do not seem very anxious to obtain their freedom, nor much pleased when they have obtained it. The free Negroes continue to live with the Negro slaves, and never with the white men, so that only when they have some special work or trade, and want to turn it to their profit, does their interest make them wish to leave the state of bondage.

DOCUMENT 2

Resolution of a Concord, Massachusetts, Town Meeting (1776)

The inhabitants of Concord—the little village where the first great battle of the Revolution occurred—responded to a request from the sitting Massachusetts legislature. The representatives wanted authorization to prepare a new state constitution, but, after debating the issue, the Concord Town Meeting decided that the writing of constitutions was properly the responsibility of a specially elected convention. The people had rights that were not dependent on the will of the legislature, and Concord wisely separated the business of governing from the task of defining those abstract rights and privileges.

At a meeting of the inhabitants of the town of Concord being free and twenty-one years of age and upwards, met by adjournment on the twenty-first day of October 1776 to take into consideration a Resolve of the Honourable House of Representatives of this State on the 17th of September last [requesting authorization to draft a new state constitution].

Resolved as follows:

1. That this State being at present destitute of a properly established form of government, it is absolutly necessary that one should be immediately formed and established.

2. That the Supreme Legislative, either in their proper capacity or in joint committee, are by no means a body proper to form and establish a constitution or form of government; for reasons following.

First, because we conceive that a Constitution in its proper idea intends a system of principles established to secure the subject in the possession and enjoyment of their rights and priviliges, against any encroachments of the governing part. Second, because the same body that forms a constitution have of consequence a power to alter it. Third, because a Constitution alterable by the Supreme Legislative is no security at all to the subject against any encroachment of the governing part on any, or on all of their rights and priviliges.

3. That it appears to this town highly necessary and expedient that a Convention or Congress be immediatly chosen, to form and establish a Constitution, by the inhabitents of the respective towns in this State, being free and twenty-one years of age

and upwards, in proportion as the Representatives of this State formerly were chosen: the Convention or Congress not to consist of a greater number than the House of Assembly of this State heretofore might consist of, except that each town and district shall have the liberty to send one Representative, or otherwise as shall appear meet to the inhabitants of this State in general.

4. That when the Convention or Congress have formed a Constitution, they adjourn for a short time and publish their proposed Constitution for the inspection and remarks of the inhabitants of this State.

5. That the honourable House of Assembly of this State be desired to recommend it to the inhabitants of the State to proceed to chuse a Convention or Congress for the purpas abovesaid as soon as possable.

CONCORD, October the 22d, 1776.

DOCUMENT 3

Constitution of Pennsylvania (1776)

Pennsylvania produced a new frame of government soon after the United States declared independence. By the standards of the eighteenth century, it was a radically democratic document. The constitution abolished property requirements for voting, creating a unicameral house of representatives, and deprived the executive council (no governor) of a veto over legislation. Like other Americans, the people of Pennsylvania insisted on drawing up a formal list of rights. Critics thought that the document had carried reform too far, and John Adams exclaimed that "the people of Pennsylvania in two years will be glad to petition the crown of Britain for reconciliation in order to be delivered from the tyranny of their Constitution." He was wrong. The constitution was not revised until 1790.

A Declaration of the Rights of the Inhabitants of the Commonwealth, or State of Pennsylvania

I. That all men are born equally free and independent, and have certain natural inherent and inalienable rights, amongst which are the enjoying and defending life and liberty, acquiring, possessing and protecting property, and pursuing and obtaining happiness and safety.

II. That all men have a natural and unalienable right to worship Almighty God according to the dictates of their own consciences and understanding: And that no man ought or of right can be compelled to attend any religious worship, or erect or support any place of worship, or maintain any ministry, contrary to, or against, his own free will and consent: Nor can any man, who acknowledges the being of a God, be justly deprived or abridged of any civil right as a citizen, on account of his religious sentiments or peculiar mode of religious worship: And that no authority can or ought to be vested in, or assumed by any power whatever, that shall in any case interfere with, or in any manner controul, the right of conscience in the free exercise of religious worship.

III. That the people of this State have the sole, exclusive and inherent right of governing and regulating the internal police of the same.

IV. That all power being originally inherent in, and consequently derived from, the people; therefore all officers of government, whether legislative or executive, are their trustees and servants, and at all times accountable to them.

V. That government is, or ought to be, instituted for the common benefit, protection and security of the people, nation or community; and not for the particular emolument or advantage of any single man, family or set of men, who are a part only of that community; And that the community hath an indubitable, unalienable and indefeasible right to reform, alter, or abolish government in such a manner as shall be by that community judged most conducive to the public weal.

VI. That those who are employed in the legislative and executive business of the State, may be restrained from oppression, the people have a right, at such periods as they may think proper, to reduce their public officers to a private station, and supply the vacancies by certain and regular elections.

VII. That all elections ought to be free; and that all free men having a sufficient evident common interest with, and attachment to the community, have a right to elect officers, or to be elected into office.

VIII. That every member of society hath a right to be protected in the enjoyment of life, liberty and property, and therefore is bound to contribute his proportion towards the expence of that protection, and yield his personal service when necessary, or an equivalent thereto: But no part of a man's property can be justly taken from him, or applied to public uses, without his own consent, or that of his legal representatives: Nor can any man who is conscien-

tiously scrupulous of bearing arms, be justly compelled thereto, if he will pay such equivalent, nor are the people bound by any laws, but such as they have in like manner assented to, for their common good.

IX. That in all prosecutions for criminal offences, a man hath a right to be heard by himself and his council, to demand the causes and nature of his accusation, to be confronted with the witnesses, to call for evidence in his favour, and a speedy public trial, by an impartial jury of the country, without the unanimous consent of which jury he cannot be found guilty; nor can he be compelled to give evidence against himself; nor can any man be justly deprived of his liberty except by the laws of the land, or the judgment of his peers.

X. That the people have a right to hold themselves, their houses, papers, and possessions free from search and seizure, and therefore warrants without oaths or affirmations first made, affording a sufficient foundation for them, and whereby any officer or messenger may be commanded or required to search suspected places, or to seize any person or persons, his or their property, not particularly described, are contrary to that right, and ought not to be granted.

XI. That in controversies respecting property, and in suits between man and man, the parties have a right to trial by jury, which ought to be held sacred.

XII. That the people have a right to freedom of speech, and of writing, and publishing their sentiments; therefore the freedom of the press ought not to be restrained.

XIII. That the people have a right to bear arms for the defence of themselves and the state; and as standing armies in the time of peace are dangerous to liberty, they ought not to be kept up; And that the military should be kept under strict subordination to, and governed by, the civil power.

XIV. That a frequent recurrence to fundamental principles, and a firm adherence to justice, moderation, temperance, industry, and frugality are absolutely necessary to preserve the blessings of liberty, and keep a government free: The people ought therefore to pay particular attention to these points in the choice of officers and representatives, and have a right to exact a due and constant regard to them, from their legislatures and magistrates, in the making and executing such laws as are necessary for the good government of the state.

XV. That all men have a natural inherent right to emigrate from one state to another that will receive them, or to form a new state in vacant countries, or in such countries as they can purchase, whenever they think that thereby they may promote their own happiness.

XVI. That the people have a right to assemble together, to consult for their common good, to instruct their representatives, and to apply to the legislature for redress of grievances, by address, petition, or remonstrance.

DOCUMENT 4

Articles of Confederation (1777)

The first framework for national government, called the Articles of Confederation, was approved in 1777. It was not until 1781, however, that the states finally ratified the Constitution. The delegates who drafted the document were fighting a war against King George III, and they had no intention of giving their own rulers too much power. In fact, they envisioned a loose federation of states. The Articles consisted of a single legislative body in which each state cast a single vote. It did not provide for an independent executive and therefore no veto over legislation. Revenue depended on the generosity of the individual states. Amendments required the unanimous consent of all states. Critics of the Articles like Alexander Hamilton and James Madison saw the Constitution of 1777 as a recipe for governmental paralysis, while defenders insisted it protected the states from domination.

To all to whom there Presents shall come, we the undersigned Delegates of the States affixed to our Names, send greeting

WHEREAS the Delegates of the United States of America, in Congress assembled, did, on the 15th day of November, in the year [1777]. . . . agree to certain Articles of Confederation and perpetual Union between the States of. . . . in the words following, viz.:

Articles of Confederation and perpetual Union between the states of New Hampshire, Massachusetts-Bay, Rhode Island and Providence Plantations, Connecticut, New-York, New-Jersey, Pennsylvania, Delaware, Maryland, Virginia, North-Carolina, South-Carolina, and Georgia.

Currency issued by the Continental Congress. When inflation decreased the value of this currency, one of the greatest weaknesses of the Continental Congress became apparent—its inability to raise taxes. The Articles of Confederation specifically prohibited the taxation of the American people.

I. The stile of this Confederacy shall be 'The United States of America'.

II. Each state retains its sovereignty, freedom, and independence, and every power, jurisdiction, and right, which is not by this Confederation expressly delegated to the United States, in Congress assembled.

III. The said states hereby severally enter into a firm league of friendship with each other, for their common defence, the security of their liberties, and their mutual and general welfare, binding themselves to assist each other, against all force offered to, or attacks made upon them, or any of them, on account of religion, sovereignty, trade, or any other pretence whatever.

IV. The better to secure and perpetuate mutual friendship and intercourse among the people of the different states in this union, the free inhabitants of each of these states, paupers, vagabonds, and fugitives from justice excepted, shall be entitled to all privileges and immunities of free citizens in the several states; and the people of each state shall have free ingress and regress to and from any other state, and shall enjoy therein all the privileges of trade and commerce, subject to the same duties, impositions and restrictions as the inhabitants thereof respectively, provided that such restriction shall not extend so far as to prevent the removal of property imported into any state, to any other state, of which the owner is an inhabitant; provided also that no imposition, duties or restriction shall be laid by any state, on the property of the United States, or either of them.

If any person guilty of, or charged with treason, felony, or other high misdemeanor in any state, shall flee from justice, and be found in any of the United States, he shall, upon demand of the Governor or executive power of the state from which he fled, be delivered up and removed to the state having jurisdiction of his offence.

Full faith and credit shall be given in each of these states to the records, acts and judicial proceedings of the courts and magistrates of every other state.

V. For the more convenient management of the general interests of the United States, delegates shall be annually appointed in such manner as the legislature of each state shall direct, to meet in Congress on the first Monday in November, in every year, with a power reserved to each state to recal its delegates, or any of them, at any time within the year, and to send others in their stead for the remainder of the year.

No state shall be represented in Congress by less than two, nor by more than seven members; and no person shall be capable of being a delegate for more than three years in any term of six years; nor shall any person, being a delegate, be capable of holding any office under the United States, for which he, or another for his benefit receives any salary, fees or emolument of any kind.

Each state shall maintain its own delegates in a meeting of the states, and while they act as members of the committee of the states.

In determining questions in the United States in Congress assembled, each state shall have one vote.

Freedom of speech and debate in Congress shall not be impeached or questioned in any court or place out of Congress, and the members of Congress shall be protected in their persons from arrests and imprisonments, during the time of their going to and from, and attendance on Congress, except for treason, felony, or breach of the peace.

VI. No state, without the consent of the United States in Congress assembled, shall send any embassy to, or receive any embassy from, or enter into any conference, agreement, alliance or treaty with any king, prince or state; nor shall any person holding any office of profit or trust under the United States, or any of them, accept of any present, emolument, office or title of any kind whatever from any king, prince or foreign state; nor shall the United States in Congress assembled, or any of them, grant any title of nobility.

No two or more states shall enter into any treaty, confederation or alliance whatever between them, without the consent of the United States in Congress assembled, specifying accurately the purposes for which the same is to be entered into, and how long it shall continue.

No state shall lay any imposts or duties, which may interfere with any stipulations in treaties, entered into by the United States in Congress assembled, with any king, prince or state, in pursuance of any treaties, already proposed by Congress, to the courts of France and Spain. . . .

The United States in Congress assembled shall also be the last resort on appeal in all disputes and differences now subsisting or that hereafter may arise between two or more states concerning boundary, jurisdiction or any other cause whatever. . . .

The United States in Congress assembled shall also have the sole and exclusive right and power of regulating the alloy and value of coin struck by their own authority, or by that of the respective states—fixing the standard of weights and measures throughout the United States—regulating the trade and managing all affairs with the Indians, not members of any of the states, provided that the legislative right of any state within its own limits be not infringed or violated—establishing or regulating post-offices from one state to another, throughout all the United States, and exacting such postage on the papers passing thro' the same as may be requisite to defray the expences of the said office—appointing all officers of the land forces, in the service of the United States, excepting regimental officers—appointing all the officers of the naval forces, and commissioning all officers whatever in the service of the United States—making rules for the government and regulation of the said land and naval forces, and directing their operations.

The United States in Congress assembled shall have authority to appoint a committee, to sit in the recess of Congress, to be denominated 'A Committee of the States', and to consist of one delegate from each state; and to appoint such other committees and civil officers as may be necessary for managing the general affairs of the United States under their direction—to appoint one of their number to preside, provided that no person be allowed to serve in the office of president more than one year in any term of three years; to ascertain the necessary sums of money to be raised for the service of the United States, and to appropriate and apply the same for defraying the public expences—to borrow money, or emit bills on the credit of the United States, transmitting every half-year to the respective states an account of their sums of money so borrowed or emitted—to build and equip a navy—to agree upon the number of land forces, and to make requisitions from each state for its quota, in proportion to the number of white inhabitants in such state. . . .

The United States in Congress assembled shall never engage in a war, nor grant letters of marque and reprisal in time of peace, nor enter into any treaties or alliances, nor coin money, nor regulate the value thereof, nor ascertain the sums and expences necessary for the defence and welfare of the United States, or any of them, nor emit bills, nor borrow money on the credit of the United States, nor appropriate money, nor agree upon the number of vessels of war, to be built or purchased, or the number of land or sea forces to be raised, nor appoint a commander in chief of the army or navy, *unless* nine states assent to the same: nor shall a question on any other point, except for adjourning from day to day be determined, unless by the votes of a majority of the United States in Congress assembled. . . .

X. The Committee of the States, or any nine of them, shall be authorized to execute, in the recess of Congress, such of the powers of Congress as the United States in Congress assembled, by the consent of nine states, shall from time to time think expedient to vest them with; provided that no power be delegated to the said Committee, for the exercise of which, by the Articles of Confederation, the voice of nine states in the Congress of the United States assembled is requisite. . . .

XIII. Every state shall abide by the determinations of the United States in Congress assembled, on all questions which by this confederation are submitted to them. And the Articles of this Confederation shall be inviolably observed by every state, and the union shall be perpetual; nor shall any alteration at any time hereafter be made in any of them; unless such alteration be agreed to in a Congress of the United States, and be afterwards confirmed by the legislatures of every state.

And Whereas it hath pleased the Great Governor of the World to incline the hearts of the legislatures we respectively represent in Congress, to approve of, and to authorize us to ratify the said articles of confederation and perpetual union. Know ye that we the undersigned delegates, by virtue of the power and authority to us given for that purpose, do by these presents, in the name and in behalf of our respective constituents, fully and entirely ratify and confirm each and every of the said articles of confederation and perpetual union, and all and singular the matters and things therin contained; And we do further solemnly plight and engage the faith of our respective constituents, that they shall abide by the determinations of the United States in Congress assembled, on all questions, which by the said confederation are submitted to them. And that the articles thereof shall be inviolably observed by the states we respectively represent, and that the union shall be perpetual. In Witness whereof we have hereunto set our hands in Congress. Done at Philadelphia in the state of Pennsylvania the ninth day of July, in the year of our Lord one Thousand seven Hundred and Seventy-eight, and in the third year of the independence of America.

DOCUMENT 5

Henry Knox, Letter to George Washington (1786)

General Henry Knox, a genial Boston bookseller who served with courage and distinction during the Revolution, had concluded by 1786 that the confederation had no future. From his perspective, the American people seemed to have surrendered to their basest, most selfish instincts, and reports reached Knox stating that weak state governments actually promoted fraud and licentiousness. For Knox, news that Daniel Shays, a veteran of the Battle of Bunker Hill(1786), had led an armed insurgency against a county courthouse in western Massachuetts, hit like a cannot shot. Even though thirteen hundred soldiers easily dispersed Shays' followers, the general feared that similar disorders might occur. He explained his growing concern to George Washington, the one leader trusted by all Americans.

I have lately been far eastward of Boston on private business, and was no sooner returned here than the commotions in Massachusetts [Shay's Rebellion] hurried me back to Boston on a public account.

Our political machine, composed of thirteen independent sovereignties, have been perpetually operating against each other and against the federal head ever since the peace. The powers of Congress are totally inadequate to preserve the balance between the respective States, and oblige them to do those things which are essential for their own welfare or for the general good. The frame of mind in the local legislatures seems to be exerted to prevent the federal constitution from having any good effect. The machine works inversely to the public good in all its parts: not only is State against State, and all against the federal head, but the States within themselves possess the name only without having the essential concomitant of government, the power of preserving the peace, the protection of the liberty and property of the citizens. On the very first impression of faction and licentiousness, the fine theoretic government of Massachusetts has given way, and its laws [are] trampled under foot. Men at a distance, who have admired our systems of government unfounded in nature, are apt to accuse the rulers, and say that taxes have been assessed too high and collected too rigidly. This is a deception equal to any that has been hitherto entertained. That taxes may be the ostensible cause is true, but that they are the true cause is as far remote from truth as light from darkness. The people who are the insurgents have never paid any or but very little taxes. But they see the weakness of government: they feel at once their own poverty compared with the opulent, and their own force, and they are de-

termined to make use of the latter in order to remedy the former.

The creed is, that the property of the United States has been protected from the confiscations of Britain by the joint exertions of all, and therefore ought to be the common property of all; and he that attempts opposition to this creed is an enemy to equality and justice, and ought to be swept from the face of the earth. In a word, they are determined to annihilate all debts public and private, and have agrarian laws, which are easily effected by the means of unfunded paper money, which shall be a tender in all cases whatever. The numbers of these people may amount, in Massachusetts, to one-fifth part of several populous countries; and to them may be added the people of similar sentiments from the States of Rhode Island, Connecticut, and New Hampshire, so as to constitute a body of twelve or fifteen thousand desperate and unprincipled men. They are chiefly of the young and active part of the community, more easily collected than kept together afterwards. But they will probably commit overt acts of treason, which will compel them to embody for their own safety. Once embodied, they will be constrained to submit to discipline for the same reason.

Having proceeded to this length, for which they are now ripe, we shall have a formidable rebellion against reason, the principle of all government, and against the very name of liberty.

This dreadful situation, for which our government have made no adequate provision, has alarmed every man of principle and property in New England. They start as from a dream, and ask what can have been the cause of our delusion? What is to give us security against the violence of lawless men? Our government must be braced, changed, or altered to secure our lives and property. We imagined that the mildness of our government and the wishes of the people were so correspondent that we were not as other nations, requiring brutal force to support the laws.

But we find that we are men,—actual men, possessing all the turbulent passions belonging to that animal, and that we must have a government proper and adequate for him.

The people of Massachusetts, for instance, are far advanced in this doctrine, and the men of property and the men of station and principle there are determined to endeavour to establish and protect them in their lawful pursuits; and, what will be efficient in all cases of internal commotions or foreign invasions, they mean that liberty shall form the basis,—liberty resulting from an equal and firm administration of law.

They wish for a general government of unity, as they see that the local legislatures must naturally and necessarily tend to retard the general government. We have arrived at that point of time in which we are forced to see our own humiliation, as a nation, and that a progression in this line cannot be a productive of happiness, private or public. Something is wanting, and something must be done, or we shall be involved in all the horror of failure, and civil war without a prospect of its termination. Every friend to the liberty of his country is bound to reflect, and step forward to prevent the dreadful consequences which shall result from a government of events. Unless this is done, we shall be liable to be ruled by an arbitrary and capricious armed tyranny, whose word and will must be law.

DOCUMENT 6

Debate over Ratification of the Constitution (1787)

The greatest political debate in the history of this nation took place during the fall and winter of 1787 and 1788. The battle over the merits of the proposed constitution engaged the talents of the most brilliant thinkers of the generation, and their arguments raised issues about the promise and perils of republican government that confront us still.

The ablest political theorists of the period maintained stable republican government required a small, homogenous population. A huge country like the United States seemed an unlikely candidate for success. The *Federalist Papers*, written by James Madison, Alexander Hamilton, and John Jay, countered these concerns, and, in the famous essay "Number 10," Madison challenged traditional thought, arguing that because the United States was so large, no single faction or interest group could possibly dominate the national government. James Wilson, a recent immigrant from Scotland and Madison's ablest ally in the Philadelphia convention, reinforced points at the heart of the federalist position.

Although the antifederalists lost the battle over ratification, they enjoyed broad popular support. They produced telling arguments against giving the federal government so much power. James Winthrop, writing as "Agrippa," ridiculed the notion that a single legal code could suit the needs of thirteen separate states. He feared that the Constitution would produce a centralized government little different from that of Great Britain.

James Madison, Federalist Paper No. 10 (1787)

November 22, 1787

To the People of the State of New York

Among the numerous advantages promised by a well constructed Union, none deserves to be more accurately developed than its tendency to break and control the violence of faction. The friend of popular governments, never finds himself so much alarmed for their character and fate, as when he contemplates their propensity to this dangerous vice. He will not fail therefore to set a due value on any plan, which, without violating the principles to which he is attached, provides a proper cure for it. . . .

. . . [I]t it may be concluded, that a pure Democracy, by which I mean, a Society, consisting of a small number of citizens, who assemble and administer the Government in person, can admit of no cure for the mischiefs of faction. A common passion or interest will, in almost every case, be felt by a majority of the whole; a communication and concern results from the form of Government itself; and there is nothing to check the inducements to sacrifice the weaker party, or an obnoxious indivdual. Hence it is, that such Democracies have ever been spectacles of turbulence and contention; have ever been found incompatible with personal security, or the rights of property; and have in general been as short in their lives, as they have been violent in their deaths. Theoretical politicians, who have patronized this species of Government, have erroneously supposed, that by reducing mankind to a perfect equality in their political rights, they would, at the same time, be perfectly equalized and assimilated in their possessions, their opinions, and their passions.

A Republic, by which I mean a Government in which the scheme of representation takes place, opens a different prospect, and promises the cure for which we are seeking. Let us examine the points in which it varies from pure Democracy, and we shall comprehend both the nature of the cure, and the efficacy which it must derive from the Union.

The two great points of difference between a Democracy and a Republic are, first, the delegation of the Government, in the latter, to a small number of citizens elected by the rest: secondly, the greater number of citizens, and greater sphere of country, over which the latter may be extended.

The effect of the first differnece is, on the one hand to refine and enlarge the public views, by passing them through the medium of a chosen body of citizens, whose wisdom may best discern the true interest of their country, and whose patriotism and love of justice, will be least likely to sacrifice it to temporary or partial considerations. Under such a regulation, it may well happen that the public voice pronounced by the representatives of the people, will be more consonant to the public good, than if pronounced by the people themselves convened for the purpose. On the other hand, the effect may be inverted. Men of factious tempers, of local prejudices, or of sinister designs, may by intrigue, by corruption or by other means, first obtain the suffrages, and then betray the interests of the people. The question resulting is, whether small or extensive Republics are most favorable to the election of proper guardians of the public weal: and it is clearly decided in favor of the latter by two obvious considerations.

In the first place it is to be remarked that however small the Republic may be, the Representatives must be raised to a certain number, in order to guard against the cabals of a few; and that however large it may be, they must be limited to a certain number, in order to guard against the confusion of a multitude. Hence the number of Representatives in the two cases, not being in proportion to that of the Constituents, and being proportionally greatest in the small Republic, it follows, that if the proportion of fit characters, be not less, in the large than in the small Republic, the former will present a greater option, and consequently a greater probability of a fit choice.

In the next place, as each Representative will be chosen by a greater number of citizens in the large than in the small Republic, it will be more difficult for unworthy candidates to practise with success the vicious arts, by which elections are too often carried; and the suffrages of the people being more free, will be more likely to centre on men who possess the most attractive merit, and the most diffusive and established characters.

It must be confessed, that in this, as in most other cases, there is a mean, on both sides of which inconveniencies will be found to lie. By enlarging too much the number of electors, you render the representative too little acquainted with all their local circumstances and lesser interests; as by reducing it too much, you render him unduly attached to these, and too little fit to comprehend and pursue great and national objects. The Federal Constitution forms a happy combination in this respect; the great and aggregate interests being referred to the national, the local and particular, to the state legislatures.

The other point of difference is, the greater number of citizens and extent of territory which may be brought within the compass of Republican, than of Democratic Government; and it is this circumstance principally which renders factious combinations less to be dreaded in the former, than in the latter. The smaller the society, the fewer probably will be the distinct parties and interests composing it; the fewer the distinct parties and interests, the more frequently will a majority be found of the same party; and the smaller the number of individuals composing a majority, and the smaller the compass within which they are placed, the more easily will they concert and execute their plans of oppression.

Extend the sphere, and you take in a great variety of parties and interests; you make it less probable that a majority of the whole will have a common motive to invade the rights of other citizens; or if such a common motive exists, it will be more difficult for all who feel it to discover their own strength, and to act in unison with each other. Besides other impediments, it may be remarked, that where there is a consciousness of unjust or dishonorable purposes, communication is always checked by distrust, in proportion to the number whose concurrence is necessary.

Hence it clearly appears, that the same advantage, which a Republic has over a Democracy, in controling the effects of faction, is enjoyed by a large over a small Republic—is enjoyed by the Union over the States composing it. Does this advantage consist in the substitution of Representatives, whose enlightened views and virtuous sentiments render them superior to local prejudices, and to schemes of injustice? It will not be denied, that the Representation of the Union will be most likely to possess these requisite endowments. Does it consist in the greater security afforded by a greater variety of parties, against the event of any one party being able to outnumber and oppress the rest? In an equal degree does the encreased variety of parties, comprised within the union, encrease this security. Does it, in fine, consist in the greater obstacles opposed to the concern and accomplishment of the secret wishes of an unjust and interested majority? Here, again, the extent of the Union gives it the most palpable advantage.

The influence of factious leaders may kindle a flame within their particular States, but will be unable to spread a general conflagration through the other States: a religious sect, may degenerate into a political faction in a part of the Confederacy; but the variety of sects dispersed over the entire face of it, must secure the national Councils against any danger from that source: a rage for paper money, for an abolition of debts, for an equal division of property, or for any other improper or wicked project, will be less apt to pervade the whole body of the Union, than a particular member of it; in the same

Daniel Shays with one of his chief officers, Jacob Shattucks. Shays, a veteran of the Battle of Bunker Hill, led a group of Massachusetts Farmers in an uprising against the Massachusetts state government in 1786. The rebellion helped convince Americans, such as George Washington, of the need for a strong central government.

proportion as such a malady is more likely to taint a particular country or district, than an entire State.

In the extent and proper structure of the Union, therefore, we behold a Republican remedy for the diseases most incident to Republican Government. And according to the degree of pleasure and pride, we feel in being Republicans, ought to be our zeal in cherishing the spirit, and supporting the character of Federalists.

James Wilson, Speech to Convention of Pennsylvania (1787)

To form a good system of government for a single city or state, however limited as to territory, or inconsiderable as to numbers, has been thought to require the strongest efforts of human genius. With

what conscious diffidence, then, must the members of the convention have revolved in their minds the immense undertaking which was before them. Their views could not be confined to a small or a single community, but were expanded to a great number of states; several of which contain an extent of territory, and resources of population, equal to those of some of the most respectable kingdoms on the other side of the Atlantick. Nor were even these the only objects to be comprehended within their deliberations. Numerous states yet unformed, myriads of the human race, who will inhabit regions hitherto uncultivated, were to be affected by the result of their proceedings. It was necessary, therefore, to form their calculations on a scale commensurate to a large portion of the globe.

For my own part, I have been often lost in astonishment at the vastness of the prospect before us. To open the navigation of a single river was lately thought, in Europe, an enterprise adequate to imperial glory. But could the commercial scenes of the Scheldt [an European river] be compared with those that, under a good government, will be exhibited on the Hudson, the Delaware, the Potowmack, and the numerous other rivers, that water and are intended to enrich the dominions of the United States?

The difficulty of the business was equal to its magnitude. No small share of wisdom and address is requisite to combine and reconcile the jarring interests, that prevail, or seem to prevail, in a single community. The United States contain already thirteen governments mutually independent. Those governments present to the Atlantick a front of fifteen hundred miles in extent. Their soil, their climates, their productions, their dimensions, their numbers are different. In many instances a difference and even an opposition subsists among their interests; and a difference and even an opposition is imagined to subsist in many more. An apparent interest produces the same attachment as a real one; and is often pursued with no less perseverance and vigour. When all these circumstances are seen and attentively considered, will any member of this honourable body be surprised, that such a diversity of things produced a proportioned diversity of sentiment? will he be surprised that such a diversity of sentiment rendered a spirit of mutual forbearance and conciliation indispensably necessary to the success of the great work? and will he be surprised that mutual concessions and sacrifices were the consequences of mutual forbearance and conciliation? When the springs of opposition were so numerous and strong, and poured forth their waters in courses so varying, need we be surprised that the stream formed by their conjunction was impelled in a direction somewhat different from that, which each of them would have taken separately?. . . .

These observations, and many others that might be made on the subject, will be sufficient to evince, that a division of the United States into a number of separate confederacies would probably be an un-

satisfactory and an unsuccessful experiment. The remaining system which the American States may adopt is, a union of them under one confederate republick. It will not be necessary to employ much time or many arguments to show, that this is the most eligible system that can be proposed. By adopting this system, the vigour and decision of a wide spreading monarchy may be joined to the freedom and beneficence of a contracted republick. The extent of territory, the diversity of climate and soil, the number, and greatness, and connexion of lakes and rivers, with which the United States are intersected and almost surrounded, all indicate an enlarged government to be fit and advantageous for them. The principles and dispositions of their citizens indicate, that in this government liberty shall reign triumphant. Such indeed have been the general opinions and wishes entertained since the era of our independence. If those opinions and wishes are as well founded as they have been general, the late convention were justified in proposing to their constituents one confederate republick, as the best system of a national government for the United States.

In forming this system, it was proper to give minute attention to the interest of all the parts; but there was a duty of still higher import—to feel and to show a prodominating regard to the superiour interests of the whole. If this great principle had not prevailed, the plan before us would never have made its appearance. The same principle that was so necessary in forming it, is equally necessary in our deliberations, whether we should reject or ratify it.

I make these observations with a design to prove and illustrate this great and important truth—that in our decisions on the work of the late convention, we should not limit our views and regards to the state of Pennsylvania. The aim of the convention was, to form a system of good and efficient government on the more extensive scale of the United States. In this, as in every other instance, the work should be judged with the same spirit with which it was performed. . . .

When a single government is instituted, the indivdiuals of which it is composed surrender to it a part of their natural independence, which they before enjoyed as men. When a confederate republick is instituted, the communities of which it is composed surrender to it a part of their political independence, which they before enjoyed as states. The principles which directed, in the former case, what part of the natural liberty of the many ought to be given up, and what part ought to be retained, will give similar directions in the latter case. The states should resign to the national government that part, and that part only, of their political liberty, which, placed in that government, will produce more good to the whole, than if it had remained in the several states. While they resign this part of their political liberty, they retain the free and generous exercise of all their other faculties as states, so far as it is compatible with the welfare of the general and superintending confederacy. . . .

These general reflections have been made in order to introduce, with more propriety and advantage, a practical illustration of the end proposed to be accomplished by the late convention.

It has been too well known—it has been too severely felt—that the present confederation is inadequate to the government and to the exigencies of the United States. The great struggle for liberty in this country, should it be unsuccessful, will probably be the last one which she will have for her existence and prosperity, in any part of the globe. And it must be confessed, that this struggle has, in some of the stages of its progress, been attended with symptoms that foreboded no fortunate issue. To the iron hand of tyranny, which was lifted up against her, she manifested, indeed, an intrepid superiority. She broke in pieces the fetters which were forged for her, and showed that she was unassailable by force. But she was environed by dangers of another kind, and springing from a very different source. While she kept her eye steadily fixed on the efforts of oppression, licentiousness was secretly undermining the rock on which she stood.

Need I call to your remembrance the contrasted scenes, of which we have been witnesses? On the glorious conclusion of our conflict with Britain, what high expectations were formed concerning us by others! What high expectations did we form concerning ourselves! Have those expectations been realized? No. What has been the cause? Did our citizens lose their perseverance and magnanimity? No. Did they become insensible of resentment and indignation at any high handed attempt, that might have been made to injure or enslave them? No. What then has been the cause? The truth is, we dreaded danger only on one side: this we manfully repelled. But on another side, danger, not less formidable, but more insidious, stole in upon us; and our unsuspicious tempers were not sufficiently attentive, either to its approach or to its operations. Those, whom foreign strength could not overpower, have well nigh become the victims of internal anarchy.

If we become a little more particular, we shall find that the foregoing representation is by no means exaggerated. When we had baffled all the menaces of foreign power, we neglected to establish among ourselves a government. that would ensure domestick vigour and stability. What was the consequence? The commencement of peace was the commencement of every disgrace and distress, that would befal a people in a peaceful state. Devoid of national power, we could not prohibit the extravagance of our importations, nor could we derive a revenue from their excess. Devoid of national power, we could not prohibit the extravagance of our importations, nor could we derive a revenue from their excess. Devoid of national importance, we could not procure for our exports a tolerable sale at foreign markets. Devoid of national credit, we saw our publick securities melt in the hands of the holders, like snow before the sun. Devoid of national dignity, we could not, in some instances, perform our treaties on our parts; and, in other instances, we could neither obtain nor compel the performance of them on the part of others. Devoid of national energy, we could not carry into execution our own resolutions, decisions, or laws.

Shall I become more particular still? The tedious detail would disgust me: nor is it now necessary. The years of languor are past. We have felt the dishonour, with which we have been covered: we have seen the destruction with which we have been threatened. We have penetrated to the causes of both, and when we have once discovered them, we have begun to search for the means of removing them. For the confirmation of these remarks, I need not appeal to an enumeration of facts. The proceedings of congress, and of the several states, are replete with them. They all point out the weakness and insufficiency of the present confederation as the cause, and an efficient general government as the only cure of our political distempers.

Under these impressions, and with these views, was the late convention appointed; and under these impressions, and with these views, the late convention met.

We now see the great end which they proposed to accomplish. It was to frame, for the consideration of their constituents, one federal and national constitution—a constitution that would produce the advantages of good, and prevent the inconveniences of bad government—a constitution, whose beneficence and energy would pervade the whole union, and bind and embrace the interests of every part—a constitution that would ensure peace, freedom, and happiness, to the states and people of America.

We are now naturally led to examine the means, by which they proposed to accomplish this end. This opens more particularly to our view the important discussion before us. But previously to our entering upon it, it will not be improper to state some general and leading principles of government, which will receive particular applications in the course of our investigations.

There necessarily exists in every government a power, from which there is no appeal; and which, for that reason, may be termed supreme, absolute, and uncontrollable. Where does this power reside? To which question, writers on different governments will give different answers. Sir William Blackstone will tell you, that in Britain, the power is lodged in the British parliament; that the parliament may alter the form of the government; and that its power is absolute and without control. The idea of a constitution, limiting and superintending the operations of legislative authority, seems not to have been accurately understood in Britain. There are, at least, no traces of practice, conformable to such a princi-

ple. The British constitution is just what the British parliament pleases. When the parliament transferred legislative authority to Henry the eighth, the act transferring it could not, in the strict acceptance of the term, be called unconstitutional.

To control the power and conduct of the legislature by an overruling constitution, was an improvement in the science and practice of government reserved to the American States.

Perhaps some politician, who has not considered, with sufficient accuracy, our political systems, would answer, that, in our governments, the supreme power was vested in the constitutions. This opinion approaches a step nearer to the truth, but does not reach it. The truth is, that, in our governments, the supreme, absolute, and uncontrollable power remains in the people. As our constitutions are superiour to our legislatures; so the people are superiour to our constitutions. Indeed the superiority, in this last instance, is much greater; for the people possess, over our constitutions, control in act, as well as in right.

The consequence is, that the people may change the constitutions, whenever, and however they please. This is a right, of which no positive institution can ever deprive them.

These important truths, sir, are far from being merely speculative: we, at this moment, speak and deliberate under their immediate and benign influence. To the operation of these truths, we are to ascribe the scene, hitherto unparalleled, which America now exhibits to the world—a gentle, a peaceful, a voluntary, and a deliberate transition from one constitution of government to another. In other parts of the world, the idea of revolutions in governments is, by a mournful and indissoluble association, connected with the idea of wars, and all the calamities attendant on wars. But happy experience teaches us to view such revolutions in a very different light—to consider them only as progressive steps in improving the knowledge of government, and increasing the happiness of society and mankind.

Oft have I viewed with silent pleasure and admiration the force and prevalence, through the United States, of this principle—that the supreme power resides in the people; and that they never part with it. It may be called the *panacea* in politics. There can be no disorder in trhe community but may here receive a radical cure. If the errour be in the legislature, it may be corrected by the constitution; if in the constitution, it may be corrected by the people. There is a remedy, therefore, for every distemper in government, if the people are not wanting to themselves. For a people wanting to themselves, there is no remedy: from their power, as we have seen, there is no appeal: to their errour, there is no superiour principle of correction.

James Winthrop, "To the People" (1787)

Having considered some of the principal advantages of the happy form of government under which it is our peculiar good fortune to live, we find by experience, that it is the best calculated of any form hitherto invented, to secure to us the rights of our persons and of our property, and that the general circumstances of the people shew an advanced state of improvement never before known. We have found the shock given by the war in a great measure obliterated, and the publick debt contracted at that time to be considerably reduced in the nominal sum. The Congress lands are fully adequate to the redemption of the principal of their debt, and are selling and populating very fast. The lands of this state, at the west, are, at the moderate price of eighteen pence an acre, worth near half a million pounds in our money. They ought, therefore, to be sold as quick as possible. An application was made lately for a large tract at that price, and continual applications are made for other lands in the eastern part of the state. Our resources are daily augmenting.

We find, then, that after the experience of near two centuries our separate governments are in full vigour. They discover, for all the purposes of internal regulation, every symptom of strength, and none of decay. The new system is, therefore, for such purposes, useless and burdensome.

Let us now consider how far it is practicable consistent with the happiness of the people and their freedom. It is the opinion of the ablest writers on the subject, that no extensive empire can be governed upon republican principles, and that such a government will degenerate to a despotism, unless it be made up of a confederacy of smaller states, each having the full powers of internal regulation. This is precisely the principle which has hitherto preserved our freedom. No instance can be found of any free government of considerable extent which has been supported upon any other plan. Large and consolidated empires may indeed dazzle the eyes of a distant spectator with their splendour, but if examined more nearly are always found to be full of misery. The reason is obvious. In large states the same principles of legislaiton will not apply to the parts. The inhabitants of warmer climates are more dissolute in their manners, and less industrious, than in colder countries. A degree of severity is, therefore, necessary with one which would cramp the spirit of the other. We accordingly find that the very great empires have always been despotick. They have indeed tried to remedy the inconveniences to which the people were exposed by local regulations; but these contrivances have never answered the end. The laws not being made by the people, who felt the inconveniences, did not suit their circumstances. It is under such tyranny that the Spanish provinces languish, and such would be our misfortune and degradation, if we should submit to have the concerns of the whole empire managed by one legislature. To promote the happiness of the people it is necessary that there should be local laws; and it is necessary that those laws should be made by the representatives of those who are immediately subject to the want of them. By endeavouring to suit both extremes, both are injured.

It is impossible for one code of laws to suit Georgia and Massachusetts. They must, therefore, legislate for themselves. Yet there is, I believe, not one point of legislation that is not surrendered in the proposed plan. Questions of every kind respecting property are determinable in a continental court, and so are all kinds of criminal causes. The continental legislature has, therefore, a right to make rules *in all cases* by which their judicial courts shall proceed and decide causes. No rights are reserved to the citizens. The laws of Congress are in all cases to be the supreme law of the land, and paramount to the constitutions of the individual states. The Congress may institute what modes of trial they please, and no plea drawn from the constitution of any state can avail. This new system is, therefore, a consolidation of all the states into one large mass, however diverse the parts may be of which it is to be composed. The idea of an uncompounded republick, on an average, one thousand miles in length, and eight hundred in breadth, and containing six miillions of white inhabitants all reduced to the same standard of morals, or habits, and of laws, is in itself an absurdity, and contrary to the whole experience of mankind. The attempt made by Great-Britain to introduce such a system, struck us with horrour, and when it was proposed by some theorist that we should be represented in partliament, we uniformly declared that one legislature could not represent so many different interests for the purposes of legislation and taxation. This was the leading principle of the revolution, and makes an essential article in our creed. All that part, therefore, of the new system, which relates to the internal government of the states, ought at once to be rejected.

DOCUMENT 7

Thomas Jefferson, Notes on the State of Virginia *(1787)*

In 1780 François Marbois, secretary of the French legation in the United States, sent a questionnaire to leading members of Congress. Marbois wanted information about the institutions and physical character of the various states. A copy of the document found its way into the hands of Thomas Jefferson, then governor of Virginia. For several years Jefferson worked on a manuscript eventually published as *Notes*. The essay is much more than a survey of Virginia's natural resources. Jefferson speculates about the future of the nation, arguing that its continuing strength depended on yeomen farmers, in other words, on free, white landowners. The Jeffersonian vision did not include blacks, at least, not as full citizens. He turned science into a tool for excluding African Americans from republican equality.

In Europe the lands are either cultivated, or locked up against the cultivator. Manufacture must therefore be resorted to of necessity not of choice, to support the surplus of their people. But we have an immensity of land courting the industry of the husbandman. Is it best then that all our citizens should be employed in its improvement, or that one half should be called off from that to exercise manufactures and handicrafts arts for the other? Those who labour in the earth are the chosen people of God, if ever he had a chosen people, whose breasts he has made his peculiar deposit for substantial and genuine virtue. It is the focus in which he keeps alive that sacred fire, which otherwise might escape from the face of the earth. Corruption of morals in the mass of cultivators is a phænomenon of which no age nor nation has furnished an example. It is the mark set on those, who not looking up to heaven, to their own soil and industry, as does the husbandman, for their subsistance, depend for it on the casualties and caprice of customers. Dependance begets subservience and venality, suffocates the germ of virtue, and prepares fit tools for the designs of ambition. This, the natural progress and consequence of the arts, has sometimes perhaps been retarded by accidental circumstances: but generally speaking, the proportion which the aggregate of the other classes of citizens bears in any state to that of its husbandmen, is the proportion of its unsound to its healthy parts, and is a good-enough barometer whereby to measure its degree of corruption. While we have land to labour then, let us never wish to see our citizens occupied at a work-bench, or twirling a distaff. Carpenters, masons, smiths, are wanting in husbandry: but, for the general operations of manufacture, let our work-shops remain in Europe. It is better to carry provisions and materials, and with them their manners and principles. The loss by the transportation of commodities across the Atlantic will be made up in happiness and permanence of government. The mobs of great cities add just so much to the support of pure government, as sores do to the strength of the human body. It is the manners and spirit of a people which preserve a republic in vigour. A degeneracy in these is a canker which soon eats to the heart of its laws and constitution.

[* * *]

It will probably be asked, Why not retain and incorporate the blacks into the state, and thus save the expence of supplying, by importation of white settlers, the vacancies they will leave? Deep rooted prejudices entertained by the whites; ten thousand recollections, by the blacks, of the injuries they have sustained; new provocations; the real distinctions which nature had made; and many other circumstances, will divide us into parties, and produce convulsions which will probably never end but in

the exterminaiton of the one or the other race.—To thse objections, which are political, may be added others, which are physical and moral. The first difference which strikes us is that of colour. Whether the black of the negro resides in the reticular membrane between the skin and scarf-skin, or in the scarf-skin itself; whether it proceeds from the colour of the blood, the colour of the bile, or from that of some other secretion, the difference is fixed in nature, and is as real as if its seat and cause were better known to us. And is this difference of no importance? Is it not the foundation of a greater or less share of beauty in the two races? Are not the fine mixtures of red and white, the expressions of every passion by greater or less suffusions of colour in the one, preferable to that eternal monotony, which reigns in the countenances, that immoveable veil of black which covers all the emotions of the other race? Add to these, flowing hair, a more elegant symmetry of form, their own judgment in favour of the whites, declared by the preference of them, as uniformly as is the preference of the Oran-ootan for the black women over those of his own species. The circumstance of superior beauty, is thought worthy attention in the propagation of our horses, dogs, and other domestic animals; why not in that of man? Besides those of colour, figure, and hair, there are other physical distinctions proving a difference of race. They have less hair on the face and body. They secrete less by the kidnies, and more by the glands of the skin,which gives them a very strong and disagreeable odour. This greater degree of transpiration renders them more tolerant of heat, and less so of cold, than the whites. Perhaps too a difference of structure in the pulmonary apparatuys, which a late ingenious experimentalist has discovered to be the principal regulator of animal heat, may have disabled them from extricating, in the act of inspiration, so much of that fluid from the outer air, or obliged them in expiration, to part with more of it. They seem to require less sleep. A black, after hard labour through the day, will be induced by the slightest amusements to sit up till midnight, or later, though knowing he must be out with the first dawn of the morning. They are at least as brave, and more adventuresome. But this may perhaps proceed from a want of forethought, which prevents their seeing a danger till it be present. When present, they do not go through it with more coolness or steadiness than the whites. They are more ardent after their female: but love seems with them to be more an eager desire, than a tender delicate mixture of sentiment and sensation. Their griefs are transient. Those numberless afflictions, which render it doubtful whether heaven has given life to us in mercy or in wrath, are less felt, and sooner forgotten with them. In general, their existence appears to participate more of sensation than reflection. To this must be ascribed their disposition to sleep when abstracted from their diversions, and unemployed in labour. An animal whose body is at rest, and who does not reflect, must be disposed to sleep of course. Comparing them by their faculties of memory, reason,a nd imagination, it appears to me, that in memory they are equal to the whites; in reason much inferior, as I think one could scarcely be found capable of tracing and comprehending the investigations of Euclid; and that in imagination they are dull, tasteless, and anomalous. It would be unfair to follow them to Africa for this investigation. We will consider them here, on the same stage with the whites, and where the facts are not apocryphal on which a judgment is to be formed. It will be right to make great allowances for the difference of condition, of education, of conversation, of the sphere in which they move. Many millions of them have been brought to, and born in America. Most of them indeed have been confined to tillage, to their own homes, and their own society: yet many have been so situated, that they might have availed themselves of the conversation of their masters; many have been brought up to the handicraft arts, and from that circumstance have always been associated with the whites. Some have been liberally educated, and all have lived in countries where the arts and sciences are cultivated to a considerable degree, and have had before their eyes samples of the best works from abroad. The Indians, with no advantages of this kind, will often carve figures on their pipes not destitute of design and merit. They will crayon out an

animal, a plant, or a country, so as to prove the existence of a germ in their minds which only wants cultivation. They astonish you with strokes of the most sublime oratory; such as prove their reasona nd sentiment strong, their imagination glowing and elevated. But never yet could I find that a black had uttered a thought above the level of plain narration; never see even an elementary trait of painting or sculpture. In music they are more generally gifted than the whites with accurate ears for tune and time, and they have been found capable of imagining a small catch. Whether they will be equal to the composition of a more extensive run of melody, or of complicated harmony, is yet to be proved. . . .

. . . The opinion, that they are inferior in the faculties of reason and imagination, must be hazarded with great diffidence. To justify a general conclusion, requires many observations, even where the subject may be submitted to the Anatomical knife, to Optical glasses, to analysis by fire, or by solvents. How much more then where it is a faculty, not a substance, we are examining; where it eludes the research of all the senses; where the conditions of its existence are various and variously combined; where the effects of those which are present or absent bid defiance to calculation; let me add too, as a circumstance of great tenderness, where our conclusion would degrade a whole race of men from the rank in the scale of beings which their Creator may perhaps have given them. To our reproach it must be said, that though for a century and a half we have had under our eyes the races of black and of red men, they have never yet been viewed by us as subjects of natural history. I advance it therefore as a suspicion only, that the blacks, whether originally a distinct race, or made distinct by time and circumstnaces, are inferior to the whites in the endowments both of body and mind. It is not against experience to suppose, that different species of the same genus, or varieties of the same species, may possess different qualifications. Will not a lover of natural history then, one who views the gradations in all the races of animals with the eye of philosophy, excuse an effort to keep those in the department of man as distinct as nature has formed them? This unfortunate difference of colour, and perhaps of faculty, is a powerful obstacle to the emancipation of these people. Many of their advocates, while they wish to vindicate the liberty of human nature, are anxious also to preserve its dignity and beauty. Some of these, embarrassed by the question "What further is to be done with them?" join themselves in opposition with those who are actuated by sordid avarice only. Among the Romans emancipation required but one effort. The slave, when made free, might mix with, without staining the blood of his master. But with us a second is necessary, unknown to history. When freed, he is to be removed beyond the reach of mixture.

DOCUMENT 8

James Wilson, An Introductory Lecture To a Course of Law Lectures (1791)

James Wilson, associate justice of the Supreme Court, considered another form of exclusion from participation in republican government. In his opening remarks on American law, Wilson raised the possibility of educating women as well as men for careers in law and politics. Most women, he assumed, could not succeed in these demanding fields. The only women who had done so had "too much of the masculine in them." Women's proper role, Wilson claimed, was in "domestick society: there the lovely and accomplished woman shines with superiour lustre." Society intended them to become republican wives and mothers, not full citizens.

I have been zealous—I hope I have not been altogether unsuccessful—in contributing the best of my endeavours towards forming a system of government; I shall rise in importance, if I can be equally successful—I will not be less zealous—in contributing the best of my endeavours towards forming a system of education likewise, in the United States. I shall rise in importance, because I shall rise in usefulness.

What are laws without manners? How can manners be formed, but by a proper education?

Methinks I hear one of the female part of my audience exclaim—What is all this to us? We have heard much of societies, of states, of governments, of laws, and of a law education. Is every thing made for your sex? Why should not we have a share? Is our sex less honest, or less virtuous, or less wise than yours?

Will any of my brethren be kind enough to furnish me with answers to these questions?—I must answer them, it seems, myself? and I mean to answer them most sincerely.

Your sex is neither less honest, nor less virtuous, nor less wise than ours. With regard to the two first of these qualities, a superiority, on our part, will not be pretended: with regard to the last, a pretension of superiority cannot be supported.

I will name three women; and I will then challenge any of my brethren to name three men superiour to them in vigour and extent of abilities. My female champions are, Semiramis of Nineveh; Zenobia, the queen of the East; and Elizabeth of England. I believe it will readily be owned, that three men of superiour active talents cannot be named.

You will please, however, to take notice, that the issue, upon which I put the characters of these three ladies, is not that they were *accomplished;* it is, that they were *able* women.

This distinction immediately reminds you, that a woman may be an able, without being an accomplished female character.

In this latter view, I did not produce the three female characters I have mentioned. I produced them as women, merely of distinguished abilities—of abilities equal to those displayed by the most able of our sex.

But would you wish to be tried by the qualities of our sex? I will refer you to a more proper standard—that of your own.

All the three able characters, I have mentioned, had, I think, too much of the masculine in them. Perhaps I can conjecture the reason. Might it not be owing, in a great measure—might it not be owing altogether to the masculine employments, to which they devoted themselves?

Two of them were able warriors: all of them were able queens; but in all of them, we feel and we regret the loss of the lovely and accomplished woman: and let me assure you, that, in the estimation of our sex, the loss of the love and accomplished woman is irreparable, even when she is lost in the queen.

For these reasons, I doubt much, whether it would be proper that you should undertake the management of publick affairs. You have, indeed, heard much of publick government and publick law: but these things were not made for themselves: they were made for something better; and of that something better, you form the better part—I mean society—I mean particularly domestick society: there the lovely and accomplished woman shines with superiour lustre.

By some politicians, society has been considered as only the scaffolding of government; very improperly, in my judgment. In the just order of things, government is the scaffolding of society: and if society could be built and kept entire without government, the scaffolding might be thrown down, without the least inconvenience or cause of regret.

Government is, indeed, highly necessary; but it is highly necessary to a fallen state. Had man continued innocent, society, without the aids of government, would have shed its benign influence even over the bowers of Paradise.

For those bowers, how finely was your sex adapted! But let it be observed, that every thing else was finished, before Heaven's "last best gift" was introduced: let it be also observed, that, in the pure and perfect commencement of society, there was a striking difference between the only two persons, who composed it. . . .

Her accomplishments indicated her destination. Female beauty is the expression of female virtue. The purest complexion, the finest features, the most elegant shape are uninteresting and insipid, unless we can discover, by them, the emotions of the mind. How beautiful and engaging, on the other hand, are the features, the looks, and the gestures, while they disclose modesty, sensibility, and every sweet and tender affection! When these appear, there is a "Soul upon the countenance." . . .

How many purposes may be served at once, if things are done in the proper way! I have been giving a recipe for the improvement and preservation of female beauty; but I find that I have, at the same time, been delivering instructions for the culture and refinement of female virtue; and have been pointing at the important purposes, which female virtue is fittedf and intended to accomplish.

If nature evinces her designs by her works; you were destined to embellish, to refine, and to exalt the pleasures and virtues of social life.

To protect and to improve social life, is, as we have seen, the end of government and law. If, therefore, you have no share in the formation, you have a most intimate connexion with the effects, of a good system of law and government.

That plan of education, which will produce, or promote, or preserve such a system, is, consequently, an object to you peculiarly important.

But if you would see such a plan carried into complete effect, you must, my amiable hearers, give it your powerful assistance. The pleasing task of forming your daughters is almost solely yours. In my plan of education for your sons, I must solicit you to cooperate. Their virtues, in a certain proportion—the refinement of their virtues, in a much greater proportion, must be moulded on your example.

In your sex, too, there is a natural, an easy, and, often, a pure flow of diction, which lays the best foundation for that eloquence, which, in a free country, is so important to ours.

The style of some of the finest orators of antiquity was originally formed on that of their mothers, or of other ladies, to whose acquaintance they had the honour of being introduced.

I have already mentioned the two Scevolæ among the illustrious Roman characters. One of them was married to Lælia, a lady, whose virtues and accomplishments rendered her one of the principal ornaments of Rome. She possessed the elegance of language in so eminent a degree, that the first speakers of the age were ambitious of her company. The graces of her unstudied elocution were the purest model, by which they could refine their own.

Cicero was in the number of those, who improved by the privilege of her conversation. In his writing, he speaks in terms of the warmest praise concerning her singular talents. He mentions also the conversation of her daughters and grand daughters, as deserving particular notice.

The province of early education by the female sex, was deemed, in Rome, an employment of so much dignity, that ladies of the first rank did not disdain it. We find the names of Aurelia and Attia, the mothers of Julius Cæsar and of Augustus, enumerated in the list of these honourable patronesses of education.

The example of the highly accomplished Cornelia, the daughter of the great Africanus, and the mother of the Gracchi, deserves uncommon attention. She shone, with singular lustre, in all these endowments and virtues that can dignify the female character.

She was, one day, visited by a lady of Campania, who was extremely fond of dress and ornament. This lady, after having displayed some very rich jewels of her own, expressed a wish to be favoured with the view of those which Cornelia had; expected to see some very superb ones, in the toilet of a lady of such distinguished birth and character. Cornelia diverted the conversation, till her sons came into the room: "These are my jewels," said she, presenting them to the Campanian lady.

Cicero had seen her letters: his expressions concerning them are very remarkable. "I have read," says he, "the letters of Cornelia, the mother of the Gracchi; and it appears, that her sons were not so much nourished by the milk, as formed by the style of their mother."

You see now, my fair and amiable hearers, how deeply and nearly interested you are in a proper plan for law education. By some of you, whom I know to be well qualified for taking in it the share, which I have described, that share will be taken. By the younger part of you, the good effects of such a plan will, I hope, be participated: for those of my pupils, who themselves shall become most estimable, will treat you with the highest degree of estimation.

Study Questions

1. Why did Americans of the revolutionary generation have so much trouble creating a strong national government?

2. What role did race play in the republican experiment?

3. Could the problems raised by the Articles of Confederation have been addressed without writing a new constitution?

4. Why did so many people see the states as an effective balance against the power of federal government?

8

Politics in the New Nation

Translating constitutional generalities into actual government policy proved more difficult than most Americans anticipated. To guide the nation through this process, they relied on George Washington, the most popular man in the United States. He got off to a promising start, nominating outstanding people—Thomas Jefferson and Alexander Hamilton, for example—to major cabinet posts. Although these loyal supporters initially assumed they were of one mind about the character of republican government, they soon found themselves fighting over specific legislation. A highly partisan press—a new element in the political life of the nation—fanned personal disagreement into full-scale party conflict. For most of the decade, many wondered whether squabbling Federalists and Republicans would destroy the Constitution.

The great political drama played before a population on the move. For almost two centuries the colonists had stayed close to the Atlantic, but soon after independence, they flooded over the Appalachians. Timothy Dwight, an observant traveler who was president of Yale College, feared the equality and lawlessness of frontier culture (Document 1). But even as he grumbled about western vulgarity, he noted how shiftless people became solid citizens once they acquired land of their own. J. P. Brissot de Warville, a French visitor, also sensed that the future strength of America lay in the settlements beyond the mountains (Document 2), but, unlike Dwight, he worried about the fate of the Native Americans who claimed this territory as their home.

No one in Washington's administration understood national finance better than Alexander Hamilton. In 1790 and 1791 he wrote three economic reports that called for the restructuring of the U.S. debt, the chartering of a national bank, and the promotion of manufacturing. Each plan involved active intervention by the federal government. Such schemes horrified Jefferson and his allies. They vowed to resist the consolidation of power, a move they thought would corrupt the United States and, in the process, emasculate the states.

At the heart of the debate were differing interpretations of the Constitution. Jefferson took a narrow view, arguing that the federal government could do nothing unless specifically authorized by the Constitution. Hamilton ridiculed this position in his masterful "Opinion on the Constitutionality of an act to establish a Bank" (Document 3). He championed a doctrine of *implied powers*. Although William

Edward Savage's 1796 nationalistic engraving, titled
"Liberty," contains the symbols of the new American
Republic. The eagle, representing power and unity,
drinks from the cup offered by the goddess, Liberty.

Maclay, a blunt Scots-Irish senator from Pennsylvania, may not have appreciated the
subtleties of Hamilton's economic program, he insisted that it had to be stopped
(Document 4). And in time, more and more people of Jeffersonian persuasion came
to share Senatory Maclay's point of view.

Differences among colleagues soon hardened into real party conflict. A crisis
occurred in 1794 when a group of farmers living in western Pennsylvania defied efforts to collect a tax on whiskey passed a few years earlier by Congress. Washington
and other Federalist leaders assumed that Republican clubs had provoked the
Whiskey Rebellion for purely partisan purposes, and the President dispatched a large
army to put down a tiny insurrection. In an address to Congress in 1794 (Document
5), Washington chastised political opponents for their disloyalty, a charge Jefferson
deeply resented (Document 6). From his perspective, the Federalists were responsible

for the nation's troubles.

The French Revolution exacerbated domestic controversy. Indeed, events in Paris unleashed radical ideologies that echoed throughout the United States. Republicans generally sympathized with the French, while the Federalists backed Great Britain, France's implacable enemy. In 1798 extreme Federalists decided to crush political dissent, passing the so-called Alien and Sedition Acts (Document 7). This vindictive legislation threatened free speech and due process. Jefferson responded in the Kentucky Resolutions (Document 8) and came close to supporting a doctrine of nullification allowing states to disregard federal laws they deemed unconstitutional.

The sirens of foreign ideologies agitated blacks as well as whites. In 1800 Gabriel Prosser, a slave, organized an insurrection in Richmond, Virginia, and while the rebellion never got off the ground, it frightened southern planters. One African American who followed Gabriel—"Ben alias Ben Woolfolk"—united traditional Christianity and radical French notions of equality into a powerful message of freedom (Document 9).

DOCUMENT 1

Timothy Dwight, Travels in New England and New York *(1821)*

Timothy Dwight's *Travels,* appeared in print a few years after his death in 1817. They were the product of a lifetime. Writing during long tours through the region, the president of Yale College recorded cultural and scientific information, often adding his own piquant comments. In this section, a visit to frontier Vermont triggers a passionate analysis of the future of western settlement.

Vermont has been settled entirely from the other states of New England. The inhabitants have, of course, the New England character, with no other difference besides what is accidental. In the formation of colonies, those who are first inclined to emigrate are usually such as have met with difficulties at home. These are commonly joined by persons who, having large families and small farms, are induced for the sake of settling their children comfortably to seek for new and cheaper lands. To both are always added the discontented, the enterprising, the ambitious, and the covetous. Many of the first, and some of all these classes, are found in every new American country within ten years after its settlement has commenced. From this period, kindred, friendship, and former neighborhood prompt others to follow them. Others still are allured by the prospect of gain presented in very new country to the sagacious from the purchase and sale of lands, while not a small number are influenced by the brilliant stories which everywhere are told concerning most tracts during the early progress of their settlement. A considerable part of all those who *begin* the cultivation of the wilderness may be determined *foresters or pioneers*. The business of these persons is no other than to cut down trees, build log houses, lay open forested grounds to cultivation, and prepare the way for those who come after them. These men cannot live in regular society. They are too idle, too talkative, too passionate, too prodigal, and too shiftless to acquire either property or character. They are impatient of the restraints of law, religion, and morality; grumble about the taxes by which rulers, ministers, and schoolmasters are supported; and complain incessantly, as well as bitterly, of the extortions of mechanics, farmers, merchants, and physicians, to whom they are always indebted. At the same time, they are usually possessed in their own view of uncommon wisdom; understand medical science, politics, and religion better than those who have studied them through life; and, although they manage their own concerns worse than any other men, feel perfectly satisfied that they could manage those of the nation far better than the agents to whom they are committed by the public. After displaying their own talents and worth, after censuring the weakness and wickedness of their superiors, after exposing the injustice of the community in neglecting to invest persons of such merit with public offices, in many an eloquent harange, uttered by many a kitchen fire, in every blacksmith's shop, and in every corner of the streets, and finding all their efforts vain, they become at length discouraged; and, under the pressure of poverty, the fear of a jail, and the consciousness of public contempt leave their native places and betake themselves to the wilderness.

Here they are obliged either to work or starve. They accordingly cut down some trees and girdle others; they furnish themselves with an ill-built log house and a worse barn, and reduce a part of the forest into fields, half enclosed and half cultivated. The forests furnish browse, and their fields yield a stinted herbage. On this scanty provision they feed a few cattle, and with these and the penurious products of their labor, eked out by hunting and fishing, they keep their families alive.

A farm thus far cleared promises immediate subsistence to a better husbandman. A log house thus built presents, when repaired with moderate exertions, a shelter for his family. Such a husbandman is therefore induced by these little advantages, where the soil and situation please him, to purchase such a farm, when he would not plant himself in an absolute wilderness. The proprietor is always ready to sell, for he loves this irregular, adventurous, half-working, and half-lounging life, and hates the sober industry and prudent economy by which his bush pasture might be changed into a farm, and himself raised to thrift and independence. The bargain is soon made. The forester, receiving more money for his improvements than he ever before possessed, and a price for the soil somewhat enhanced by surrounding settlements, willingly quits his house to build another like it, and his farm to girdle trees, hunt, and saunter in another place. His wife accompanies him only from a sense of duty or necessity, and secretly pines for the quiet, orderly, friendly society to which she orginally bade a reluctant farewell. Her husband in the meantime becomes less and less a civilized man, and almost everything in the family which is amiable and meritorious is usually the result of her principles, care, and influence.

The second proprietor is commonly a *farmer*, and with an industry and spirit deserving no small commendation changes the desert into a fruitful field.

This change is accompllished much more rapidly in some places than in others as various causes, often accidental, operate. In some instances a settlement is begun by farmers, and assumes the aspect of regular society from its commencement. This to some extent is always the fact, and the greater number of the first planters are probably of this description; but some of them also are foresters, and sometimes a majority. . . .

The class of men who have been the principal subject of these remarks have already straggled onward from New England, as well as from other parts of the Union, to Louisiana. In a political view, their emigration is of very serious utility to the ancient settlements. All countries contain restless inhabitants: men impatient of labor; men who will contract debts without intending to pay them, who had rather talk than work, whose vanity persuades them that they are wise, and prevents them from knowing that they are fools, who are delighted with innovation, who think places of power and profit due to their peculiar merits, who feel that every change from good order and established society will be beneficial to themselves, who have nothing to lose, and therefore expect to be gainers by every scramble; and who, of course, spend life in disturbing others with the hope of gaining something for themselves. Under despotic governments they are awed into quiet; but in every free community they create, to a greater or less extent, continual turmoil, and have often overturned the peace, liberty, and happiness of their fellow citizens. In the Roman commonwealth, as before in the republics of Greece, they were emptied out as soldiers upon the surrounding countries, and left the sober inhabitants in comparative quiet at home. It is true, they often threw these states into confusion, and sometimes overturned the government. But if they had not been thus thrown off from the body politic, its life would have been of a momentary duration. As things actually were, they finally ruined all these states. For some of them had, as some of them always will have, sufficient talents to do mischief; at time, very extensive. . . .

Formerly the energetic government established in New England, together with the prevailing high sense of religion and morals, and the continually pressing danger from the French and the savages, compelled the inhabitants into habits of regularity and good order, not surpassed perhaps in the world. But since the American Revolution, our situation has become less favorable to the existence, as well as to the efficacy, of these great means of internal peace. The former exact and decisive energy of the government has been obviously weakened. From our ancient dangers we have been delivered, and the deliverance was a distinguished blessing; but the sense of danger regularly brings with it a strong conviction that safety cannot be preserved without exact order and a ready submission to lawful authority.

The institutions and the habits of New England, more I suspect than those of any other country,

have prevented or kept down this noxious disposition; but they cannot entirely prevent either its existence or its effects. In mercy, therefore, to the sober, industrious, and well-disposed inhabitants, Providence has opened in the vast western wilderness a retreat sufficiently alluring to draw them away from the land of their nativity. We have many troubles even now, but we should have many more if this body of foresters had remained at home.

It is however to be observed that a considerable number even of these people become sober, industrious citizens merely by the acquisition of property. The love of property to a certain degree seems indispensable to the existence of sound morals. I have never had a servant in whom I could confide, except such as were desirous to earn and preserve money. The conveniences and the character attendant on the possession of property fix even these restless men at times when they find themselves really able to accumulate it, and persuade them to a course of regular industry. I have mentioned that they sell the soil of their first farms at an enhanced price, and that they gain for the improvements on them what, to themselves at least is a consderable sum. The possession of this money removes, perhaps for the first time, the despair of acquiring property, and awakens the hope and the wish to acquire more. The secure possession of property demands every moment the hedge of law, and reconciles a man originally lawless to the restraints of government. Thus situated, he sees that reputation also is within his reach. Ambition forces him to aim at it, and compels him to a life of sobriety and decency. That his children may obtain this benefit, he is obliged to send them to school and to unite with those around him in supporting a schoolmaster. His neighbors are disposed to build a church and settle a minister. A regard to his own character, to the character and feelings of his family, and very often to the solicitations of his wife prompts him to contribute to both these objects; to attend, when they are compassed, upon the public worship of God; and perhaps to become in the end a religious man.

DOCUMENT 2

Jacques Pierre Brissot de Warville, New Travels in the United States of America (1788)

Brissot was a curious figure. Having risen from humble origins through what one historian called "the netherworld of hack journalism," the Frenchman achieved a certain notoriety for his advocacy of universal humanity. A visit to America sparked his imagination, and his vision of the West—strikingly different from Timothy Dwight's—captures the nation's optimism. After returning to revolutionary Paris, Brissot backed a losing political faction, and in 1793 he died on the guillotine.

I must here describe to you these American frontiersmen, who are undoubtedly destined to change the face of this part of the world. The frontiersman likes hunting and prefers it to farming. He raises only what he needs for his own use or to pay for his pleasures. Detesting work and any sort of ties and with no attachment to the place he inhabits, he loves adventure and is easily enticed by descriptions of better opportunities and a finer country somewhere else. He enjoys fighting and is ready and willing to go off to war in Canada or Louisiana, but he will not enroll for more than a year, for he is also a husband and father and he likes some home life at least for a part of the year.

The frontiersman is courageous, daring, unafraid of death, and contemptuous of the Indians. He can sleep as soundly in the middle of a forest as he would surrounded by neighbors. When a sudden Indian raid alarms a settlement and a family is murdered, people within a range of two or three miles may worry, but no one else is concerned. The Indians almost never attack except in small parties, and as soon as the alarm is given all the Americans in the area get together and go off to hunt these unhappy savages, whom they are slowly decimating, for the Indians are miserably bad fighters and they are always defeated in the end.

The Indians most to be feared are those along the shores of Lake Erie, the Creeks, the Cherokees, the Chahtas and the Chickasaws. They have recently been waging a cruel war against the inhabitants of Georgia and Cumberland. . . .

It cannot be denied that the majority of their faults are the result of their contact with Europeans, who have taught them dishonesty. Never would the tomahawk have killed so cruelly had all the American frontiersmen been as peaceable and as honorable as the Quakers. The following story is but one example of the deceit practiced by Europeans. In one of the states an agreement was signed with the Indians according to which they would sell for a given sum of money as much land as a man could cover from sunrise to sunset. The English sent for a man reputed the fastest runner in America, who managed to cover three times as much ground as an ordinary man could have done. The Indians were furious at being tricked and immediately began a war.

The Indians' affection for the French is touching and indicative of their virtues and of the gratitude of which they are capable. A Frenchman can travel among them from Canada to Illinois without weapons and in complete security. The Indians can tell by his appearance, by his skin, and by his speech to what nation he belongs, and they entertain him as a brother. But if they find him in the company of Americans, he suffers the same cruelty as the Americans, whom they detest.

This hatred, which seems almost ineradicable, permits no hope that a lasting harmony will ever prevail between the two peoples. Congress is taking, however, wise precautions to put an end to fighting and war. Henceforth no private individual and no state may buy land from the Indians. Laws have been passed severely punishing Americans who hunt on Indian territory. Various treaties have been signed with the largest and most respected Indian tribes, such as the Creeks, who are commanded by the famous McGillivray [a mixed-blood Creek leader]. Congress, under the leadership of Washington, has undertaken to pay them an annual subsidy of $1,500 for the land they have lost by the new treaty. You will also be pleased to hear that in order to encourage agriculture among the Indians Congress has promised to give them seeds, cattle, tools, and commissioners to instruct them.

These steps have been taken in the hope of slowly inducing the Indians to be peaceable but not with any expectation of leading them to adopt the ways of European civilization. Many examples discourage any such attempt. There have been cases of Indians who have been taken from their tribes in childhood, educated in schools, and raised among Europeans until they reached the age of twenty, who at their first visit to their own people took off their European dress and reverted to the independent Indian way of life, despite all efforts to stop them.

While making every effort to assure peace, Congress has not failed to take wise precautions to prevent Indian raids. Fort Franklin defends the frontiers of Pennsylvania and the Ohio is dotted with forts: Fort Harmar at the mouth of the Muskingum, Fort Steuben at the rapids of the Ohio, Post Vincennes on the Wabash, etc. All these posts contain well-trained troops, consisting of young volunteers who enlist for three years and who at the end of this time settle on lands in the area that are given to them, thus guaranteeing the security of the territory and at the same tiem contributing to its prosperity.

This change in policy by the American govern-

ment will undoubtedly benefit the Indians, for the government is essentially peaceable by nature. It will, however, cause an upsurge in the Indian population, and then either the Indians will become civilized and be assimilated by the Americans or else a thousand causes will bring about their annihilation.

There is therefore no need to fear that the danger of the Indians will check the drive of the Americans in their mass progress toward the south. Everyone hopes that once navigation on the Mississippi becomes free, enormous markets will become available for the products which Americans produce in abundance and which are needed by the Spanish colonies. Will the Spaniards open this navigation willingly? Will the Americans have to force them to do so? This is the question. Negotiations are in progress, but they have been dragging on for four years. The suspicion exists that certain American states, fearing an emigration which would leave them stripped of population, are secretly backing the Spaniards. It is this covert support of the Spanish position which has given birth to the proposal that navigation on the Mississippi be closed for twenty-five years on condition that Americans have free trade with Spain. Virginia and Maryland, although they have the most to fear from western competition, have opposed this proposal on the ground that it is derogatory to the honor of the United States, and the majority of the other states have concurred.

The suspicions that Westerners have of the real intentions of the American government and of Congress are construed by some people as a sign that the Union will not last long and that there will be secession, particularly since the English of Canada are trying to persuade the Westerners to unite with them.

But I believe, for many reasons, that the Union will endure. The largest part of the land in the West belongs to men who live in the East; the continuous migrations from state to state keep the ties strong; and, finally, as it is in the interest of both Eastern and Western states to establish trade on a large scale with South America and to expand across the Mississippi, they must and will remain united in order to achieve these objectives. . . .

Some distance from the Mississippi and along its navigable tributaries the Natchitoches, the Opelousas, and the Atakapas are languishing, their numbers not increasing, on a great plain 150 miles wide and 600 miles long containing vast natural meadows, forests, and arable land whose riches are equal to those of the most fertile countries in the world. Transport into these wonderful valleys the hardworking citizens of Massachusetts or the orderly and sober Quakers, and what immense riches will they draw from the bosom of this bountiful land! They will produce wealth which, overflowing into the rest of the world, will make basic foodstuffs less expensive, increase employment, and reduce the number of paupers. The indolence and ignorance which condemn so beautiful a country to be an empty wasteland are digging the graves of unborn generations.

I sometimes imagine myself living a hundred years from now, and I see these wild forests replaced, not by cities, but by scattered farms stretching without interruption from New Hampshire to Quito. I see happiness and labor hand in hand. I see beauty adorning the daughters of nature, liberty and virtue rendering government and laws almost unnecessary, sweet tolerance replacing the cruel Inquisition. I see a festival in which Peruvians, Mexicans, Free Americans, and Frenchmen embrace one another as brothers, anathematizing tyranny and blessing the reign of liberty which brings all men into universal harmony. But what will become of the mines and the slaves? The mines will be shut. The slaves will be the brothers of their masters, and they will deserve to be their equals by sharing their knowledge and their way of life. But what will men do without gold, that cynosure of universal greed? Is it not right for a free people to seek it if they must use the hands of slaves to wrest it from the earth. Will a free people ever be without some token by which they can exchange their goods? Gold has served despotism better than it has liberty, and freedom can always find a less dangerous medium of exchange. Our speculators are far from understanding that two revolutions are being prepared in the New World, revolutions which will change completely the commercial theories and practices of Europe. There will be the opening of a canal between the Atlantic and the Pacific and the abandonment of the mines of Peru.

DOCUMENT 3

Alexander Hamilton, Final Version of "An Opinion on the Constitutionality of an Act to Establish a Bank" (1791)

Although Congress passed Hamilton's bill to establish a national bank of the United States, President Washington considered vetoing the legislation on constitutional grounds. Before doing so, however, he requested written opinions from the members of his cabinet. Jefferson's rambling attack on the bank was not one of his most persuasive performances. By contrast, in only a few days, Hamilton prepared a decisive essay, assuring the president that the Constitution justified issuing charters to national banks. He boldly articulated a doctrine of *implied powers*, an interpretation of the Constitution that neither Madison nor Jefferson had anticipated. Hamilton's "loose construction" carried the day, and Washington signed the bank bill into law.

The Secretary of the Treasury having perused with attention the papers containing the opinions of the Secretary of State and Attorney General [Edmund Randolph and Thomas Jefferson] concerning the constitutionality of the bill for establishing a National Bank proceeds according to the order of the President [George Washington] to submit the reasons which have induced him to entertain a different opinion.

It will naturally have been anticipated that, in performing this task he would feel uncommon solicitude. Personal considerations alone arising from the reflection that the measure originated with him would be sufficient to produce it: The sense which he has manifested of the great importance of such an institution to the successful administration of the department under his particular care; and an expectation of serious ill consequences to result from a failure of the measure, do not permit him to be without anxiety on public accounts. But the chief solicitude arises from a firm persuasion, that principles of construction like those espoused by the Secretary of State and the Attorney General would be fatal to the just & indispensible authority of the United States.

In entering upon the argument it ought to be premised, that the objections of the Secretary of State and Attorney General are founded on a general denial of the authority of the United States to erect corporations. The latter indeed expressly admits, that if there be any thing in the bill which is not warranted by the constitution, it is the clause of incorporation.

Now it appears to the Secretary of the Treasury, that this *general principle* is *inherent* in the very *definition* of *Government* and *essential* to every step of the progress to be made by that of the United States; namely—that every power vested in a Government is in its nature *sovereign*, and includes by *force* of the *term*, a right to employ all the *means* requisite, and fairly *applicable* to the attainment of the *ends* of such power; and which are not precluded by restrictions & exceptions specified in the constitution; or not immoral, or not contrary to the essential ends of political society.

This principle in its application to Government in general would be admitted as an axiom. And it will be incumbent upon those, who may incline to deny it, to *prove* a distinction; and to shew that a rule which in the general system of things is essential to the preservation of the social order is inapplicable to the United States.

The circumstances that the powers of sovereignty are in this country divided between the National and State Governments, does not afford the distinction required. It does not follow from this, that each of the *portions* of powers delegated to the one or to the other is not sovereign *with regard to its proper objects*. It will only *follow* from it, that each has sovereign power as to *certain things*, and not as to *other things*. To deny that the Government of the United States has sovereign power as to its declared purposes & trusts, because its power does not extend to all cases, would be equally to deny, that the State Governments have sovereign power in any case; because their power does not extend to every case. The tenth section of the first article of the constitution exhibits a long list of very important things which they may not do. And thus the United States would furnish the singular spectacle of a *political society* without *sovereignty*, or of a people *governed* without *government*.

If it would be necessary to bring proof to a proposition so clear as that which affirms that the powers of the federal government, *as to its objects*, are sovereign, there is a clause of its constitution which would be decisive. It is that which declares, that the constitution and the laws of the United States made in pursuance of it, and all treaties made or which shall be made under their authority shall be the supreme law of the land. The power which can create the *Supreme law* of the land, in any case, is doubtless sovereign *as to such case*.

This general & indisputable principle puts at once an end to the *abstract* question—Whether the United States have power to *erect a corporation?* that is to say, to give a *legal* or *artificial capacity* to one or more persons, distinct from the natural. For it is unquestionably incident to *sovereign power* to erect corporations, and consequently to *that* of the United Strates, in *relation to the objects* intrusted to the management of the government. The difference is this—where the authority of the government is general, it can create corporations in *all cases;* where it is confined to certain branches of legislation, it can create corporations only in those cases.

Here then as far as concerns the reasonings of the Secretary of State & the Attorney General, the affirmative of the constitutionality of the bill might be permitted to rest. It will occur to the President that the principle here advanced has been untouched by either of them. . . .

It is not denied, that there are *implied*, as well as *express* powers, and that the former are as effectually delegated as the latter. And for the sake of accuracy it shall be mentioned, that there is another class of powers, which may be properly denominated *resulting* powers. It will not be doubted that if the United States should make a conquest of any of the territories of its neighbours, they would possess sovereign jurisdiction over the conquered territory. This would rather be a result from the whole mass of the powers of the government & from the nature of political society, than a consequence of either of the powers specially enumerated.

But be this as it may, it furnishes a striking illustration of the general doctrine contended for it. It shews an extensive case, in which a power of erecting corporations is either implied in, or would result from some or all of the powers, vested in the National Government. The jurisdiction acquired over

such conquered territory would certainly be competent to every species of legislation.

To return—It is conceded, that implied powers are to be considered as delegated equally with express ones.

Then it follows, that as a power of erecting a corporation may as well be *implied* as any other thing; it may as well be employed as an *instrument* or *mean* of carrying into execution any of the specified powers, as any other instrument or mean whatever. The only question must be, in this as in every other case, whether the mean to be employed, or in this instance the corporation to be erected, has a natural relation to any of the acknowledged objects or lawful ends of the government. Thus a corporation may not be erected by congress, for superintending the police of the city of Philadelphia because they are not authorised to *regulate* the *police* of that city; but one may be erected in relation to the collection of the taxes, or to the trade with foreign countries, or to the trade between the States, or with the Indian Tribes, because it is the province of the federal government to regulate those objects & because it is incident to a general *sovereign* or *legislative power* to *regulate* a thing, to employ all the means which relate to its regulation to the *best* & *greatest advantage*.

A strange fallacy seems to have crept into the manner of thinking & reasoning upon the subject. Imagination appears to have been unusually busy concerning it. An incorporation seems to have been regarded as some great, independent, substantive thing—as a political end of peculiar magnitude & moment; whereas it is truly to be considered as a *quality, capacity,* or *mean* to an end. Thus a mercantile company is formed with a certain capital for the purpose of carrying on a particular branch of business. Here the business to be prosecuted is the *end;* the association in order to form the requisite capital is the primary mean. Suppose that an incorporation were added to this; it would only be to add a new *quality* to that association; to give it an artificial capacity by which it would be enabled to prosecute the business with more safety & convenience.

That the importance of the power of incorporaton has been exaggerated, leading to erroneous conclusions, will further appear from tracing it to its origin. The roman law is the source of it, according to which a *voluntary* association of individuals at *any time* or *for any purpose* was capable of producing it. In England, whence our notions of it are immediately borrowed, it forms a part of the executive authority, & the exercise of it has been often *delegated* by that authority. Whence therefore the ground of the supposition, that it lies beyond the reach of all those very important portions of sovereign power, legislative as well as executive, which belong to the government of the United States?

To this mode of reasoning respecting the right of employing all the means requisite to the execution of the specified powers of the Government, it is objected that none but *necessary* & proper means are to be employed, & the Secretary of State [Jefferson] maintains, that no means are to be considered as *necessary*, but those without which the grant of the power would be *nugatory*. Nay so far does he go in his restrictive interpretation of the word, as even to make the case of *necessity* which shall warrant the constitutional exercise of the power to depend on *casual* & *temporary* circumstances, an idea which alone refutes the construction. The *expediency* of exercising a particular power, at a particular time, must indeed depend on *circumstance* but the constitutional right of exercising it must be uniform & invariable—the same to day, as to morrow.

All the arguments therefore against the constitutionality of the bill derived from the accidental existence of certain State-banks: institutions which *happen* to exist to day, & for ought that concerns the government of the United States, may disappear to morrow, must not only be rejected as fallacious, but must be viewed as demonstrative, that there is a *radical* source of error in the reasoning.

It is essential to the being of the National government, that so erroneous a conception of the meaning of the word *necessary*, should be exploded.

It is certain, that neither the grammatical, or popular sense of the term requires that construction. According to both, *necessary* often means no more than *needful*, *requisite*, *incidental*, *useful*, or *conducive to*. It is a common mode of expression to say, that it

is *necessary* for a government or a person to do this or that thing, when nothing more is intended or understood, than that the interests of the government or person require, or will be promoted, by the doing of this or that thing. The imagination can be at no loss for exemplifications of the use of the word in this sense.

And it is the true one in which it is to be understood as used in the constitution. The whole turn of the clause containing it, indicates that it was the intent of the convention, by that clause to give a liberal latitude to the exercise of the specified powers. The expressions have peculiar comprehensiveness. They are—"to make *all laws*, necessary & proper for *carrying into execution* the foregoing powers & all *other powers* vested by the constituion in the *government* of the United States, or in any *department* or *officer* thereof." To understand the word as the Secretary of State does, would be to depart from its obvious & popular sense, and to give it a *restrictive* operation; an idea never before entertained. It would be to give it the same force as if the word *absolutely* or *indispensibly* had been prefixed to it.

Such a construction would beget endless uncertainty & embarassment. The cases must be palpable & extreme in which it could be pronounced with certainty, that a measure was absolutely necessary, or one without which the exercise of a given power would be nugatory. There are few measures of any government, which would stand so severe a test. To insist upon it, would be to make the criterion of the exercise of any implied power a *case of extreme necessity*; which is rather a rule to justify the overleaping of the bounds of constitutional authority, than to govern the ordinary exercise of it.

It may be truly said of every government, as well as of that of the United States, that it has only a right, to pass such laws as are necessary & proper to accomplish the objects intrusted to it. For no government has a right to do *merely what it pleases*. Hence by a process of reasoning similar to that of the Secretary of State, it might be proved, that neither of the State governments has a right to incorporate a bank. It might be shewn, that all the public business of the State, could be performed without a bank, and inferring thence that it was unnecessary it might be argued that it could not be done, because it is against the rule which has been just mentioned. A like mode of reasoning would prove, that there was no power to incorporate the Inhabitants of a town, with a few to a more perfect police: For it is certain, that an incorporation may be dispensed with, though it is better to have one. It is to be remembered, that there is no *express* power in any State constitution to erect corporations.

The *degree* in which a measure is necessary, can never be a test of the *legal* right to adopt it. That must ever be a matter of opinion; and can only be a test of expediency. The *relation* between the *measure* and the *end*, between the *nature* of *the mean* employed towards the execution of a power and the object of that power, must be the criterion of constitutionality not the more or less of *necessity* or *utility*. . . .

This restrictive interpretation of the word *necessary* is also contrary to this sound maxim of construction namely, that the powers contained in a constitution of government, especially those which concern the general administration of the affairs of a country, its finances, trade, defence & ought to be construed liberally, in advancement of the public good. This rule does not depend on the particular form of a government or on the particular demarkation of the boundaries of its powers, but on the nature and objects of government itself. The means by which national exigencies are to be provided for, national inconveniences obviated, national prosperity promoted, are of such infinite variety, extent and complexity, that there must, of necessity, be great latitude of discretion in the selection & application of those means. Hence consequently, the necessity & propriety of exercising the authorities intrusted to a government on principles of liberal construction. . . .

The truth is that difficulties on this point are inherent in the nature of the federal constitution.

They result inevitably from a division of the legislative power. The consequence of this division is, that there will be cases clearly within the power of the National Government; others clearly without its power; and a third class, which will leave room for controversy & difference of opinion, & concerning which a reasonable latitude of judgment must be allowed.

But the doctrine which is contended for is not chargeable with the consequence imputed to it. It does not affirm that the National government is sovereign in all respects, but that it is sovereign to a certain extent: that is, to the extent of the objects of its specified powers.

It leaves therefore a criterion of what is constitutional, and of what is not so. This criterion is the *end* to which the measure relates as a *mean*. If the end be clearly comprehended within any of the specified powers, & if the measure have an obvious relation to that end, and is not forbidden by any particular provision of the constitution—it may safely be deemed to come within the compass of the national authority. There is also this further criterion which may materially assist the decision. Does the proposed measure abridge a preexisting right of any State, or of any individual? If it does not, there is a strong presumption in favour of its constitutionality; & slighter relations to any declared object of the constitution may be permitted to turn the scale. . . .

A hope is entertained, that it has by this time been made to appear, to the satisfaction of the President, that a bank has a natural relation to the power of collecting taxes; to that of borrowing money; to that of regulating trade; to that of providing for the common defence: and that as the bill under consideration contemplates the government in the light of a joint proprietor of the stock of the bank, it brings the case within the provision of the clause of the constitution which immediately respects the property of the United States.

DOCUMENT 4

[William Maclay], "For the Independent Gazetteer" (1790)

Pennsylvania selected William Maclay as one of its first senators. Although he supported ratification of the Constitution, he soon found himself at odds with colleagues who wanted to strengthen the federal government. Maclay took particular dislike to Hamilton, whom he called a "damnable villain." In this unsigned journal article, the senator employs heavy-handed satire to warn constituents about the trickery taking place in the nation's capital.

Mr. PRINTER,

I am a poor distressed woman [the United States of America], who for the thirteen or fourteen years since I kept house, have had as great a variety of fortune as ever beset any female. Glorious gleams of sunshine indeed have I had, and happiness ever seemed in my reach; yet by the mismanagement of servants, in brakeing cups and saucers, spoiling provisions, &c. I think I am likely to be ruined. A few days ago I expected to put an end to all my troubles, by sending for a worthy gentleman [George Washington], who had often taken me out of the gutter, when I considered myself as irretrievably fallen. Hearing he was at hand, I requested my neighbour (as good a man I thought as could be) to brush the furniture, and sweep the house, where I used to lodge my best friends. Now could you think it, Sir? Off he runs, and buys such an heap of pots and pans, and dishes and ladles, as run me to ten or twelve pounds of expence. Good Lord! and all this after my being so much in debt already. I determined not to pay him. But what of that? *Sawny* [Alexander Hamilton] the servant, who had the keeping of the trifle of cash I was possessed of, the moment my back was turned, gave him the money. Was there ever such a trick? People tell me the Grand Jury [Congress] should indict him; but la Sir, the Jury know all about it, and I am afraid will take no notice of him, but lye by, till it suits them too, to get a slap at me.

Mr. Printer, I think I am not deficient in the qualities of my head; my heart I know to be possessed of the principles of rectitude. Is it not dreadful that my concerns should be knocked about at this rate, every body doing what they please with me? After describing my situation, you cannot expect me to tell my name, but pray publish my case, which is a plain one. Perhaps some humane person may direct me how to get out of my difficulties.

DOCUMENT 5

George Washington, Sixth Annual Address to Congress (1794)

After President Washington led fifteen hundred militiamen into the woods of Pennsylvania against farmers protesting a whiskey excise tax, he delivered a message to Congress concerning the rebellion. Washington blamed Republican political clubs for promoting the civil unrest. He apparently believed that the opposition party had dispatched French agents to undermine the authority of the federal government. Washington's address stated that the Whiskey Rebellion had been "fomented by combinations of men, who . . . have disseminated, form an ignorance or perversion of facts, suspicions, jealousies, and accusations of the whole government."

Sixth Annual Address To Congress

United States, November 19, 1794

Fellow Citizens of the Senate and of the House of Representatives: When we call to mind the gracious indulgence of Heaven, by which the American People became a nation; when we survey the general prosperity of our country, and look forward to the riches, power, and happiness, to which it seems destined; with the deepest regret do I announce to you, that during your recess, some of the citizens of the United States have been found capable of an insurrection. It is due, however, to the character of our government, and to its stability, which cannot be shaken by the enemies of order, freely to unfold the course of this event.

During the session of the year one thousand seven hundred and ninety, it was expedient to exercise the legislative power, granted by the constitution of the United States, "to lay and collect excises." In a majority of the States, scarcely an objection was heard to this mode of taxation. In some, indeed, alarms were at first conceived, until they were banished by reason and patriotism. In the four western counties of Pennsylvania, a prejudice,

fostered and embittered by the artifice of men, who labored for an ascendency over the will of others, by the guidance of their passions, produced symptoms of riot and violence. It is well known, that Congress did not hesitate to examine the complaints which were presented, and to relieve them, as far as justice dictated, or general convenience would permit, But the impression, which this moderation made on the discontented, did not correspond, with what it deserved. The arts of delusion were no longer confined to the efforts of designing individuals.

The very forbearance to press prosecutions was misinterpreted into a fear of urging the execution of the laws; and associations of men began to denounce threats against the officers employed. From a belief, that by a more formal concert, their operation might be defeated, certain self-created societies assumed the tone of condemnation. Hence, while the greater part of Pennsylvania itself were conforming themselves to the acts of excise, a few counties were resolved to frustrate them. It was now perceived, that every expectation from the tenderness which had been hitherto pursued, was unavailing, and that further delay could only create an opinion of impotency or irresolution in the government. Legal process was, therefore, delivered to the marshal, against the rioters and delinquent distillers.

No sooner was he understood to be engaged in this duty, than the vengeance of armed men was aimed at *his* person, and the person and property of the inspector of the revenue. They fired upon the marshal, arrested him, and detained him for some time, as a prisoner. He was obliged, by the jeopardy of his life, to renounce the service of other process, on the west side of the Allegeny mountain; and a deputation was afterwards sent to him to demand a surrender of that which he *had* served. A numerous body repeatedly attacked the house of the inspector, seized his papers of office, and finally destroyed by fire, his buildings, and whatsoever they contained. Both of these officers, from a just regard to their safety, fled to the seat of government; it being avowed, that the motives to such outrages were to compel the resignation of the inspector, to withstand by force of arms the authority of the United States, and thereby to extort a repeal of the laws of excise, and an alteration in the conduct of government.

Upon the testimony of these facts, an associate Justice of the Supreme Court of the United States notified to me, that "in the counties of Washington and Allegeny, in Pennsylvania, laws of the United States were opposed, and the execution thereof obstructed by combinations, too powerful to be suppressed by the ordinary course of judicial proceedings, or by the powers vested in the marshal of that district." On this call, momentous in the extreme, I sought and weighed, what might best subdue the crisis. On the one hand, the judiciary was pronounced to be stripped of its capacity to enforce the laws; crimes, which reached the very existence of social order, were perpetrated without controul, the friends of government were insulted, abused, and overawed into silence, or an apparent acquiescence; and the yield to the treasonable fury of so small a portion of the United States, would be to violate the fundamental principle of our constitution, which enjoins that the will of the majority shall prevail. On the other, to array citizen against citizen, to publish the dishonor of such excesses, to encounter

the expense, and other embarrassments of so distant an expedition, were steps too delicate, too closely interwoven with many affecting considerations, to be lightly adopted. I postponed, therefore, the summoning of the militia immediately into the field. But I required them to be held in readiness, that if my anxious endeavours to reclaim the deluded, and to convince the malignant of their danger, should be fruitless, military force might be prepared to act, before the season should be too far advanced.

My Proclamation of the 7th of August last was accordingly issued, and accompanied by the appointment of Commissioners, who were charged to repair to the scene of insurrection. They were authorized to confer with any bodies of men, or individuals. They were instructed to be candid and explicit, in stating the sensations, which had been excited in the Executive, and his earnest wish to avoid a resort to coercion. To represent, however, that without submission, coercion *must* be the resort; but to invite them, at the same time, to return to the demeanor of faithful citizens, by such accommodations as lay within the sphere of the executive power. Pardon, too, was tendered to them by the government of the United States, and that of Pennsylvania, upon no other condition, than a satisfactory assurance of obedience to the laws.

Although the report of the commissioners marks their firmness and abilities, and must unite all virtuous men, by shewing, that the means of conciliation have been exhausted, all of those who had committed or abetted the tumults, did not subscribe the mild form, which was proposed, as the atonement; and the indications of a peaceable temper were neither sufficiently general, nor conclusive, to recommend or warrant, a further suspension of the march of the militia.

Thus, the painful alternative could not be discarded. I ordered the militia to march, after once more admonishing the insurgents, in my proclamation of the 25th of September last.

It was a task too difficult to ascertain with precision, the lowest degree of force, competent to the quelling of the insurrection. From a respect, indeed, to œconomy, and the ease of my fellow citizens belonging to the militia, it would have gratified me to accomplish such an estimate. My very reluctance to ascribe too much importance to the opposition, had its extent been accurately seen, would have been a decided inducement to the smallest efficient numbers. In this uncertainty, therefore, I put in motion fifteen thousand men, as being an army, which according to all human calculation, would be prompt, and adequate in every view; and might perhaps, by rendering resistance desperate, prevent the effusion of blood. Quotas had been assigned to the states of New-Jersey, Pennsylvania, Maryland, and Virginia; the governor of Pennsylvania having declared on this occasion, an opinion which justified a requisition to the other states.

As commander in chief of the militia, when called into the actual service of the United States, I have visited the places of general rendezvous, to obtain more exact information, and to direct a plan for ulterior movements. Had there been room for a persuasion, that the laws were secure from obstruction; that the civil magistrate was able to bring to justice such of the most culpable, as have not embraced the proffered terms of amnesty, and may be deemed fit objects of example; that the friends to peace and good government were not in need of that aid and countenance, which they ought always to receive, and I trust, ever will receive, against the vicious and turbulent; I should have caught with avidity the opportunity of restoring the militia to their families and home. But succeeding intelligence has tended to manifest the necessity of what has been done; it being now confessed by those who were not inclined to exaggerate the ill-conduct of the insurgents, that their malevolence was not pointed merely to a particular law; but that a spirit, inimical to all order, has actuated many of the offenders. If the state of things had afforded reason for the continuance of my presence with the army, it would not have been withholden. But every appearance assuring such an issue, as will redound to the reputation and strength of the United States, I have judged it most proper, to resume my duties at the seat of government, leaving the chief command with the governor of Virginia.

Still, however, as it is probable, that in a commotion like the present, whatsoever may be the pretence, the purposes of mischief and revenge may not be laid aside; the stationing of a small force for a certain period in the four western counties of Pennsylvania will be indispensable; whether we contemplate the situation of those, who are connected with the execution of the laws; or of others who may have exposed themselves by an honorable attachment to them. . . .

While there is cause to lament, that occurrences of this nature should have disgraced the name, or interrupted the tranquility of any part of our community, or should have diverted to a new application, any portion of the public resources, there are not wanting real and substantial consolations for the misfortune. It has demonstrated, that our prosperity rests on solid foundations; by furnishing an additional proof, that my fellow citizens understand the true principles of government and liberty: that they feel their inseparable union: that notwithstanding all the devices which have been used to sway them from their interest and duty, they are now as ready to maintain the authority of the laws against licentious invasions, as they were to defend their rights against usurpation. It has been a spectacle, displaying to the highest advantage, the value of Republican Government, to behold the most and least wealthy of our citizens standing in the same ranks as private soldiers; pre-eminently distinguished by being the army of the constitution; undeterred by a march of three hundred miles over rugged mountains, by the approach of an inclement season, or by any other discouragement. Nor ought I to omit to acknowledge the efficacious and patriotic co-operation, which I have experienced from the chief magistrates of the states, to which my requisitions have been addressed.

To every description, indeed, of citizens let praise be given. But let them persevere in their affectionate vigilance over that precious depository of American happiness, the constitution of the United States. Let them cherish it too, for the sake of those, who from every clime are daily seeking a dwelling in our land. And when in the calm moments of reflection, they shall have retraced the origin and progress of the insurrection, let them determine whether it has not been fomented by combinations of men, who, careless of consequences, and disregarding the unerring truth, that those who rouse, cannot always appease a civil convulsion, have disseminated, from an ignorance of perversion of facts, suspicions, jealousies, and accusations of the whole government.

Having thus fulfilled the engagement, which I took, when I entered this office, "to the best of my ability to preserve, protect, and defend the constitution of the United States," on you, Gentlemen, and the people by whom you are deputed, I rely for support.

In the arrangements, to which the possibility of a similar contingency will naturally draw your attention, it ought not to be forgotten, that the militia laws have exhibited such striking defects, as could not have been supplied but by the zeal of our citizens. Besides the extraordinary expense and waste, which are not the least of the defects, every appeal to those laws is attended with a doubt of its success.

The devising and establishing of a well regulated militia, would be a genuine source of legislative honor, and a perfect title to public gratitude. I, therefore, entertain a hope, that the present session will not pass, without carrying to its full energy the power of organizing, arming, and disciplining the militia; and thus providing, in the language of the constitution, for calling them forth to execute the laws of the union, suppress insurrections, and repel invasions.

As auxiliary to the state of our defence, to which Congress can never too frequently recur, they will not omit to enquire whether the fortifications, which have been already licensed by law, be commensurate with our exigencies. . . .

An estimate of the necessary appropriations, including the expenditures into which we have been driven by the insurrection, will be submitted to Congress.

Gentlemen of the Senate, and of the House of Representatives: The mint of the United States has entered upon the coinage of the precious metals; and considerable sums of defective coins and bullion have been lodged with the director by individuals. There is a pleasing prospect that the institution will, at no remote day, realize the expectation which was originally formed of its utility.

In subsequent communications, certain circumstances of our intercourse with foreign nations, will be transmitted to Congress. However, it may not be unseasonable to announce that my policy in our foreign transactions has been, to cultivate peace with all the world; to observe treaties with pure and absolute faith; to check every deviation from the line of impartiality; to explain what may have been misapprehended; and having thus acquired the right, to lose no time in acquiring the ability, to insist upon justice being done to ourselves.

Let us unite, therefore, in imploring the Supreme Ruler of nations, to spread his holy protection over these United States: to turn the machinations of the wicked to the confirming of our constitution: to enable us at all times to root out internal sedition, and put invasion to flight: to perpetuate to our country that prosperity, which his goodness has already conferred, and to verify the anticipations of this government being a safe guard to human rights.

DOCUMENT 6

Thomas Jefferson, Letter to James Madison (1794)

Like Washington, Jefferson had an opinion on the Whiskey Rebellion. But far from blaming Republicans, Jefferson blamed the "infernal" excise law itself. Jefferson saw three errors: the first "was to admit it by the Constitution; the 2d, to act on that admission; the 3d & last will be, to make it the instrument of dismembering the Union. . . ." Jefferson feared that since "detestation of the excise law is universal, and has now associated to it a detestation of the government," the result would be "that separation which perhaps was a very distant & problematical event, is now near, & certain, & determined in the mind of every man."

. . . . The denunciation of the democratic societies is one of the extraordinary acts of boldness of which we have seen so many from the fraction of monocrats. It is wonderful indeed, that the President should have permitted himself to be the organ of such an attack on the freedom of discussion, the freedom of writing, printing & publishing. It must be a matter of rare curiosity to get at the modifications of these rights proposed by them, and to see what line their ingenuity would draw between democratical societies, whose avowed object is the nourishment of the republican principles of our constitution, and the society of the Cincinnati, *a self-created* one, carving out for itself hereditary distinctions, lowering over our Constitution eternally, meeting together in all parts of the Union, periodically, with closed doors, accumulating a capital in their separate treasury, corresponding secretly & regularly, & of which society the very persons denouncing the democrats are themselves the fathers, founders, & high officers. Their sight must be perfectly dazzled by the glittering of crowns & coronets, not to see the extravagance of the proposition to suppress the friends of general freedom, while those who wish to confine that freedom to the few, are permitted to go on in their principles & practices. I here put out of sight the persons whose misbehavior has been taken advantage of to slander the friends

of popular rights; and I am happy to observe, that as far as the circle of my observation & information extends, everybody has lost sight of them, and views the abstract attempt on their natural & constitutional rights in all it's nakedness. I have never heard, or heard of, a single expression or opinion which did not condemn it as an inexcusable aggression. And with respect to the transactions against the excise law, it appears to me that you are all swept away in the torrent of governmental opinions, or that we do not know what these transactions have been. We know of none which, according to the definitions of the law, have been anything more than riotous. There was indeed a meeting to consult about a separation. But to consult on a question does not amount to a determination of that question in the affirmative, still time to the acting on such a determination; but we shall see, I suppose, what the court lawyers, & courtly judges, & would-be ambassadors will make of it. The excise law is an infernal one. The first error was to admit it by the Constitution; the 2d, to act on that admission; the 3d & last will be, to make it the instrument of dismembering the Union, & setting us all afloat to chuse which part of it we will adhere to. The information of our militia, returned from the Westward, is uniform, that tho the people there let them pass quietly, they were objects of their laughter, not of their fear; that 1000 men could have cut off their whole force in a thousand places of the Alleganey; that their detestation of the excise law is universal, and has now 'associated to it a detestation of the government; & that separation which perhaps was a very distant & problematical event, is now near, & certain, & determined in the mind of every man. I expected to have seen some justification of arming one part of the society against another; of declaring a civil war the moment before the meeting of that body which has the sole right of declaring war; of being so patient of the kicks & scoffs of our enemies, & rising at a feather against our friends; of adding a million to the public debt & deriding us with rec-ommendations to pay it if we can &c., &c. But the part of the speech which was to be taken as a justifi-cation of the armament, reminded me of parson Saunders demonstration why minus into minus make plus. After a parcel of shreds of stuff from Æsop's fables and Tom Thumb, he jumps all at once into his Ergo minus multiplied into minus make

plus. Just so the 15,000 men enter after the fables, in the speech. —However, the time is coming when we shall fetch up the leeway of our vessel. The changes in your house, I see, are going on for the better, and even the Augean herd over your heads are slowly purging off their impurities. Hold on then, my dear friend, that we may not shipwreck in the meanwhile. I do not see, in the minds of those with whom I converse, a greater affliction than the fear of your retirement; but this must not be, unless to a more splendid & a more efficacious post. There I should rejoice to see you; I hope I may say, I shall rejoice to see you. I have long had much in my mind to say to you on that subject. But double delicacies have kept me silent. I ought perhaps to say while I would not give up my own retirement for the empire of the universe, how I can justify wishing one whose happiness I have so much at heart as yours, to take the front of the battle which is fighting for my secu-rity. This would be easy enough to be done, but not at the heel of a lengthy battle.

DOCUMENT 7

The Alien and Sedition Acts (1798)

From time to time in this nation's long history, federal authorities have tried to si-lence their opponents. Those who attack free speech and due process usually claim that the ends justify the means. The Federalists succumbed to such a sordid logic in 1798, passing a group of bills known collectively as the Alien and Sedition Acts. Although the Federalists claimed that they were acting for the good of the country, they were clearly intent on punishing the Jeffersonians, a party that seemed to have promoted dangerous French ideologies.

The Alien Act

June 25, 1798. Statute II., Chap. LVIII.—An Act Concerning Aliens

SECTION I. *Be it enacted by the Senate and House of Representatives of the United States of America in Congress assembled,* That it shall be lawful for the President of the United States at any time during the continuance of this act, to *order* all such *aliens* as he shall judge dangerous to the peace and safety of the United States, or shall have reasonable grounds to suspect are concerned in any treasonable or secret machinations against the government thereof, to depart out of the territory of the United States, within such time as shall be expressed in such order, which order shall be served on such alien by delivering him a copy thereof, or leaving the same at his usual abode, and returned to the office of the Secretary of State, by the marshal or other person to whom the same shall be directed. And in case any alien, so ordered to depart, shall be found at large within the United States after the time limited in such order for his departure, and not having obtained a *license* from the President to reside therein, or having obtained such *license* shall not have conformed thereto, every such alien shall, on conviction thereof, be imprisoned for a term not exceeding three years, and shall never after be admitted to become a citizen of the United States. *Provided always and be it further enacted,* that if any alien so ordered to depart shall prove to the satisfaction of the President, by evidence to be taken before such person or persons as the President shall direct who are for that purpose hereby authorized to administer oaths, that no injury or danger to the United States will arise from suffering such alien to reside therein, the President may grant a *license* to such alien to remain within the United States for such time as he shall judge proper, and at such place as he may designate. And the President may also require of such alien to enter into a bond to the United States, in such penal sum as he may direct, with one or more sufficient sureties to the satisfaction of the person authorized by the President to take the same, conditioned for the good behavior of such alien during his residence in the United States, and not violating his license, which license the President may revoke whenever he shall think proper.

SEC. 2. *And be it further enacted,* That is shall be lawful for the President of the United States, whenever he may deem it necessary for the public safety, to order to be removed out of the territory thereof, any alien who may or shall be in prison in pursuance of this act; and to cause to be arrested and sent out of the United States such of those aliens as shall have been ordered to depart therefrom and shall not have obtained a license as aforesaid, in all cases where, in the opinion of the President, the public safety requires a speedy removal. And if any alien so removed or sent out of the United States by the President shall voluntarily return thereto, unless by permission of the President of the United States, such alien on conviction thereof, shall be imprisoned so long as, in the opinion of the President, the public safety may require.

SEC. 3. *And be it further enacted,* That every master or commander of any ship or vessel which shall come into any port of the United States after the first day of July next, shall immediately on his arrival make report in writing to the collector, or other chief officer of the customs of such port, of all aliens, if any, on board his vessel, specifying their names, age, the place of nativity, the country from which they shall have come, the nation to which they belong and owe allegiance, their occupation and a description of their persons, as far as he shall be informed thereof, and on failure, every such master and commander shall forfeit and pay three hundred dollars, for the payment whereof on default of such master or commander, such vessel shall also be holden, and may by such collector or other officer of the customs be detained. And it shall be the duty of such collector, or other officer of the customs, forthwith to transmit to the office of the department of state true copies of all such returns.

SEC. 4. *And be it further enacted,* That the circuit and district courts of the United States, shall respectively have cognizance of all crimes and offences against this act. And all marshals and other officers of the United States are required to execute all precepts and orders of the President of the United States issued in pursuance or by virtue of this act.

SEC. 5. *And be it further enacted,* That it shall be lawful for any alien who may be ordered to be removed from the United States, by virtue of this act, to take with him such part of his goods, chattels, or other property, as he may find convenient; and all property left in the United States by any alien, who may be removed, as aforesaid, shall be, and remain subject to his order and disposal, in the same manner as if this act had not been passed.

SEC. 6. *And be it further enacted,* That this act shall continue and be in force for and during the term of two years from the passing thereof.

APPROVED, June 25, 1798.—*Statutes at Large of the United States,* ed. 1850, Vol. I., pp. 570–572.

The Second Alien Act

July 6, 1798. Statute II., Chap. LXVI.—An Act respecting Alien Enemies

SECTION 1. *Be it enacted by the Senate and House of Representatives of the United States of America in Congress assembled,* That whenever there shall be a declared war between the United States and any foreign nation or government, or any invasion or predatory incursion shall be perpetrated, attempted, or threatened against the territory of the United States, by any foreign nation or government, and the President of the United States shall make public proclamation of the event, all natives, citizens, denizens, or subjects of the hostile nation or government, being males of the age of fourteen years and upwards, who shall be within the United States, and not actually naturalized, shall be liable to be apprehended, restrained, secured and removed, as alien enemies. And the President of the United States shall be, and he is hereby authorized, in any event, as aforesaid, by his proclamation thereof or other public act, to direct the conduct to be observed, on the part of the United States, towards the aliens who shall become liable, as aforesaid; the manner and degree of the restraint to which they shall be subject, and in what cases, and upon what security their residence shall be permitted, and to provide

for the removal of those, who, not being permitted to reside within the United States, shall refuse or neglect to depart therefrom; and to establish any other regulations which shall be found necessary in the premises and for the public safety: Provided, that aliens resident within the United States, who shall become liable as enemies, in the manner aforesaid, and who shall not be chargeable with actual hostility, or other crime against the public safety, shall be allowed for the recovery, disposal, and removal of their goods and effects, and for their departure, the full time which is, or shall be stipulated by any treaty, where any shall have been between the United States and the hostile nation or government, of which they shall be natives, citizens, denizens or subjects: and when no such treaty shall have existed, the President of the United States may ascertain and declare such reasonable time as may be consistent with the public safety, and according to the dictates of humanity and national hospitality.

SEC. 2. *And be it further enacted,* That after any proclamation shall be made as aforesaid, it shall be the duty of the several courts of the United States, and of each state, having criminal jurisdiction, and of the several judges and justices of the courts of the United States, and they shall be, and are hereby respectively, authorized upon complaint, against any alien or alien enemies, as aforesaid, who shall be resident and at large within such jurisdiction or district, to the danger of the public peace or safety, and contrary to the tenor or intent of such proclamation, or other regulations which the President of the United States shall and may establish in the premises, to cause such alien or aliens to be duly apprehended and convened before such court, judge or justice; and after a full examination and hearing on such complaint, and sufficient cause therefor appearing, shall and may order such alien or aliens to be removed out of the territory of the United States, or to give such sureties for their good behaviour, or to be otherwise restrained, conformably to the proclamation or regulations which shall or may be established as aforesaid, and may imprison, or otherwise secure such alien or aliens, until the order which shall and may be made, as aforesaid, shall be performed.

SEC. 3. *And be it further enacted,* That it shall be the duty of the marshal of the district in which any alien enemy shall be apprehended, who by condemnment of the United States, or by the order of any court judge or justice, as aforesaid, shall be required to depart, and to be removed, as aforesaid, to provide therefor, and to execute such order, by himself or his deputy, or other discreet person or persons to be employed by him, by causing a removal of such alien out of the territory of the United States; and for such removal the marshal shall have the warrant of the President of the United States, or of the court, judge or justice ordering the same, as the case may be.

APPROVED, July 6, 1798.—*Statutes at Large of the United States,* ed. of 1850, Vol. I., p. 577.

The Sedition Act

July 14, 1798. Chap. LXXIV.—An Act in addition to the act, entitled "An Act for the punishment of certain crimes against the United States"

SECTION I. *Be it enacted by the Senate and House of Representatives of the United States of America, in Congress assembled,* That if any persons shall unlawfully combine or conspire together, with intent to oppose any measure or measures of the government of the United States, which are or shall be directed by proper authority, or to impede the operation of any law of the United States, or to intimidate or prevent any person holding a place of office in or under the government of the United States, from undertaking, performing or executing, his trust or duty; and if any person or persons, with intent as aforesaid, shall counsel, advise or attempt to procure any insurrection, riot, unlawful assembly, or combination, whether such conspiracy, threatening, counsel, advice, or attempt shall have the proposed effect or not, he or they shall be deemed guilty of a high misdemeanor, and on conviction, before any

court of the United States having jurisdiction thereof, shall be punished by a fine not exceeding five thousand dollars, and by imprisonment during a term not less than six months nor exceeding five years; and further, at the discretion of the court may be holden to find sureties for his good behaviour in such sum, and for such time, as the said court may direct.

SEC. 2. *And be it further enacted,* That if any person shall write, print, utter or publish, or shall cause or procure to be written, printed, uttered or published, or shall knowingly and willingly assist or aid in writing, printing, uttering or publishing any false, scandalous and malicious writing or writings against the government of the United States, or the President of the United States, with intent to defame the said government, or either house of the said Congress, or the said President, or to bring them, or either of them, into contempt or disrepute; or to excite against them, or either or any of them, the hatred of the good people of the United States, or to stir up sedition within the United States, or to excite any unlawful combinations therein, for opposing (or resisting any law of the United States,) or any act of the President of the United States, done in pursuance of any such law, or of the powers in him vested by the Constitution of the United States, or to resist, oppose, or defeat any such law or act, or to aid, encourage or abet any hostile designs of any foreign nation against the United States, their people or government, then such person, being thereof convicted before any court of the United States having jurisdiction thereof, shall be punished by a fine not exceeding two thousand dollars, and by imprisonment not exceeding two years.

SEC. 3. *And be it further enacted and declared,* That if any person shall be prosecuted under this act, for the writing or publishing any libel aforesaid, it shall be lawful for the defendant, upon the trial of the cause, to give in evidence in his defence, the truth of the matter contained in the publication charged as a libel. And the jury who shall try the cause, shall have a right to determine the law and the fact, under the direction of the court, as in other cases.

SEC. 4. *And be it further enacted*, That this act shall continue and be in force until the third day of March, one thousand eight hundred and one, and no longer: *Provided*, that the expiration of the act shall not prevent or defeat a prosecution and punishment of any offence against the law, during the time it shall be in force.

APPROVED, July 14, 1798.—*Statutes at Large of the United States*, ed., of 1850, Vol. I., p. 596.

DOCUMENT 8

Thomas Jefferson, "The Kentucky Resolutions" (1798)

Following passage of the Alien and Sedition Acts, Jefferson and Madison drafted separate protests known as the Kentucky and Virginia Resolutions. Jefferson wrote the Kentucky Resolutions in November 1798, and in his deep anger over the Federalist legislation, he flirted with a doctrine of nullification, a position that threatened the survival of the Union. Jefferson envisioned the United States as a compact. In this agreement the states allowed the federal government only those powers specifically granted in the Constitution. The Hamiltonian argument for "implied powers" struck him as dangerous nonsense, and while they had some reservations about Jefferson's statement, the legislators of Kentucky declared the Alien and Sedition Acts unconstitutional.

1. *Resolved*, That the several States composing the United States of America, are not united on the principle of unlimited submission to their General Government; but that, by a compact under the style and title of a Constitution for the United States, and of amendments thereto, they constituted a General Government for special purposes,—delegated to that government certain definite powers, reserving, each State to itself, the residuary mass of right to their own self-government; and that whensoever the General Government assumes undelegated powers, its acts are unauthoritative, void, and of no force; that to this compact each State acceded as a State, and is an integral party, its co-States forming, as to itself, the other party: that the government created by this compact was not made the exclusive or final judge of the extent of the powers delegated to itself; since that would have made its discretion, and not the Constitution, the measure of its powers; but that, as in all other cases of compact among powers having no common judge, each party has an equal right to judge for itself, as well of infractions as of the mode and measure of redress.

2. *Resolved*, That the Constitution of the United States, having delegated to Congress a power to punish treason, counterfeiting the securities and current coin of the United States, piracies, and felonies committed on the high seas, and offences against the law of nations, and no other crimes whatsoever; and it being true as a general principle, and one of the amendments to the Constitution having also declared, that "the powers not delegated

Political dissent, particularly in the early years of the Republic, sometimes ended in violence. This fistfight between Republican Matthew Lyon and Federalist Roger Griswold took place on the floor of the House of Representatives on February 15, 1798.

to the United States by the Constitution, nor prohibited by it to the States, are reserved to the States respectively, or to the people," therefore the act of Congress, passed on the 14th day of July, 1798, and intituled "An Act in addition to the act intituled An Act for the punishment of certain crimes against the United States," as also the act passed by them on the—day of June, 1798, intituled "An Act to punish frauds committed on the bank of the United States," (and all their other acts which assume to create, define, or punish crimes, other than those so enumerated in the Constitution,) are altogether void, and of no force; and that the power to create, define, and punish such other crimes is reserved, and, of right, appertains solely and exclusively to the respective States, each within its own territory.

3. *Resolved,* That it is true as a general principle, and is also expressly declared by one of the amendments to the Constitution, that "the powers not delegated to the United States by the Constitution, nor prohibited by it to the States, are reserved to the States respectively, or to the people;" and that no power over the freedom of religion, freedom of speech, or freedom of the press being delegated to the United States by the Constitution, nor prohibited by it to the States, all lawful powers respecting the same did of right remain, and were reserved to the States or the people: that thus was manifested their determination to retain themselves the right of judging how far the licentiousness of speech and of the press may be abridged without lessening their useful freedom, and how far those abuses which cannot be separated from their use should be tolerated, rather than the use be destroyed. And thus also they guarded against all abridgment by the United States of the freedom of religious opinions and exercises, and retained to themselves the right of protecting

the same, as this State, by a law passed on the general demand of its citizens, had already protected them from all human restraint or interference. And that in addition to this general principle and express declaration, another and more special provision has been made by one of the amendments to the Constitution, which expressly declares, that "Congress shall make no law respecting an establishment of religion, or prohibiting the free exericse thereof, or abridging the freedom of speech or of the press:" thereby guarding in the same sentence, and under the same words, the freedom of religion, of speech, and of the press: insomuch, that whatever violated either, throws down the sanctuary which covers the others, and that libels, falsehood, and defamation, equally with heresy and false religion, are withheld from the cognizance of federal tribunals. That, therefore, the act of Congress of the United States, passed on the 14th day of July, 1798, intituled "An Act in addition to the act intituled An Act for the punishment of certain crimes against the United States, which does abridge the freedom of the press, is not law, but is altogether void, and of no force.

4. *Resolved,* That alien friends are under the jurisdiction and protection of the laws of the State wherein they are: that no power over them has been delegated to the United States, nor prohibited to the individual States, distinct from their power over citizens. And it being true as a general principle, and one of the amendments to the Constitution also declared, that "the powers not delegated to the United States by the Constitution, nor prohibited by it to the States, are reserved to the States respectively, or to the people," the act of the Congress of the United States, passed on the—day of July, 1798, intituled "An Act concerning aliens," which assumes powers over alien friends, not delegated by the Constitution, is not law, but is altogether void, and of no force.

5. *Resolved,* That in addition to the general principle, as well as the express declaration, that powers not delegated are reserved, another and more special provision, inserted in the Constitution from abundant caution, has declared that "the migration or importation of such persons as any of the States now existing shall think proper to admit, shall not be prohibited by the Congress prior to the year 1808;" that this commonwealth does admit the migration of alien friends, described as the subject of the said act concerning aliens: that a provision against prohibiting their migration, is a provision against all acts equivalent thereto, or it would be nugatory: that to remove them when migrated, is equivalent to a prohibition of their migration, and is, therefore, contrary to the said provision of the Constitution, and void.

6. *Resolved,* That the imprisonment of a person under the protection of the Laws of this commonwealth, on his failure to obey the simple *order* of the President to depart out of the United States, as is undertaken by said act intituled "An Act concerning aliens," is contrary to the Constitution, one amendment to which has provided that "no person shall be deprived of liberty without due process of law;" and that another having providing that "in all criminal prosecutions the accused shall enjoy the right to public trial by an impartial jury, to be informed of the nature and cause of the accusation, to be confronted with the witnesses against him, to have compulsory process for obtaining witnesses in his favor, and to have the assistance of counsel for his defence," the same act, undertaking to authorize the President to remove a person out of the United States, who is under the protection of the law, on his own suspicion, without accusation, without jury, without public trial, without confrontation of the witnesses against him, without hearing witnesses in his favor, without defence, without counsel, is contrary to the provision also of the Constitution, is therefore not law, but utterly void, and of no force: that transferring the power of judging any person, who is under the protection of the laws, from the courts to the President of the United States, as is undertaken by the same act concerning aliens, is against the article of the Constitution which provides that "the judicial power of the United States shall be vested in courts, the judges of which shall hold their offices during good behavior;" and that the said act is void for that reason also. And it is further to be noted, that this transfer of judiciary power

is to that magistrate of the General Government who already possesses all the Executive, and a negative on all legislative powers.

7. *Resolved,* That the construction applied by the General Government (as is evidenced by sundry of their proceedings) to those parts of the Constitution of the United States which delegate to Congress a power "to lay and collect taxes, duties, imports, and excises, to pay the debts, and provide for the common defence and general welfare of the United States," and "to make all laws which shall be necessary and proper for carrying into execution the powers vested by the Constitution in the government of the United States, or in any department or officer thereof," goes to the destruction of all limits prescribed to their power by the Constitution: that words meant by the instrument to be subsidiary only to the execution of limited powers, ought not to be so construed as themselves to give unlimited powers, nor a part to be so taken as to destroy the whole residue of that instrument: that the proceedings of the General Government under color of these articles, will be a fit and necessary subject of revisal and correction, at a time of greater tranquillity, while those specified in the preceding resolutions call for immediate redress.

8th. *Resolved,* That a committee of conference and correspondence be appointed, who shall have in charge to communicate the preceding resolutions to the legislatures of the several States; to assure them that this commonwealth continues in the same esteem of their friendship and union which it has manifested from that moment at which a common danger first suggested a common union: that it considers union, for specified national purposes, and particularly to those specified in their late federal compact, to be friendly to the peace, happiness and prosperity of all the States; that faithful to that compact, according to the plain intent and meaning in which it was understood and acceded to by the several parties, it is sincerely anxious for its preservation: that it does also believe, that to take from the States all the powers of self-government and transfer them to a general and consolidated government,

without regard to the special delegations and reservations solemnly agreed to in that compact, is not for the peace, happiness or prosperity of these States; and that therefore this commonwealth is determined, as it doubts not its co-States are, to submit to undelegated, and consequently unlimited powers in no man, or body of men on earth: that in cases of an abuse of the delegated powers, the members of the General Government, being chosen by the people, a change by the people would be the constitutional remedy; but, where powers are assumed which have not been delegated, a nullification of the act is the rightful remedy: that every State has a natural right in cases not within the compact, (asus non fœderis,) to nullify of their own authority all assumptions of power by others within their limits: that without this right, they would be under the dominion, absolute and unlimited, of whatsoever might exercise this right of judgment for them: that nevertheless, this commonwealth, from motives of regard and respect for its co-States, has wished to communicate with them on the subject: that with them alone it is proper to communicate, they alone being parties to the compact, and solely authorized to judge in the last resort of the powers exercised under it, Congress being not a party, but merely the creature of the compact, and subject as to its assumptions of power to the final judgment of those by whom, and for whose use itself and its powers were all created and modified: that if the acts before specified should stand, these conclusions would flow from them; that the General Government may place any act they think proper on the list of crimes, and punish it themselves whether enumerated or not enumerated by the Constitution as cognizable by them: that they may transfer its cognizance to the President, or any other person, who may himself be the accuser, counsel, judge and jury, whose *suspicions* may be the evidence, his *order* the sentence, his *officer* the executioner, and his breast the sole record of the transaction: that a very numerous and valuable description of the inhabitants of these States being, by this precedent, reduced, as outlaws, to the absolute dominion of one man, and the bar-

The Federal Plan Most Solid & Secure
Americans Their Freedom Will Endure
All Arts Shall Flourish in Columbus Land
And All her Sons Join as One Social Band

SOCIETY of PEWTERERS

SOLID AND PURE

Many artisans banded together in support of the new Constitution and national government. Ordinary workers concluded that a strong central government could more easily levy tariffs to regulate foreign trade than could individual states.

rier of the Constitution thus swept away from us all, no rampart now remains against the passions and the powers of a majority in Congress to protect from a like exportation, or other more grievous punishment, the minority of the same body, the legislatures, judges, governors, and counsellors of the States, nor their other peaceable inhabitants, who may venture to reclaim the consitutional rights and liberties of the States and people, or who for other causes, good or bad, may be obnoxious to the views, or marked by the suspicions of the President, or be thought dangerous to his or their election, or other interests, public or personal: that the friendless alien has indeed been selected as the safest subject of a first experiment; but the citizen will soon follow, or rather, has already followed, for already has a sedition act marked him as its prey: that these and successive acts of the same character, unless arrested at the threshold, necessarily drive these States into revolution and blood, and will furnish new calumnies against republican government, and new pretexts for those who wish it to be believed that man cannot be governed but by a rod of iron: that it would be a dangerous delusion were a confidence in the men of our choice to silence our fears for the safety of our rights: that confidence is everywhere the parent of despotism—free government is founded in jealousy, and not in confidence; it is jealousy and not confidence which prescribes limited constitutions, to bind down those whom we are obliged to trust with power: that our Constitution has accordingly fixed the limits to which, and no further, our confidence may go; and let the honest advocate of confidence read the alien and sedition acts, and say if the Constitution has not been wise in fixing limits to the government it created, and whether we should be wise in destroying those limits. Let him say what the government is, if it be not a tyranny, which the men of our choice have conferred on our President, and the President of our choice has assented to, and accepted over the friendly strangers to whom the mild spirit of our country and its laws have pledged hospitality and protection: that the men of our choice have more respected the bare *suspicions* of the President, than the solid right of innocence, the claims of justification, the sacred force of truth, and the forms and substance of law and justice. In questions of power, then, let no more be heard of confidence in man, but bind him down from mischief by the chains of the Constitution. That this commonwealth does therefore call on its co-States for an expression of their sentiments on the acts concerning aliens, and for the punishment of certain crimes herein before specified, plainly declaring whether these acts are or are not authorized by the federal compact. And it

doubts not that their sense will be so announced as to prove their attachment unaltered to limited government, whether general or particular. And that the rights and liberties of their co-States will be exposed to no dangers by remaining embarked in a common bottom with their own. That they will concur with this commonwealth in considering the said acts as so palpably against the Constitution as to amount to an undisguised declaration that that compact is not meant to be the measure of the powers of the General Government, but that it will proceed in the exercise over these States, of all powers whatsoever: that they will view this as seizing the rights of the States, and consolidating them in the hands of the General Government, with a power assumed to bind the States, not merely as the cases made federal, (casus fœderis,) but in all cases whatsoever, by laws made, not with their consent, but by others against their consent: that this would be to surrender the form of government we have chosen, and live under one deriving its powers from its own will, and not from our authority; and that the co-States, recurring to their natural right in cases not made federal, will concur in declaring these acts void, and of no force, and will each take measures of its own for providing that neither these acts, nor any others of the General Government not plainly and intentionally authorized by the Constitution, shall be exercised within their respective territories.

9th. *Resolved,* That the said committee be authorized to communicate by writing or personal conferences, at any times or places whatever, with any person or person who may be appointed by any one or more co-States to correspond or confer with them; and that they lay their proceedings before the next session of Assembly.

Study Questions

1. What difference did the party conflicts of the 1790s make to the people described by Timothy Dwight and Brissot?

2. Why was the federal government so ill-equipped to deal with political conflict? Why would anyone mistake party competition for treason?

3. Is it helpful for historians to describe the federalists as "conservatives," the republicans as "progressives"?

4. Jefferson and Hamilton were the two dominant political theorists of the decade. Describe the character of their differences.

9

The Jeffersonian State

Thomas Jefferson's inauguration as president in 1801 marked the ascendancy of the Republican Party. Sometimes termed the "Revolution of 1800," Jefferson's moment of triumph triggered no riots in the streets, no attempted coup by disgruntled Federalists, no threats of secession from the Union, indeed, nothing but the peaceful transfer of power from the leaders of one party to those of the opposition. Jefferson and his friends soon discovered that victory brought the burden of responsibility. Once in office, Jeffersonians—often called Democrats—found it hard to govern the nation according to principles they had championed during the 1790s.

Most Americans—even those who had most fiercely resisted Jefferson's election—interpreted his success in symbolic terms. Although the new president was a Virginian planter who owned many slaves, he seemed to speak for ordinary white citizens. Wherever they lived, these people defended their independence and equality against all challengers, and they measured a person's worth more by the money he had made than by his family's genealogy. Charles William Janson, an English traveler, confronted aggressive republicans on the streets of Philadelphia and in the backwoods of Georgia (Document 1) and among other things, learned that a strong current of racism often accompanied the popular egalitarian rhetoric.

Jefferson professed a desire to heal festering political wounds. In his First Inaugural Address (Document 2), directed at "Friends and Fellow Citizens," the new president reminded former opponents that their responsibility to the republic far outweighed loyalty to party. "We are all republicans: we are all federalists," he declared. During the early days of his first administration, people expressed curiosity about the man who now occupied the White House. Margaret Bayard Smith, a young married woman who came from a Federalist family, expected to encounter a "violent democrat, the vulgar demagogue, the bold atheist and profligate man" (Document 3). But, in fact, Jefferson charmed Smith as well as many other former enemies. In his memoirs, Jefferson's slave Isaac described living with a master who just happened to be president of the United States (Document 4).

Western expansion tested Jefferson's constitutional principles. In 1803 France offered to sell the entire Louisiana Territory for only $15 million. The acquisition doubled the size of the United States. When American negotiators asked the French foreign minister how much land they had actually purchased, he answered ambiguously, "You have made a noble bargain for yourself, and I suppose you will make the most of it." And, of course, they did. A happy Jefferson immediately requested congressional approval.

While the purchase won universal acclaim, the president worried that perhaps his administration had exceeded its proper authority. After all, the Constitution did not specifically mention buying new territories and incorporating foreign citizens. The president contemplated proposing a constitutional amendment. Correspondence with trusted friends and advisers (Document 5), however, persuaded Jefferson of the need for pragmatism in interpreting the Constitution. The creation of a great American empire generated considerably less excitement among the Indians, who thought the West was theirs. In a poignant autobiography (Document 6), Black Hawk, the famous Sauk chief, recounted the pain of being cheated out of land by unscrupulous representatives of the U. S. government.

After 1800 the Federalists steadily lost whatever popular support they may have once enjoyed. In New England, however, they remained a potent political force. No Federalist was more sharp-tongued than Fisher Ames, a Massachusetts lawyer who interpreted political events in stark conspiratorial terms (Document 7). Jefferson and his successor, James Madison, fumbled their way from one diplomatic disaster to another, a chain of events that led finally to a declaration of war against Great Britain. This conflict, called the War of 1812, crippled New England shipping and drove surviving Federalists to distraction. In the fall of 1814, regional leaders organized the Hartford Convention (Document 8). While New Englanders did not openly advocate secession, they demanded constitutional amendments reflecting their special interests within the nation. When the convention delegates reached Washington with their resolutions, everyone was celebrating the American victory at New Orleans and in no mood to placate New Englanders, who Republicans accused of attempting to dismember the Union.

DOCUMENT 1

Charles William Janson, The Stranger in America: Containing Observations Made During a Long Residence in that Country (1807)

Charles W. Janson, an Englishman who lived in the United States for thirteen years, never quite adjusted to the egalitarian spirit that energized ordinary Americans. After several business failures, Janson returned to Great Britain, and the censorious tone pervading this selection may reflect personal disappointment. Whatever his experiences may have been, Janson shared with many American contemporaries an uneasiness about republican culture. It seemed crude and disorderly, and of course, terribly "uncongenial to English habits."

Arrived at your inn, let me suppose, like myself, you had fallen in with a landlord, who at the moment would condescend to *take the trouble* to procure you refreshment after the family hour, and that no *pig*, or other trifling circumstance called off his attention, he will sit by your side, and enter in the most familiar manner into conversation; which is prefaced, of course, with a demand of your business, and so forth. He will then start a political question (for here every individual is a politican), force your answer, contradict, deny, and, finally, be ripe for a quarrel, should you not acquiesce in all his opinions. When the homely meal is served up, he will often place himself opposite to you at the table, at the same time declaring, that "though he thought he had eaten a hearty dinner, yet he will pick a bit with you." Thus will he sit, drinking out of your glass, and of the liquor you are to pay for, belching in your face, and committing other excesses still more indelicate and disgusting. Perfectly inattentive to your accommodation, and regardless of your appetite, he will dart his fork into the best of the dish, and leave you to take the next cut. If you arrive at the dinner-hour, you are seated with "mine hostess" and her dirty children, with whom you have often to scramble for a plate, and even the servants of the inn; for liberty and equality level all ranks upon the road, from the host to the hostler. The children, imitative of their free and polite papa, will also seize your drink, slobber in it, and often snatch a dainty bit from your plate. This is esteemed wit, and consequently provokes a laugh, at the expence of those who are paying for the board. No check must be given to these demonstrations of unsophisticated nature; for the smallest rebuke will bring down a severe animadversion from the parent. Many are the instances that could be pointed out, where the writer has undergone these mortifications, and if Mr. Winterbottom has ever travelled in the country

parts of the United States, he can, if he pleases, attest the truth of these observations.

"The American farmer, (says this gentleman) has more simplicity and honesty—we more art and chicanery; they have more of nature, and we more of the world. Nature, indeed, formed our features and intellects very much alike; but while we have metamorphosed the one, and contaminated the other, they have retained and preserved the natural symbols of both."

If we credit these assertions, we must admit that the inhabitants of the new world, far excel us, also, in mental acquirements; but I take the very contrary to be the fact. A republican spirit makes them forward and impertinent—a spirit of trade renders them full of chicanery—and under a shew of liberty, they are commonly tyrants to each other. This is observable at their public meetings, when the fumes of whisky or apple-brandy begin to operate—the more opulent will lord it over his poor neighbor; while the robust will attack the weak, till the whole exhibits a scene of riot, blasphemy, and intoxication. . . .

Among the females, a stranger may soon discover the pertness of republican principles. Divested, from that cause, of the blushing modesty of the country girls of Europe, they will answer a familiar question from the other sex with the confidence of a French Mademoiselle. I would not, however, be understood to question their chastity, of which they have as large a portion as Europeans; my object is merely to shew the force of habit, and the result of education.

The arrogance of domestics in this land of republican liberty and equality, is particularly calculated to excite the astonishment of strangers. To call persons of this description *servants*, or to speak of their *master* or *mistress*, is a grievous affront. Having called one day at the house of a gentleman of my acquaintance, on knocking at the door, it was opened by a servant-maid, whom I had never before seen, as she had not been long in his family. The following is the dialogue, word for word, which took place on this occasion:—"Is your master at home?"—"I have no master."—"Don't you live here?"—"I *stay* here."—"And who are you then?"—"Why, I am Mr. ———'s *help*. I'd have you to know, *man*, that I am no *sarvant*; none but *negers* are *sarvants*." . . .

To return to the city of Washington—I have re-marked, that on my return to London, the first general enquiry of my friends is respecting this far-famed place. The description given of it by interested scribblers, may well serve to raise an Englishman's curiosity, and lead him to fancy the capital of Columbia a terrestrial paradise.

The entrance, or avenues, as they are pompously called, which lead to the American seat of government, are the worst roads I passed in the country; and I appeal to every citizen who has been unlucky enough to travel the stages north and south leading to the city, for the truth of the assertion. I particularly allude to the mail stage road from Bladensburg to Washington, and from thence to Alexandria. In the winter season, during the sitting of Congress, every turn of your waggon wheel (for I must again observe, that there is no such thing in the country as what we call a stage coach, or a postchaise,) is for many miles attended with danger. The roads are never repaired; deep ruts, rocks, and stumps of trees, every minute impede your progress, and often threaten your limbs with dislocation.

Arrived at the city, you are struck with its grotesque appearance. In one view from the capitol hill, the eye fixes upon a row of uniform houses, ten or twelve in number, while it faintly discovers the adjacent tenements to be miserable wooden structures, consisting, when you approach them, of two or three rooms one above another. Again, you see the hotel, which was vauntingly promised, on laying the foundation, to rival the large inns in England. This, like every other private adventure, failed: the walls and the roof remain, but not a window! and, instead of accommodating the members of Contress, and travellers of distinction, as proposed, a number of the lowest order of Irish have long held the title

of *naked possession*, from which, were it ever to become an object, it would be difficult to eject them. Turning the eye, a well finished edifice presents itself, surrounded by lofty trees, which never felt the stroke of the axe. The president's house, the offices of state, and a little theatre, where an itinerant company repeated, during a part of the last year, the lines of Shakespeare, Otway, and Dryden, to empty benches, terminate the view of the Pennsylvania, or Grand Avenue.

Speculation, the life of the American, embraced the design of the new city. Several companies of speculators purchased lots, and began to build handsome streets, with an ardor that soon promised a large and populous city. Before they arrived at the attic story, the failure was manifest; and in that state at this moment are the walls of many scores of houses begun on a plan of elegance. In some parts, purchasers have cleared the wood from their grounds, and erected temporary wooden buildings; others have fenced in their lots, and attempted to cultivate them; but the sterility of the land laid out for the city is such, that this plan has also failed. The country adjoining consists of woods in a state of nature, and in some places of mere swamps, which give the scene a curious patch-work appearance. The view of the noble river Potomack, which the eye can trace till it terminates at Alexandria, is very fine. The navigation of the river is good from the bay of Chesapeak, till the near approach to the city, where bars of sand are formed, which every year encroach considerably on the channel. The frigate which brought the Tunisian embassy, grounded on one of these shoals, and the barbarians were obliged to be landed in boats. This is another great disadvantage tothe growth of the city. It never can become a place of commerce, while Baltimore lies on one side, and Alexandria on the other; even admitting the navigation to be equally good—nor can the wild and uneven spot laid out into streets be cleared and levelled for building upon, for many years, even with the most indefatigable exertions.

The capitol, of which two wings are now finished, is of hewn stone, and will be a superb edifice, worthy of its name. The architect who built the first wing, left the country soon after its completion; the corresponding part was carried on under the direction of Mr. Latrobe, an Englishman; from whose taste and judgment much may be expected in finishing the centre of the building: the design of which, as shewn to me by Doctor Thornton, is truly elegant.

The president's house, of which a correct view is given in the frontispiece to this volume, is situated one mile from the Capitol, at the extremity of Pennsylvania Avenue. The contemplated streets of this embryo city are called avenues, and every state gives name to one. That of Pennsylvania is the largest; in fact I never heard of more than that and the New Jersey Avenue, except some houses uniformly built, in one of which lives Mr. Jefferson's printer, John Harrison Smith, a few more of inferior note, with some public-houses, and here and there a little *grog-shop*, this boasted avenue is as much a wilderness as Kentucky, with this disadvantage, that the soil is good for nothing. Some half-starved cattle browsing among the bushes, present a melancholy spectacle to a stranger, whose expectation has been wound up by the illusive description of speculative writers. So very thinly is the city peopled, and so little is it frequented, that quails and other birds are constantly shot within a hundred yards of the Capitol, and even during the sitting of the houses of congress. . . .

Neither park, nor mall, neither churches, theatres, nor colleges, could I discover so lately as the summer of 1806. A small place has indeed been erected since in the Pennsylvania Avenue, called a theatre, in which Mr. Green and the Virginia company of comedians were nearly starved the only season it was occupied, and were obliged to go off to Richmond during the very height of the sitting of congress. Public offices on each side of the president's house, uniformly built of brick, may also, perhaps, have been built subsequent to that period. That great man who planned the city, and after whom it is named, certainly entertained the hopes that it would at some future period equal ancient Rome in splendor and magnificence. Among the regulations for building were these—that the houses

should be of brick or stone—the walls to be at least thirty feet high, and to be built parallel to the line of the street.

The president's house is certainly a neat but plain piece of architecture, built of hewn stone, said to be of a better quality than Portland stone, as it will cut like marble, and resist the change of the seasons in a superior degree. Only part of it is furnished; the whole salary of the president would be inadequate to the expence of completing it in a style of suitable elegance. Rooms are fitted up for himself, an audience chamber, and apartments for Mr. Thomas Man Randolph, and Mr. Epps, and their respective families, who married two of his daughters, and are members of the house of representatives.

The ground around it, instead of being laid out in a suitable style, remains in its ancient rude state, so that, in a dark night, instead of finding your way to the house, you may, perchance, fall into a pit, or stumble over a heap of rubbish. The fence round the house is of the meanest sort; a common post and rail enclosure. This parsimony destroys every sentiment of pleasure that arises in the mind, in viewing the residence of the president of a nation, and is a disgrace to the country.

Though the permanent seat of government has been fixed at Washington, its progress has been proved to be less rapid than any other new settlement supported only by trade. The stimulus held out by the presence of congress has proved artificial and unnatural. After enumerating the public buildings, the private dwelling-houses of the officers of government, the accommodations set apart for the members of the legislature, and the temporary tenements of those dependent on them, the remainder of this boasted city is a mere wilderness of wood and stunted shrubs, the occupants of barren land. Strangers after viewing the offices of state, are apt to enquire for the city, while they are in its very centre.

One of the greatest evils of a republican form of government is a loss of that subordination in society which is essentially necessary to render a country agreeable to foreigners. To the well-informed, this defect is irksome, and no remedy for it can be applied. The meaning of liberty and equality, in the opinion of the vulgar, consists in impudent freedom, and uncontrolled licentiousness; while boys assume the airs of full-grown coxcombs. This is not to be wondered at, where most parents make it a principle never to check those ungovernable passions which are born with us, or to correct the growing vices of their children. Often have I, with horror, seen boys, whose dress indicated wealthy parents, intoxicated, shouting and swearing in the public streets. In the use of that stupefying weed, tobacco, apeing their fathers, they smoke segars to so immoderate a degree, that sickness, and even death, has been the consequence. . . .

Literature is yet at a low ebb in the United States. During my stay in Philadelphia, where the small portion of genius is chiefly to be found, I heard of very few literary characters, superior to the political scribblers of the day. Joseph Dennie, and Mr. Brown, of that city, with Mr. Fessenden, of Boston, are men of genius. The former is editor of a literary periodical paper, called "The Port-Folio," a publication which would do credit to the most polished nation in Europe. Its contemporary prints make politics their principal object; the Port-Folio embraces the belles lettres, and cultivates the arts and sciences. The editor, when he touches upon the state of his country, speaks in the cause of federalism; and, from his great abilities, he is consequently obnoxious to the ruling party. The government had long endeavored to control the federal prints, and had already ineffectually prosecuted some of the editors. At length, they denounced Mr. Dennie, who was indicted and tried at Philadelphia, for publishing the following political strictures:—

"A democracy is scarcely tolerable at any period of national history. Its omens are always sinister, and its powers are unpropitious. With all the lights of experience blazing before our eyes, it is impossible not to discern the futility of this form of government. It was weak and wicked in Athens. It was bad in Sparta, and worse in Rome. It has been tried in France, and has terminated in despotism. It was tried in England, and rejected with the utmost loathing and abhorrence. It is on its trial here, and the issue will be civil war, desolation, and anarchy. No wise man but discerns its imperfections; no good man but shudders at its miseries; no honest man but proclaims its fraud; and no brave man but draws his sword against its force. The institution of a scheme of polity, so radically contemptible and vicious, is a memorable example of what the villainy of some men can devise, the folly of others receive, and both establish, in despite of reason, reflection, and sensation."

This paragraph was copied into the federal papers throughout the union, and it became extremely obnoxious to the democratic party. The trial greatly interested all ranks; but, after much time being consumed, and much party spirit evinced by the contending advocates, Mr. Dennie was acquitted. He gives a sketch of the trial in the Port-Folio, and thus concludes:— "The causes of this prosecution, the spirit of the times, and the genius of the commonwealth, must be obvious to every observer. The editor inscribes *vici* on the white shield of his innocence, but is wholly incapable of vaunting at the victory!" . . .

Printing and bookselling have of late years been extended to the most remote parts of the country. Several newspapers are printed in Kentucky; and almost every town of more than a few score houses, in every state, has a printing-office, from which the news is disseminated. There is no tax whatever on the press, and consequently every owner of one can print a newspaper with little risk, among a people who are all politicians. These sheets are the utmost limits of literature in most country towns, and they furnish ample food for disputation. Several hundred different newspapers are daily distributed by the public mail, in all parts, to subscribers, at the small charge of one or two cents, at most, for postage; but printers exchange their papers with each other, by that mode, free of any charge. I have often seen a printer receive as many newspapers by one mail, as would fill the room of several hundred letters.

DOCUMENT 2

Thomas Jefferson, "First Inaugural Address" (1801)

At the strike of noon on March 4, 1801, Thomas Jefferson began walking down New Jersey Avenue toward the Capitol, where he was to be sworn in as the third president of the United States. As befitted a leader of the Republican Party, the occasion was simple. He carried his Inaugural Address, a document that had gone through several drafts and represented Jefferson's most polished prose. Although he delivered the speech in an inaudible mumble, Jefferson produced a document of enduring significance. As a biographer explained, "The genius of the address lay in its seemingly artless elevation of the Republican creed to a creed of Americanism."

Friends and Fellow Citizens:

Called upon to undertake the duties of the first executive office of our country, I avail myself of the presence of that portion of my fellow citizens which is here assembled to express my grateful thanks for the favor with which they have been pleased to look toward me, to declare a sincere consciousness that the task is above my talents, and that I approach it with those anxious and awful presentiments which the greatness of the charge and the weakness of my powers so justly inspire. A rising nation, spread over a wide and fruitful land, traversing all the seas with the rich productions of their industry, engaged in commerce with nations who feel power and forget right, advancing rapidly to destinies beyond the reach of mortal eye—when I contemplate these transcendent objects and see the honor, the happiness, and the hopes of this beloved country committed to the issue and the auspices of this day, I shrink from the contemplation and humble myself before the magnitude of the undertaking. Utterly indeed should I despair did not the presence of many whom I here see remind me that in the other high authorities provided by our Constitution I shall find resources of wisdom, of virtue, and of zeal on which to rely under all difficulties. To you then, gentlemen, who are charged with the sovereign functions of legislation, and to those associated with you, I look

with encouragement for that guidance and support which may enable us to steer with safety the vessel in which we are all embarked amidst the conflicting elements of a troubled world.

During the contest of opinion through which we have passed, the animation of discussions and of exertions has sometimes worn an aspect which might impose on strangers unused to think freely and to speak and to write what they think. But this being now decided by the voice of the nation, enounced according to the rules of the Constitution, all will of course arrange themselves under the will of the law and unite in common efforts for the common good. All, too, will bear in mind this sacred principle that, though the will of the majority is in all cases to prevail, that will, to be rightful, must be reasonable; that the minority possess their equal rights, which equal laws must protect and to violate which would be oppression. Let us then, fellow citizens, unite with one heart and one mind; let us restore to social intercourse that harmony and affection without which liberty, and even life itself, are but dreary things. And let us reflect that, having banished from our land that religious intolerance under which mankind so long bled and suffered, we have yet gained little if we countenance a political intolerance as despotic, as wicked, and capable of as bitter and bloody persecutions. During the throes and

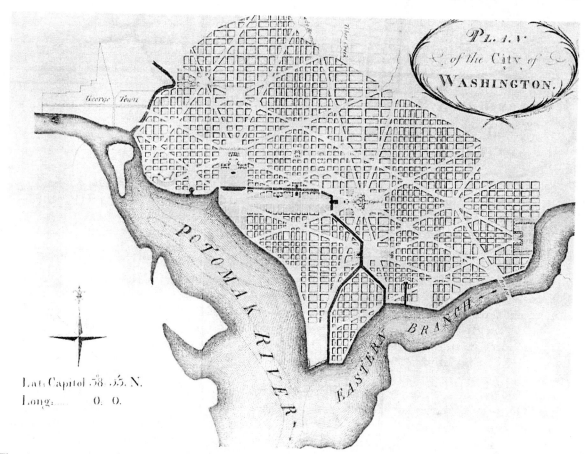

This plan by Pierre L'Enfant for the new capital of Washington was first published in 1792. The government was officially transferred to the District of Columbia in 1800.

convulsions of the ancient world, during the agonizing spasms of infuriated man, seeking through blood and slaughter his long-lost liberty, it was not wonderful that the agitation of the billows should reach even this distant and peaceful shore, that this should be more felt and feared by some and less by others, and should divide opinions as to measures of safety.

But every difference of opinion is not a difference of principle. We have called by different names brethren of the same principle. We are all republicans; we are all federalists. If there be any among us who would wish to dissolve this Union or to change its republican form, let them stand undisturbed as monuments of the safety with which error of opinion may be tolerated, where reason is left free to combat it. I know, indeed, that some honest men fear that a republican government cannot be strong; that this government is not strong enough. But would the honest patriot, in the full tide of successful experiment, abandon a government which has so far kept us free and firm, on the theoretic and visionary fear that this government, the world's best hope, may by possibility want energy to preserve itself? I trust not. I believe this, on the contrary, the strongest government on earth. I believe it the only one where every man, at the call of the law, would fly to the standard of the law and would meet invasions of the public order as his own personal concern. Sometimes it is said that man cannot be trusted with the government of himself. Can he then be trusted with the government of others? Or have we found angels, in the form of kings, to govern him? Let history answer this question.

Let us then, with courage and confidence, pursue our own federal and republican principles, our attachment to Union and representative government. Kindly separated by nature and a wide ocean from the exterminating havoc of one quarter of the globe; too high-minded to endure the degradations of the others; possessing a chosen country, with room enough for our descendants to the thousandth and thousandth generation; entertaining a due sense of our equal right to the use of our own faculties, to the acquisitions of our own industry, to honor and confidence from our fellow citizens, resulting not from birth but from our actions and their sense of them; enlightened by a benign religion, professed indeed and practiced in various forms, yet all of them including honesty, truth, temperance, gratitude, and the love of man; acknowledging and adoring an overruling Providence which, by all its dispensations, proves that It delights in the happiness of man here and his greater happiness hereafter; with all these blessings, what more is necessary to make us a happy and a prosperous people? Still one thing more, fellow citizens—a wise and frugal government which shall restrain men from injuring one another, shall leave them otherwise free to regulate their own pursuits of industry and improvement, and shall not take from the mouth of labor the bread it has earned. This is the sum of good government, and this is necessary to close the circle of our felicities.

About to enter, fellow citizens, on the exercise of duties which comprehend everything dear and valuable to you, it is proper you should understand what I deem the essential principles of our government and, consequently, those which ought to shape its administration. I will compress them within the narrowest compass they will bear, stating the gen-

eral principle but not all its limitations: Equal and exact justice to all men, of whatever state or persuasion, religious or political; peace, commerce, and honest friendship with all nations, entangling alliances with none; the support of the State governments in all their rights, as the most competent administrations for our domestic concerns and the surest bulwarks against anti-republican tendencies; the preservation of the general government in its whole constitutional vigor, as the sheet anchor of our peace at home and safety abroad; a jealous care of the right of election by the people, a mild and safe corrective of abuses which are lopped by the sword of revolution where peaceable remedies are unprovided; absolute acquiescence in the decisions of the majority, the vital principle of republics from which there is no appeal but to force, the vital principle and immediate parent of despotism; a well-disciplined militia, our best reliance in peace and for the first moments of war till regulars may relieve them; the supremacy of the civil over the military authority; economy in the public expense, that labor may be lightly burdened; the honest payment of our debts and sacred preservation of the public faith; encouragement of agriculture, and of commerce as its handmaid; the diffusion of information, and arraignment of all abuses at the bar of the public person, under the protection of the habeas corpus; and trial by juries, impartially selected. These principles form the bright constellation which has gone before us and guided our steps through an age of revolution and reformation. The wisdom of our sages and blood of our heroes have been devoted to their attainment; they should be the creed of our political faith, the text of civic instruction, the touchstone by which to try the services of those we trust; and should we wander from them in moments of error or of alarm, let us hasten to retrace our steps and to regain the road which alone leads to peace, liberty, and safety.

I repair then, fellow citizens, to the post you have assigned me. With experience enough in subordinate offices to have seen the difficulties of this, the greatest of all, I have learned to expect that it will rarely fall to the lot of imperfect man to retire from this station with the reputation and the favor which bring him into it. Without pretensions to that high confidence you reposed in our first and great revolutionary character, whose pre-eminent services had entitled him to the first place in his country's love and destined for him the fairest page in the volume of faithful history, I ask so much confidence only as may give firmness and effect to the legal administration of your affairs. I shall often be thought wrong by those whose positions will not command a view of the whole ground. I ask your indulgence for my own errors, which will never be intentional, and your support against the errors of others who may condemn what they would not if seen in all its parts. The approbation implied by your suffrage is a great consolation to me for the past, and my future solicitude will be to retain the good opinion of those who have bestowed it in advance, to conciliate that of others by doing them all the good in my power, and to be instrumental to the happiness and freedom of all.

Relying then on the patronage of your good will, I advance with obedience to the work, ready to retire from it whenever you become sensible how much better choice it is in your power to make. And may that Infinite Power which rules the destinies of the universe lead our councils to what is best and give them a favorable issue for your peace and prosperity.

DOCUMENT 3

Margaret Bayard Smith Meets Thomas Jefferson (1801)

In these two documents—one a letter, the other a selection from her reminiscences—Margaret Bayard Smith captures the excitement of Jefferson's first days in office. She was a young woman recently married to a man engaged by Jefferson to edit a new Republican newspaper. Her father had been a prominent Federalist in Philadelphia, however, and he seems to have filled her mind with negative images of the third president. Jefferson proved her father wrong, and Margaret and her husband became leading figures in Washington social life.

Margaret Bayard Smith to Miss Susan B. Smith (1801)

Let me write to you my dear Susan, e're that glow of enthusiasm has fled, which now animates my feelings; let me congratulate not only you, but all my fellow citizens, on an event which will have so auspicious an influence on their political welfare. I have this morning witnessed one of the most interesting scenes, a free people can ever witness. The changes of administration, which in every government and in every age have most generally been epochs of confusion, villainy and bloodshed, in this our happy country take place without any species of distraction, or disorder. This day, has one of the most amiable and worthy men taken that seat to which he was called by the voice of his country. I cannot describe the agitation I felt, while I looked around on the various multitude and while I listened to an address, containing principles the most correct, sentiments the most liberal, and wishes the most benevolent, conveyed in the most appropriate and elegant language and in a manner mild as it was firm. If doubts of the integrity and talents of Mr. Jefferson ever existed in the minds of any one, methinks this address must forever eradicate them. The Senate chamber was so crowded that I believe not another creature could enter. On one side of the house the Senate sat, the other was resigned by the representatives to the ladies. The roof is arched, the room half circle, every inch of ground was occupied. It has been conjectured by several gentlemen whom I've asked, that there was near a thousand persons within the walls. The speech was delivered in so low a tone that few heard it. Mr. Jefferson had given your Brother a copy early in the morning, so that on coming out of the house, the paper was distributed immediately. Since then there has been a constant succession of persons coming for the papers.

Margaret Bayard Smith, "Reminiscences" (1800)

"And is this," said I, after my first interview with Mr. Jefferson, "the violent democrat, the vulgar demagogue, the bold atheist and profligate man I have so often heard denounced by the federalists? Can this man so meek and mild, yet dignified in his manners, with a voice so soft and low, with a countenance so benignant and intelligent, can he be that daring leader of a fraction, that disturber of the peace, that enemy of all rank and order?" Mr. Smith, indeed, (himself a democrat) had given me a very different description of this celebrated individual; but his favourable opinion I attributed in a great measure to his political feelings, which led him zealously to support and exalt the party to which he belonged, especially its popular and almost idolized leader. Thus the virulence of party-spirit was somewhat neutralized, nay, I even entertained towards him the most kindly dispositions, knowing him to be not only politically but personally friendly to my husband; yet I did believe that he was an ambitious

and violent demagogue, coarse and vulgar in his manners, awkward and rude in his appearance, for such had the public journals and private conversations of the federal party represented him to be.

In December, 1800, a few days after Congress had for the first time met in our new Metropolis, I was one morning sitting alone in the parlour, when the servant opened the door and showed in a gentleman who wished to see my husband. The usual frankness and care with which I met strangers, were somewhat checked by the dignified and reserved air of the present visitor; but the chilled feeling was only momentary, for after taking the chair I offered him in a free and easy manner, and carelessly throwing his arm on the table near which he sat, he turned towards me a countenance beaming with an expression of benevolence and with a manner and voice almost femininely soft and gentle, entered into conversation on the commonplace topics of the day, from which, before I was conscious of it, he had drawn me into observations of a more personal and interesting nature. I know not how it was, but there was something in his manner, his countenance and voice that at once unlocked my heart, and in answer to his casual enquiries concerning our situation in our *new home*, as he called it, I found myself frankly telling him what I liked or disliked in our present circumstances and abode. I knew now who he was, but the interest with which he listened to my artless details, induced the idea he was some intimate acquaintance or friend of Mr. Smith's and put me perfectly at my ease; in truth so kind and conciliating were his looks and manners that I forgot he was not a friend of my own, until on the opening of the door, Mr. Smith entered and introduced the stranger to me as *Mr. Jefferson.*

I felt my cheeks burn and my heart throb, and not a word more could I speak while he remained. Nay, such was my embarrassment I could scarcely listen to the conversation carried on between him and my husband. For several years he had been to me an object of peculiar interest. In fact my destiny, for on his success in the pending presidential election, or rather the success of the democratic party, (their interests were identical) my condition in life, my union with the man I loved, depended. In addition to this personal interest, I had long participated in my husband's political sentiments and anxieties, and looked upon Mr. Jefferson as the corner stone on which the edifice of republican liberty was to rest, looked upon him as the champion of human rights, the reformer of abuses, the head of the republican party, which must rise or fall with him, and on the triumph of the republican party I devoutly believed the security and welfare of my country depended. Notwithstanding those exalted views of Mr. Jefferson as a political character; and ardently eager as I was for his success, I retained my previously conceived ideas of the coarseness and vulgarity of his appearance and manners and was therefore equally awed and surprised, on discovering the stranger whose deportment was so dignified and gentlemanly, whose language was so refined, whose voice was so gentle, whose countenance was so benignant, to be no other than Thomas Jefferson. How instantaneously were all these preconceived prejudices dissipated, and in proportion to their strength, was the reaction that took place in my opinions and sentiments. I felt that I had been the victim of prejudice, that I had been unjust. The revolution of feeling was complete and from that moment my heart warmed to him with the most affectionate interest and I implicitly believed all that his friends and my husband believed and which the after experience of many years confirmed. Yes, not only was he great, but a truly good man!

DOCUMENT 4

"*Memoirs of a Monticello Slave, as Dictated to Charles Campbell by Isaac*" (1847)

Recalling Jefferson in 1847, his former slave Isaac offers in this document a private perspective on the man at the time of his ascendance to the presidency. Isaac portrays Jefferson in a warm, respectful light while detailing the sumptuous life of Monticello, his travels with the new president, and his own start in metalsmithing, a vocation encouraged by his master and from which he was allowed to gain a portion of the profits. Isaac lived into his seventies and continued to ply his trade in Petersburg, Virginia, until his death in 1849.

Old Master was never seen to come out before breakfast—about 8 o'clock. If it was warm weather he wouldn't ride out till evening: studied upstairs till bell ring for dinner. When writing he had a copyin' machine. While he was a-writin' he wouldn't suffer nobody to come in his room. Had a dumb-waiter; when he wanted anything he had nothin' to do but turn a crank and the dumb-waiter would bring him water or fruit on a plate or anything he wanted. Old Master had abundance of books; sometimes would have twenty of 'em down on the floor at once—read fust one, then tother. Isaac has often wondered how Old Master came to have such a mighty head; read so many of them books; and when they go to him to ax him anything, he go right straight to the book and tell you all about it. He talked French and Italian. Madzay talked with him; his place was called Colle. General Redhazel (Riedesel) stayed there. He (Mazzei) lived at Monticello with Old Master some time. Didiot, a Frenchman, married his daughter Peggy, a heavy chunky looking woman—mighty handsome. She had a daughter Frances and a son Francis; called the daughter Franky. Mazzei brought to Monticello Antonine, Jovanini, Francis, Modena, and Belligrini, all gardeners. My Old Master's garden was monstrous large: two rows of palings, all 'round ten feet high.

Mr. Jefferson had a clock in his kitchen at Monticello; never went into the kitchen except to wind up the clock. He never would have less than eight covers at dinner if nobody at table but himself. Had from eight to thirty-two covers for dinner. Plenty of wine, best old Antigua rum and cider; very fond of wine and water. Isaac never heard of his being disguised in drink. He kept three fiddles; played in the afternoons and sometimes arter supper. This was in his early time. When he begin to git so old, he didn't play. Kept a spinnet made mostly in shape of a harpsichord; his daughter played on it. Mr. Fauble, a Frenchman that lived at Mr. Walker's, a music man, used to come to Monticello and tune it. There was a *fortepiano* and a guitar there. Never seed anybody play on them but the French people. Isaac never could git acquainted with them; could hardly larn their names. Mr. Jefferson always singing when ridin' or walkin'; hardly see him anywhar outdoors but what he was a-singin'. Had a fine clear voice, sung minnits (minuets) and sich; fiddled in the parlor. Old Master very kind to servants.

The fust year Mr. Jefferson was elected President, he took Isaac on to Philadelphia. He was then about fifteen years old; traveled on horseback in company with a Frenchman named Joseph Rattiff and Jim Hemings, a body servant. Fust day's journey they went from Monticello to old Nat Gordon's, on the Fredericksburg road, next day to Fredericksburg, then to Georgetown, crossed the Potomac there, and so to Philadelphia—eight days a-goin'. Had two ponies and Mr. Jefferson's tother riding horse Odin. Mr. Jefferson went in the phaeton. Bob Hemings drove; changed horses on the road. When they got to Philadelphia, Isaac stayed three days at Mr. Jefferson's house. Then he was bound prentice to one Bringhouse, a tinner; he lived in the direction of the Waterworks. Isaac remembers seeing the image of a woman thar holding a goose in her hand—the water spouting out of the goose's mouth. This was the head of Market Street. Bringhouse was a short, mighty small, neat-made; treated Isaac very well. Went thar to larn the tinner's trade. Fust week larnt to cut out and sodder; make little pepper boxes and graters and sich, out of scraps of tin, so as not to waste any till he had larnt. Then to making cups. Every Sunday Isaac would go to the President's house—large brick house, many windows; same house Ginral Washington lived in before when he was President. Old Master used to talk to me mighty free and ax me, "How you come on Isaac, larning de tin business?" As soon as he could make cups pretty well, he carred three or four to show him. Isaac made four dozen pint cups a day and larnt to tin copper and sheets (sheet iron)—make 'em tin. He lived four years with Old Bringhouse. One time Mr. Jefferson sent to Bringhouse to tin his copper kittles and pans for kitchen use; Bringhouse sent Isaac and another prentice thar—a white boy named Charles; can't think of his other name. Isaac was the only black boy in Bringhouse's shop. When Isaac carred the cups to his Old Master to show him, he was mightily pleased. Said, "Isaac you are larnin mighty fast; I bleeve I must send you back to Vaginny to car on the tin business. You is growin too big; no use for you to stay here no longer."

DOCUMENT 5

Constitutionality of the Louisiana Purchase (1803)

Like many Americans, Jefferson believed that the United States would eventually acquire substantial western territories. The opportunity came more swiftly than anyone anticipated. Spain transferred Louisiana to France in 1801, and after a French army dispatched to the Caribbean succumbed to tropical disease, Napoleon tired of the whole business. In his words, "Damn sugar, damn coffee, damn colonies.... I renounce Louisiana." Napoleon's decision suddenly made the dream of westward expansion a real possibility. However welcome the opportunity may have been, the Louisiana Purchase raised serious problems for the president. As the correspondence in this section reveals, Republicans eager for empire had to square territorial ambitions with the letter of the Constitution.

Thomas Jefferson to John C. Breckinridge

Monticello, Aug. 12, 1803

DEAR SIR,—The enclosed letter, tho' directed to you, was intended to me also, and was left open with a request, that when perused, I would forward it to you. It gives me occasion to write a word to you on the subject of Louisiana, which being a new one, an interchange of sentiments may produce correct ideas before we are to act on them.

Our information as to the country is very incompleat; we have taken measures to obtain it in full as to the settled part, which I hope to receive in time for Congress. The boundaries, which I deem not admitting question, are the high lands on the western side of the Mississippi enclosing all it's waters, the Missouri of course, and terminating in the line drawn from the northwestern point of the Lake of the Woods to the nearest source of the Missipi, as lately settled between Gr Britain and the U S. We have some claims to extend on the sea coast Westwardly to the Rio Norte or Bravo, and better, to go Eastwardly to the Rio Perdido, between Mobile & Pensacola, the antient boundary of Louisiana. These claims will be a subject of negociation with

Spain, and if, as soon as she is at war, we push them strongly with one hand, holding out a price in the other, we shall certainly obtain the Floridas, and all in good time. In the meanwhile, without waiting for permission, we shall enter into the exercise of the natural right we have always insisted on with Spain, to wit, that of a nation holding the upper part of streams, having a right of innocent passage thro' them to the ocean. We shall prepare her to see us practise on this, & she will not oppose it by force.

Objections are raising to the Eastward against the vast extent of our boundaries, and propositions are made to exchange Louisiana, or a part of it, for the Floridas. But, as I have said, we shall get the Floridas without, and I would not give one inch of the waters of the Mississippi to any nation, because I see in a light very important to our peace the exclusive right to it's navigation, & the admission of no nation into it, but as into the Potomak or Delaware, with our consent & under our police. These federalists see in this acquisition the formation of a new confederacy, embracing all the waters of the Missipi, on both sides of it, and a separation of it's Eastern waters from us. These combinations depend on so many circumstances which we cannot foresee, that I place little reliance on them. We have seldom

No one knew the exact size of the Louisiana Territory when Congress purchased it from Napoleon for $15 million. President Jefferson sent Meriwether Lewis and William Clark—depicted here with Native Americans of the Missouri Valley—to survey the peoples and resources of the West.

seen neighborhood produce affection among nations. The reverse is almost the universal truth. Besides, if it should become the great interest of those nations to separate from this, if their happiness should depend on it so strongly as to induce them to go through that convulsion, why should the Atlantic States dread it? But especially why should we, their present inhabitants, take side in such a question? When I view the Atlantic States, procuring for those on the Eastern waters of the Missipi friendly instead of hostile neighbors of it's Western waters, I do not view it as an Englishman would the procuring future blessing for the French nation, with whom he has no relations of blood or affection. The future inhabitants of the Atlantic & Missipi States will be our sons. We leave them in distinct but bordering establishments. We think we see their happiness in their union, & we wish it. Events may prove it otherwise; and if they see their interest in

separation, why should we take side with our Atlantic rather than our Missipi descendants? It is the elder and the younger son differing. God bless them both, & keep them in union, if it be for their good, but separate them, if it be better. The inhabited part of Louisiana, from Point Coupée to the sea, will of course be immediately a territorial government, and soon a State. But above that, the best use we can make of the country for some time, will be to give establishments in it to the Indians on the East side of the Missipi, in exchange for their present country, and open land offices in the last, & thus make this acquisition the means of filling up the Eastern side, instead of drawing off it's population. When we shall be full on this side, we may lay off a range of States on the Western bank from the head to the mouth, & so, range after range, advancing compactly as we multiply.

This treaty must of course be laid before both

Houses, because both have important functions to exercise respecting it. They, I presume, will see their duty to their country in ratifying & paying for it, so as to secure a good which would otherwise probably be never again in their power. But I suppose they must then appeal to *the nation* for an additional article to the Constitution, approving & confirming an act which the nation had not previously authorized. The constitution has made no provision for our holding foreign territory, still less for incorporating foreign nations into our Union. The Executive in seizing the fugitive occurrence which so much advances the good of their country, have done an act beyond the Constitution. The Legislature in casting behind them metaphysical subtleties, and risking themselves like faithful servants, must ratify & pay for it, and throw themselves on their country for doing for them unauthorized what we know they would have done for themselves had they been in a situation to do it. It is the case of a guardian, investing the money of his ward in purchasing an important adjacent territory; & saying to him when of age, I did this for your good; I pretend to no right to bind you: you may disavow me, and I must get out of the scrape as I can: I thought it my duty to risk myself for you. But we shall not be disavowed by the nation, and their act of indemnity will confirm & not weaken the Constitution, by more strongly marking out its lines.

We have nothing later from Europe than the public papers give. I hope yourself and all the Western members will make a sacred point of being at the first day of the meeting of Congress; for *vestra res agitur.*

Accept my affectionate salutations & assurances of esteem & respect.

Thomas Jefferson to Wilson Cary Nicholas

Monticello, Sep. 7, 1803
DEAR SIR,—Your favor of the 3d was delivered me at court; but we were much disappointed at not seeing you here, Mr. Madison & the Gov. being here at the time. I enclose you a letter from Monroe on the subject of the late treaty. You will observe a hint in it, to do without delay what we are bound to do. There is reason, in the opinion of our ministers, to believe, that if the thing were to do over again, it could not be obtained, & that if we give the least opening, they will declare the treaty void. A warning amounting to that has been given to them, & an unusual kind of letter written by their minister to our Secretary of State, direct. Whatever Congress shall think it necessary to do, should be done with as little debate as possible, & particularly so far as respects the constitutional difficulty. I am aware of the force of the observations you make on the power given by the Constn to Congress, to admit new States into the Union, without restraining the subject to the territory then constituting the U S. But when I consider that the limits of the U S are precisely fixed by the treaty of 1783, that the Constitution expressly declares itself to be made for the U S, I cannot help believing the intention was to permit Congress to admit into the Union new States, which should be formed out of the territory for which, & under whose authority alone, they were then acting. I do not believe it was meant that they might receive England, Ireland, Holland, &c. into it, which would be the case on your construction. When an instrument admits two constructions, the one safe, the other dangerous, the one precise, the other indefinite, I prefer that which is safe & precise. I had rather ask an enlargement of power from the nation, where it is found necessary, than to assume it by a construction which would make our powers boundless. Our peculiar security is in possession of a written Constitution. Let us not make it a blank paper by construction. I say the same as to the opinion of those who consider the grant of the treaty making power as boundless. If it is, then we have no Constitution. If it has bounds, they can be no others than the definitions of the power which that instrument gives. It specifies & delineates the operations permitted to the federal government, and gives all the powers necessary to carry these into execution. Whatever of these enumerated objects is proper for a law, Congress may make the law;

whatever is proper to be executed by way of a treaty, the President & Senate may enter into the treaty; whatever is to be done by a judicial sentence, the judges may pass the sentence. Nothing is more likely than that their enumeration of powers is defective. This is the ordinary case of all human works. Let us go on then perfecting it, by adding, by way of amendment to the Constitution, those powers which time & trial show are still wanting. But it has been taken too much for granted, that by this rigorous construction the treaty power would be reduced to nothing. I had occasion once to examine its effect on the French treaty, made by the old Congress, & found that out of thirty odd articles which that contained, there were one, two, or three only which could not now be stipulated under our present Constitution. I confess, then, I think it important, in the present case, to set an example against broad construction, by appealing for new power to the people. If, however, our friends shall think differently, certainly I shall acquiesce with satisfaction; confiding, that the good sense of our country will correct the evil of construction when it shall produce ill effects.

No apologies for writing or speaking to me freely are necessary. On the contrary, nothing my friends can do is so dear to me, & proves to me their friendship so clearly, as the information they give me of their sentiments & those of others on interesting points where I am to act, and where information & warning is so essential to excite in me that due reflection which ought to precede action. I leave this about the 21st, and shall hope the District Court will give me an opportunity of seeing you.

Accept my affectionate salutations, & assurances of cordial esteem & respect.

Thomas Paine to John C. Breckinridge

I know little and can learn but little of the extent and present population of Louisiana. After the cession be completed and the territory annexed to the United States it will, I suppose, be formed into states, one, at least, to begin with. The people, as I have said, are new to us and we to them and a great deal will depend on a right beginning. As they have been transferred backward and forward several times from one European Government to another it is natural to conclude they have no fixed prejudices with respect to foreign attachments, and this puts them in a fit disposition for their new condition. The established religion is roman; but in what state it is as to exterior ceremonies (such as processions and celebrations), I know not. Had the cession to France continued with her, religion I suppose would have been put on the same footing as it is in that country, and there no ceremonial of religion can appear on the streets or highways; and the same regulation is particularly necessary now or there will soon be quarrels and tumults between the old settlers and the new. The Yankees will not move out of the road for a little wooden Jesus stuck on a stick and carried in procession nor kneel in the dirt to a wooden Virgin Mary. As we do not govern the territory as provinces but incorporated as states, religion there must be on the same footing it is here, and Catholics have the same rights as Catholics have with us and no others. As to political condition the Idea proper to be held out is, that we have neither conquered them, nor bought them, but formed a Union with them and they become in consequence of that union a part of the national sovereignty.

The present Inhabitants and their descendants will be a majority for some time, but new emigrations from the old states and from Europe, and intermarriages, will soon change the first face of things, and it is necessary to have this in mind when the first measures shall be taken. Everything done as an expedient grows worse every day, for in proportion as the mind grows up to the full standard of sight it disclaims the expedient. America had nearly been ruined by expedients in the first stages of the revolution, and perhaps would have been so, had not *Common Sense* broken the charm and the Declaration of Independence sent it into banishment.

DOCUMENT 6

Black Hawk, "Life of Black Hawk" (1833)

In 1832, Black Hawk (1767–1838), whose Native American name was Ma-ka-tai-me-she-kia-kiak, led a band of Sauk and Fox Indians in a fight to reclaim lands in Illinois and Wisconsin that the Indians believed Americans had stolen in 1804. Desperate and hungry, they were no match for the U. S. Army, which hunted down and killed most of Black Hawk's group at The Battle of Bad Axe in western Wisconsin. In this document, Black Hawk, dictating his autobiography through a federal interpreter, remembers the coming of the "American father" to the midwestern prairie and the land swindle that Black Hawk called "the origin of all our difficulties."

We generally paid a visit to St. Louis every summer; but, in consequence of the protracted war in which we had been engaged, I had not been there for some years. Our difficulties having all been settled, I concluded to take a small party, that summer, and go down to see our Spanish father. We went—and on our arrival, put up our lodges where the market-house now stands. After painting and dressing, we called to see our Spanish father, and were well received. He gave us a variety of presents, and plenty of provisions. We danced through the town as usual, and its inhabitants all seemed to be well pleased. They appeared to us like brothers—and always gave us good advice.

On my next, and *last*, visit to my Spanish father, I discovered, on landing, that all was not right: every countenance seemed sad and gloomy! I inquired the cause, and was informed that the Americans were coming to take possession of the town and country!—and that we should then lose our Spanish father! This news made myself and band sad—because we had always heard bad accounts of the Americans from Indians who had lived near them!—and we were sorry to lose our Spanish father, who had always treated us with great friendship.

A few days afterwards, the Americans arrived. I took my band, and went to take leave, for the last time, of our father. The Americans came to see him also. Seeing them approach, we passed out at one door, as they entered another—and immediately started, in canoes, for our village on Rock river—not liking the change any more than our friends appeared to, at St. Louis.

On arriving at our village, we gave the news, that strange people had taken St. Louis—and that we should never see our Spanish father again! This information made all our people sorry!

Some time afterwards, a boat came up the river, with a young American chief, and a small party of soldiers. We heard of them, (by runners,) soon after he had passed Salt river. Some of our young braves watched him every day, to see what sort of people he had on board! The boat, at length, arrived at Rock river, and the young chief came on shore with his interpreter—made a speech, and gave us some presents! We, in return, presented him with meat, and such provisions as we could spare.

We were all well pleased with the speech of the young chief. He gave us good advice; said our American father would treat us well. He presented us an American flag, which was hoisted. He then requested us to pull down our *British flags*—and give him our *British medals*—promising to send us others on his return to St. Louis. This we declined, as we wished to have *two Fathers!*

When the young chief started, we sent runners to the Fox village, some miles distant, to direct them to treat him well as he passed—which they did. He went to the head of the Mississippi, and then returned to St. Louis. We did not see any Americans again for some time,—being supplied with goods by British traders.

We were fortunate in not giving up our medals—for we learned afterwards, from our traders, that the chiefs high up on the Mississippi, who gave theirs, never received any in exchange for them. But the fault was not with the young American chief. He was a good man, and a great brave—and died in his country's service.

Some moons after this young chief descended the Mississippi, one of our people killed an American—and was confined, in the prison at St. Louis, for the offence. We held a council at our village to see what could be done for him,—which determined that Quàsh-quà-me, Pà-she-pa-ho, Oú-che-quà-ka, and Hà-she-quar-hi-qua, should go down to St. Louis, see our American father, and do all they could to have our friend released: by paying for the person killed—thus covering the blood, and satisfying the relations of the man murdered! This being the only means with us of saving a person who had killed another—and we *then* thought it was the same way with the whites!

The party started with the good wishes of the whole nation—hoping they would accomplish the object of their mission. The relatives of the prisoner blacked their faces, and fasted—hoping the Great Spirit would take pity on them, and return the hus-

band and father to his wife and children.

Quàsh-quà-me and party remained a long time absent. They at length returned, and encamped a short distance below the village—but did not come up that day—nor did any person approach their camp! They appeared to be dressed in *fine coats*, and had *medals!* From these circumstances, we were in hopes that they had brought good news. Early the next morning, the Council Lodge was crowded—Quàsh-quà-me and party came up, and gave us the following account of their mission:

"On their arrival at St. Louis, they met their American father, and explained to him their business, and urged the release of their friend. The American chief told them he wanted land—and they had agreed to give him some on the west side of the Mississippi, and some on the Illinois side opposite the Jeffreon. When the business was all arranged, they expected to have their friend released to come home with them. But about the time they were ready to start, their friend was let out of prison, who ran a short distance, and was *shot dead!* This is all they could recollect of what was said and done. They had been drunk the greater part of the time they were in St. Louis."

This is all myself or nation knew of the treaty of 1804. It has been explained to me since. I find, by that treaty, all our country, east of the Mississippi, and south of the Jeffreon, was ceded to the United States for *one thousand dollars* a year! I will leave it to the people of the United States to say, whether our nation was properly represented in this treaty? or whether we received a fair compensation for the extent of country ceded by those *four* individuals? I could say much about this treaty, but I will not, at this time. It has been the origin of all our difficulties.

DOCUMENT 7

Fisher Ames, "The Republican. No. II" (1804)

After Jefferson's election in 1800, many former opponents moderated their attacks on Republicanism. But Fisher Ames (1758–1808) was not among them. An acerbic Massachusetts lawyer, Ames championed strong central authority and reviled egalitarianism. He claimed that the federal government should be built on an aristocracy of "the wise and good and opulent." Ames served in the House of Representatives for three terms. Illness cut short his political career, and in retirement he wrote stinging blasts against the "Southern Jacobins," his term for Republican leaders who mouthed radical philosophies while holding slaves.

We justly consider the condition of civil liberty as the most exalted to which any nation can aspire; but high as its rank is, and precious as are its prerogatives, it has not pleased God, in the order of his providence, to confer this preeminent blessing, except upon a very few, and those very small, spots of the universe. The rest sit in darkness, and as little desire the light of liberty, as they are fit to endure it.

We are ready to wonder, that the best gifts are the most sparingly bestowed, and rashly to conclude, that despotism is the decree of heaven, because by far the largest part of the world lies bound in its fetters. But either on tracing the course of events in history, or on examining the character and passions of man, we shall find that the work of slavery is his own, and that he is not condemned to wear chains till he has been his own artificer to forge them. We shall find that society cannot subsist, and that the streets of Boston would be worse than the lion's den, unless the appetites and passions of the violent are made subject to an adequate control. How much control will be adequate to that end, is a problem of no easy solution beforehand, and of no sort of difficulty after some experience. For all who have any thing to defend, and all indeed who have nothing to ask protection for but their lives, will desire that protection; and not only acquiesce, but rejoice in the progress of those slave-making intrigues and tumults, which at length assure to society its repose, though it sleeps in bondage. Thus it will happen, and as it is the course of nature, it cannot be resisted, that there will soon or late be control and government enough.

It is also obvious, that there may be, and probably will be, the least control and the most liberty there, where the turbulent passions are the least excited, and where the old habits and sober reasons of the people are left free to govern them.

Hence it is undeniably plain, that the mock patriots, the opposers of Washington and the Constitution, from 1788 to this day, who, under pretext of being the people's friends, have kept them in a state of continual jealousy, irritation, and discontent, have deceived the people, and perhaps themselves, in regard to the tendency of their principles and conduct; for instead of lessening the pressure of government, and contracting the sphere of its powers, they have removed the field-marks that bounded its exercise, and left it arbitrary and without limits. The passions of the people have been kept in agitation, till the influence of truth, reason, and the excellent habits we derive from our ancestors is lost or greatly impaired; till it is plain, that those, whom manners and morals can no longer govern, must be governed by force; and that force a dominant faction derives from the passions of its adherents; on that alone they rely.

Take one example, which will illustrate the case

as well as a hundred; the British treaty [Jay's Treaty 1793] was opposed by a faction, headed by six or eight mob leaders in our cities, and a rabble, whom the arts of these leaders had trained for their purpose. Could a feeble government, could mere truth and calm reason, pointing out the best public interest, have carried that treaty through, and effected its execution in good faith, had not the virtue and firmness of Washington supplied an álmost superhuman energy to its powers at the moment? No treaty made by the government has ever proved more signally beneficial. The nature of the treaty, however, is not to the point of the present argument. Suppose a mob opposition had defeated it, and confusion, if not war, had ensued, the confusion that very society is fated to suffer, when, on a trial of strength, a faction in its bosom is found stronger than its government; on this supposition, and that the conquering faction had seized the reins of power, is it to be believed that they would not instantly provide against a like opposition to their own treaties? Did they not so provide, and annex Louisiana, and squander millions in a week? Have we not seen in France, how early and how effectually the conqueror takes care to prevent another rival from playing the same game, by which he himself prevailed against his predecessor?

Let any man, who has any understanding, exercise it to see that the American jacobin party, by rousing the popular passions, inevitably augments the powers of government, and contracts within narrower bounds, and on a less sound foundation, the privileges of the people.

Facts, yes facts, that speak in terror to the soul, confirm this speculative reasoning. What limits are there to the prerogatives of the present administration? and whose business is it, and in whose power does it lie, to keep them within those limits? Surely not in the senate: the small States are now in vassalage, and they obey the nod of Virginia. Not in the judiciary: that fortress, which the Constitution had made too strong for an assault, can now be reduced by famine. The Constitution, alas! that sleeps with Washington, having no mourners but the virtuous, and no monument but history. Louisiana, in open and avowed defiance of the Constitution, is by treaty to be added to the union; the bread of the children of the union is to be taken and given to the dogs.

Judge then, good men and true, judge by the effects, whether the tendency of the intrigues of the party was to extend or contract the measure of popular liberty. Judge whether the little finger of Jefferson is not thicker than the loins of Washington's administration; and, after you have judged, and felt the terror that will be inspired by the result, then reflect how little your efforts can avail to prevent the continuance, nay, the perpetuity of his power. Reflect, and be calm. Patience is the virtue of slaves, and almost the only one that will pass for merit with their masters.

DOCUMENT 8

Report of a Joint Committee of the General Assembly of Connecticut (1814)

President Madison's inept handling of the War of 1812 angered New Englanders. An ill-conceived embargo on trade seriously harmed the region's commercial interests, and when British troops occupied several villages in the present state of Maine, the Republican administration seemed indifferent to local problems of defense. The assemblies of the separate New England states considered a proper response to what they saw as the tyranny of federal government. In their session, the legislators of Connecticut debated the merits of holding a regional convention, and as their statement reveals, it did not require much persuasion for them to send delegates to a meeting designed to mount a protest consistent "WITH OUR OBLIGATIONS AS MEMBERS OF THE NATIONAL UNION."

At a General Assembly of the State of Connecticut, holden at New-Haven, in said state, on the second Thursday of October, in the year of our Lord one thousand eight hundred and fourteen.

To the Honourable the General Assembly now in session. The committee to whom was referred the speech of his excellency the governor, with the documents accompanying the same, and also his excellency's message, presenting a communication from the governour of Massachusetts; further report,—

That the condition of this state demands the most serious attention of the Legislature. We lately enjoyed, in common with the other members of the national confederacy, the blessings of peace. The industry of our citizens, in every department of active life, was abundantly rewarded; our cities and villages exhibited indications of increasing wealth; and the foreign relations of the Union secured our safety and nourished our prosperity.

The scene is now reversed. We are summoned to the field of war, and to surrender our treasures for our defence. The fleets of a powerful enemy hover on our coasts; blockade our harbours; and threaten our towns and cities with fire and desolation.

When a commonwealth suddenly falls from a state of high prosperity, it behoves the guardians of its interests to inquire into the cause of its decline, and, with deep solicitude, to seek a remedy.

In the latter part of the last century, a spirit of daring enterprise—impatient of restraint—regardless of the sanctions of religion—hostile to human happiness, and aspiring to supreme power—overturned many ancient governments; made Europe a scene of carnage, and threatened with ruin all which was valuable in the civilized world. The history of its progress and decline is familiar to every

mind. Nations without the reach of the immense physical power which it embodied, were tainted by its corruptions; and every state and province in christendom has felt its baneful influences. By the pure principles inherited from our fathers, conducive, at once, to the preservation of liberty and order, this state has been eminently exempt, in its interior policy, from this modern scourge of nations. In thus withstanding this potent adversary of all ancient establishments, while many monarchies have been subverted, we have exhibited to the world the highest evidence that a free constitution is not inconsistent with the strength of civil government, and that the virtue of a people is the best preservation of both.

Occupying a comparatively small territory, and naturally associating, during the revolutionary war, with states whose views were identified with ours, our interests and inclinations led us to unite in the great national compact, since defined and consolidated by the constitution of the United States. We had justly anticipated, from that union the preservation and advancement of our dearest rights and interests; and while the father of his country, and those other great and wise men,—who, mindful of their high duties, and regardless of local and party considerations, consulted the happiness of the commonwealth, guided our councils, we were not disappointed in our expectations. The federal government, in which our own venerable statesmen were conspicuous, was revered in every nation. An American in foreign lands, was honoured for his country's sake: a rich and virtuous population was rapidly reducing the limits of our extensive wilderness; and the commerce of America was in every sea.

But a coalition, not less evident than if defined by the articles of a formal treaty, arose between the national administration and that fearful tyrant in Europe, who was aspiring to the dominion of the world. No means, however destructive to the commerce and hazardous to the peace of this country, were left unattempted, to aid his efforts and unite our interests and destinies with his. From this fatal cause, we are bereft of the respectable standing we once held in the councils of the nation; impoverished by a long course of commercial restrictions; involved in an odious and disastrous war; and subjected to all the complicated calamities which we now deplore.

Thus driven from every object of our best hopes, and bound to an inglorious struggle in defence of our dwellings from a public enemy; we had no apprehension, much as we had suffered from the national government, that it would refuse to yield us such protection as its treasures might afford. Much less could we doubt, that those disbursements, which might be demanded of this state, would be passed to our credit on the books of the treasury. Such however has not been the course adopted by the national agents. All supplies have been withdrawn from the militia of this state, in the service of the United States. The groundless pretext for this unwarrantable measure, was, their submission to an officer assigned them by the commander in chief, in perfect conformity with military usage, and the principles of a request from the President himself, under which a party of them was detached. The injustice of that measure, by which we were compelled to sustain alone the burden of supplying and paying our own forces, in the service of the United States—a service rendered necessary to defend our territory from invasion—is highly aggravated by the consideration, that the dangers which called them to the field, and the concentration of the enemy's forces on our coasts, have resulted from the ships of the United States having taken refuge in our waters. Were this the only instance evincive of the disregard of the administration to the just claims and best interests of this state,—the only ground to fear that we are forgotten in their councils, except as

subjects of taxation and oppression,—we should choose to consider it an instance anomalous and solitary—still yield them our confidence, and hope for protection to the extent of their power, in this session of unusual calamity.

Protection is the first, and most important claim of these states on the government of the nation. It is a primary condition, essential to the very obligation of every compact between rulers and their subjects. To obtain that, as a principal object, Connecticut became a member of the national confederacy. In a defensive war, a government would stand justified, after making a fair application of its powers to that important end;—for it could do no more. But when a government hastily declares war, without providing the indispensable means of conducting it—want of means is no apology for refusing protection. In such a case, the very declaration of war, is, of itself, a breach of the sacred obligation; inasmuch as the loss of protection by the subject, is the natural and inevitable consequence of the measure. When that war annihilates the only revenues of the nation, the violation of the original contract is still more palpable. If waged for foreign conquest, and the wreck of the national treasures devoted to a fruitless invasion of the enemy's territory, the character of the act is more criminal, but not more clear.

Whatever may be the disposition of the national Executive towards this state, during the sequel of the war, such is the condition of the public finances, that constant and very great advances must be made from our state treasury, to meet the expenditures necessary for our own defence.

But the utmost efforts of this state, under the most favourable circumstances for raising revenue, would be hardly adequate to the costly operations of defending, against a great naval power, a sea-coast of more than one hundred and twenty miles in length; much less, at this inauspicious period, when the distresses of the people are enhanced by the embarrassments of our monied institutions, and the circulating medium constantly diminishing, can any thing be spared consistently with our safety. Yet the national government are dooming us to enormous taxation, without affording any just confidence that

Created by cartoonist Alexander Anderson, the Ograbme (embargo spelled backwards) snapping turtle is shown here grabbing an American tobacco smuggler. The controversial embargo was intended to exert pressure on Great Britain and France by depriving them of American goods, but the embargo backfired when U.S. businesses began to go bankrupt.

we shall share in the expenditures of the public revenue. The invasion of Canada is perseveringly pursued, our coasts left defenceless, and the treasures of the country exhausted on more favoured points of the national frontier. To meet those demands, and, at the same time, to defend ourselves, is impossible. Whatever we may contribute, we have no reasonable ground to expect protection in return.

The people of this state have no disloyalty to the interests of the Union. For their fidelity and patriotism, they may appeal, with confidence, to the national archives from the commencement of the revolutionary war.

In achieving the independence of the nation, they bore an honourable part. Their contingent in men and money has ever been promptly furnished, when constitutionally required. Much as they lament the present unnatural hostilities with Great Britain, they have, with characteristic obedience to lawful authority, punctually paid the late taxes imposed by the general government. On every lawful demand of the national Executive, their well-disciplined militia have resorted to the field. The public enemy, when invading their shores, has been met at the water's edge, and valiantly repulsed. They duly appreciate the great advantages which would result from the federal compact, were the government administered according to the sacred principles of the constitution. They have not forgotten the ties of confidence and affection, which bound these states to each other during their toils for independence;— nor the national honour and commercial prosperity, which they mutually shared, during the happy years of a good administration. They are, at the same time, conscious of their rights and determined to defend them. Those sacred liberties—those inestimable institutions, civil and religious, which their venerable fathers have bequeathed them, are, with the blessing of Heaven, to be maintained at every hazard, and never to be surrendered by tenants of the soil which the ashes of their ancestors have consecrated.

"In what manner the multiplied evils, which we feel and fear, are to be remedied, is a question of the highest moment, and deserves the greatest consideration. The documents transmitted by his excellency the Governor of Massachusetts, present, in the opinion of the committee, an eligible method of combining the wisdom of New-England, in devising, on full consultation, a proper course to be adopted, consistent with our obligations to the United States. The following [is] . . . therefore, respectfully submitted.

"Resolved, That seven persons by appointed Delegates from this state, to meet the delegates of the Commonwealth of Massachusetts, and of any other of the New-England states, at Hartford, on the 15th day of December next, and confer with them on the subjects proposed by a resolution of said Commonwealth, communicated to this legislature, and upon any other subjects which may come before them, for the purpose of devising and recommending such measures for the safety and welfare of these states, AS MAY CONSIST WITH OUR OBLIGATIONS AS MEMBERS OF THE NATIONAL UNION.

Study Questions

1. In what sense did Jefferson's election as president in 1800 mark a "revolution"?

2. In his first Inaugural Address, Jefferson claimed that "We are all Republicans: we are all Federalists." What did he mean? Did he really think that party conflict would cease?

3. Did the Louisiana Purchase raise serious questions of constitutionality? Were the Republicans acting consistently with their own principles?

4. Interpret closely Charles Janson's conversation with a servant maid. Why is she so eager to distinguish herself from African-Americans?

❧   ❧

10

Early Industrial Transformations

Known as the "Era of Good Feelings," the years after the conclusion of the War of 1812 achieved greater political harmony than the republic had seen since President Washington's first administration. This period also marked the beginning of a major shift in the structure of capitalism throughout the United States. For most of their history, Americans had been farmers, producing basic necessities for their families and selling small surpluses in highly localized markets. Commerce between the different regions was difficult, in some cases almost impossible. All this changed after 1815. New forms of transportation—canals and road systems, for example—connected distant Americans. Banks offered innovative forms of credit. And in towns scattered across the northern states, small factories announced the birth of robust internal markets for domestic manufactures.

Economic change occurred slowly. It would be a mistake to anticipate full-scale industrialization, a stage of development not reached for another half-century. For people who experienced the early phases of this transformation, however, the shifts seemed dramatic. Men and women who cultivated western lands no longer saw themselves as pioneers; they were commercial farmers, exchanging staple crops over long distances for items manufactured in the East. Evidence of economic strength—indeed, of possible national self-sufficiency—fueled the spirit of nationalism, for a full fifty years after declaring independence, Americans finally appeared ready to break free from the commercial yoke of British colonialism. No wonder a young congressman, John C. Calhoun, exclaimed, "Let us, then, bind the nation together with a perfect system of roads and canals. Let us conquer space."

In 1816 Jacob Bigelow, a distinguished Harvard professor, endorsed the growing optimism of the American people (Document 1). Like other thoughtful commentators, Bigelow welcomed change, calling on citizens trained in science to lead the way. Perhaps no achievement of the period brought Americans greater satisfaction than completion of the Erie Canal, a magnificent engineering feat connecting the Hudson River to Lake Erie, a distance of 364 miles. Contemporaries bubbled with pride. They also appreciated rising land prices and entrepreneurial opportunities (Document 2). As an official at the 1818 groundbreaking in Rome, New York, observed, the "expense and labor of this great undertaking, bears no proportion to its utility."

Technological innovation further stimulated economic growth. Western farmers employed iron and steel plows to break the soil, shipping their crops to market on fast steamships, invented by Robert Fulton. In the factories of the Northeast, the development of interchangeable parts—a process associated primarily with Eli Whitney and Simeon North—brought greater efficiency to manufacturing. The reorganization of production forced American laborers to specialize, a change in the character of the work culture that undermined the position of skilled craftsmen. Eager to increase productivity and develop guns that could be repaired easily, the federal government encouraged gunsmiths at the Springfield, Massachusetts, armory to perform specific tasks and to create interchangeable parts for the weapons (Document 3).

In this expansive environment economic planning acquired patriotic character. In Congress, Henry Clay put forward his "American System," a complex blueprint for economic development. Clay advocated high tariffs to protect domestic manufacturing and internal improvements to stimulate a home market. The American System held out the possibility of making the nation economically self-sufficient and free from dependence on Europe. When political opponents attacked elements of Clay's grand plan of 1832, the Kentucky orator rose in passionate defense (Document 4). A newspaper article singing the praises of manufacturing in Ohio suggests how rapidly the economic culture of the United States was changing (Document 5).

The earliest and most successful industrial ventures produced textiles. Factories located in southern New England installed power looms and spinning machinery. The labor force required to operate these mills consisted largely of young, unmarried women, the daughters of local farmers. They accepted positions for different reasons, but many wanted to earn enough money to start a family. In other words, they did not regard factory work as a career. Although early mill owners professed a desire to make the work rewarding, female laborers often complained of long hours and low pay (Document 6).

DOCUMENT 1

Jacob Bigelow, "Inaugural Address" (1816)

In 1816 Jacob Bigelow (1786–1879), a leading botanist and noted physician, was the Rumfort Professor of Medicine at Harvard. He used the occasion to review the material progress of the United States—particularly New England—and, like many contemporaries writing on this topic, Bigelow expressed great optimism about the future of a businesslike republic.

Human ingenuity, in all ages of the world, has been directed to the acquisition of power. The simple bodily strength, with which nature has endowed every one; the inventions which we have sought out

to extend and improve our physical ability; the craft and subtlety with which we learn to operate on our fellow-beings have been strikingly employed, at all times, for the promotion of this object. Those men have been great, who have brought others under their dominion; who have swayed them by their eloquence, or influenced them by the ascendency of their character; or who, by enlarging the boundaries of human knowledge, have increased the extent of their own resources, and obtained a control over the creation around them.

Power, when acquired, may have centered and terminated with the individual, or it may have become the common stock of society, and descended from one age to another. In this respect, we find a remarkable difference between the civil and the philosophical history of the world. The power which men and nations exercise in regard to each other, is temporary and transient. The greatest individuals have lived to see the decline of every thing upon which their greatness reposed. Societies and political institutions, which have been distinguished in their ascent, have been not less remarkable in their fall. Those nations and governments which, in former times, have subdued their competitors and controlled, for a time, the destinies of a great portion of the world; are now erased from the list of empires, and, perhaps, recognized only in name. . . .

The portion of country in which it is our fortune to live, is not one of exuberant soil and spontaneous plenty. The summer of New-England does not elicit a second burden from our trees, nor is even our annual harvest exempt from the contingency of failure. Winter maintains here a long and late influence upon the seasons, and frosts are visiting us in the latest breezes of spring. Our territory is interrupted by extensive masses of rock, and broken by mountains intractable to cultivation. Our thin and penurious soil rests upon beds of granite, upon flint and sand, which drain it of its moisture, while themselves afford no pabulum for its vegetation. Whatever is raised from the bosom of the earth must be extorted by assiduous and painful culture, and a labourious vigilance is necessary to insure the fruits of the year.

Yet has this part of our country become the most populous and enlightened in the continent upon which we live. The very causes which seemed at variance with our prosperity, have proved its most

powerful promoters. A vigor and hardihood of character have grown up, out of the evils which they had to combat; and a spirit of enterprise and perseverance, unknown in more luxurious climates, has become the characteristic of our population. The intelligence and the untiring application which were at first the offspring of necessity, have eventually exhibited ample fruits in the features of our land. Cultivated grounds and ornamental dwellings, wealthy cities and flourishing institutions have arisen upon a spot, where nature was never lavish of her gifts. . . .

In science and the arts, notwithstanding the infancy of our institutions, and the embarrassment which most individuals experience from the necessity of attending to the calls of business, we have not been wholly without improvement, and are perhaps not destitute of a name. The researches of most of our ingenious men have had utility for their object. They have been performed in intervals taken from professional duties, and have been impeded by a deficiency of books and means. We have had little of the parade of operation, yet we have sometimes seen the fruits of silent efficiency and perseverance. We have had few learned men, but many useful ones. We have not often seen individuals among us, like the laborious Germans, spending their lives in endless acquisitions, while perhaps themselves add little to the general stock of knowledge; yet we have had men of original talents, who have been fortunate enough to discover some province in which they were qualified to be serviceable to their country and mankind. We have had ingenious mechanicians, skilful projectors, profound mathematicians, and men well versed in the useful learning of their time. The progress of our internal improvements, and the high state of the mechanic arts among us, as well as in our sister states, has entitled us to the character of a nation of inventors. The individuals who have originated and promoted such improvements, have often been men unambitious of fame, whose lives have past in obscurity; yet there have sometimes been those among us, whose labours have attracted the honorable notice of foreigners, and reflected lustre upon the country of their birth. It has even been our fortune to impose obligations on others, and there are services of our citizens which are now better known than their names. There are some things which, if gathered from the ashes of obscurity, might serve to shed a gleam upon our literary reputation, and to make known at least the light they have kindled for others. It is a fact perhaps not generally realized, that the American Philosophical Society at Philadelphia, the Royal Society of Great Britain, and the Royal Institution of London, all of them are in a measure indebted for their birth and first foundation to natives or inhabitants of New-England.

DOCUMENT 2

Building the Erie Canal

Although Americans had long contemplated opening a water route between the eastern states and the West, it was not until 1817 that the ambitious project actually began. The legislature of New York raised money for the Erie Canal, which officially opened in 1825. The canal represented a spectacular engineering achievement. It was ten times longer than any other canal in the United States. Situated mostly on flat ground, the Erie Canal connected Buffalo and Albany, making it much cheaper to haul heavy freight between eastern urban centers and western farms. While the canal was not a financial success, it symbolized American ingenuity. The documents in this section offer different perspectives on the meaning of the Erie Canal.

Extract from the Albany Daily Advertiser (1819)

The last two days have presented in this village, a scene of the liveliest interest; and I consider it among the privileges of my life to have been present to witness it. On Friday afternoon I walked to the head of the grand canal, the eastern extremity of which reaches within a very short distance of the village, and from one of the slight and airy bridges which crossed it, I had a sight that could not but exhilirate and elevate the mind. The waters were rushing in from the westward, and coming down their untried channel towards the sea. Their course, owing to the absorption of the new banks of the canal, and the distance they had to run from where the stream entered it, was much slower than I had anticipated; they continued gradually to steal along from bridge to bridge, and at first only spreading over the bed of the canal, imperceptibly rose and washed its sides with a gentle wave. It was dark before they reached the eastern extremity; but at sunrise next morning, they were on a level, two feet and a half deep throughout the whole distance of thirteen miles. The interest manifested by the whole country, as this new internal river rolled its first waves through the state, cannot be described. You might see the people running across the fields, climbing on trees and fences, and crowding the bank of the canal to gaze upon the welcome sight. A

The original Erie Canal was 363 miles long, 40 feet wide, and about 4 feet deep, with 84 locks. The canal, shown here near its completion in 1825, helped to make New York City one of the strongest commercial centers in the nation.

boat had been prepared at Rome, and as the waters came down the canal, you might mark their progress by that of this new Argo, which floated triumphantly along the Hellespont of the west, accompanied by the shouts of the peasantry, and having on her deck a military band. At nine the next morning, the bells began a merry peal, and the commissioners in carriages, proceeded from Bagg's hotel, to the place of embarkation.

The governor, accompanied by Gen. Van Rensselaer, Rev. Mr. Stansbury, of Albany, Rev. Dr. Blatchford, of Lansingburgh, Judge Miller, of Utica, Mr. Holly, Mr. Seymour, Judge Wright, Col. Lansing, Mr. Childs, Mr. Clark, Mr. Bunner, and a large company of their friends, embarked, at a quarter past nine, and were received with the roll of the drum, and the shouts of a large multitude of spectators. The boat, which received them, is built for pas-

sengers;—is sixty-one feet in length, and seven and an half feet in width;—having two rising cabins, of fourteen feet each, with a flat deck between them. In forty minutes the company reached Whitesborough, a distance of two miles and three quarters; the boat being drawn by a single horse, which walked on the towing path, attached to a tow rope, of about sixty feet long. The horse travelled, apparently, with the utmost ease. The boat, though literally loaded with passengers, drew but fourteen inches water. A military band played patriotic airs.

From bridge to bridge, from village to village, the procession was saluted with cannon, and every bell whose sound could reach the canal, swung, as with instinctive life, as it passed by. At Whitesborough, a number of ladies embarked, and heightened, by their smiles, a scene which wanted but this to make it complete.

"To the Honourable Senate and House of Representatives of the United States in Congress, the Representation of the [Canal] Commissioners of the State of New-York" (1817)

That the Legislature of the said state, in April last, passed an act to provide for the improvement of their internal navigation, of which act we take the liberty of transmitting herewith a copy. In this it will be seen that a board of commissioners is constituted, and that, among other duties enjoined upon them, they are required to make application to the government of the United States, for cessions, grants or donations of lands or money, for the purpose of aiding in opening a communication, by means of canals, between the navigable waters of Hudson's river and lake Erie, and the said navigable waters and lake Champlain. To fulfil this requisition, then, is the object of this address.

Next to the establishment and security of the right to self-government, we flatter ourselves that no subject requiring legislative interference, can be found more interesting than the one which we are charged to lay before your honourable body. And we venture to solicit your favourable consideration of it, in full confidence that an enlightened public spirit may justly give to it such a pleasure of patronage as cannot fail to produce signal benefits to the nation.

The benefits to be acquired by the United States, from the construction of these canals, will most obviously and immediately affect their pecuniary and political interests. More remotely, indeed, they will exert a favourable influence upon every object embraced within the scope of an enlightened and paternal policy. If we consider the extent and fertility of our territory northwest of the Ohio; the large proportion of it, which yet remains unsold; the disposition and the ability which our eastern fellow-citizens possess to purchase and to improve it, we cannot be insensible of the great pecuniary advantage which would result from opening to them a safe, easy, and economical passage into that territory. Every dollar saved to them, in the expenses of removing thither, would operate to enhance the value of the public

lands, and, at the same time, to hasten their settlement: and it is obvious, that a canal from the Hudson to lake Erie would save a very large portion of these expenses. The number of persons to be affected by this consideration, cannot be accurately stated. It certainly would not be small. We are well assured, that in the course of one year, since the war, more than twelve thousand new settlers, almost exclusively from the east, have established themselves within the limits of this state west of the Genesee river.

Whatever adds to the value of all that land produces must increase the value of land itself. To a country, which depends upon a distant market for the sale of its surplus productions, it is of great importance to afford every possible facility of transportation; for all that is taken from the expense of transportation is added to the value of the articles transported: and by cheapening the rate of carriage, many articles are rendered valuable which would otherwise be worthless.

Moreover, if habit or the necessary accommodation of life, require that such a country should consume foreign goods to the amount of all its surplus productions, it is evident that the landholder there enjoys a two-fold benefit in every increased facility of transportation. Perhaps the whole of the country between the great lakes, the Mississippi, and the Ohio (certainly the greater part of it,) would derive from the completion of our principal canal greater advantages for distant communication than any country, so far inland, has hitherto enjoyed, comparably greater than that country can ever from any other means. Regarded, then, merely measure of pecuniary wisdom, we trust your honourable body will make such an appropriation in favour of it as will ensure its accomplishment.

But considerations of a political nature seem to us, most urgently to recommend the construction of these canals. The great influence exercised over the western Indians, even in our own territory, by the subjects of a foreign government, we have always had numerous reasons to wish destroyed. This influence depends materially, upon establishments erected for the promotion of the fur trade. Any measure that would open, between one of our sea ports and the region where furs are collected, a road in all respects preferable to any other, besides drawing to our own citizens a profitable commerce, would tend, eventually, to the subversion of that influence, and, in the mean time, offer to us important facilities for controlling it.

The trade carried on between our country and the Canadian provinces is already considerable, and is rapidly growing. The fruits of the earth from the southern shores of Erie and Ontario, and from the borders of Champlain, find their way to the ports of our northern neighbours cheaper than they can to any, which offers a market, of our own, and are there exchanged for the various commodities of foreign countries. This trade is, indeed, profitable to many of our citizens who engage in it, but it is much more so to the British. Subject to their control, they direct it to the advancement of all their public interests. And it is no mean instrument of that advancement. It is evidently the vital spirit of their internal navigation, which it cannot fail to exalt into a consequence that may hereafter greatly affect us. Would not the prosecution of our projects to complete effect, result immediately in giving to the citizens of the United States the entire profits of this trade, and to government all the security and influence connected with a thickly settled frontier, and a most decided superiority of shipping on the lakes?

Nothing can be more certain, than that the continance of our Union is essential to our freedom. The mean of this continuance are to be found only in the strength of our common interests. Whatever extends and consolidates these interests, then must be of distinguished importance to government: and can any thing be imagined more efficaciously conducive to these objects, than opening to distant sections of our country the means of easy and profitable intercourse? Virtuous and enlightened men among us, have long delighted themselves with looking forward to the period, when a canal communication between the Hudson and lake Erie would afford, to halt the United States, more ample means of promoting every social interest, than have heretofore, in any country, been furnished by the accomplishment of any human enterprise.

The advantages of canals were not entirely unknown to ancient governments. Among them, the wisest and most powerful executed works of this kind, in every direction through their territories, for the purposes of agriculture, commerce, and war. The vestiges of many of these are still discoverable, and they are doubtless to be reckoned among the most impressive memorials that remain of ancient greatness. When we recollect the instrumentality which canals have formerly exhibited in collecting the blessings of wealth, strength, and a crowded population for every country through which they passed, and see those very countries, by the neglect and ruin of them, reduced to their original barrenness, can we suppress a conviction of their immense utility? But, it is not alone from history, and the faint traces of them which have survived the lapse of many centuries, that the advantages of these improvements are to be known. There are proofs more conclusive. Our own times furnish them. In contemplating the present state of Europe, it is impossible not to be struck with the number and extent of her canals. And we perceive that they abound most in those countries where the wants of the social state and the means of power, have been most diligently explored, and are most profoundly understood. We see them ever enabling extensive empires to hold in speedy administration, to every public object, all the resources of their remote sections; and, at the same time, increasing those resources prodigiously by the economical exchanges of which they are the occasion. Experience is always a safe guide. It is especially to be trusted when it has been acquired in the midst of difficulties and dangers, and has been sanctioned by the wisdom of different nations. If, then, in the pressing exigencies of recent events, when every power of national defence and annoyance has been exerted, when all the capacities of men, as individuals, and in political combination, have been remarkably evolved, we observe in that quarter of the globe, a perpetually growing attention to the subject of canals, is it not expedient, is it not wise for us to engage in making them? No country is more susceptible of all their benefits than ours: none of larger extent presents fewer impediments to their construction. They constitute improvements peculiarly fit for a republic. They contribute equally to the safety and opulence of the people, and the reputation and resources of the government. They are equally desirable in reference to the employments of peace, and the operations of war. In whatever light they are viewed, they seem to combine the substantial glories of the most splendid and permanent utility.

But if the execution of those of which we are the advocates, be impracticable, or would involve an expense inappropriate to their value, they can have no claim upon the favour of the national legislature. On these topics we entertain no doubts. The minute examination which has been made this season, under our superintendents, of all the lands which these canals will traverse, has convinced us that an expenditure not exceeding ten millions of dollars would be sufficient to perfect them. Shall they remain unattempted? The state of New-York is not unaware of her interests, nor disinclined to prosecute them; but where those of the general government are united with hers, and seem to be paramount, she deems it her duty to ask for their assistance. Wherefore, in her behalf, we solicit your honourable body to make such an appropriation, in lands or money, to aid in the construction of these canals, as you, in your wisdom may think reasonable and just.

James F. Cooper, Notions of the Americans (1840)

Five-and-twenty years ago engineers from Europe began to make their appearance in America. They brought with them the rules of science, and a competent knowledge of the estimates of force, and the adaptation of principles to results; but they brought them, all calculated to meet the contingencies of the European man. Experience showed that they neither knew how to allow for the difficulties of a novel situation, nor for the excess of intellect they were enabled to use. Their estimates were always wild, uncertain, and fatal, in a country that was still experimenting. But five-and-twenty years ago was too soon for canals in America. It was wise to wait

for a political symptom in a country where a natural impulse will always indicate the hour for action. Though five-and-twenty, or twenty, or even fifteen years, were too soon, still ten were not. Ten years ago, demonstrations had been made which enabled keen observers to detect that the time for extraordinary exertion had come. The great western canal of New-York was conceived and planned. But instead of seeking for European engineers, a few of the common surveyors of the country were called to the aid of those who were intrusted with the duty of making the estimates; and men of practical knowledge, who understood the people with whom they had to deal, and who had tutored their faculties in the thousand collisions of active life, were brought to the task as counsellors. The result is worthy of grave attention. The work, in its fruits and in its positive extent, exceeded any thing of a similar nature ever attempted in Christendom. The authority to whom responsibility was due, was more exacting than any of our hemisphere. Economy was inculcated to a degree little known in other nations; and, in short, greater accuracy than usual was required under circumstances apparently the least favourable to attain it. Now, this canal was made (with such means) at a materially less cost, in infinitely less time, and with a boldness in the estimates, and an accuracy in the results, that were next to marvellous. There was not a man of any reputation for science employed in the work. But the utmost practical knowledge of men and of things was manifested in the whole of the affair. The beginning of each year brought its estimate of the expense, and of the profits, and the close its returns, in wonderful conformity. The labour is completed, and the benefit is exceeding the hopes of the most sanguine.

In this sketch of the circumstances under which the New-York canal has been made, we may trace the cause of the prodigious advance of this nation. Some such work as this was necessary to demonstrate to the world, that the qualities which are so exclusively the fruits of liberty and of a diffused intelligence, have an existence elsewhere than in the desires of the good. Without it, it might have been said the advance of America is deceptive; she is doing no more than our own population could do under circumstances that admitted of so much display, but she will find the difference between felling trees, and burning forests, and giving the finish which denotes the material progress of society. The mouths of such critics are now silenced. The American can point to his ploughs, to his ships, to his canals, to his bridges, and, in short, to every thing that is useful in his particular state of society, and demand, where a better or cheaper has been produced, under any thing like circumstances of equality?

It is vain to deny the causes of the effects of the American system. . . . since they rest on principles that favour the happiness and prosperity of the human race. We should not cavil about names, nor minor distinctions, in governments, if the great and moving principles are such as contemplate the improvement of the species in the masa and not in exclusive and selfish exceptions. . . .

The construction of canals, on a practical scale, the mining for coal, the exportation of cotton goods, and numberless other improvements, which argue an advancing state of society, have all sprung into existence within the last dozen years. It is a knowledge of these facts, with a clear and sagacious understanding of their immense results, coupled with the exciting moral causes, that render the American sanguine, aspiring, and confident in his anticipations. He sees that his nation lives centuries in an age, and he feels no disposition to consider himself a child, because other people, in their dotage, choose to remember the hour of his birth.

How pitiful do the paltry criticisms on an inn, or the idle, and, half the time, vulgar comments on the vulgarity of a *parvenu*, become, when objects and facts like these are pressing themselves on the mind! I have heard it said, that there are European authors who feel a diffidence of contracting acquaintances with American gentlemen, because they feel a consciousness of having turned the United States into ridicule! I can tell these unfortunate subjects of a precipitate opinion, that they may lay aside their scruples. No American of any character, or knowledge of his own country, can feel any thing but commiseration for the man who has attempted to throw ridicule on a nation like this. The contest is too unequal to admit of any doubt as to the result, and the wiser way will be for these Quixotes in literature to say and think as little as possible about their American tilting match, in order that the world may not liken their lances to that used by the hero of La Mancha, and their helmets to barbers' basins.

DOCUMENT 3

American State Papers, Military Affairs, "Description of the United States Armory at Springfield, Massachusetts" (1819)

In late 1819, Major James Dalliba inspected the Springfield Armory. Dalliba provided Congress with a glowing report of the Armory's success in producing cheap, reliable guns. Dalliba praised the Armory for developing interchangeable parts—which permitted guns to be fixed on the front rather than returned to the manufacturer for repair—and for promoting specialized labor by the workers. He did, however, note a disadvantage of specialized labor: although "each workman becomes an adept at his part," the consequence was that "not one of them becomes a finished armorer." In other words, such a worker, although skilled, "cannot make a fire-arm."

At Springfield, in the county of Hampden, and commonwealth of Massachusetts, the United States have as extensive establishment for the manufacture of arms. "The original site of this manufactory is also a military post, which is a perfectly level elevated plat, situated about half a mile east of the village, from which there is a gradual ascent, flanked on the north by a deep ravine, and on the south by a less considerable one, with an extensive plain spreading in the rear, the adjacent parts being uncovered, fronting on the brow of the declivity, and commanding an extensive and beautifully variegated landscape."

At the armory on the hill "there is one brick building, 204 by 32 feet, two stories high, divided into eight rooms, occupied by lock filers, stuckers, and finishers. One brick forging shop, 130 by 32 feet, of one story, containing eleven double forges, used for forging the limbs of locks," breech pins, screw pins, ramrods, "and repair tools." One brick building, 60 by 32 feet, two stories high, with a paved cellar under the whole, used for storing iron, steel, oil, &c; the first story is occupied as offices for superintendent, master armorer, and clerks; the second story, forming a large and spacious hall, is devoted to religious worship, and as a chapel was dedicated to the service of God, on the 13th day of May, 1817, by the Rev. Titus Strong, of Greenfield. One building, 100 by 40 feet, two stories high, also of brick, for the deposite of arms; two military stores; a carpenter's shop; a file cutter's shop; a coal and proof house; and brick shop, fire proof, 32 by 16 feet, with three furnaces, one for hardening ramrods, one for nealing work, and one for a brass foundry; two stores for forged work, one for files, and seventeen dwelling houses. One pay office, ordinance yard, magazine, block house, and lumber yard. On the large shop first mentioned is a handsome cupola and bell, from which is an interesting view of Connecti-

cut river and the surrounding country.

The aforesaid buildings are arranged northerly of the great State road leading to Boston, bordering on a large flat square piece of ground, fenced and set out with trees, around which is a road about 60 feet wide, leading to several dwelling houses occupied by the officers and workmen; the whole assuming a handsome and regular appearance.

In this establishment are employed from 240 to 250 workmen, who complete on an average about forty-five muskets daily. The works may be increased to almost any extent. The water privileges already owned by the United States will warrant the extension to thirty thousand stands annually.

This extensive manufactory is under the direction of a principal, who is styled superintendent, who has the chief management of the business of the armory; provides, contracts for, and purchases all stock, tools, and materials necessary for manufacturing arms; engages the workmen, determines their wages, and prescribes the necessary regulations for the local government of the establishment. To aid him in the important duties of the armory, there are allowed a master armorer, who manages the mechanical operations, and is held accountable for all stores, tools, and materials put under his charge for the use of the armory, and for the correct workmanship of the muskets, and a paymaster and storekeeper, whose duty it is to liquidate and pay all debts contracted by the superintendent for the armory, and receive the finished arms, for which he is held accountable, as well as for all other public property delivered him. Each of the above officers is allowed a clerk, to aid in keeping all accounts. There is also a foreman, or assistant master armorer, to each principal branch of the work, viz: of forged work, one inspector of welded, bored, and ground barrels, mounting bayonets and ramrods; one of the lock filers; one of the stockers; and one of the finishers. They are severally held accountable for all stock, tools and parts of work, delivered them for their respective departments, who severally hold the individual workmen responsible for all stock, tools, or parts of work delivered to them. Each assistant master armorer, or foreman is inspector in the several branches, and is responsible for the faithful and correct performance of the work. Each individual puts on the work he executes his own private mark, as do the inspectors, when they examine and approve of the various parts of the musket. Thus, in case of any defect, the delinquent may readily be found. Monthly returns of work are made to the superintendent, from which the monthly pay-roll is made. . . .

The situation of this establishment is remarkably pleasant and healthy; being sixty miles from the nearest seaport in a thickly inhabited country, it is perfectly safe from an invading foe, and still has water communication to within a few rods of the armory. Materials for the manufacturing of arms may be obtained in great abundance, on reasonable terms. The number of arms completed in the year 1817 exceeded 13,000, with an increase of the several parts of the musket; and the works are so arranged, that in the year 1818 15,000 stands may be made by the same number of hands, (250, including officers,) and for about the same expense. Good professional armorers, in considerable numbers, can at any time be added to the works, if necessary, for reasonable wages. The necessaries of life are abundant, and can at all times be procured at a moderate price.

On the whole, it is believed that there is not a situation in the United States where arms can be made for a sum, and where so many important advantages combine, as renders this station eligible for a grand national establishment. . . .

The number of workmen now employed is 244, viz:

7 Barrel welders, who work by the piece. 10 Polishers, who work by the piece.
7 Barrel borers, who work by the piece. 9 Drillers, millers, and turners, who work by the piece.
5 Lock forgers, who work by the piece. 5 Barrel finishers, who work by the piece.
2 Bayonet forgers, who work by the piece.
42 Lock filers, who work by the piece.
8 Mounting forgers, who work by the piece.
12 Mounting filers, who work by the piece.
2 Gun rod forgers, who work by the piece.
35 Stockers, who work by the piece.
6 Trip hammer's men, who work by the piece.
14 Finishers, who work by the piece.
18 Forgemen and trip hammer men's assistants, who work by the piece. 52 Jobbers, or those men who work by the day including carpenters and nullwrights.
10 Grinders, who work by the piece.

The number of jobbers ordinarily employed is forty; it being now increased, in consequence of the building a forge for making bar iron from the scraps, &c. made at the works.

The price paid for the working of each piece have been settled by the superintendent, upon the result of each experiment. It is calculated that good industrious men will be able to earn $1 40 per day. Upon this basis the prices have been established. The workmen earn now from $20 to $60 per month; such is the difference in the skill, industry, and ambition of men of the same trade. There are, however, but three or four in the 244 who are up to $60 per month. The average price paid is about $35 per month, or about $1 35 per day, allowing that they work twenty-five days in the month.

The jobbers are men who work by the day, and are paid $1 to $1 75 per day when they work. The usual price given to all sorts of mechanics is $1 40 per day.

The prices paid to the workmen, on the whole, are not high. "The times are hard," and the wages of mechanics are now generally high in every part of the Northern States. The prices paid to ordinary mechanics is that State of New York for the two past years is $1 37 1/2 per day; to first rate workmen $1 50; and to some few of known skill and smartness $1 75; to master workmen, to direct and oversee, $2 per day; and to master builders from $3 to $5 per day. So that by comparison, considering the mechanics at Springfield are generally first rate workmen and respectable citizens, the prices now given appear to be rather under those ordinarily paid to mechanics in this part of the United States.

I obtained a table of prices paid for working each piece, in part, or in whole, as the piece is either worked in part or wholly by the same man; but as it is lengthy, and as it can be obtained at any time of the superintendent if required, I think it not worth while to embrace it in this report. There are a hundred and forty things to be done by the workmen by the piece, and as many prices for doing them.

The plan of having the work done by the piece is, undoubtedly, the best of all possible plans, provided there is a strict attention paid to the inspection of the several parts, before they pass from one workman to another. It gives this advantage, that every man is paid according to his merit; it excites ambition and industry, and brings into operation and usefulness the otherwise dormant powers of the mind. It has a moral, good tendency upon the workmen, and at the same, or a far less price, gives annually to the Government a much greater number of arms. Where it is practicable, this plan is pursued; but there are some kinds of the work that cannot be done by the piece.

General arrangement of workmen to the several branches of business

The general arrangement of the workmen to their work is the best that can be adopted for the United States, but not so for the interest of the workmen; that is, each man is kept at one particular kind of work, and is not shifted. For instance, one man is always kept at forging locks, another at filing them, and so on for the other parts. One man is kept at putting the parts of the lock together, and finishing them; another at drilling them; another at milling the pins; another at slitting the heads; another at polishing the parts of the lock. One is kept grinding barrels; another at turning; another at sighting, and another at breeching them, &c.

By this arrangement, it will readily be perceived that each workman becomes an adept at his part. He works with greater facility, and *does the work much*

better than one *could* who worked at all the parts. This is undoubtedly the best method for Government. The consequence, however, to the workmen is, that not one of them becomes a finished armorer. If he is always employed at the Government factories, it is no matter for him; he is, in fact, the better for it, for he does more work, and gets more money; but if he wishes to set up business for himself, he has got no trade; he cannot make a fire-arm. . . .

Process and method of executing the work generally

It has already been observed, that each part of the work is done by particular men, and, in addition to the advantages there stated to be derived from this method, it will be proper further to remark, that the great desideratum, uniformity of work, is thus more nearly obtained. To obtain continually from the United States' armories, and from contractors, arms made precisely to one pattern in all the detail of parts, is very desirable; but it is believed that perfection in this subject is not attainable. One thing, I believe, is most clear to all those officers who have turned their attention to this point, that we ought to arrive as *near* to perfection as time, money, the want of arms, reason, and good sense will allow. To what extent shall we try? and when shall we be satisfied? are, it is thought, the proper questions to be decided. That a few pieces might be made so perfect, that if they were taken to pieces, and the several parts of the locks, the stocks, barrels, and mounting thrown into a pile promiscuously, they might again be put together when the parts should be alternatively changed, is believed, provided each similar part was made by the same man: but if the similar parts were made by different men, which must always by the case where a great number are made even at one factory, it is not believed practicable even to make a small number prefect; and as the parts must be made by different men where the arms are made at different factories, and as the United States have, and will have, different factories employed, it is believed to be impossible to attain universal perfection. Different men have different visions; they do not see alike, and they do not feel alike; and, as the accuracy of parts depends upon the vision and feeling of the workmen, the parts made by them must vary. Admitting that arms to any extent could be made perfectly alike in all their parts, would it be advisable? Being governed in this decision, as we must be, by the before-mentioned considerations, of money, time, want of arms, and reason, it is believed it would not be advisable. Why? Because the muskets would cost at least $30 each, instead of $12 50; and because about three years instead of one would be required to make an equal number of arms; and because the country wants arms as fast as they can be made; and lastly, because, if perfection were attained in the muskets, the real advantage gained in the country would be proportionably very far short of the expense. What is the advantage of having all the similar parts precisely alike? This: that when they are damaged, the several parts that remain good can be put together, and good arms be made out of bad ones. *In practice*, what parts would be thus put together, if they were perfectly alike? and who would do it? Let us see, and then we can judge of the advantage. Arms damaged in service would be turned over to, or collected by the quartermaster, or some other proper officer of the army. Arms are wanted; new ones cannot be obtained; some officer or soldier of the army would be directed to overhaul the damaged arms in *possession of that army*, and make out as many good ones as he could. What parts, if damaged, would he, with his *skill and tools*, replace? If other parts would fit, he can exchange and replace bayonets, ramrods, barrels, stocks, cocks, and whole locks—nothing more. He can never replace the parts of locks or mounting, except hands, which are seldom damaged or lost. Then it follows that locks and mounting must go to the repairing shops to be repaired, if they are all alike. The workmen in the repairing shops are armorers, and have tools. If the parts requiring to be changed want a little altering or filing, they are able to do it, to make them fit; so that, if the parts of the locks and mounting are so nearly alike that the repairer is able to make them fit with his tools, it is all that is required. The following objects, then, only

seem necessary to be attained in the manufacture of small arms, viz: that the barrels, stocks, whole locks, cocks, bayonets, and ramrods should each fit every musket; and that the several parts of the locks and mounting should be made so nearly alike, that they could be fitted at the repairing shops. Consequently, when this is attained, we shall have done all we ought to wish for. This is not yet done, but it is believed *to be practicable*. The most important of the individual objects is to have the bayonets all fit every musket. Bayonets are more likely to get lost or broken than any other parts of the musket, and hence much difficulty has been experienced. This is proved by the result of repairing arms damaged in the last war. Last year I had at this post, Rome, and Vergennes, six thousand stands of repaired arms, in every other way complete but wanting bayonets and ramrods, and only about three thousand wanted the rods. There were probably about thirty thousand stands repaired, and about five hundred stands condemned altogether. From this it appears that about one-fifth of the whole wanted the bayonets, either by loss or not fitting, about one-tenth the rods, and only about one-sixtieth the other parts altogether. This deficiency of bayonets was made up by getting six thousand made at Springfield, and sent to the repairing shops. In this great difficulty was experienced, on account of the different sizes of sockets required. Twelve different sizes of patterns were sent to the forgers, and then each class of sizes had to be altered individually at the repairing shops, to fit the barrels. Hence it appears evident, that the first and most important object in the manufacture of muskets is, to cause all the bayonets to fit the same gun, and all the barrels to fit the same bayonets.

In order to attain this grand object of uniformity of parts, the only method which can accomplish it has been adopted at Springfield, but it requires to be perfected, viz: making each part to fit a standard gauge. The master armorer has a set of standard patterns and gauges. The foremen of shops and branches and inspectors have each a set for the parts formed in their respective shops; and each workman has those that are required for the particular part at which he is at work. These are all made to correspond with the original set, and are tried by them occasionally, in order to discover any variation that may have taken place in using. They are made of hardened steel. The workman makes every similar piece to fit the same gauge, and, consequently, every similar piece must be nearly of the same size and form. If this method is continued, and the closest attention paid to it by the master workmen, inspectors, workmen, and superintendent, the desired object will finally be attained. The method practised at Springfield, of inspecting each part before the parts are put together, or before it goes to another workman, to be put through another process, has a great influence on the workman; it does much towards improving the work generally, and towards obtaining a uniformity of parts, and consequently a uniformity of muskets, and is undoubtedly the best possible method. If a part does not pass inspection, it goes back to the workman, either to be improved, or deducted from his wages. His interest compels him to do it well. It is on account of this method that the arms made at the national armories are, and will be, superior to those made on contract. In the latter case, the arm is finished before inspection, and, if a part is condemned, the whole piece, valued at $13 or $14, is condemned. The inspector cannot, from this cause, avoid feeling a reluctance in condemning the arms he is set to inspect; his feeling will be towards the contractor; and, from a slight neglect in one particular part, he will seldom condemn the musket; and thus he will receive arms, among which, perhaps, there is not one without some defect; whereas, if the same inspector were to inspect the same parts as they were made, he would condemn them, because he would think that the loss would be but trifling, and it would be incurred by the workman, who ought to bear the loss of his own bad work; and if all the parts of a musket were to be condemned in this way, the loss would be divided between, perhaps, a dozen or fifteen men, instead of falling upon one. An inspector is more

likely to condemn a trifling thing than a valuable one, for a small defect.

In the method and process of executing the work at Springfield, I have reason to believe, both from inquiry and a comparison of the arms now made with those made before the late war, that great improvements have been made. How much credit is due for this to the superintendent, and how much to the colonel of ordinance, I have not the means of judging; but there is a credit due somewhere.

To give in detail the process of each part of the musket, from the raw material to the finishing shop, would occupy too much room to be embraced in this report. I shall, therefore, not attempt it. I will only observe that, as far as I can judge, the arrangements are good, and, with some intended changes in the shops, cannot probably be bettered. There must necessarily be in such establishments a good deal of passing of parts of muskets from one shop to another; but the whole is accomplished at Springfield by one two-horse team, which passes round to the different shops but twice in each day.

On the subject of uniformity of arms I will make one more remark: that, in order to accomplish this object throughout the Union, it will be necessary to have a set of original patterns and gauges of each and every part of the musket, sealed and kept in the Ordnance Office at Washington, and to cause those of the superintendent of each factory to be sent occasionally to that office, to be compared with them, and fitted anew, if required. This remark will hold good with every thing else in the Union that requires uniformity of construction. Hence, we may, be fair inference, deduce the great importance of the present organization and arrangement of the Ordnance Department to the country. The great advantage of placing the armories under the direction of such a permanent corps and such a head is already felt and acknowledged at Springfield, both by the officers and citizens.

DOCUMENT 4

Henry Clay, "Defense of the American System" (1832)

Henry Clay (1777–1852), congressman from Kentucky, fought for the interests of the West. After the War of 1812, Clay advanced an ambitious plan for national economic development at federal expense, known as the "American System." The central element in Clay's blueprint was a high tariff on foreign imports. Restrictions on free trade, he maintained, would free Americans from dependence on British manufacturers. Moreover, the tariff would stimulate domestic industries by protecting them from competition. Worried about the growth of sectionalism in the United States, Clay hoped that his American System would unite people of different regions. If they did so, he was confident that the United States would rise "to that height to which God and nature had destined it." When opponents later attacked Clay's scheme, suggesting that the Constitution did not allow for federal spending on domestic improvements, the Kentucky congressman launched a spirited defense.

I have now to perform the more pleasing task of exhibiting an imperfect sketch of the existing state of the unparalleled prosperity of the country. On a general survey, we behold cultivation extended, the arts flourishing, the face of the country improved; our people fully and profitably employed, and the public countenance exhibiting tranquility, contentment and happiness. And if we descend into particulars, we have the agreeable contemplation of a people out of debt, land rising slowly in value, but in a secure and salutary degree; a ready though not extravagant market for all the surplus productions of our industry; innumerable flocks and herds browsing and gamboling on ten thousand hills and plains, covered with rich and verdant grasses; our cities expanded, and whole villages springing up, as it were, by enchantment; our exports and imports increased and increasing; our tonnage, foreign and coastwise, swelling and fully occupied; the rivers of our interior animated by the perpetual thunder and lightning of countless steam-boats; the currency sound and abundant; the public debt of two wars nearly redeemed; and, to crown all, the public treasury overflowing, embarrassing Congress, not to find subjects

of taxation, but to select the objects which shall be liberated from the impost. If the term of seven years were to be selected, of the greatest prosperity which this people have enjoyed since the establishment of their present constitution, it would be exactly that period of seven years which immediately followed the passage of the tariff of 1824.

This transformation of the condition of the country from gloom and distress to brightness and prosperity, has been mainly the work of American legislation, fostering American industry, instead of allowing it to be controlled by foreign legislation, cherishing foreign industry. The foes of the American System, in 1824, with great boldness and confidence, predicted, 1st. The ruin of the public revenue, and the creation of a necessity to resort to direct taxation. The gentleman from South Carolina, (General Hayne,) I believe, thought that the tariff of 1824 would operate a reduction of revenue to the large amount of eight millions of dollars. 2d. The destruction of our navigation. 3d. The desolation of commercial cities. And 4th. The augmentation of the price of objects of consumption, and further decline in that of the articles of our exports.

Every prediction which they made has failed—utterly failed. Instead of the ruin of the public revenue, with which they then sought to deter us from the adoption of the American System, we are now threatened with its subversion, by the vast amount of the public revenue produced by that system. . . .

If the system of protection be founded on principles erroneous in theory, pernicious in practice—above all if it be unconstitutional, as is alledged, it ought to be forthwith abolished, and not a vestage of it suffered to remain. But, before we sanction this sweeping denunciation, let us look a little at this system, its magnitude, its ramifications, its duration, and the high authorities which have sustained it. We shall see that its foes will have accomplished comparatively nothing, after having achieved their present aim of breaking down our iron-founderies, our woollen, cotton, and hemp manufactories, and our sugar plantations. The destruction of these would, undoubtedly, lead to the sacrifice of immense capital, the ruin of many thousands of our fellow citizens, and incalculable loss to the whole community. But their prostration would not disfigure, nor produce greater effect upon the *whole* system of protection, in all its branches, than the destruction of the beautiful domes upon the capitol would occasion to the magnificent edifice which they surmount. Why, sir, there is scarcely an interest, scarcely a vocation in society, which is not embraced by the beneficence of this system.

It comprehends our coasting tonnage and trade, from which all foreign tonnage is absolutely excluded.

It includes all our foreign tonnage, with the inconsiderable exception made by the treaties of reciprocity with a few foreign powers.

It embraces our fisheries, and all our hardy and enterprising fishermen.

It extends to almost every mechanic and: to tanners, cordwainers, tailors, cabinet-makers, hatters, tinners, brass-workers, clock-makers, coach-makers, tallow-chandlers, trace-makers, rope-makers, cork-cutters, tobacconists, whip-makers, paper-makers, umbrella-makers, glass-blowers, stocking-weavers, butter-makers, saddle and harness-makers, cutlers,

brush-makers, book-binders, dairy-men, milk-farmers, black-smiths, type-founders, musical instrument-makers, basket-makers, milliners, potters, chocolate-makers, floor-cloth-makers, bonnet-makers, hair-cloth-makers, copper-smiths, pencil-makers, bellows-makers, pocket book-makers, card-makers, glue-makers, mustard-makers, lumber-sawyers, saw-makers, scale-beam-makers, scythe-makers, wood-saw-makers, and many others. The mechanics enumerated, enjoy a measure of protection adapted to their several conditions, varying from twenty to fifty per cent. The extent and importance of some of these artizans may be estimated by a few particulars. The tanners, curriers, boot and shoe-makers, and other workers in hides, skins and leather, produce an ultimate value per annum of forty millions of dollars; the manufacturers of hats and caps produce an annual value of fifteen millions; the cabinet-makers twelve millions; the manufacturers of bonnets and hats for the female sex, lace, artificial flowers, combs, &c. seven millions; and the manufacturers of glass, five millions.

It extends to all lower Louisiana, the Delta of which might as well be submerged again in the Gulf of Mexico, from which it has been a gradual conquest, as now to be deprived of the protecting duty upon is great staple.

It effects the cotton planter himself, and the tobacco planter, both of whom enjoy protection.

The total amount of the capital vested in sheep, the land to sustain them, wool, woollen manufacturers, and woollen fabrics, and the subsistence of the various persons directly or indirectly employed in the growth and manufacture of the article of wool, is estimated at one hundred and sixty-seven millions of dollars, and the number of persons at one hundred and fifty thousand.

The value of iron, considered as a raw material, and of its manufacturers, is estimated at twenty-six millions of dollars per annum. Cotton goods, exclusive of the capital vested in the manufacture, and of the cost of the raw material, are believed to amount annually, to about twenty millions of dollars.

These estimates have been carefully made, by practical men of undoubted character, who have brought together and embodied their information. Anxious to avoid the charge of exaggeration, they have sometimes placed their estimates below what was believed to be the actual amount of these interests. With regard to the quantity of bar and other iron annually produced, it is derived from the known works themselves; and I know some in western States which they have omitted in their calculations. . . .

When gentlemen have succeeded in their design of an immediate or gradual destruction of the American System, what is their substitute? Free trade? Free trade! The call for free trade is as unavailing as the cry of a spoiled child, in its nurse's arms, for the moon, or the stars that glitter in the firmament of heaven. It never has existed, it never will exist. Trade implies, at least two parties. To be free, it should be fair, equal and reciprocal. But if we throw our ports wide open to the admission of foreign productions, free of all duty, what ports of any other foreign nation shall we find open to the free admission of our surplus produce? We may break down all barriers to free trade on our part, but the work will not be complete until foreign powers shall have removed theirs. There would be freedom on one side, and restrictions, prohibitions and exclusions on the other. The bolts, and the bars, and the chains of all other nations will remain undisturbed. It is, indeed, possible, that our industry and commerce would accommodate themselves to this unequal and unjust, state of things; for, such is the flexibility of our nature, that it bends itself to all circumstances. The wretched prisoner incarcerated in a jail, after a long time becomes reconciled to his solitude, and regularly notches down the passing days of his confinement.

Gentlemen deceive themselves. It is not free trade that they are recommending to our acceptance. It is in effect, the British colonial system that we are invited to adopt; and, if their policy prevail, it will lead substantially to the re-colonization of these States, under the commercial dominion of Great Britain. . . .

Gentlemen are greatly deceived as to the hold which this system has in the affections of the people of the United States. They represent that it is the policy of New England, and that she is most benefitted by it. If there be any part of this Union which has been most steady, most unanimous, and most determined in its support, it is Pennsylvania. Why is not that powerful State attacked? Why pass her over, and aim the blow at New England? New England came reluctantly into the policy. In 1824 a majority of her delegation was opposed to it. From the largest State of New England there was but a solitary vote in favor of the bill. That enterprising people can readily accommodate their industry to any policy, provided it be *settled*. They supposed this was fixed, and they submitted to the decrees of government. And the progress of public opinion has kept pace with the developments of the benefits of the system. Now, all New England, at least in this house (with the exception of one small still voice) is in favor of the system. In 1824 all Maryland was against it; now the majority is for it. Then, Louisiana, with one exception, was opposed to it; now, without any exception, she is in favor of it. The march of public sentiment is to the South. Virginia will be the next convert; and in less than seven years, if there be no obstacles from political causes, or prejudices industriously instilled, the majority of eastern Virginia will be, as the majority of western Virginia now is, in favor of the American System. North Carolina will follow later, but not less certainly. Eastern Tennessee is now in favor of the system. And finally, its doctrines will pervade the whole Union, and the wonder will be, that they ever should have been opposed.

DOCUMENT 5

"The Western Country," Extracts from Letters Published in Niles' Weekly Register *(1816)*

In 1816 Ohio was still a young state. As letters taken from regional newspapers dramatically reveal, however, the Ohio economy had already taken the first steps toward industrialization. The documents not only list—almost as if they were gamescores—the different business enterprises recently established in the southern part of the state but also capture the sense of pride that Americans felt about rapid economic growth.

The western country continues to rise in population and importance with unabated rapidity. This town has been, since the war, full to overflowing; many being obliged to leave it after coming from the Eastern states, not being able to get a *room* to dwell in. More houses will be built this summer than during the last three years together. Manufactories of several important kinds are establishing, among which is a steam grist and saw mill. The surveyor general is making arrangements for laying out, agreeably to late acts of Congress, towns at the Lower Rapids of Sandusky, and at the Rapids of the Miami of the Lakes. The local situation of the latter cannot but render it a most important place. It will be situated at some point within the reservation of twelve miles square, to which vessels of a small tonnage can ascend, and as near the foot of the rapids as may be. I believe the time not very distant when the wealth and resources of the western country will be brought almost to your doors, by means of an extensive inland navigation through the lakes and the grand canal proposed to be made in New York. It will be an easy matter to connect the Miami of the Lakes and the Miami of the Ohio by a canal, the face of the country between the head of the navigation of each of those rivers being quite level. What an extensive inland navigation would then be opened!—from New Orleans to the Hudson!

The whole of that fine tract in Indiana territory, generally called Harrison's purchase, is now surveyed, and will be offered for sale. That part in Jeffesonville district to commence on the first Monday in September next; and that part in Vincennes district on the second Monday in the same month. This tract contains near *three millions of acres* of excellent land; and is, perhaps, the greatest body of good land in the western country. Indiana will be settled as fast as Ohio.

To the foregoing it is pleasant to add the following abstract of an account of the town of Mount Pleasant in Ohio, from the Western Herald.

The town of Mount Pleasant, in Jefferson country, in 1806, containing only seven families, living mostly in cabins—*last summer* it had between 80 and 90 families and about 500 souls, besides journeymen and laborers, transient persons, and its private buildings were mostly of brick.

There were 7 stores; 3 taverns; 3 saddler's, 3 hatter's, 4 blacksmith's, 4 weaver's, 6 boot and shoe maker's, 8 carpenter's, 3 tailor's, 3 cabinet maker's, 1 baker's, 1 apothecary's, and 2 waggon maker's shops—2 tanneries; 1 shop for making wool carding machines; 1 with a machine for spinning wool; 1 manufactory for spinning thread from *flax;* 1 nail factory; 2 wool carding machines. The public buildings were—1 meeting house belonging to the society of Friends, or Quakers, built of brick, two-stories high, with galleries, 92 feet by 60; 1 brick school house, 46 by 22 feet; and 1 brick markethouse, 32 by 16.

Within the distance of six miles from the town were—9 merchant mills; 1 grist mills; 12 saw mills; 1 paper mill, with 2 vats; 1 woolen factory, with 4 looms, and 2 fulling mills.

DOCUMENT 6

Letters of John and Elizabeth Hodgdon (1840)

Women who left their households to enter the mills of New England in the nineteenth century found mixed blessings there. They faced long hours and a regimented life, but also found a sense of independence in their new work and hard-earned wages. In the following letters, a mill worker tells her family about life there and plans for staying on to earn more.

Dear sister,

I take this time to write you a few lines as I have a good opportunity. I thank you for your letter you sent sister and myself; and I find you have not forgotten me (your unworthy Brother). As you wrote to me about never working there again I hope you will never be under the necessity of it but I hope you will not put to[o] much dependence on your absent fri[e]nd for you know not neather do any of us what time will bring forth but God alone knows and if we put our trust in him he will bring all things for the best. Therefore let us look to him alone and he will brings things out right. You said if I mistake not you have not seen a well day since your absence. I am sorry to hear that for it pained me to the hart and brought me to reflect on myself when sick from home. But it was not so hard for me having a sister to comfort me in my illness. I suppose sister that I shall come after you if nothing particular prevents me. So you can give your notice when you please and send us word and we will move you home as you say.

Yours with respect Sarah D Hodgdon

Your most affectionate brother John B. Hodgdon

I have forgoten one thing; Mr Hays Lydias father Layes at the point of Deth. He has a feaver and has been sick about or little over a week. His fri[e]nds have given him up and the Doctor says it is a doutful case.

Dear Sister

Do not think I have forgotten you because I have not written for there has always been something to prevent me so that I could not write & the alarm concerning the small pet entirely ceased soon after you went away & I thought you would probably hear of it therefore I did not feel so anxious about writing as if it had been otherwise.

Sister Sarah I suppose you feel by this time as though you had worked long enough in the factory & I should think the money you wrote me you had earned with what you had before would be as much as you would need to spend during this year, you know. The patterns you sent me I do not like very much. Respecting Florence bonnets I think they are to[o] costly for us & in fact they last too long; but if

TIME TABLE OF THE LOWELL MILLS,

To take effect on and after Oct. 21st, 1851.

The Standard time being that of the meridian of Lowell, as shown by the regulator clock of JOSEPH RAYNES, 43 Central Street.

	From 1st to 10th inclusive.				From 11th to 20th inclusive.					From 21st to last day of month.			
	1st Bell	2d Bell	3d Bell	Eve.Bell	1st Bell	2d Bell	3d Bell	Eve.Bell		1st Bell	2d Bell	3d Bell	Eve.Bell
January,	5.00	6.00	6.50	*7.30	5.00	6.00	6.50	*7.30		5.00	6.00	6.50	*7.30
February,	4.30	5.30	6.40	*7.30	4.30	5.30	6.25	*7.30		4.30	5.30	6.15	*7.30
March,	5.40	6.00		*7.30	5.20	5.40		*7.30		5.05	5.25		6.35
April,	4.45	5.05		6.45	4.30	4.50		6.55		4.30	4.50		7.00
May,	4.30	4.50		7.00	4.30	4.50		7.00		4.30	4.50		7.00
June,	"	"		"	"	"		"		"	"		"
July,	"	"		"	"	"		"		"	"		"
August,	"	"		"	"	"		"		"	"		"
September,	4.40	5.00		6.45	4.50	5.10		6.30		5.00	5.20		*7.30
October,	5.10	5.30		*7.30	5.20	5.40		*7.30		5.35	5.55		*7.30
November,	4.30	5.30	6.10	*7.30	4.30	5.30	6.20	*7.30		5.00	6.00	6.25	*7.30
December,	5.00	6.00	6.45	*7.30	5.00	6.00	6.50	*7.30		5.00	6.00	6.50	*7.30

*Excepting on Saturdays from Sept. 21st to March 20th inclusive, when it is rung at 20 minutes after sunset.

YARD GATES.

Will be opened at ringing of last morning bell, of meal bells, and of evening bells; and kept open Ten minutes.

MILL GATES.

Commence hoisting Mill Gates, Two minutes before commencing work.

WORK COMMENCES,

At Ten minutes after last morning bell, and at Ten minutes after bell which "rings in" from Meals.

BREAKFAST BELLS.

During March "Ring out".........at....7.30 a. m..........."Ring in" at 8.05 a. m.
April 1st to Sept. 20th inclusive ....at ....7.00 " "......... " at 7.35 " "
Sept. 21st to Oct. 31st inclusive.....at ....7.30 " "......... " at 8.05 " "
Remainder of year work commences after Breakfast.

DINNER BELLS.

" Ring out"...... ....12.30 p. m.........."Ring in".... 1.05 p. m.

In all cases, the *first* stroke of the bell is considered as marking the time.

B. H. Penhallow, Printer, 28 Merrimack Street.

Eli Whitney's cotton gin, invented in 1793, greatly expanded the supply of cotton, making it possible for entrepreneurs such as Francis Cabot Lowell to increase the production of cloth. This eleven-hour-a-day, six-days-a week schedule for workers at the Lowell textile mills in Massachusetts illustrates how hard laborers had to work during the Industrial Revolution to make a decent living.

you think you should prefer them I have not a word to say. I think it will not be possible for me to go down while you work there so if you make any purchases I have only so say satisfy yourself & I assure you I shall not be dissatisfied. Study what will be profitable & becoming for us the ensuing season if we should live to enjoy it which may it be the pleasure & will of Divine Providence that we may & be blest in fully realizing what our fond hopes now anticipate.

You say you want to come home when we all think you have staid long enough but we do not know better than you or so well either when you have earned as much as you will want to spend. Yet it is Mothers opinion & mine that you have already as much as you will probably want to spend if you lay it out to good advantage which we doubt not but you will. We want you to make arrangements to suit yourself to give your notice as soon as you please & settle all up & send us word so that we may know when to send for you or move you home as you say.

All are well in this place excepting Mr Hayes of whom John has wrote. It is really a distressed house & an affecting scene to see relatives weeping over him. All the children are at home excepting Ichabod whom they expect next Wednesday. Moses was over here last Friday after Aunt Liberty to go & take care of him but she could not go. He said he wished you was at home that he might get you to go & said something about going down after you. But I should advise you not to go if he did but dont you let him know that I said any thing against it. Yet I think on the whole that he will not go for you now the doing is so bad and the house is already quite full.

Be sure to send us word as soon as you learn how your time is limited. Give my love to Lucy & accept much to yourself.

From your affectionate sister
Elizabeth K. Hodgdon

Study Questions

1. What was the connection between economic growth and nationalism in the United States?

2. What was innovative about the production of guns at the Springfield Armory?

3. Why might people living in different regions of the United States have supported Henry Clay's American System?

4. How did working in the textile mills affect the lives of young American women?

11

Jacksonian Democracy

The second quarter of the nineteenth century witnessed an unprecedented expansion of popular participation in politics accompanied by tributes to the virtue of government for and by the ordinary citizen. The man who came to embody the growing democratic spirit and thus symbolized the era was Andrew Jackson. Raised in the backwoods of North Carolina, he fought as an adolescent in the Revolutionary War and later gained renown as an Indian fighter and the victor in the Battle of New Orleans (1815).

Although Jackson acquired wealth and slaves in the new state of Tennessee, his image as a tough-as-nails man of the people made him a natural for politics. Jackson lost in his first bid for the presidency in 1824 to the New England Whig John Quincy Adams, even though Jackson polled more popular votes in a four-candidate race. When Jackson swept into office with a clear electoral and popular majority in 1828, a new era of mass politics began. The politician who did not pay heed to public opinion in this age of high voter turnout and few restrictions on white male suffrage did so at his own peril (Document 1).

What it meant actually to represent the interests of the "common man," however, became the subject of much contention during the Age of Jackson. While serving two terms as president, Jackson did not hesitate to use either the power of the executive branch against other branches of government or the authority of the federal government against the states. Two crises captured Jackson's governing style: his battle against the Bank of the United States and the Nullification Crisis of 1832–1833. The president's hostility to the bank stemmed from opposition to what he saw as the unfair granting of special privileges to private citizens. Thus, he vetoed the bill sent to him by Congress to recharter the bank (Document 2). His easy re-election against the pro-bank Henry Clay demonstrated public approval of his decision.

The Nullification Crisis tested Jackson's mettle in another way. South Carolina organized a convention to void the applicability of federal tariffs designed to protect northern manufacturers from foreign competition by imposing import taxes on many items. Such a policy, according to southern planters, unfairly penalized their region, which had no trouble selling its commodities on the world market. South Carolina's unilateral rejection of the act aroused Jackson's ire. He persuaded

JACKSON TICKET

Honor and gratitude to the man who has filled
the measure of his country's glory—*Jefferson*

FOR THE ASSEMBLY
GEORGE H. STEUART,
JOHN V. L. McMAHON.

An 1828 campaign poster for political candidates identified with Andrew Jackson. A hero of the War of 1812,
Jackson was depicted as a champion of democracy and
the common man. As president, he strengthened the
Democratic party, and ambitious politicians throughout
the nation echoed his attack on special privilege.

Congress to pass the Force Bill, giving him the power to take military action against
the nullifiers if necessary (Document 3). Such a threat compelled South Carolina to
accept a compromise tariff, which Jackson signed into law.

Jackson's actions and the style of democratic politics he encouraged provoked
criticism. His opponents ultimately came together in the Whig Party, which offered a
platform geared to government-sponsored commercial development and greater respect for traditional social hierarchy. Whigs also bemoaned the effects of what they
perceived as demagoguery and pandering (Document 4). In practice, of course, Whig
politicians aggressively competed for support from all sectors of society, thus contributing much to Jacksonian political culture. Jacksonian democracy, moreover,
penetrated deep into society. Writers like Walt Whitman looked back over the period as one of robust expansion in which every man and woman made his or her valuable contribution (Document 5). Indeed, from one perspective, the salience of the
ordinary citizen across the vast and growing American landscape defined a unique

national character.

While for many white men the door to entry into the rough-and-tumble world of Jacksonian democracy required only a hard and well-timed push (Document 6), for other men and women opportunities were scarcer and even diminishing. Laborers in the expanding northern urban manufacturing sector faced low wages, episodic unemployment, and overcrowded living conditions. Male workers, though sympathetic to the even worse conditions under which many women labored, often proved wary of female competition in the marketplace (Document 7); they also remained indifferent to the plight of millions of black slaves.

The limits of Jacksonian democracy became strikingly apparent to American Indians during the period. In the 1830s the federal government forced thousands of southeastern Indians to march from their homes in Georgia or Alabama across the Mississippi and on to Oklahoma territory (Document 8). Disease and death accompanied the Indians on their westward Trail of Tears.

DOCUMENT 1

Michel Chevalier, Society, Manners and Politics in the United States (1834)

In 1834, the French minister of the interior dispatched to the United States Michel Chevalier, who reported on American society in a series of letters. The contract between the character of public opinion in Europe and America particularly impressed the visitor. In the United States, Chevalier observed, public opinion was a democratic phenomenon, the powerful voice of "the farmer and the mechanic."

Public opinion has not the same arbiters here as in European societies; what is called public opinion in Europe, is the generally current opinion among the middling and higher classes, that of the merchants, manufacturers, men of letters, and statesmen, of those who, having inherited a competency, devote their time to study, the fine arts, and unfortunately too often, to idleness. These are the persons who govern public opinion in Europe, who have seats in the chambers, fill public offices, and manage or direct the most powerful organs of the press. They are the polite and cultivated, who are accustomed to self-control, most inclined to scepticism from fanaticism, and on their guard against the impulses of enthusiasm; to whose feelings all violence is repugnant, all rudeness and all brutality offensive; who cherish moderation often even to excess and prefer compromises and half-measures. . . .

The minority, which in Europe decides public opinion and by this means is sovereign, is here deposed, and having been successively driven from post to post, had come to influence opinion only in a few saloons in the large cities, and to be itself under as strict guardianship as minors, women, and idiots. Until the accession of General Jackson, it had, however, exercised some influence over all the Presidents, who were generally scholars, and all of whom, aside from their party connections, were attached to it by family and social relations, and by their habits of life. Up to the present time, this class had also preserved some influence over the two houses; but it has now completely broken with the President, or rather the President has broken with it; it has no longer any credit, except with one of the Houses, because the Senate still consists of men whom it may claim as belonging to it by their superior intelligence, education, and property. The democracy does not fail, therefore, to stigmatize the Senate as an aristocratic body, and to call it the House of Lords The mass, which in Europe bears the pack and receives the law, has here put the pack on the back of the enlightened and cultivated class, which among us on the other hand, has the upper hand. The farmer and the mechanic are the lords of the New World; public opinion is *their* opinion; the public will is *their* will; the President is their choice, *their* agent, *their* servant. If it is true that the depositaries of power in Europe have been too much exposed to use it in promoting their own interests, without consulting the wishes and the welfare of the mass beneath them, it is no less true that the classes which held the sceptre in America are equally tainted with selfishness, and that they take less pains to disguise it. In a word, North America is Europe with its head down and its feet up. European society, in London and Paris as well as at St. Petersburg, in the Swiss republic as well as in the Austrian empire, is aristocratical in this sense, that, even after all the great changes of the last fifty years, it is still founded more or less absolutely on the principle of inequality or a different of ranks. American society is essentially and radically a democracy, not in name merely but in deed. In the United States the democratic spirit is infused into all the national habits, and all the customs of society; it besets and startles at every step the foreigner, who, before landing in the country, had no suspicion to what a degree every nerve and fibre had been steeped in aristocracy by a European education. It has effaced all distinctions, except that of colour; for here a shade in the hue of the skin separates men more widely than in any other country in the world. It pervades all places, one only excepted, and that the very one which in Catholic Europe is consecrated to equality, the church; here all whites are equal, every where, except in the presence of Him, in whose eyes, the distinctions of this world are vanity and nothingness. Strange inconsistency! Or rather solemn protest, attesting that the principle of rank is firmly seated in the human heart by the side of the principle of equality, that it must have its place in all countries and under all circumstances!

Democracy everywhere has no soft words, no suppleness of forms; it has little address, little of management it is apt to confound moderation with weakness, violence with heroism. Little used to self-control, it gives itself unreservedly to its friends, and sets them up as idols to whom it burns incense; it utters its indignation and its suspicions against those of whom it thinks that it has cause for complaint, rudely, and in a tone of anger and menace. It is intolerant towards foreign nations: the American democracy in particular, bred up in the belief that the nations of Europe groan ignobly under the yoke of absolute despots, looks upon them with a mixture of pity and contempt. When it throws a glance beyond the Atlantic it affects the superior air of a freeman looking upon a herd of slaves. Its pride kindles at the idea of humbling the monarchical principle in the person of the "tyrants who tread Europe under foot." . . .

DOCUMENT 2

Andrew Jackson, Veto of the Bank Bill (1832)

Andrew Jackson believed that the Bank of the United States, a publicly chartered but privately controlled institution that held the federal government's deposits and controlled the nation's credit system, subverted the principles of democracy and advanced the interests of the few over the many. In his veto message of a congressional bill to renew the bank's charter, scheduled to expire in 1836, Jackson played on nationalist and class themes to persuade Congress to sustain his decision. Not only did they do so, but his victory in the ensuing presidential election allowed Jackson to pursue controversial and economically destabilizing antibank policies during the institution's final years.

To the Senate:

The bill "to modify and continue" the act entitled "An act to incorporate the subscribers to the Bank of the United States" was presented to me on the 4th July instant. Having considered it with that solemn regard to the principles of the Constitution which the day was calculated to inspire, and come to the conclusion that it ought not to become a law, I herewith return it to the Senate, in which it originated, with my objections.

A bank of the United States is in many respects convenient for the Government and useful to the people. Entertaining this opinion, and deeply impressed with the belief that some of the powers and privileges possessed by the existing bank are unauthorized by the Constitution, subversive of the rights of the States, and dangerous to the liberties of the people, I felt it my duty at an early period of my Administration to call the attention of Congress to the practicability of organizing an institution combining all its advantages and obviating these objections. I sincerely regret that in the act before me I can perceive none of those modifications of the bank charter which are necessary, in my opinion, to make it compatible with justice, with sound policy, or with the Constitution of our country.

The present corporate body, denominated the president, directors, and company of the Bank of

the United States, will have existed at the time this act is intended to take effect twenty years. It enjoys an exclusive privilege of banking under the authority of the General Government, a monopoly of its favor and support, and, as a necessary consequence, almost a monopoly of the foreign and domestic exchange. The powers, privileges, and favors bestowed upon it in the original character, by increasing the value of the stock far above its par value, operated as a gratuity of many millions to the stockholders. . . .

It is not our own citizens only who are to receive the bounty of our Government. More than eight millions of the stock of this bank are held by foreigners. By this act the American Republic proposes virtually to make them a present of some millions of dollars. For these gratuities to foreigners and to some of our own opulent citizens the act secures no equivalent whatever. . . .

It is not conceivable how the present stockholders can have any claim to the special favor of the Government. The present corporation has enjoyed its monopoly during the period stipulated in the original contract. If we must have such a corporation, why should not the Government sell out the whole stock and thus secure to the people the full market value of the privileges granted? Why should not Congress create and sell twenty-eight millions of stock, incorporating the purchasers with all the

Jackson's veto of the recharter bill for the Bank of the United States, as well as his removal of government funds from the bank, led his political opponents to charge that he was abusing presidential power. Jackson questioned the bank's constitutionality and was angered by political opposition from some of the bank's officers. While Jackson's withdrawal of government funds effectively crippled the Bank of the United States, he did little to provide for a new national banking policy.

powers and privileges secured in this act and putting the premium upon the sales into the Treasury?

But this act does not permit competition in the purchase of this monopoly. It seems to be predicated on the erroneous idea that the present stockholders have a prescriptive right not only to the favor but to the bounty of Government. It appears that more than a fourth part of the stock is held by foreigners and the residue is held by a few hundred of our own citizens, chiefly of the richest class. For their benefit does this act exclude the whole American people from competition in the purchase of this monopoly and dispose of it for many millions less than it is worth. This seems the less excusable because some of our citizens not now stockholders petitioned that the door of competition might be opened, and offered to take a charter on terms much more favorable to the Government and country. . . .

It is to be regretted that the rich and powerful too often bend the acts of government to their selfish purposes. Distinctions in society will always exist under every just government. Equality of talents, of education, or of wealth can not be produced by human institutions. In the full enjoyment of the gifts of Heaven and the fruits of superior industry, economy, and virtue, every man is equally entitled to protection by law; but when the laws undertake to add to these natural and just advantages artificial distinctions, to grant titles, gratuities, and exclusive privileges, to make the rich richer and the potent more powerful, the humble members of society—the farmers, mechanics, and laborers—who have neither the time nor the means of securing like favors to themselves, have a right to complain of the injustice of their Government. There are no necessary evils in government. Its evils exist only in its abuses. If it would confine itself to equal protection, and, as Heaven does its rains, shower its favors alike on the high and the low, the rich and the poor, it would be an unqualified blessing. In the act before me there seems to be a wide and unnecessary departure from these just principles.

Nor is our Government to be maintained or our Union preserved by invasions of the rights and powers of the several States. In thus attempting to make our General Government strong we make it weak. Its true strength consists in leaving individuals and States as much as possible to themselves—in making itself felt, not in its power, but in its beneficence; not in its control, but in its protection; not in binding the States more closely to the center, but leaving each to move unobstructed in its proper orbit.

Experience should teach us wisdom. Most of the difficulties our Government now encounters and most of the dangers which impend over our Union have sprung from an abandonment of the legitimate objects of Government by our national legislation, and the adoption of such principles as are embodied in this act. Many of our rich men have not been content with equal protection and equal benefits, but have besought us to make them richer by act of Congress. By attempting to gratify their desires we have in the results of our legislation arrayed section against section, interest against interest, and man against man, in a fearful commotion which threatens to shake the foundations of our Union. It is time to pause in our career to review our principles, and if possible revive that devoted patriotism and spirit of compromise which distinguished the sages of the Revolution and the fathers of our Union. If we can not at once, in justice to interests vested under improvident legislation, make our Government what it ought to be, we can at least take a stand against all new grants of monopolies and exclusive privileges, against any prostitution of our Government to the advancement of the few at the expense of the many, and in favor of compromise and gradual reform in our code laws and system of political economy.

DOCUMENT 3

The Force Bill (1833)

J ackson found Congress cooperative in his effort to assert federal supremacy over the individual states during the Nullification Crisis. South Carolinian John C. Calhoun, Jackson's vice president during his first term, encouraged his home state openly to defy the so-called tariff of abominations, which taxed imports, to the advantage of northern manufacturers but not southern planters. The Force Bill passed by Congress to crush any resistance to tariff collection in South Carolina helped facilitate a compromise tariff that returned South Carolina peaceably to the federal fold.

An Act further to provide for the collection of duties on imports.

Be it enacted by the Senate and House of Representatives of the United States of America, in Congress assembled, That whenever, by reason of unlawful obstructions, combinations, or assemblages of persons, it shall become impracticable, in the judgment of the President, to execute the revenue laws, and collect the duties on imports in the ordinary way, in any collection district, it shall and may be lawful for the President to direct that the custom-house for such district be established and kept in any secure place within some port or harbour of such district, either upon land or on board any vessel; and, in that case, it shall be the duty of the collector to reside at such place, and there to detain all vessels and cargoes arriving within the said district until the duties imposed on said cargoes, by law, be paid in cash, deducting interest according to existing laws; and in such cases it shall be unlawful to take the vessel or cargo from the custody of the proper officer of the customs, unless by process from some court of the United States; and in case of any attempt otherwise to take such vessel or cargo by any force, or combination, or assemblage of persons too great to be overcome by the officers of the customs, it shall and may be lawful for the President of the United States, or such person or persons as he shall have empowered for that purpose, to employ such part of the land or naval forces, or militia of the United States, as may be deemed necessary for the purpose of preventing the removal of such vessel or cargo, and protecting the officers of the customs in retaining the custody thereof.

SEC. 2. *And be it further enacted,* That the jurisdiction of the circuit courts of the United States shall extend to all cases, in law or equity, arising under the revenue laws of the United States, for which other provisions are not already made by law; and if any person shall receive any injury to his person or property for or on account of any act by him done, under any law of the United States, for the protection of the revenue or the collection of duties on imports, he shall be entitled to maintain suit for damage therefor in the circuit court of the United States in the district wherein the party doing the injury may reside, or shall be found. And all property taken or detained by any officer or other person under authority of any revenue law of the United States, shall be irrepleviable, and shall be deemed to be in the custody of the law, and subject only to the orders and decrees of the courts of the United States having jurisdiction thereof. And if any person shall dispossess or rescue, or attempt to dispossess or rescue, any property so taken or detained as aforesaid, or shall aid or assist therein, such person shall be deemed guilty of a misdemeanour . . .

SEC. 5. *And be it further enacted,* That whenever the President of the United States shall be officially informed, by the authorities of any state, or by a judge of any circuit or district court of the United States, in the state, that, within the limits of such state, any law or laws of the United States, or the execution thereof, or of any process from the courts of the United States, is obstructed by the employment of military force, or by any other unlawful means, too great to be overcome by the ordinary course of judicial proceeding, or by the powers vested in the marshal by existing laws, it shall be lawful for him, the President of the United States, forthwith to issue his proclamation, declaring such fact or information, and requiring all such military and other force forthwith to disperse; and if at any time after issuing such proclamation, any such opposition or obstruction shall be made, in the manner or by the means aforesaid, the President shall be, and hereby is, authorized, promptly to employ such means to suppress the same, and to cause the said laws or process to be duly executed . . .

SEC. 6. *And be it further enacted,* That in any state where the jails are not allowed to be used for the imprisonment of persons arrested or committed under the laws of the United States, or where houses are not allowed to be so used, it shall and may be lawful for any marshal, under the direction of the judge of the United States for the proper district, to use other convenient places, within the limits of said state, and to make such other provision as he may deem expedient and necessary for that purpose.

SEC. 8. *And be it further enacted,* That the several provisions contained in the first and fifth sections of this act, shall be in force until the end of the next session of Congress, and no longer.

APPROVED, March 2, 1833.

DOCUMENT 4

Nicholas Biddle, Commencement Address (1835)

Jackson's policies and political style helped persuade his opponents to join the Whig Party. Among Jackson's critics was Nicholas Biddle, embattled president of the bank of the United States. In his speech to the graduating class of the College of New Jersey, Biddle did not mention the Bank or Jackson, concentrating instead on what he regarded as the debasement of American politics by those who sought to pander to the popular passions of the moment. He offered his hope that education, self-restraint, and principle still had a role to play in the nation's public life.

In our country, too many young men rush into the arena of public life without adequate preparation. They go abroad because their home is cheerless. They fill their minds with the vulgar excitement of what they call politics, for the want of more genial stimulants within. Unable to sustain the rivalry of more disciplined intellects, they soon retire in disgust and mortification, or what is far worse, persevere after distinctions which they can now obtain only by artifice. They accordingly take refuge in leagues and factions—they rejoice in stratagems—they glory in combinations,—weapons all these, by which mediocrity revenges itself on the uncalculating manliness of genius—and mines its way to power. Their knowledge of themselves inspires a low estimate of others. They distrust the judgment and the intelligence of the community, on whose passions alone they rely for advancement—and their only study is to watch the shifting currents of popular prejudice, and be ready at a moment's warning to follow them. For this purpose, their theory is, to have no principles and to give no opinions, never to do any thing so marked as to be inconsistent with doing the direct reverse—and never to say any thing not capable of contradictory explanations. They are thus disencumbered for the race—and as the ancient mathematician could have moved the world if he had had a place to stand on, they are sure of success if they have only room to turn. Accordingly, they worship cunning, which is only the counterfeit of wisdom, and deem themselves sagacious only because they are selfish. They believe that all generous sentiments of love of country, for which they feel no sympathy in their own breasts, are hollow pretences in others—that public life is a game in which success depends on dexterity—and that all government is a mere struggle for place. They thus disarm ambition of its only fascination, the desire of authority in order to benefit the country; since they do not seek places to obtain power, but power to obtain places. Such persons may rise to great official stations—for high offices are like the tops of the pyramids, which reptiles can reach as well as eagles. But though they may gain places, they never can gain honors—they may be politicians—they never can become statesmen. The mystery of their success lies in their adroit management of our own weakness—just as the credulity of his audience makes half the juggler's skill. Personally and singly, objects of indifference, our collected merits are devoutly adored when we acquire the name of "the people." Our sovereignty, our virtues, our talents, are the daily themes of eulogy: they assure us that we are the best and wisest of the human race—that their highest glory is to be the instruments of our pleasure, and that they will never act nor think nor speak but as we direct them. If we name them to executive stations, they promise to execute only what we desire—if we send them to deliberative bodies, they engage never to deliberate, but be guided solely by the light of our intuitive wisdom. Startled at first by language, which, when addressed to other sovereigns, we are accustomed to ridicule for its abject sycophancy, constant repetition makes it less incredible. By degrees, although we may not believe all the praise, we cannot doubt the praiser, till at last we become so spoiled by adulation, that truth is unwelcome. If it comes from a stranger, it must be prejudice—if from a native, scarce less than treason; and when some unhappy traveller ventures to smile at follies which we will not see or dare not acknowledge, instead of disregarding it, or being amused by it, or profiting by it, we resent it as an indignity to our sovereign perfections. This childish, sensitiveness would be only ludicrous if it did not expose us to the seduction of those who flatter us only till they are able to betray us—as men praise what they mean to sell—treating us like pagan idols, caressed till we have granted away our power—and then scourged for our impotence. Their pursuit of place has alienated them from the walks of honest industry—their anxiety for the public fortunes has dissipated their own. With nothing left either in their minds or means to retreat upon; having no self esteem, and losing that of others, when they cease to possess authority, they acquire a servile love of sunshine—a dread of being what is called unpopular, that makes them the ready instruments of any chief who promises to be the strongest. They degenerate at last into mere demagogues, wandering about the political common, without a principle or a dollar, and anxious to dispose to the highest bidder of their only remaining possession, their popularity. If successful, they grow giddy with the frequent turns by which they rose, and wither into obscurity. If they miscalculate—if they fall into that fatal error—a minority—retirement, which is synonymous with disgrace, awaits them, while their more fortunate rivals, after flourishing for a season in a gaudy and feverish notoriety, are eclipsed by some fresher demagogue, some more popular man of the people. Such is the melancholy history of many persons, victims of an abortive ambition, whom more cultivation might have rendered useful and honorable citizens.

Above this crowd and beyond them all stands that character which I trust many of you will become—a real American statesman.

For the high and holy duty of serving his country, he begins by deep and solitary studies of its constitution and laws, and all its great interests. These studies are extended over the whole circumference of knowledge—all the depths and shoals of the human passions are sounded to acquire the mastery over them. The solid structure is then strengthened and embellished by familiarity with ancient and modern languages—with history, which supplies the treasures of old experience—with eloquence, which gives them attraction—and with the whole of that wide miscellaneous literature, which spreads over them all a perpetual freshness and variety. These acquirements are sometimes reproached by the ignorant as being pedantry. They would be pedantic if they intruded into public affairs inappropriately, but in subordination to the settled habits of the individual, they add grace to the strength of his general character, as the foliage ornaments the fruit that ripens beneath it. They are again denounced as weakening the force of native talent, and contrasted disparagingly with what are called rough and strong minded men. But roughness is no necessary attendant on strength; the true steel is not weakened by the highest polish—just as the scymetar of Damascus, more flexible in the hands of its master, inflicts a keener wound than the coarsest blade. So far from impairing the native strength of the mind, at every moment this knowledge is available. In the play of human interests and passions, the same causes ever influence the same results; what has been, will again be, and there is no contingency of affairs on which the history of the past may not shed its warning light on the future. The modern languages bring him into immediate contract with the living science and the gifted minds of his remote contemporaries. All the forms of literature, which are but the varied modifications in which the human intellect develops itself, contribute to reveal to him its structure and its passions—and these endowments can be displayed in a stateman's career only by eloquence—itself a master power, attained only by cultivation, and never more requiring it than now, when its influence is endangered by its abuse. Our institutions require and create a multitude of public speakers and writers—but, without culture, their very numbers impede their excellence—as the wild richness of the soil throws out an unweeded and rank luxuriance. Accordingly, in all that we say or write about public affairs, a crude abundance is the disease of our American style . . .

For this idle waste of words—at once a political evil and a social wrong—the only remedy is study. The last degree of refinement is simplicity; the highest eloquence is the plainest; the most effective style is the pure, severe and vigorous manner, of which the great masters are the best teachers.

DOCUMENT 5

Walt Whitman, Preface to Leaves of Grass (1855)

Coming of age in the Jacksonian era, poet Walt Whitman attempted to capture the legacy that decades of democratic culture had wrought. In his path-breaking volume of poetry, *Leave of Grass*, Whitman sought to incorporate into his art the variety of experiences of ordinary men and women in an accessible, unpretentious style. The preface to the first edition of that volume, published in 1855, directly addressed his belief that American life and American letters had new stories to tell, which were not dependent on the cultivated manners or closed traditions of the past.

William Sidney Mount's "The Power of Music." This canvas set in Mount's native Long Island depicts a somewhat romanticized vision of American rural life. Unlike many contemporary artists, Mount regularly included African Americans in his paintings.

The Americans of all nations at any time upon the earth have probably the fullest poetical nature. The United States themselves are essentially the greatest poem. In the history of the earth hitherto the largest and most stirring appear tame and orderly to their ampler largeness and stir. Here at last is something in the doings of man that corresponds with the broadcast doings of the day and night. Here is not merely a nation but a teeming nation of nations. Here is action untied from strings necessarily blind to particulars and details magnificently moving in vast masses. Here is the hospitality which forever indicates heroes. . . . Here are the roughs and beards and space and ruggedness and nonchalance that the soul loves. Here the performance disdaining the trivial unapproached in the tremendous audacity of its crowds and groupings and the push of its perspective spreads with crampless and flowing breadth and showers its prolific and splendid extravagance. One sees it must indeed own the riches of the summer and winter, and need never be bankrupt while corn grows from the ground or the orchards drop apples or the bays contain fish or men beget children upon women.

Other states indicate themselves in their deputies . . . but the genius of the United States is not best or most in its executives or legislatures, nor in its ambassadors or authors or colleges or churches or parlors, nor even in its newspapers or inventors . . . but always most in the common people. Their manners speech dress friendships—the freshness and candor of their physiognomy—the picturesque looseness of their carriage . . . their deathless attachment to freedom—their aversion to anything indecorous or soft or mean—the practical acknowledgment of the citizens of one state by the citizens of all other states—the fierceness of their roused resentment—their curiosity and welcome of novelty—their self-esteem and wonderful sympathy—their susceptibility to a slight—the air they have of persons who never knew how it felt to stand in the presence of superiors—the fluency of their speech—their delight in music, the sure symptom of manly tenderness and native elegance of soul . . . their good temper and openhandedness—the terrible significance of their elections—the President's taking off his hat to them not they to him—these too are unrhymed poetry. It awaits the gigantic and generous treatment worthy of it.

The largeness of nature or the nation were monstrous without a corresponding largeness and generosity of the spirit of the citizen. Not nature nor swarming states nor streets and steamships nor prosperous business nor farms nor capital nor learning may suffice for the ideal of man . . . nor suffice the poet. No reminiscences may suffice either. A live nation can always cut a deep mark and can have the best authority the cheapest . . . namely from its own soul. This is the sum of the profitable uses of individuals or states and of present action and grandeur and of the subjects of poets.—As if it were necessary to trot back generation after generation to the eastern records! As if the beauty and sacredness of the demonstrable must fall behind that of the mythical! As if men do not make their mark out of any times! As if the opening of the western continent by discovery and what has transpired since in North and South America were less than the small theatre of the antique or the aimless sleepwalking of the middle ages! The pride of the United States leaves the wealth and finesse of the cities and all returns of commerce and agriculture and all the magnitude of geography or shows the exterior victory to enjoy the breed of fullsized men or one fullsized man unconquerable and simple.

The American poets are to enclose old and new for America is the race of races. Of them a bard is to be commensurate with a people. To him the other continents arrive as contributions . . . he gives them reception for their sake and his own sake. His spirit responds to his country's spirit . . . he incarnates its geography and natural life and rivers and lakes. . . .

To him enter the essences of the real things and past and present events—of the enormous diversity of temperature and agriculture and mines—the tribes of red aborigines—the weatherbeaten vessels entering new ports or making landings on rocky coasts—the first settlements north or south—the rapid stature and muscle—the haughty defiance of '76, and the war and peace and formation of the constitution . . . the union always surrounded by blatherers and always calm and impregnable—the perpetual coming of immigrants—the warſhem'd cities and superior marine—the unsurveyed interior—the loghouses and clearings and wild animals and hunters and trappers . . . the free commerce—the fisheries and whaling and gold-digging—the endless gestation of new states—the convening of Congress every December, the members duly coming up from all climates and the uttermost parts . . . the noble character of the young mechanics and of all free American workmen and workwomen . . . the general ardor and friendliness and enterprise—the perfect equality of the female with the male . . . the large amativeness—the fluid movement of the population—the factories and mercantile life and labor-saving machinery—the Yankee swap—the New-York firemen and the target excursion—the southern plantation life—the character of the northeast and of the northwest and southwest—slavery and the tremulous spreading of hands to protect it, and the stern opposition to it which shall never cease till it ceases or the speaking of tongues and the moving of lips cease. For such the expression of the American poet is to be transcendent and new. It is to be indirect and not direct or descriptive or epic. Its quality goes through these to much more. Let the age and wars of other nations be chanted and their eras and characters be illustrated and that finish the verse. Not so the great psalm of the republic. Here the theme is creative and has vista. Here comes one among the wellbeloved stonecutters and plans with decision and science and sees the solid and beautiful forms of the future where there are now no solid forms.

DOCUMENT 6
Niles' Weekly Register (1835)

The dominant political parties of the era, the Democratic and the Whig, were not monolithic. Moreover, political contestants did not feel constrained to follow orderly procedures or pursue their goals solely with the gentle arts of persuasion. *Niles' Weekly Register* of Baltimore passed along to its readers an account from New York of a nomination battle between the so-called Loco-Focos and the established Democratic Party organization in New York City. The working-class Loco-Focos wished to see hard coinage replace bank notes as a means of payment. They thus waged war not only on the Bank of the United States, opposed by Jackson and his followers, but also on state banks, which the president did favor. In the nominating fight chronicled here by a sympathetic newspaper, however, policy issues appear to have given way to spirited tactical maneuvering.

Grand Row—At Tammany Hall, New York

From the Daily Advertiser—opposition

The great republican family was called together last evening in general meeting, to hear the report of the nominating committee. The flag was displayed during the day, the bills were posted up in all parts of the city, and the building was illuminated at sundown. Seven o'clock was the appointed hour, and long before that time large crowds assembled in front of the building, and continued to increase till about ten minutes before 7; a sudden peal of hurrahs announced that an entry had been effected by those who were for supporting the ticket nominated by the committee. A rush of course from the outside followed, and we followed in the crowd, and when we arrived in the room, we found the worthy alderman of the twelfth ward, (Varian) in the chair, and banners floating about the stage over his head, on which were appropriately inscribed, "the TIMES must change ere we give up our POST." Another run thus, "hear him, Joel Curtis." Another with Ferris's name at the head, together with the other candidates on the Haskell ticket. a third was peculiarly required; it thus run, "*support the chair*," which the audience seemed as peculiarly inclined to disregard.

From the opening of the door until we entered, the clamot was as usual *a la mode* Tammany, so deafening that not one word could be heard. Twice the chairman lost his underpinning, and twice he recovered his place after the time alluded to. The flag, bearing Job Haskell's name, was ingloriously prostrate for a moment, but it emerged again with new effulgence, midst clamors, hisses and groans. A sudden rush for the private door by about thirty individuals, announced that the chairman had finished his duties; and a cry that the "regular tickets had adjourned," and that the nomination was carried, but by whom or when, as was usual in such cases, it was not announced, closed the farce on one side.

Alexander Ming then mounted the table with a flag headed "Ferrie for congress!" and kept his position very well; and it was soon very evident that the sovereigns had ascertained that he was on the right

side, and therefore the people were disposed to hear him. But, before he began his harangue, the stoppers were put to the gas lights, and the front part of the hall was in total darkness. But the Haskell luminaries were not to be frustrated in this way, and in a moment the platform was lined with fifty sperm lights; and thus the old trick would not take. *This was complete glory*—and the cheers were tremendous.

Rodney S. Church, esq, mounted the table while Ming was putting matters to rights, and when the audience found he was of the orthodox party they listened to him. He said the people spake, let there be light and there is light, and those who love darkness rather than light have put out the light because their deeds are evil. Here Mr. C. entered into the merits of his patriotism; said he never had any of the people's money; had been a democrat ever since he was twenty-one years of age; helped to fight the battle to put down the bank, and where, in 1832, when the panic was over the land, was Gideon Lee? Was he at his post. (No! no! three cheers.) He went for democracy and against all banks, and "go to your wards, go to your wards," vociverated he, "go and vote, and (here the candle in his hand went out, but did not diminish his eloquence), vote down the democrats who have aristocracy in their hearts but democracy on their tongues."

"Three cheers for the Evening Post," cried Ming and the Post had them long and hearty. "Three groans for Ringgold," cried out somebody. "D—n Gid. Lee," said a third. But the groans came long and awful, and poor Ringgold might almost have read his fate. "Sharpe is a friend to col. Stone, aint he? Didn't he petition for the Pearl street bank last year? Down with him!" By this time Ming rallied with his resolutions; and he was determined to have and give fair play. He read off the usual number that are annually administered to the pure democracy, and took the question separately, to which there was about half a dozen dissentients in the crowds; but the working men's party, (so they would call themselves), as far as we could judge, formed seven-eighths of the audience, save and except the whigs who came as lookers-on in Venice." Ming called for "three cheers for Job Haskell," which were responded to. Indeed the whole of the sovereigns seemed disposed to support Job, and to hold the leaders to their doctrines about the banks, &c.

A new, and somewhat unknown democrat, here mounted that part of the chairman's underpinning which remained—his name we understand was McLaughlin—he had a foreign accent but he understood the constitution perfectly, and determined to stick to it through thick and thin for the sake of the people and their posterity. In the meantime, some fellow thought that the people outside ought to have a part of the fun, and insisted on it that the flag with Haskell's name should be stuck out of the window which caused a little interruption. However, the people outside were called upon for their ayes and noes on Ferris' nomination, by somebody at the window, who put the question, but it is supposed that there was so much of the old leaven of federalism outside, that the hurrah could not be got up. "Who's got it! who's got it?" cried a son of Hibernia. Is it Mr. Gade Lee or Mr. Alderman Ferris who's going to congress?" "Charcoal! charcoal!" said the mob outside—and so Job was honored with a flag outside once more. Mr. Ming started that a motion had been made to adjourn; but the people indignantly refused to let off the aristocracy so cheap. Resolutions were then passed in favor of Martin Van Buren and Richard M. Johnson; and a motion made, that the democracy, for their triumph, should form a procession, with the Ferris banner "waving over them," which was carried. But the lights which the people had obtained, and which they very unceremoniously and sacrilegiously had taken from the transparency of the old hero, in front of the hall, were getting short from too much use, and from having been cut up into too many pieces on the agrarian plan of division, so that the people were compelled to resort to further pillage of untouched candles, when they were very unceremoniously charged by some person in authority with being robbers, and taking away what didn't, according to the conservative doctrines, belong to them.

This was resented by a young democrat, who charged the man in authority with having put out his own lights, and now wished to put out the peoples; but he must look out or his own would get knocked in. The effect was magical, showing clearly the majesty of the people. No further opposition to the public voice was manifested and the procession and crowd retired, amidst cries of "no monopolies, fall in, fall in, no aristocracy," and sundry other equally important clamors. Where they went, or how far or how fast they went, or how long their candles lasted is not known by the latest information. When their luminaries were so near the sockets which nature had furnished all true republicans with, resort was had to a stick, on which the candle was tied with a string—evincing in the mind of the holder a strong determination not to suffer the liberties of the great republic to be extinguished, as long as the spermaceti held out.

From the clamor as long as alderman Varian was in the chair, it was utterly impossible to hear a single word that was uttered. As far as an opinion could be formed, the sovereign people are decidedly opposed to the old fashioned mode of having every thing cut and dried, through the back door entrance, and putting out the gas lights will hereafter be considered very aristocratic, being no doubt emblematic of the desire of the old leaders to put out the regular fire of liberals. Besides, the people seemed determined not to be old-generalized, even though it was at the expense of general Jackson's and his horse's transparency, and the other standing rebukes on the aristocracy, which grace Tammany Hall.

DOCUMENT 7

Female Industry Association, from the New York Herald (1845)

Partisan politics could not satisfy all the concerns of ordinary men and women in the Age of Jackson. Indeed, the growth of a working class to staff the growing manufacturing base of northeastern cities gave rise to unions seeking better wages and working conditions. Lacking voting rights and at times spurned by their male counterparts, some women nonetheless organized to place their concerns before employers and the public. Here a New York newspaper reports on the efforts of the Female Industry Association in 1845.

Seldom or never did the Superior Court of the City Hall contain such an array of beauty under suffering, together with common sense and good order, as it did yesterday, on the occasion of the meeting of the female industrial classes, in their endeavors to remedy the wrongs and oppressions under which they labor, and, for some time past, have labored. At the hour appointed for the adjourned meeting, four o'clock, about 700 females, generally of the most interesting age and appearance, were assembled; and, after a trifling delay, a young lady stepped forward, and in rather a low, diffident tone, moved that Miss Gray take the Chair, which, having been put and carried in the usual business-like way—

Miss Gray (a young woman, neatly dressed, of some 22 or 24 years of age, fair complexion, interesting, thoughtful and intelligent cast of countenance) came forward from the back part of the room. She proceeded to make a few observations on the nature and objects of their movements and intentions, and stated that, finding the class she belonged to were unable to support themselves, honestly and respectably, by their industry, under the present prices they received for their work, had, therefore, come to the determination of endeavoring to obtain something better, by appealing to the public at large, and showing the amount of sufferings under which they at present labored. She then went on to give instances of what wages they were in the habit of receiving in different branches of the business in which she was engaged, and mentioned several employers by name who only paid them from $.10 to $.18 per day; others, who were proficient in the business, after 12 or 14 hours hard labor, could only get about $.25 per day; one employer offered them $.20 per day, and said that if they did not take it, he would obtain girls from Connecticut who would work for less even than what he offered. The only employer who had done them justice was Mr. Beck, of Fourteenth street, who only allowed his girls to be out about two hours, when he complied with their reasonable demands. He was a man who was worthy of the thanks of every girl present, and they wished him health, wealth, and happiness. How was it possible that on such an income they could support themselves decently and honestly, let alone supporting widowed mothers, and some two, three, or four helpless brothers and sisters, which many of them had. Pieces of work for which they last year got seven shillings, this year they could only get three shillings.

A female stepped forward . . . and enquired if the association was confined to any one branch of business, or was it open to all who were suffering under like privations and injustice?

The Chairwoman observed that it was opened to

all who were alike oppressed, and it was only by a firm cooperation they could accomplish what they were laboring for.

Another female of equally interesting appearance (Mrs. Storms) then came forward and said that it was necessary the nature and objects of the party should be distinctly understood, particularly by those who were immediately interested; their own position should be fully known. If the supply of labor in the market was greater than the demand, it followed as a matter of course that they could not control the prices; and, therefore, it would be well for those present to look around them and see into what other channels they could turn their industry with advantage. There were many branches of business in which men were employed that they could as well fill. Let them memorialize the merchants in the dry goods department, for instance, and show them this also. That there were hundreds of females in this city who were able to keep the books as well as any man in it. There were various other branches of business in which men were employed for which females alone were suitable and intended. Let these men go to the fields and seek their livelihood as men ought to do, and leave the females their legitimate employment. There were the drapers also, and a number of other branches of trade in which females could be as well if not better and more properly employed. By these means, some thousands would be afforded employment in branches much more valuable to themselves and the community generally. She then proceeded to recommend those present to be moderate in their demands, and not to ask for more than the circumstances of trade would warrant, for if they acted otherwise, it would tend to their more ultimate ruin. Under present circumstances, a very few years broke down their constitutions, and they had no other resource but the alms-house, and what could bring this about sooner than the bread and water diet and rough shelter, which many of them at present were obliged to put up with.

The proceedings of the previous meeting were then read and approved of.

A number of delegates from the following trades entered their names to act as a Committee to regulate future proceedings: tailoresses, plain and coarse sewing, shirt makers, book-folders and stitchers, cap makers, straw workers, dress makers, crimpers, fringe and lace makers, &c.

The following preamble and resolutions were agreed to:

Whereas, the young women attached to the different trades in the city of New York, having toiled a long time for a remuneration totally inadequate for the maintenance of life, and feeling the truth of the Gospel assertion, that "the laborer is worthy of his hire," have determined to take upon themselves the task of asserting their rights against unjust and mercenary employers. It must be remembered by those to whom we address ourselves, that our object is not extortion; our desire, not to reap advantages which will be denied to our employers. The boon we ask is founded upon right, alone! The high prices demanded by tradesmen for their goods renders them amply able to advance wages to a standard, which, while it obviates the present cause of complaint, will render laborers only the more cheerful at their work, and still more earnest and willing to serve their employers. The scarcity of employment, and the low rates of pay which have so long prevailed, have, undoubtedly driven many virtuous females to courses which might, otherwise, have been avoided. Many of the female operatives of this city have families dependent upon their exertions; aged fathers and mothers—young brothers—helpless sisters, who, but for their exertions, must inevitably starve, or betake themselves to that scarcely less horrible alternative—the poor house! Such a picture is enough to bestir the most inert to active exertion; the love of life is a passion inherent in us all, and we feel persuaded that we need no better excuse for the movement to which the glaring injustice of our employers has driven us! . . .

DOCUMENT 8

Memorial of the Delegation of the Cherokee Nation (1840)

Besides slavery (see Chapter 14), nowhere did the limits and contradictions of Jacksonian Democracy reveal themselves more starkly than in Indian-white relations. The eviction of Creeks, Cherokees, and other southern tribes from Georgia, Alabama, and Mississippi occurred despite the Supreme Court's ruling that Indians had rights to their lands and despite Indian appeals to federal authority. Those Indians who did not move west voluntarily after tribal leaders signed coerced treaty agreements were forced to emigrate, often with deadly consequences.

The Cherokee Nation was removed; though, on their first capture by troops of the American republic, estates, large and small, were, upon the instant, seized and sold to any sordid adventurer, at large commissions to the auctioneers, and next to nothing for the owners; though, in the sudden and forced gathering of the people into separate masses by those troops, children were abruptly severed from doating parents who never met them more; though even the young husband was doomed to know that his wife, whom he was not permitted to protect, nor even to behold, had to pause before the rough soldier, on the road to a military camp, and, under these maddening circumstances, hear the first cry of her infant; though vast multitudes of both sexes and of all ages, ever, until then, habituated to domestic comforts, were sickened by the wretchedness and unwholesomeness of being congregated in open fields, and crowded under tents, during the most scorching heat of summer, and thousands of those nearest and dearest to many of us at length sunk into miserable graves: yes, though all these aggravations clustered around us on every side, still the drooping Cherokees were cheered on finding their armed captors eventually withdrawn, and their conduct into exile transferred to persons among themselves in whom they could confide. The welcome

change was hailed by them as the harbinger of a realization of the promise that the United States would secure to them elsewhere that national independence, that exemption from intrusive meddlers, from prying and lying tale bearers, and from military protection of the few to overawe the many, from which the ill-starred peculiarities of their previous position had for ever debarred them in the home whence they had departed. A few of their compatriots found themselves circumscribed in the chase by the advancing change in the modes of life, not only all around, but within their native country, and that these few sought hunting grounds in the far west. The place they chose was, at that time, the property of Spain; it passed into the hands of the United States, from whom, when the policy was arising to remove the Indians, our mother-country east of the Mississippi purchased it that her absent children might not be disturbed: thus began the nucleus around which successive emigrants gathered, until at length its boundaries were outstretched by treaty for all Cherokees who might thenceforward follow. At the time the entire nation bent its course towards the region in question, about (as nearly as can be ascertained) one-sixth was generally designated as the western Cherokees. These facts will be well remembered by your honorable bodies, and your memorialists only state them to render their story more distinct.

The Cherokee Nation was removed. The great majority now found themselves on the prairies of the far west. There were many sick; there were many who could not even taste the unwholesome pittance of food furnished by their captors, and against which their conductors had remonstrated, but in vain. . . .

Your memorialists would not have considered the fabrications of which they have spoken as entitled to notice, had it not been for the consequences they must bring upon their important embassy, unless those consequences are averted by your honorable bodies. Your memorialists most humbly represent, that, if some mode of settling the concerns of the Cherokees with the United States is not presently adopted, their people will be reduced to ruin and despair; and it is their ardent hope that your honorable bodies will assist them to prevent such a result as all must deprecate, and not permit any pretence, however plausibly urged, to exclude us from being heard in the name of our people. The greater portion of them will, presently, be without food, as the period for supplying the new emigrants with rations is just expiring. They have no means; they have not so much as the implements of husbandry; and their arms, which were taken from them some years ago, having never been restored, as promised, they cannot supply themselves with game. The existing relations between us and the United States are so ambiguous, and capable of such opposite constructions, that even an obligation which is assumed to preserve peace, and to prevent intestine commotion, is, at this very moment, so exercised as to create the very evils it professes to remedy, and to defeat the very principle of recognising the power of the majority, which the Cherokees are instructed to consider as the principle of the United States in their dealings regarding them. We ask that these ambiguities may be cleared away. When our

eastern country was lately taken from us without the consent of the majority, and the great mass of our people captured, they said that it was hard; but they were the weaker, and would not resist. They were doubted, but not a hand was raised; and now, those who have survived are in the west. We have done our part. We have given up all. What has been done by the United States? Nothing. Notwithstanding these things, have we yet acted towards the United States otherwise than with the meekest spirit of endurance? No one can say we ever did. We implore the great Republic to remember this in our favor; and we will then echo in its praise the benison of the Savior God himself: "Blessed are the peacemakers."

Your memorialists, therefore, humbly state that, having full powers from the Cherokee people to bring all questions between them and the United States to a close, they have been waiting for some time in Washington, for the purpose—

1st. Of obtaining indemnification for the country which has been taken away from them east of the Mississippi, and for the loss of private property, and for injuries sustained, in their forced removal.

2d. Of establishing a satisfactory definition of the tenure under which they are to hold their lands in the west.

3d. Of procuring some specific stipulations of the relations which are to exist between them and the United States. And,

4th. Of bringing the balance yet due for the expenses of their recent emigration under General Scott to an immediate settlement.

And your memorialists throw themselves on the humanity and justice of your honorable bodies, as the only resource now left for the arrangement of these momentous affairs, to open the door for their relief, by such action as the wisdom of your honorable bodies may devise, and the circumstances of our case urgently demand.

Study Questions

1. Whose interpretation of American society—Chevalier's, Biddle's, or Whitman's—most accurately describes the nation in this period?

2. On what issues did public opinion have a controlling voice in Jacksonian politics? Which issues were less responsive to public opinion?

3. In what ways was President Jackson a representative figure of the age that bears his name?

4. How important a role did economic concerns play in the political contests and crises examined in this chapter?

5. What factors led to the exclusion of Indians from Jacksonian democracy?

12

Reforming Society

The expansive capitalism and contentious democracy of the Jacksonian era encouraged many Americans to look with increased scrutiny at their society's moral foundations. Men and women reacted to the shifting demands of the developing society by asking age-old questions about how to achieve a righteous social order and how to regulate the role of the individual within that order. Spiritual issues—such as how to harvest more souls for Christ—often gave rise to temporal issues, including alcohol consumption, education, and gender roles.

For native-born Protestants, white settlements' push across the Appalachian Mountains threatened to sever ties between organized eastern Christianity and the frontier. A second Great Awakening and the proliferation of competing Protestant denominations spreading the word of God by way of massive outdoor revivals—often called camp meetings—provided an effective method for gathering converts across wide stretches of territory. With varying degrees of emotionalism and intellectualism, orthodoxy and experimentation, traveling preachers stimulated listeners to look after their own souls. Revivalism, as one of its proponents argued, was an essential method to guide sinners toward redemption in a world full of "Backslidden Christians" (Document 1). The first large frontier camp meetings took place in early nineteenth-century Kentucky (Document 2) and quickly became the model for large-scale revivals.

Reformers also placed a new emphasis on personal responsibility and the sanctity of the family. Temperance became a key article of faith for many reformers. Trends such as the separation of the workplace from the home, the movement of employers and laborers to separate neighborhoods, the growth of Irish and German immigration, and increased competition for profits in the manufacturing sector raised fears that traditional social controls were weakening. Crusaders against the consumption of alcohol condemned the use of spirits as a threat to family values and honest government. Indeed, the extraordinary personal freedom granted to native and foreign-born alike brought home to reformers the pressing need for restraints on individual behavior (Document 3).

Women played a crucial role in both articulating and implementing the new spirit of reform. As men increasingly earned income outside the home, writers deemphasized the economic role of women and the family, especially within a burgeoning middle class. Instead, women and their ministers began to see the home as a repository of moral values, a site where mothers could cultivate industriousness and duty to church, community, and country (Document 4).

Yet, for some women, the rhetoric of domestic power rang false. In an age of both democratic ferment and social reform, such women asked whether division of gender roles, which they equated with female subordination, was the most logical or equitable means of organizing society. Moreover, if women had such a strong moral sense, why should they leave public life to men? Thus the era saw the founding of women's rights and suffrage movements (Document 5).

The nascent women's rights movement demonstrated that the reform spirit naturally generated permutations and forms of protest not easily contained by a single moral agenda. In New England, so-called Transcendentalist philosophers like Ralph Waldo Emerson and Henry David Thoreau embodied and contested the spirit of the time by championing the supremacy of the individual conscience over the claims of society (Document 6). In a different vein, Catholics, made up largely of immigrants, embraced some aspects of American society, voting generally for Democratic Party candidates, while suspecting that other aspects, like public schools (Document 7) and temperance, were aimed at undermining their own traditional beliefs and practices.

Meanwhile, other Americans began to experiment with entirely new religious beliefs and social organizations. Most notably in upstate New York, a region undergoing rapid economic development, men and women launched innovative quests for moral perfection. Such endeavors often turned on its head the Protestant ethic of sober accumulation of private property. Some groups prepared for the imminent millenial return of Christ, others such as the Mormons, founded entirely new branches of Christianity, while others tried radical experiments in communal living (Document 8). These experiments demonstrated the impossibility of placing institutional checks on religious and social creativity in the young republic.

DOCUMENT 1

Charles G. Finney, "What a Revival of Religion Is" (1835)

Beginning in the 1820s, Charles G. Finney began organizing revival meetings in upstate New York. He went on to become one of the most prominent and powerful advocates of mainstream Protestant revivalism, founding Oberlin College on the Ohio frontier to train ministers who would continue to stoke the revivalistic spirit. In this document, Finney reflects on the vital importance of revivalism in maintaining a Christian society. He believed that the benefits of religious emotionalism outweighed the acknowledged risk of excesses.

❦　❧

Look back at the history of the Jews, and you will see that God used to maintain religion among *them* by special occasions, when there would be a great excitement, and people would turn to the Lord. And after they had been thus revived, it would be but a short time before there would be so many counteracting influences brought to bear upon them, that religion would decline, and keep on declining, till God could have time—so to speak—to shape the course of events so as to produce another excitement, and then pour out his Spirit again to convert sinners. Then the counteracting causes would again operate, and religion would decline, and the nation would be swept away in the vortex of luxury, idolatry, and pride.

There is so little *principle* in the church, so little firmness and stability of purpose, that unless they are greatly excited, they will not obey God. They have so little knowledge, and their principles are so weak, that unless they are excited, they will go back from the path of duty, and do nothing to promote the glory of God. The state of the world is still such, and probably will be till the millennium is fully come, that religion must be mainly promoted by these excitements. How long and how often has the experiment been tried, to bring the church to act steadily for God, without these periodical excitements! Many good men have supposed, and still suppose, that the best way to promote religion, is to go along *uniformly*, and gather in the ungodly gradually, and without excitement. But however such reasoning may appear in the abstract, *facts* demonstrate its futility. If the church were far enough advanced in knowledge, and had stability of principle enough to *keep awake*, such a course would do; but the church is so little enlightened, and there are so many counteracting causes, that the church will not go steadily to work without a special excitement. As the millennium advances, it is probable that these periodical excitements will be unknown. Then the church will be enlightened, and the counteracting causes removed, and the entire church will be in a state of habitual and steady obedience to God. The entire church will stand and take the infant mind, and cultivate it for God. Children will be trained up

in the way they should go, and there will be no such torrents of worldliness, and fashion, and covetousness, to bear away the piety of the church, as soon as the excitement of a revival is withdrawn.

It is very desirable it should be so. It is very desirable that the church should go on steadily in a course of obedience without these excitements. Such excitements are liable to injure the health. Our nervous system is so strung that any powerful excitement, if long continued, injures our health and unfits us for duty. If religion is ever to have a pervading influence in the world, it can't be so; this spasmodic religion must be done away. Then it will be uncalled for. Christians will not sleep the greater part of the time, and once in a while wake up, and rub their eyes, and bluster about, and vociferate, a little while, and then go to sleep again. Then there will be no need that ministers should wear themselves out, and kill themselves, by their efforts to roll back the flood of worldly influence that sets in upon the church. But as yet the state of the Christian world is such, that to expect to promote religion without excitements is unphilosophical and absurd. The great political, and other worldly excitements that agitate Christendom, are all unfriendly to religion, and divert the mind from the interests of the soul. Now these excitements can only be counteracted by *religious* excitements. And until there is religious principle in the world to put down irreligious excitements, it is in vain to try to promote religion, except by counteracting excitements. This is true philosophy, and it is a historical fact.

It is altogether improbable that religion will ever make progress among *heathen* nations except through the influence of revivals. The attempt is now making to do it by education, and other cautious and gradual improvements. But so long as the laws of mind remain what they are, it cannot be done in this way. There must be excitement sufficient to wake up the dormant moral powers, and roll back the tide of degradation and sin. And precisely so far as our own land approximates to heathenism, it is impossible for God or man to promote religion in such a state of things but by powerful excitements.—This is evident from the fact that this has always been the way

Charles Finney had an optimistic view of human ability and encouraged people to become good Christians by overcoming such social ills as slavery. Revivalist meetings, of the sort pictured here also provided rural people with a strong sense of community and an emotionally fulfilling sense of self.

in which God has done it. God does not create these excitements, and choose this method to promote religion for nothing, or without reason. Where mankind are so reluctant to obey God, they will not act until they are excited. For instance, how many there are who know that they ought to be religious, but they are afraid if they become pious they shall be laughed at by their companions. Many are wedded to idols, others are procrastinating repentence, until they are settled in life, or until they have secured some favorite worldly interest. Such persons never will give up their false shame, or relinquish their ambitious schemes, till they are so excited that they annot contain themselves any longer. . . .

It presupposed that the church is sunk down in a backslidden state, and a revival consists in the return of the church from her backslidings, and in the conversion of sinners.

1. A revival always includes conviction of sin on the part of the church. Backslidden professors cannot wake up and begin right away in the service of God, without deep searchings of heart. The fountains of sin need to be broken up. In a true revival, Christians are always brought under such convictions; they see their sins in such a light, that often they find it impossible to maintain a hope of their acceptance with God. It does not always go to that extent; but there are always, in a genuine revival, deep convictions of sin, and often cases of abandoning all hope.

2. Backslidden Christians will be brought to repentence. A revival is nothing else than a new beginning of obedience to God. Just as in the case of a converted sinner, the first step is a deep repentance, a breaking down of heart, a getting down into the dust before God, with deep humility, and forsaking of sin.

3. Christians will have their faith renewed. While they are in their backslidden state they are blind to the state of sinners. Their hearts are as hard as marble. The truths of the Bible only appear like a dream. They admit it to be all true; their conscience and their judgment assent to it; but their faith does not see it standing out in bold relief, in all the burning realities of eternity. But when they enter into a revival, they no longer see men as trees walking, but they see things in that strong light which will renew the love of God in their hearts. This will lead them to labor zealously to bring others to him. They will feel grieved that others do not love God, when they love him so much. And they will set themselves feelingly to persuade their neighbors to give him their hearts. So their love to men will be renewed. They will be filled with a tender and burning love for souls. They will have a longing desire for the salvation of the whole world. They will be in agony for individuals whom they want to have saved; their friends, relations, enemies. They will not only be

urging them to give their hearts to God, but they will carry them to God in the arms of faith, and with strong crying and tears beseech God to have mercy on them, and save their souls from endless burnings.

4. A revival breaks the power of the world and of sin over Christians. It brings them to such vantage ground that they get a fresh impulse towards heaven. They have a new foretaste of heaven, and new desires after union to God; and the charm of the world is broken, and the power of sin overcome.

5. When the churches are thus awakened and reformed, the reformation and salvation of sinners will follow, going through the same stages of conviction, repentance, and reformation. Their hearts will be broken down and changed. Very often the most abandoned profligates are among the subjects. Harlots, and drunkards, infidels, and all sorts of abandoned characters, are awakened and converted. The worst part of human society are softened, and reclaimed, and made to appear as lovely specimens of the beauty of holiness. . . .

Mankind are accustomed to read the countenances of their neighbors. Sinners often read the state of a Christian's mind in his eyes. If his eyes are full of levity, or worldly anxiety and contrivance, sinners read it. If they are full of the Spirit of God, sinners read it; and they are often led to conviction by barely seeing the countenance of Christians.

An individual once went into a manufactory to see the machinery. His mind was solemn, as he had been where there was a revival. The people who labored there all knew him by sight, and knew who he was. A young lady who was at work saw him, and whispered some foolish remark to her companion, and laughed. The person stopped and looked at her with a feeling of grief. She stopped, her thread broke, and she was so much agitated she could not join it. She looked out at the window to compose herself, and then tried again; again and again she strove to recover her self-command. At length she sat down, overcome with her feelings. The person then approached and spoke with her; she soon manifested a deep sense of sin. The feeling spread through the establishment like fire, and in a few

hours almost every person employed there was under conviction, so much so, that the owners, though worldly men, were astounded, and requested to have the works stop and have a prayer meeting; for they said it was a great deal more important to have these people converted than to have the works go on. And in a few days, the owners and nearly every person employed in the establishment were hopefully converted. The eye of this individual, his solemn countenance, his compassionate feeling, rebuked the levity of the young woman, and brought her under conviction of sin; and this whole revival followed, probably in a great measure, from so small an incident.

If Christians have deep feeling on the subject of religion themselves, they will produce deep feeling wherever they go. And if they are cold, or light and trifling, they inevitably destroy all deep feeling, even in awakened sinners. . . .

You see the error of those who are beginning to think that religion can be better promoted in the world without revivals, and who are disposed to give up all efforts to produce religious excitements. Because there are evils arising in some instances out of great excitements on the subject of religion, they are of opinion that it is best to dispense with them altogether. This cannot, and must not be. True, there is danger of abuses. In cases of great *religious* as well as all other excitements, more or less incidental evils may be expected of course. But this is no reason why they should be given up. The best things are always liable to abuses. Great and manifold evils have originated in the providential and moral governments of God. But these *foreseen* perversions and evils were not considered a sufficient reason for giving them up. For the establishment of these governments was on the whole the best that could be done for the production of the greatest amount of happiness. So in revivals of religion, it is found by experience, that in the present state of the world, religion cannot be promoted to any considerable extent without them. The evils which are sometimes complained of, when they are real, are incidental, and of small importance when compared with the amount of good produced by revivals. The sentiment should not be admitted by the church for a moment, that revivals may be given up. It is fraught with all that is dangerous to the interests of Zion, is death to the cause of missions, and brings in its train the damnation of the world.

DOCUMENT 2

Richard McNemar, The Kentucky Revival, or a Short History of the Late Extraordinary Out-Pouring of the Spirit of God, in the Western States of America (1808)

Richard McNemar (1770–1839) brought the full force of the Second Great Awakening to the Kentucky frontier. Like other evangelical ministers of the region, the Presbyterian McNemar preached a highly emotional brand of Calvinism, which had an effect on ordinary men and women that was both immediate and remarkable. They literally felt the terrible burden of sin, and, in the process of obtaining a new birth in Christ, some of them experienced involuntary body movements, behavior that McNemar and his allies saw as a sign of religious authenticity but that critics found unsettling, even repellent.

The first extraordinary appearances of the power of God in the late revival, began about the close of the last century, in Logan and Christian counties; on the waters of Gasper and Red Rivers. And in the spring of 1801, the same extraordinary work broke out in Mason county, upper part of Kentucky; of which I was an eye witness, and can therefore, with greater confidence, testify what I have heard, seen and felt.

It first began in individuals who had been under deep convictions of sin, and great trouble about their souls, and had fasted and prayed, and diligently searched the scriptures, and had undergone distresses of mind inexpressibly sore, until they had obtained a comfortable hope of salvation. And from seeing and feeling the love of Christ, and his willingness to save all that would forsake their sins and turn to God through him; and feeling how freely his love and goodness flowed to them, it kindled their love to other souls, that were lost in their sins; and an ardent desire that they might come and partake of that spiritual light, life, and comfort, which appeared infinite in its nature, and free to all. And under such an overpowering weight of the divine goodness, as tongue could not express, they were constrained to cry out, with tears and trembling, and testify a full and free salvation in Christ, for all that would come; and to warn their fellow-creatures of the danger of continuing in sin; and entreating them in the most tender and affectionate manner, to turn from it; and seek the Lord, in sure and certain hope that he would be found.

Under such exhortations, the people began to be affected in a very strange manner. At first they were taken with an inward throbbing of heart; then with weeping and trembling: from that to crying out, in apparent agony of soul; falling down and swooning away till every appearance of animal life was suspended, and the person appeared to be in a trance. From this state they would recover under different sensations. . . .

And here a new scene was opened, while some trembled like one in a fit of the ague; wept or cried out, lamenting their distance from God, and exposedness to his wrath; others were employed in praying with them, encouraging them to believe on the Son of God—to venture upon his promise—give up their wicked rebellious heart, just as it was; for God to take it away, and given them a heart of flesh;—singing, hymns, and giving thanks to God, for the display of his power, without any regard to former rules of order. At this, some were offended and withdrew from the assembly, determined to oppose it, as a work of the wicked one. But all their objections, only tended to open the way for the true nature and spirit of the work to shine out; and encourage the subjects of it, to set out with warmer zeal to promote it. Accordingly a meeting was appointed a few evenings after; to which a crowd of awakened souls flocked, and spent the whole night in singing hymns, praying, and exhorting one another, &c. At this meeting, one man was struck down and lay for about an hour, in the situation above mentioned. This put the matter beyond dispute, that the work was supernatural; and the outcry which it raised against sin, confirmed a number in the belief that it was from above.

From small beginnings, it gradually spread. The news of these strange operations flew about, and attracted many to come and see; who were convinced, not only from seeing and hearing, but feeling; and carried home the testimony, that it was the living work of God. This stirred up others, and brought out still greater multitudes. And these strange exercises still increasing, and having no respect to any stated hours of worship, it was found expedient to encamp on the ground, and continue the meeting day and night. To these encampments the people flocked in hundreds and thousands, on foot, on horseback, and in waggons and other carriages.

At first appearance, those meetings exhibited nothing to the spectator, but a scene of confusion that could scarce be put into human language. They were generally opened with a sermon; near the close of which, there would be an unusual out-cry; some bursting forth into loud ejaculations of prayer, or thanksgiving for the truth. Others breaking out in emphatical sentences of exhortation. Others flying to their careless friends, with tears of compassion, beseeching them to turn to the Lord. Some struck with terror, and hastening through the croud to make their escape, or pulling away their relations.—Others, trembling, weeping and crying out for the Lord Jesus to have mercy upon them: fainting and swooning away, till every appearance of life was gone, and the extremities of the body assumed the coldness of a dead corpse.—Others surrounding them with melodious songs, or fervent prayers for their happy resurrection, in the love of Christ.—Others collecting into circles around this variegated scene, contending with arguments for and against. And under such appearances, the work would continue for several days and nights together. . . .

The next general camp-meeting was held at Concord, in the county of Bourbon, about the last of May, or beginning of June. The number of people was supposed to be about 4,000, who attended on this occasion. There were present seven Presbyterian ministers, four of whom were opposed to the work and spoke against it until the fourth day about noon, the evidence then became so powerful, that they all professed to be convinced that it was the work of God; and one of them addressed the assembly with tears, acknowledging that notwithstanding they had long been praying to the Lord to pour out his spirit, yet when it came they did not know it, but wickedly opposed the answer of their own prayers. On this occasion, no sex nor color, class nor description, were exempted from the pervading influence of the spirit; even from the age of eight months to sixty years, there were evident subjects of this marvellous operation.

The meeting continued five days and four nights; and after the people generally scattered from the ground, numbers convened in different places and continued the exercise much longer. And even where they were not collected together, these wonderful operations continued among every class of people and in every situation; in their houses and fields, and in their daily employments, falling down and crying out under conviction, or singing and shouting with unspeakable joy, were so common, that the whole country round about, seemed to be leavened with the spirit of the work. . . .

The people among whom the revival began, were generally Calvinists, and altho' they had been long praying in words for the out-pouring of the spirit, and believed that God had *"foreordained whatsoever comes in to pass;"* yet, when it *came to pass* and their prayer was answered, and the spirit began to flow like many waters, from a cloud of witnesses, and souls were convicted of sin and cried for mercy, and found hope and comfort in the news of a Saviour; they rose up and quarreled with the work, because it did not *come to pass* that the subjects of it were willing to adopt their soul stupifying creed. Those who had laboured and travailed to gain some solid hope of salvation, and had ventured their souls upon the covenant of promise, and felt the living zeal of eternal love; could not, dare not preach that salvation was restricted to a certain *definite number;* nor insin-

uate that any being which God had made, was, by the Creator, laid under the dire necessity of being damned forever. The love of a Saviour constrained them to testify, that one had died for all. This truth, so essential to the first ray of hope in the human breast, was like a dead fly in the ointment of the apothecary, to the Calvinist; hence all this trembling, weeping and groaning under sin, rejoicing in the hope of deliverance and turning from the former practice of it, sent forth a disagreeable savor. Yet these exercises would no doubt, have passed for a good work of God, had they appeared as seals to their doctrine of election, imperfection, and final perseverance. But every thing appeared new, and to claim no relation to the old bed of sand upon which they had been building; and rather than quit the old foundation, they chose to reject, oppose and persecute the truth, accompanied with all that evidence which many of them were obliged to acknowledge was divine. . . .

DOCUMENT 3

Lyman Beecher, Six Sermons on Intemperance (1828)

Lyman Beecher stands with Finney as one of the most prominent proponents of religious awakening. A Congregational minister, Beecher addressed a variety of reform issues, including temperance. In these excerpts from a volume of lectures on intemperance, Beecher excoriated the consumption of alcohol as a threat to not only the moral but also the economic and political fiber of the United States.

But of all the ways to hell, which the feet of deluded mortals tread, that of the intemperate is the most dreary and terrific. The demand for artificial stimulus to supply the deficiencies of healthful aliment, is like the rage of thirst, and the ravenous demand of famine. It is famine: for the artificial ex-

citement has become as essential now to strength and cheerfulness, as simple nutrition once was. But nature, taught by habit to require what once she did not need, demands gratification now with a decision inexorable as death, and to most men as irresistible. The denial is a living death. The stomach, the head, the heart, and arteries, and veins, and every muscle, and every nerve, feel the exhaustion, and the restless, unutterable wretchedness which puts out the light of life, and curtains the heavens, and carpets the earth with sackcloth. All these varieties of sinking nature, call upon the wretched man with trumpet tongue, to dispel this darkness, and raise the ebbing tide of life, by the application of the cause which produced these woes, and after a momentary alleviation will produce them again with deeper terrors, and more urgent importunity; for the repetition, at each time renders the darkness deeper, and the torments of self-denial more irresistible and intolerable.

At length, the excitability of nature flags, and stimulants of higher power, and in greater quantities, are required to rouse the impaired energies of life, until at length the whole process of dilatory murder, and worse than purgatorial suffering, having been passed over, the silver cord is loosed, the golden bowl is broken, the wheel at the cistern stops, and the dust returns to the earth as it was, and the spirit to God who gave it.

These sufferings, however, of animal nature, are not to be compared with the moral agonies which convulse the soul. It is an immortal being who sins, and suffers; and as his earthly house dissolves, he is approaching the judgment seat, in anticipation of a miserable eternity. He feels his captivity, and in anguish of spirit clanks his chains and cries for help. Conscience thunders, remorse goads, and as the gulf opens before him, he recoils, and trembles, and weeps, and prays, and resolves, and promises, and reforms, and "seeks it yet again,"—again resolves, and weeps, and prays, and "seeks it yet again!" Wretched man, he has placed himself in the hands of a giant, who never pities, and never relaxes his iron gripe. He may struggle, but he is in chains. He may cry for release, but it comes not; and lost! lost! may be inscribed upon the door posts of his dwelling.

In the mean time these paroxsyms of his dying moral nature decline, and a fearful apathy, the harbinger of spiritual death, comes on. His resolution fails, and his mental energy, and his vigorous enterprise; and nervous irritation and depression ensue. The social affections lose their fulness and tenderness, and conscience loses its power, and the heart its

sensibility, until all that was once lovely and of good report, retires and leaves the wretch abandoned to the appetites of a ruined animal. In this deplorable condition, reputation expires, business falters and becomes perplexed, and temptations to drink multiply as inclination to do so increases, and the power of resistance declines. And now the vortex roars, and the struggling victim buffets the fiery wave with feebler stroke, and warning supplication, until despair flashes upon his soul, and with an outcry that pierces the heavens, he ceases to strive, and disappears. . . .

Upon national industry the effects of intemperance are manifest and mischievous.

The results of national industry depend on the amount of well-directed intellectual and physical power. But intemperance paralyses and prevents both these springs of human action.

In the inventory of national loss by intemperance, may be set down—the labor prevented by indolence, by debility, by sickness, by quarrels and litigation, by gambling and idleness, by mistakes and misdirected effort, by improvidence and wastefulness, and by the shortened date of human life and activity. Little wastes in great establishments constantly occurring may defeat the energies of a mighty capital. But where the intellectual and muscular energies are raised to the working point daily by ardent spirits, until the agriculture, and commerce, and arts of a nation move on by the power of artificial stimulus, that moral power cannot be maintained, which will guaranty fidelity, and that physical power cannot be preserved and well directed, which will ensure national prosperity. The nation whose immense enterprise is thrust forward by the stimulus of ardent spirits, cannot ultimately escape debility and bankruptcy. . . .

The prospect of a destitute old age, or of a suffering family, no longer troubles the vicious portion of our community. They drink up their daily earnings, and bless God for the poor-house, and begin to look upon it as, of right, the drunkard's home, and contrive to arrive thither as early as idleness and excess will give them a passport to this sinecure of vice. Thus is the insatiable destroyer of industry marching through the land, rearing poor-houses, and augmenting taxation: night and day, with sleepless activity, squandering property, cutting the sinews of industry, undermining vigor, engendering disease, paralysing intellect, impairing moral principle, cutting short the date of life, and rolling up a national debt, invisible, but real and terrific as the debt of England: continually transferring larger and larger bodies of men, from the class of contributors to the national income, to the class of worthless consumers. . . .

The effects of intemperance upon civil liberty may not be lightly passed over.

It is admitted that intelligence and virtue are the pillars of republican institutions, and that the illumination of schools, and the moral power of religious institutions, are indispensable to produce this intelligence and virtue.

But who are found so uniformly in the ranks of irreligion as the intemperate? Who like these violate the Sabbath, and set their mouth against the heavens—neglecting the education of their families—and corrupting their morals? Almost the entire amount of national ignorance and crime is the offspring of intemperance. Throughout the land, the intemperate are hewing down the pillars, and undermining the foundations of our national edifice. Legions have besieged it, and upon every gate the battle-axe rings; and still the sentinels sleep.

Should the evil advance as it has done, the day is not far distant when the great body of the laboring classes of the community, the bones and sinews of the nation, will be contaminated; and when this is accomplished, the right of suffrage becomes the engine of self-destruction. For the laboring classes constitute an immense majority, and when these are perverted by intemperance, ambition needs no better implements with which to dig the grave of our liberties, and entomb our glory.

Such is the influence of interest, ambition, fear, and indolence, that one violent partisan, with a handful of disciplined troops, may overrule the influence of five hundred temperate men, who act without concert. Already is the disposition to temporize, to tolerate, and even to court the intemperate, too apparent, on account of the apprehended retribution of their perverted suffrage. The whole power of law, through the nation, sleeps in the statute book, and until public sentiment is roused and concentrated, it may be doubted whether its execution is possible.

Where is the city, town, or village, in which the laws are not openly violated, and where is the magistracy that dares to carry into effect the laws against the vending or drinking of ardent spirits? Here then an aristocracy of bad influence has already risen up, which bids defiance to law, and threatens the extirpation of civil liberty. As intemperance increases, the power of taxation will come more and more into the hands of men of intemperate habits and desperate fortunes; of course the laws gradually will become subservient to the debtor, and less efficacious in protecting the rights of property. This will be a vital stab to liberty—to the security of which property is indispensable. For money is the sinew of war—and when those who hold the property of a nation cannot be protected in their rights, they will change the form of government, peaceably if they may, by violence if they must.

DOCUMENT 4

"Early Habits of Industry," The Mother's Magazine *(1834)*

Changes in work and class structure accompanied America's economic expansion during the first half of the nineteenth century. The growing segment of middle-class women found that their homes had ceased to be a primary location of economic production. Yet some believed that inculcating strong "habits of industry" at home was essential to the success of husbands and sons in the competitive marketplace. A new ideology of motherhood developed, stressing the separate roles of men and women and the home's importance as the moral center for an industrializing society. Promoting this ideology were new magazines aimed at women such as *The Mother's Magazine,* in which the following article appeared.

If, as a distinguished writer has observed, "Man is a bundle of habits," there is perhaps scarcely a subject to which maternal influence should be more unceasingly directed, than the early formation of right habits. And probably there is no one habit more important in a character formed for usefulness, than that of industry and regular application to business.

This habit should be commenced at a very early period; long before the little ones can be very profitable from the fruits of their industry. I know it is often alleged that the labour and care of teaching young children various useful employments, is greater than all the benefits which may be expected to result. But this, I believe, is a fact only in regard to a few of their first lessons.

I have a friend, who is both a gentleman and a scholar. For the sake of employment, his father required his little son, from the early age of eight years, to copy all his letters. I have often heard this friend ascribe his business talent, which, in regard to despatch, punctuality, and order, is seldom equalled, to his father's unremitting efforts, to keep him, at stated intervals, regularly employed.

In the formation of character, I had almost said, habits are every thing. Could the whole amount of knowledge, which a young man has acquired, just entering professional life, after nine years laborious preparatory study, have been at once imparted to his mind, without any effort on his part, the value to him would be immeasurably less than the slow process by which it was acquired. The *mental discipline,* the *intellectual habits,* are worth even more to him than the knowledge gained.

But the importance of a habit may perhaps be best ascertained by its practical result. We refer mothers to the annals of great and good men, in all ages of the world, who have been the benefactors of mankind. By attention to their early history, it will be found, that their learning and talents are not merely the effects of genius, as many suppose, but are the precious fruits of which industry and persevering application were the early bud. The Bible furnishes impressive examples on this subject. Adam in a state of innocence, was required to "dress the garden, and to keep it."

The glorified beings in heaven rest not day nor night. It is said of the great exemplar of the Christian, that "he went about doing good." We are both instructed and warned by such scripture passages as the following: Ex. xx. 9. Eccl. ix. 10: v. 12. Prov. xxiv. 30—34: xx. 4. Ezekiel x. 49. Rom. xii. 11. 2 Thess. v. 10—12. Rev. vii. 15.

When habits of industry and personal effort have been faithfully cherished, it will not be difficult to cultivate those of benevolence and self-denial. Children should be early encouraged and induced to contribute to the various institutions of benevolence in our country; but let it never be done without an effort, and a sacrifice, on their part. They should be made to feel, with David, that "they will not offer to the Lord a sacrifice which costs them nothing."

It is a principle which they may easily apprehend, and one that will be of great value in forming their future characters. At a very early age they can be made to understand something of the wants and woes of the heathen world; and when their sympathies are excited, instruct them in what manner they may begin to aid in sending abroad the blessings of salvation.

Mothers may encourage their little ones to resolve how much they will endeavour to earn in this way, and for such purposes in a year. Let a little book of accounts be prepared for them, in which all their little earnings shall regularly be entered, and as soon as they are able, let them keep these accounts themselves. In this way, several useful habits may be associated,—children may be thus early taught that money is valuable, rather as enabling them to do good, than as a means of selfish or sensual gratification.

The want of suitable regular employment for children, particularly for boys, is an evil extensively felt and deplored, especially by men in professional life, and the inhabitants of large cities and populous villages. Perhaps there is no one class of persons in our country, so highly favored in this particular as *farmers;* and it is one of the peculiar blessings of their condition, of which I fear they are not sufficiently aware, to be suitably grateful.

But in respect to others, a remedy must be supplied, or their children will be ruined. If all other resources fail, it is better to consider a regular portion of each day as "a time to cast away stones, and a time to gather stones together," to be again dispersed for the same object, rather than indulge or connive at habits of idleness.

At one of the most respectable colleges in New-England, the President and Professors have had the wisdom and precaution for a number of years, regularly to send their sons, during a considerable portion of each year, among their friends in the country, to labor on farms. The boys themselves are delighted with the plan, and all the judicious commend it, as affording the most healthful, improving, and pleasant employment. And probably even greater attainments are made in their studies, than if constantly confined in school the whole year. And perhaps not the least advantage which will result, will be found in giving to them an athletic frame, and a sound and vigorous constitution.

But in respect to daughters, the evil cannot be so great. The *domestic duties* of every family furnish sufficient employment to give a habit of industry to our daughters. And with these duties, it is disgraceful for any young lady to be wholly unacquainted; not less disgraceful, certainly, than to be ignorant of her alphabet; if the value of knowledge is to be estimated by its practical utility.

Whenever a young lady becomes herself the mistress of a family, no matter how elevated her station may be, "looking well to the ways of her household" is her *profession.*

What would be thought of the physician, or the pastor, who should enter upon his profession, ignorant of the duties it involved, because he was rich enough to employ a substitute? A knowledge of domestic duties in its various branches and operations, are indispensable for females, and mothers are held responsible, that their daughters acquire it, by a systematic and thorough course of training.

DOCUMENT 5

"Declaration of Sentiments," Seneca Falls Convention (1848)

The reforming spirit and the celebration of women as society's moral guardians generated other more radical interpretations of the role of women in a changing social order. Female participation in moral crusades such as temperance and the abolition of slavery (see Chapter 13) stimulated some women to question the legally limited public role assigned to them. A women's convention met at Seneca Falls, New York, to raise the banner for equal rights. The "Declaration of Sentiments" quite consciously borrowed the language and form of the Declaration of Independence.

Elizabeth Cady Stanton (left) with Susan B. Anthony (c. 1870). Stanton and Anthony formed the National Woman's Suffrage Association to work for a constitutional amendment to extend the franchise to women and to press for national changes affecting women's education and employment.

When, in the course of human events, it becomes necessary for one portion of the family of man to assume among the people of the earth a position different from that which they have hitherto occupied, but one to which the laws of nature and of nature's God entitle them, a decent respect to the opinions of mankind requires that they should declare the causes that impel them to such a course.

We hold these truths to be self-evident: that all men and women are created equal; that they are endowed by their Creator with certain inalienable rights; that among these are life, liberty, and the pursuit of happiness; that to secure these rights governments are instituted, deriving their just powers from the consent of the governed. Whenever any form of government becomes destructive of these ends, it is the right of those who suffer from it to refuse allegiance to it, and to insist upon the institution of a new government, laying its foundation on such principles, and organizing its powers in such form, as to them shall seem most likely to effect their safety and happiness. Prudence, indeed, will dictate that governments long established should not be changed for light and transient causes; and accordingly all experience hath shown that mankind are more disposed to suffer, while evils are sufferable, than to right themselves by abolishing the forms to which they were accustomed. But when a long train of abuses and usurpations, pursuing invariably the same object evinces a design to reduce them under absolute despotism, it is their duty to throw off such government, and to provide new guards for their future security. Such has been the patient sufferance of the women under this government, and such is now the necessity which constrains them to demand the equal station to which they are entitled.

The history of mankind is a history of repeated injuries and usurpations on the part of man toward woman, having in direct object the establishment of an absolute tyranny over her. To prove this, let facts be submitted to a candid world.

He has never permitted her to exercise her inalienable right to the elective franchise.

He has compelled her to submit to laws, in the formation of which she had no voice.

He has withheld from her rights which are given to the most ignorant and degraded men—both natives and foreigners.

Having deprived her of this first right of a citizen, the elective franchise, thereby leaving her without representation in the halls of legislation, he has oppressed her on all sides.

He has made her, if married, in the eye of the law, civilly dead.

He has taken from her all right in property, even to the wages she earns.

He has made her, morally, an irresponsible being, as she can commit many crimes with impunity, provided they be done in the presence of her husband. In the covenant of marriage, she is compelled to promise obedience to her husband, he becoming, to all intents and purposes, her master—the law giving him power to deprive her of her liberty, and to administer chastisement.

He has so framed the laws of divorce, as to what shall be the proper causes, and in case of separation, to whom the guardianship of the children shall be given, as to be wholly regardless of the happiness of women—the law, in all cases, going upon a false supposition of the supremacy of man, and giving all power into his hands.

After depriving her of all rights as a married woman, if single, and the owner of property, he has taxed her to support a government which recognizes her only when her property can be made profitable to it.

He has monopolized nearly all the profitable employments, and from those she is permitted to follow, she receives but a scanty remuneration. He closes against her all the avenues to wealth and distinction which he considers most honorable to himself. As a teacher of theology, medicine, or law, she is not known.

He has denied her the facilities for obtaining a thorough education, all colleges being closed against her.

He allows her in Church, as well as State, but a subordinate position, claiming Apostolic authority for her exclusion from the ministry, and, with some exceptions, from any public participation in the affairs of the Church.

He has created a false public sentiment by giving to the world a different code of morals for men and women, by which moral delinquencies which exclude women from society, are not only tolerated, but deemed of little account in man.

He has usurped the prerogative of Jehovah himself, claiming it as his right to assign for her a sphere of action, when that belongs to her conscience and to her God.

He has endeavored, in every way that he could, to destroy her confidence in her own powers, to lessen her self-respect, and to make her willing to lead a dependent and abject life.

Now, in view of this entire disfranchisement of one-half the people of this country, their social and religious degradation—in view of the unjust laws above mentioned, and because women do feel themselves aggrieved, oppressed, and fraudulently deprived of their most sacred rights, we insist that they have immediate admission to all the rights and privileges which belong to them as citizens of the United States.

In entering upon the great work before us, we anticipate no small amount of misconception, misrepresentation, and ridicule; but we shall use every instrumentality within our power to effect our object. We shall employ agents, circulate tracts, petition the State and National legislatures, and endeavor to enlist the pulpit and the press in our behalf. We hope this Convention will be followed by a series of Conventions embracing every part of the country.

DOCUMENT 6

Ralph Waldo Emerson, "Self-Reliance" (1841)

Among the lasting legacies of this era of spiritual searching is the writing of a group of New England intellectuals often called Transcendentalists. These thinkers sought a dispassionate evaluation of the rapidly developing American landscape. They simultaneously questioned and voiced some of society's dominant values. In the following passage from Ralph Waldo Emerson's 1841 essay "Self-Reliance," the Concord, Massachusetts, philosopher criticized the proliferation of moral reform organizations, trumpeting instead the superiority of the independent mind.

Whoso would be a man, must be a nonconformist. He who would gather immortal palms must not be hindered by the name of goodness, but must explore if it be goodness. Nothing is at last sacred but the integrity of your own mind. Absolve you to yourself, and you shall have the suffrage of the world. I remember an answer which when quite young I was prompted to make to a valued adviser who was wont to importune me with the dear old doctrines of the church. On my saying, "What have I to do with the sacredness of traditions, if I live wholly from within?" my friend suggested,—"But these impulses may be from below, not from above." I replied, "They do not seem to me to be such; but if I am the Devil's child, I will live then from the Devil." No law can be sacred to me but that of my nature. Good and bad are but names very readily transferable to that or this; the only right is what is after my constitution; the only wrong what is against it. A man is to carry himself in the presence of all opposition as if every thing were titular and ephemeral but he. I am ashamed to think how easily we capitulate to badges and names, to large societies and dead institutions. Every decent and well-spoken individual affects and sways me more than is right. I ought to go upright and vital, and speak the rude truth in all ways. If malice and vanity wear the coat of philanthropy, shall that pass? If an angry bigot assumes this bountiful cause of Abolition, and comes to me with his last news from Barbadoes, why should I not say to him, 'Go love thy infant; love thy wood-chopper; be good-natured and modest; have that grace; and never varnish your hard, uncharitable ambition with this incredible tenderness for black folk a thousand miles off. Thy love afar is spite at home.' Rough and graceless would be such greeting, but truth is handsomer than the affection of love. Your goodness must have some edge to it,—else it is none. The doctrine of hatred must be preached, as the counteraction of the doctrine of love, when that pules and whines. I shun father and mother and wife and brother when my genius calls me. I would write on the lintels of the door-post, *Whim.* I hope it is somewhat better than whim at last, but we cannot spend the day in explanation. Expect me not to show cause why I seek or why I exclude company. Then again, do not tell me, as a good man did to-day, of my obligation to put all poor men in good situations. Are they *my* poor? I tell thee, thou foolish philanthropist, that I grudge the dollar, the dime, the cent I give to such men as do not belong to me and to whom I do not belong. There is a class of persons to whom by all spiritual affinity I am bought and sold; for them I will go to prison if need be; but your miscellaneous popular charities; the education at college of fools; the building of meeting-houses to the vain end to which many now stand; alms to sots, and the thousand-fold Relief Societies;—though I confess with shame I sometimes succumb and give the dollar, it is a wicked dollar, which by and by I shall have the manhood to withhold. . . .

What I must do is all that concerns me, not what the people think. This rule, equally arduous in actual and in intellectual life, may serve for the whole distinction between greatness and meanness. It is the harder because you will always find those who think they know what is your duty better than you know it. It is easy in the world to live after the world's opinion; it is easy in solitude to live after our own; but the great man is he who in the midst of the crowd keeps with perfect sweetness the independence of solitude. . . .

A foolish consistency is the hobgoblin of little minds, adored by little statesmen and philosophers and divines. With consistency a great soul has simply nothing to do. He may as well concern himself with his shadow on the wall. Speak what you think now in hard words and to-morrow speak what to-morrow thinks in hard words again, though it contradict every thing you said to-day.—'Ah, so you shall be sure to be misunderstood.'—Is it so bad then to be misunderstood? Pythagoras was misunderstood, and Socrates, and Jesus, and Luther, and Copernicus, and Galileo, and Newton, and every pure and wise spirit that ever took flesh. To be great is to be misunderstood.

DOCUMENT 7

"Petition of the Catholics of New York" (1840)

Among the most prized reforms of native-born Protestant elites was the institution of a system of public education. Men like Beecher and Horace Mann believed that, without a proper democratic education, immigrants and other members of the lower classes would have neither the skills nor the values to take a productive place in American society. While not necessarily disagreeing with the importance of educating the young, many Catholics feared that school systems operated by Protestants would undermine Catholic teachings and inculcate Protestant interpretations of history and religion. In New York, a group of Catholics petitioned the city's aldermen to provide funds for church-sponsored schools so as to relieve this apprehension.

The Petition of the Catholics of New York,
Respectfully represents:

That your Petitioners yield to no class in their performance of, and disposition to perform all the duties of citizens.—They bear, and are willing to bear, their portion of every common burden; and feel themselves entitled to a participation in every common benefit.

This participation, they regret to say, has been denied them for years back, in reference to Common School Education in the city of New York, except on conditions with which their conscience, and, as they believe their duty to God, did not, and do not leave them at liberty to comply. . . .

Your Petitioners only claim the benefit of this principle in regard to the public education of their children. They regard the public education which the State has provided as a common benefit, in which they are most desirous and feel that they are entitled to participate; and therefore they pray your Honorable Body that they may be permitted to do so, without violating their conscience.

But your Petitioners do not ask that this prayer be granted without assigning their reasons for preferring it.

In ordinary cases men are not required to assign the motives of conscientious scruples in matters of this kind. But your petitioners are aware that a large, wealthy and concentrated influence is directed against their claim by the Corporation called the Public School Society. . . .

This Society, however, is composed of gentlemen of various sects, including even one or two Catholics. But they profess to exclude all sectarianism from their schools. If they do not exclude sectarianism, they are avowedly no more entitled to the school funds than your petitioners, or any other denomination of professing Christians. If they do, as they profess, exclude sectarianism, then your petitioners contend that they exclude Christianity— and leave to the advantage of infidelity the tendencies which are given to the minds of youth by the influence of this feature and pretension of their system.

If they could accomplish what they profess, other denominations would join your petitioners in remonstrating against their schools. But they do not accomplish it. Your petitioners will show your Honorable Body that they do admit what Catholics call sectarianism, (although others may call it only religion), in a great variety of ways. . . .

The Public School Society, in their report for the year 1832, page 10, describe the effect of these "early religious instructions," without, perhaps, intending to do so; but yet precisely as your petitioners have witnessed it, in such of their children as attended those schools. *"The age at which children are usually sent to school affords a much better opportunity to mould their minds to peculiar and exclusive forms of faith than any subsequent period of life."* In page 11, of the same report, they protest against the injustice of supporting "religion in any shape" by public money; as if the "early religious instruction" which they had themselves authorized in their schools, five years before, was not "religion in some shape," and was not supported by public taxation. They tell us again, in more guarded language, "The Trustees are deeply impressed with the importance of imbuing the youthful mind with religious impressions, and they have endeavored to attain this object, as far as the nature of the institution will admit." Report of 1837...

Even the reading of the Scriptures in those schools your petitioners cannot regard otherwise than as sectarian; because Protestants would certainly consider as such the introduction of the Catholic Scriptures, which are different from theirs, and the Catholics have the same ground of objection when the Protestant version is made use of.

Your petitioners have to state further, as grounds of their conscientious objections to those schools, that many of the selections in their elementary reading lessons contain matter prejudicial to the Catholic name and character. The term "POPERY" is repeatedly found in them. This term is known and employed as one of insult and contempt towards the Catholic religion, and it passes into the minds of children with the feeling of which it is the outward expression. Both the historical and religious portions of the reading lessons are selected from Protestant writers, whose prejudices against the Catholic religion render them unworthy of confidence in the mind of your petitioners, at least so far as their own children are concerned....

For these reasons, and others of the same kind, your petitioners cannot, in conscience, and consistently with their sense of duty to God, and to their offspring, intrust the Public School Society with the office of giving "a right direction to the minds of their children." And yet this Society claims that office, and claims for the discharge of it the Common School Funds, to which your petitioners, in common with other citizens, are contributors. In so far as they are contributors, they are not only deprived to the damage and detriment of their religion, in the minds of their own children, and of the rising generation of the community at large. The contest is between the *guaranteed* rights, civil and religious, of the citizen on the one hand, and the pretensions of the Public School Society on the other; and whilst it has been silently going on for years, your petitioners would call the attention of your Honorable Body to its consequences on that class for whom the benefits of public education are most essential—the children of the poor.

This class (your petitioners speak only so far as relates to their own denomination), after a brief experience of the schools of the Public School Society, naturally and deservedly withdrew all confidence from it. Hence the establishment by your petitioners of schools for the education of the poor. The expense necessary for this, was a second taxation, required not by the laws of the land, but by the no less imperious demands of their conscience.

They were reduced to the alternative of seeing their children growing up in entire ignorance, or else taxing themselves anew for private schools, whilst the funds provided for education, and contributed in part by themselves, were given over to the Public School Society, and by them employed as has been stated above....

Your petitioners have to deplore, as a consequence of this state of things, the ignorance and vice to which hundreds, nay thousands of their children are exposed. They have to regret, also, that the education which they can provide, under the disadvantages to which they have been subjected, is not as efficient as it should be. But should your Honorable Body be pleased to designate their schools as entitled to receive a just proportion of the public funds which belong to your petitioners in common with other citizens, their schools could be improved for those who attend, others now growing up in ignorance could be received, and the ends of the Legislature could be accomplished—a result which is manifestly hopeless under the present system.

DOCUMENT 8

Bible Communism

Among the more radical voices of moral reformation was John Humphrey Noyes, though he was far from alone in experimenting in new forms of communal living in this period. Noyes's "Bible Communism"—put into practice at the Oneida Community—called for an end to marriage in favor of shared sexual relations among specially selected members as well as an abolition of private property. He listed the principles of his quest for Christian perfectionism in the following passages.

John Humphrey Noyes, Speech to the Convention of Perfectionists (1845)

Dear Brethren:

As I am prevented from meeting with you in person I will place at your disposal a contribution to the deliberations of the convention in writing.

My attention has been turned of late to the symptoms of advancing conviction on the subject of holiness which are manifesting themselves in the churches, and I see much occasion for rejoicing and hope. . . . Charles G. Finney, the center of the revival spirit, was first affected and compelled to take an advanced position. He drew after him a large body of influential followers and a theological seminary. Now Dr. Beecher, the leader that stands next after Finney in spiritual power, has submitted partially to the truth; and he too draws after him a large body of influential followers and a theological seminary.

I am well aware that Finney and Beecher have not come in line with us and with the Primitive Church on the high grounds of the new covenant. Their advance is but half way; but no hope and expectation are that the work of conviction will forward to conversion.

Let us now ask ourselves, brethren, what line of conduct is marked out for us. I will briefly give my judgment on the question. In the first place I think we ought to feel that the post assigned to us is that of the body-guard of the gospel. We must stand firm

for perfect freedom from sin, for security, and for confession. These are the essentials of the new covenant. If we steadfastly abide by the gospel which proclaims these victories of faith, the masses that have begun to move will sure come to it at last.

In the next place we must purge our own ranks of semi-Perfectionism. I have seen many indications within the last year, that there is a class bearing the name of Perfectionist claiming fellowship among us and even assuming to be inspired leaders and teachers, who exert their influence more or less openly and directly against justification, security and confession of salvation from sin. Such men have no right to a place among us. They are not with us in spirit, but with the half converted masses that are moving toward us. Let us draw the line between them and us, that we may fully discharge our responsibilities as God's banner-guard in the coming conflict.

Finally it behooves us to take away all stumbling-blocks from the path of those who are approaching the gospel; to put away childish things; to frown on disorder, fanaticism and licentiousness; to give place among us as fast as possible to the order and discipline of the Primitive Church.

In the Kingdom of God, marriage does not exist. On the other hand there is no proof in the Bible nor in reason that the distinction of sex will ever be abolished. Matt. 22:29–30.

The Oneida Community of New York was one of many social-utopia experiments launched between the 1820s and 1850s. Many of these communities were started by those who had rejected orthodox Protestantism in favor of new types of religious and spiritual experience. Leaders of the Oneida community, argued that since they were free from sin, they were exempt from traditional moral teachings, even those governing sexual relations.

John Humphrey Noyes, "Bible Communism" (1849)

In the Kingdom of God the intimate union that in the world is limited to the married pair extends through the whole body of communicants; without however excluding special companionships founded on special adaptability. John 17:21.

The situation on the day of Pentecost shows the practical tendency of heavenly influences. "All that believed were together, and had all things common; and sold their possessions and goods, and parted them to all, as every man had need."

Communism on the day of Pentecost extended only to goods, it is true. But the same spirit that abolished property in goods would, if allowed full scope, abolish property in persons. Paul expressly places property in goods and property in persons in the same category, and speaks of them together as ready to be abolished by the Kingdom of God.

The Communism of the day of Pentecost is not to be regarded as temporary and circumstantial. The seed of heavenly unity fell into the earth and was buried for a time, but in the harvest at the second coming of Christ it was reproduced and became the universal, eternal principle of the invisible church.

The abolishment of appropriation is involved in the very nature of a true relation to Christ. Appropriation is a branch of egotism. But the grand mystery of the gospel is vital union with Christ, which is the extinguishment of egotism at the center.

The abolishment of worldly restrictions on sexual union is involved in the anti-legality of the gospel. It is incompatible with the perfected freedom, toward which Paul's gospel of "grace without law" leads, that a person should be allowed to love in all directions, and yet be forbidden to express love except in one direction.

The abolishment of marriage is involved in Paul's doctrine of the end of ordinances. Marriage is a worldly ordinance. Christians are dead to the world by the death of Christ. The same reasoning which authorized the abolishment of the Jewish ordinances makes also an end of marriage. . . .

The plea that marriage is founded in nature will not bear investigation. Experience testifies that the human heart is capable of loving more than one at the same time. It is not the loving heart but the green-eyed claimant of the loving heart that sets up the one-love theory.

A system of Complex Marriage will open the prison doors to the victims both of marriage and celibacy: to the married who are oppressed by lust, tied to uncongenial nature separated from their natural mates; to the unmarried who are withered by neglect, diseased by unnatural abstinence, plunged into prostitution by desires that find no lawful outlet. . . .

The chain of evils which holds humanity in ruin has four links: first, a breach with God; second, a disruption of the sexes, involving a special curse on woman; third, oppressive labor, bearing specially on man; fourth, death. The chain of redemption begins with reconciliation with God, proceeds to a restoration of true relations between the sexes, then to a reform of the industrial system, and ends with victory over death.

It was the special function of the Apostolic Church to break up the worldly ecclesiastical system and reopen full communication with God. It is the special function of the present church, availing itself first of the work of the Apostolic Church by union with it and a re-development of its theology, to break up the worldly social system and establish true sexual and industrial relations.

From what precedes it is evident that no one should attempt to revolutionize sexual morality before settlement with God. Holiness, communism of love, association in labor, and immortality must come in their true order. . . .

Sexual shame is factitious and irrational. The more reform that arises from the sentiment of shame attempts hopeless war with nature. Its policy is to prevent pruriency keeping the mind in ignorance of sexual subjects, while nature is constantly thrusting those subjects upon the mind. The only way to elevate love is to clear away the false, debasing associations that usually crowd around it, and substitute true, beautiful ones.

The foregoing principles furnish motives for Association. They develop in a larger partnership the same attraction that draw and bind together a marriage partnership. A Community home, where love is honored and cultivated, will be much more attractive than an ordinary home as the Community outnumbers a pair. . . .

The men and women are called to usher in the Kingdom of God will be guided not merely by theoretical truth but by direct communication with the heavens, as were Abraham, Moses, David, Paul. This will be called a fanatical principle. But it is clearly a Bible principle, and we must place it on high above all others as the palladium of conservatism in the introduction of the new social order.

Study Questions

1. How would you compare the competing visions of the "moral society" presented in this chapter? Which were most compatible?

2. What were the underlying economic assumptions of the individual reformers?

3. What role did women play in the various reform efforts? How could the same culture give rise to an ideology of women's separate social role and the notion of women's equality?

4. Which was more important to moral reformers of this period: the needs of the community or the rights of the individual? How did the various authors resolve conflict between the two?

❧   ❧

13

Sectional Crisis

The United States developed rapidly during the second quarter of the nineteenth century. Territorial expansion, population growth, and economic might had multiple causes. The annexation of Texas, the cession of the vast areas of California and the Southwest, and settlement of the long simmering dispute with Great Britain over the Pacific Northwest brought new regions under the American flag. Meanwhile, territories on either side of the Mississippi River continued to gain statehood. The dramatic expansion of railroad mileage, especially in the North, gave a boost to the nation's commercial life, extending ever farther the link between farm and factory, produce and market.

As more and more land fell under cultivation, and as more and more factories sprung up, thousands of immigrants poured into American cities and Americans of both old and new stock spread across the continent. Even before the most striking signs of America's growth became evident, acute foreign observers took notice of the apparent interdependence of the young nation's regions, as well as its people's desire for personal advancement and material reward (Document 1).

Yet the same elements that made for dynamic, broad-based growth also heightened the potential for discord between regions. For even though Americans from both North and South sought to exploit the economic potential of the growing nation, they employed entirely different labor systems to do so. Free labor dominated the North, in which both factory and farm employed the additional hands necessary to make production profitable in exchange for wages. In theory at least, such wages provided the necessary funds for men to establish their own independent households over time. The South by contrast brought much of its new land under cultivation through the use of African American slaves, who from generation to generation spent their lives attached to white households and who could be sold between white masters as the calculus of profit and loss dictated. Although Northerners may have recognized as familiar the ambitions of their Southern neighbors, they commented disapprovingly on the apparent lack of commercial diversity even amid the booming cotton economy (Document 2).

The contrast between Northern and Southern ways of life took on increasingly acrimonious political dimensions as migrants sought to place their distinct imprint on the western territories. The admission of each new state and organization of each new western territory held the potential for political controversy, as the traditional balance between slave states and free states came into question. With the population of the North growing much faster than that of the South, white southerners feared that if the North ever achieved a majority in the U.S. Senate, the slave economy's ability to expand would end, thus threatening the southern racial caste system in general. White northerners for their part, wanted to extend the reach of free labor, rejecting contact with slavery's peculiar social, political, and judicial institutions, and with the black slaves themselves.

As members of Congress and senators found it increasingly difficult to compromise in drawing the lines between slave and free soil, the U.S. Supreme Court became drawn directly into the conflict. Rather than soothing sectional tempers, the Court's 1857 Dred Scott decision (Document 3) only inflamed matters by categorically upholding the right of slaveholders to carry their slaves into states and territories that did not recognize slavery. Northern politicians, especially those like Abraham Lincoln in the new antislavery Republican Party, seized on the Dred Scott decision to underscore the important crossroads to which the issue of slavery had brought the nation (Document 4).

At the center of the controversy lay the slaves themselves. Escaped slaves and free northern blacks, along with white abolitionist allies, had attempted to raise the consciousness of Americans about the injustice of human bondage for years (Document 5). Though only a tiny fraction of Northerners ever joined abolitionist organizations, the charged political atmosphere of the 1850s widened the audience for antislavery opinions. Thus, Harriet Beecher Stowe's novel *Uncle Tom's Cabin*, at once vivid, sentimental, and openly scornful of slavery, struck a powerful chord (Document 6).

In the face of mounting criticism and moral scrutiny, Southern intellectuals mounted a campaign in their own defense. They sought to justify slavery on both humanitarian and economic grounds at once. Moreover, they contemplated the possibility that their region's economy, rather than that of the North held the key to America's and, if necessary, their own independent future (Document 7).

Slaves themselves seldom had the opportunity to voice opinions about the future of their section or their country. Nonetheless, their own experiences challenged the efforts of white America to rationalize, sentimentalize, or trivialize their plight (Document 8).

DOCUMENT 1

Alexis de Tocqueville, Democracy in America *(1831)*

De Tocqueville, French intellectual and social critic, came to America in the early 1830s to observe American social and political life. In his classic two-volume study, *Democracy in America,* he reflected on a wide variety of issues stimulated by his American sojourn, including the connections and contrasts among the North, the South, and the West, the American preoccupation with success, and the emergence of a wage labor, manufacturing economy.

It is indeed easy to discover different interests in the different parts of the Union, but I am unacquainted with any that are hostile to one another. The Southern states are almost exclusively agricultural. The Northern states are more peculiarly commercial and manufacturing. The states of the West are at the same time agricultural and manufacturing. In the South the crops consist of tobacco, rice, cotton, and sugar; in the North and the West, of wheat and corn. These are different sources of wealth, but union is the means by which these sources are opened and rendered equally advantageous to all.

The North, which ships the produce of the Anglo-Americans to all parts of the world and brings back the produce of the globe to the Union, is evidently interested in maintaining the confederation in its present condition, in order that the number of American producers and consumers may remain as large as possible. The North is the most natural agent of communication between the South and the West of the Union on the one hand, and the rest of the world on the other; the North is therefore interested in the union and prosperity of the South and the West, in order that they may continue to furnish raw materials for its manufactures, and cargoes for its shipping.

The South and the West, on their side, are still more directly interested in the preservation of the Union and the prosperity of the North. The produce of the South is, for the most part, exported beyond seas; the South and the West consequently stand in need of the commercial resources of the North. They are likewise interested in the maintenance of a powerful fleet by the Union, to protect them efficaciously. The South and the West have no vessels, but willingly contribute to the expense of a navy, for if the fleets of Europe were to blockage the ports of the South and the delta of the Mississippi, what would become of the rice of the Carolinas, the tobacco of Virginia, and the sugar and cot-

ton that grow in the valley of the Mississippi? Every portion of the Federal budget does, therefore, contribute to the maintenance of material interests that are common to all the federated states.

The Free-Soil party, organized for the 1848 presidential campaign, was a short-lived political group which opposed the spread of slavery into the territories newly acquired from Mexico. Although the Free-Soil candidate Martin Van Buren, lost the election, Free-Soilers managed to obtain enough of the Democratic Party to ensure the victory of Whig candidate Zachary Taylor over Democrat Lewis Cass.

Independently of this commercial utility, the South and the West derive great political advantages from their union with each other and with the North. The South contains an enormous slave population, a population which is already alarming and still more formidable for the future. The states of the West occupy a single valley; the rivers that intersect their territory rise in the Rocky Mountains or in the Alleghenies, and fall into the Mississippi, which bears them onwards to the Gulf of Mexico. The Western states are consequently entirely cut off, by their position, from the traditions of Europe and the civilization of the Old World. The inhabitants of the South, then, are indeed to support the Union in order to avail themselves of its protection against the blacks; and the inhabitants of the West, in order not to be excluded from a free communication with the rest of the globe and shut up in the wilds of central America. The North cannot but desire the maintenance of the Union in order to remain, as it now is, the connecting link between that vast body and the other parts of the world. . . .

The American of the North sees no slaves around him in his childhood; he is even unattended by free servants, for he is usually obliged to provide for his own wants. As soon as he enters the world, the idea of necessity assails him on every side; he soon learns to know exactly the natural limits of his power; he never expects to subdue by force those who withstand him; and he knows that the surest means of obtaining the support of his fellow creatures is to win their favor. He therefore becomes patient, reflecting, tolerant, slow to act, and persevering in his designs.

In the Southern states the more pressing wants of life are always supplied; the inhabitants, therefore, are not occupied with the material cares of life, from which they are relieved by others; and their imagination is diverted to more captivating and less definite objects. The American of the South is fond of grandeur, luxury, and renown, of gayety, pleasure, and, above all, of idleness; nothing obliges him to exert himself in order to subsist; and as he has no necessary occupations, he gives way to indolence and does not even attempt what would be useful.

But the equality of fortunes and the absence of slavery in the North plunge the inhabitants in those material cares which are disdained by the white population of the South. They are taught from infancy to combat want and to place wealth above all the pleasures of the intellect or the heart. The imagination is extinguished by the trivial details of life, and the ideas become less numerous and less general, but far more practical, clearer, and more precise. As prosperity is the sole aim of exertion, it is excellently well attained; nature and men are turned to the best pecuniary advantage; and society is dexterously made to contribute to the welfare of each of its members, while individual selfishness is the source of general happiness. . . .

In America I saw the freest and most enlightened men placed in the happiest circumstances that the world affords; it seemed to me as if a cloud habitually hung upon their brow, and I thought them serious and almost sad, even in their pleasures.

The chief reason for this contrast is that the former do not think of the ills they endure, while the latter are forever brooding over advantages they do not possess. It is strange to see with what feverish ardor the Americans pursue their own welfare, and to watch the vague dread that constantly torments them lest they should not have chosen the shortest path which may lead to it.

A native of the United States clings to this world's goods as if he were certain never to die; and he is so hasty in grasping at all within his reach that one would suppose he was constantly afraid of not living long enough to enjoy them. He clutches everything, he holds nothing fast, but soon loosens his grasp to pursue fresh gratifications.

In the United States a man builds a house in which to spend his old age, and he sells it before the roof is on; he plants a garden and lets it just as the trees are coming into bearing; he brings a field into tillage and leaves other men to gather the crops; he embraces a profession and gives it up; he settles in a place, which he soon afterwards leaves to carry his changeable longings elsewhere. If his private affairs leave him any leisure, he instantly plunges into the vortex of politics; and if at the end of a year of unremitting labor he finds he has a few days' vacation, his eager curiosity whirls him over the vast extent of the United States, and he will travel fifteen hundred miles in a few days to shake off his happiness. Death at length overtakes him, but it is before he is weary of his bootless chase of that complete felicity which forever escapes him.

At first sight there is something surprising in this strange unrest of so many happy men, restless in the midst of abundance. The spectacle itself, however, is as old as the world; the novelty is to see a whole people furnish an exemplification of it.

Their taste for physical gratifications must be regarded as the original source of that secret disquietude which the actions of the Americans betray and of that inconsistency of which they daily afford fresh examples. He who has set his heart exclusively upon the pursuit of worldly welfare is always in a hurry, for he has but a limited time at his disposal to reach, to grasp, and to enjoy it. The recollection of the shortness of life is a constant spur to him. Besides the good things that he possesses, he every instant fancies a thousand others that death will prevent him from trying if he does not try them soon. This thought fills him with anxiety, fear, and regret and keeps his mind in ceaseless trepidation, which leads him perpetually to change his plans and his abode.

If in addition to the taste for physical well-being a social condition be added in which neither laws nor customs retain any person in his place, there is a great additional stimulant to this restlessness of temper. Men will then be seen continually to change their track for fear of missing the shortest cut to happiness. . . .

The poor have few means of escaping from their condition and becoming rich, but the rich are constantly becoming poor, or they give up business when they have realized a fortune. Thus the elements of which the class of the poor is composed are fixed, but the elements of which the class of the rich is composed are not so. To tell the truth, though there are rich men, the class of rich men does not exist; for these rich individuals have no feelings or purposes, no traditions or hopes, in common; there are individuals, therefore, but no definite class.

Not only are the rich not compactly united among themselves, but there is no real bond between them and the poor. Their relative position is not a permanent one; they are constantly drawn together or separated by their interests. The workman is generally dependent on the master, but not on any particular master; these two men meet in the factory, but do not know each other elsewhere; and while they come into contact on one point, they stand very far apart on all others. The manufacturer asks nothing of the workman but his labor; the workman expects nothing from him but his wages. The one contracts no obligation to protect nor the other to defend, and they are not permanently connected either by habit or by duty. The aristocracy created by business rarely settles in the midst of the manufacturing population which it directs; the object is not to govern that population, but to use it. And aristocracy thus constituted can have no great hold upon those whom it employs, and even if it succeeds in retaining them at one moment, they escape the next; it knows not how to will, and it cannot act.

The territorial aristocracy of former ages was either bound by law, or thought itself bound by usage, to come to the relief of its serving-men and to relieve their distresses. But the manufacturing aristocracy of our age first impoverishes and debases the men who serve it and then abandons them to be supported by the charity of the public. This is a natural consequence of what has been said before. Between the workman and the master there are frequent relations, but no real association.

DOCUMENT 2

A Northerner Looks at the South

Olmsted, a writer, reformer, and sometime farmer originally from Connecticut, wrote an exhaustive three-volume study of the South based on his travels through the region. He sharply criticized the southern slave-based economic system for its inability to produce the extensive commercial and cultural institutions of his native region. He also offered acute observations on the conditions of slavery itself, treating with skepticism the master class's claim that it cared for the slaves themselves in a paternalistic fashion.

Frederick Law Olmsted, A Journey in the Seaboard Slave States (1856)

The territorial Government of Alabama was established in 1816, and in 1818 she was admitted as a State into the Union. In 1820, her population was 128,000; in 1850, it had increased to 772,000; the increase of the previous ten years having been 30 per cent (that of South Carolina was 5 per cent; of Georgia, 31; Mississippi, 60; Michigan, 87; Wisconsin, 800). A large part of Alabama has yet a strikingly frontier character. Even from the State-house, in the fine and promising town of Montgomery, the eye falls in every direction upon a dense forest, boundless as the sea, and producing in the mind the same solemn sensation. Towns frequently referred to as important points in the stages of your journey, when you reach them, you are surprised to find consist of not more than three or four cabins, a tavern or grocery, a blacksmith's shop, and a stable.

A stranger once meeting a coach, in which I was riding, asked the driver whether it would be prudent for him to pass through one of these places, that we had just come from; he had heard that there were more than fifty cases of small-pox in the town. "There ain't fifty people in the town, nor within ten mile on't," answered the driver, who was a northerner. The best of the country roads are but little better than open passages for strong vehicles through the woods, made by cutting away the trees.

The greater number of planters own from ten to twenty slaves only, though plantations on which from fifty to a hundred are employed are not uncommon, especially on the rich alluvial soils of the southern part of the State. Many of the largest and most productive plantations are extremely unhealthy in summer, and their owners seldom reside upon them, except temporarily. Several of the larger towns, like Montgomery, remarkable in the midst of the wilderness which surrounds them, for the neatness and tasteful character of the houses and gardens which they contain, are in a considerable degree, made up of the residences of gentlemen who own large plantations in the hotter and less healthful parts of the State. Many of these have been educated in the older States, and with minds enlarged and liberalized by travel, they form, with their families, cultivated and attractive society.

Much the larger proportion of the planters of the State live in log-houses, some of them very neat and comfortable, but frequently rude in construction, not *chinked*, with windows unglazed, and wanting in many of the commonest conveniences possessed by the poorest class of Northern farmers and laborers of the older States. Many of those who live in this way, possess considerable numbers of slaves, and are every year buying more. Their early frontier life seems to have destroyed all capacity to enjoy many of the usual luxuries of civilized life.

The slave trade caused the tragic breakup of many African American families. Graphic images of the sale of black men and women brought the horror of slavery into the homes of Northern whites and fanned support for abolition.

Notwithstanding the youth of the State, there is a constant and extensive emigration from it, as well as immigration to it. Large planters, as their stock increases, are always anxious to enlarge the area of their land, and will often pay a high price for that of any poor neighbor, who, embarrassed by a debt, can be tempted to move on. There is a rapid tendency in Alabama, as in the older Slave States, to the enlargement of plantations. The poorer class are steadily driven to occupy poor land, or move forward on to the frontier.

Frederick Law Olmsted, A Journey in the Back Country (1860)

Once again, during the afternoon, I had the pleasure of witnessing a scene similar to those described in the first volume, in the same locality, the joyful welcome of white people, returning to their plantation, by their house-servants; and again I noticed the comparative indifference of the field-hands or common slaves, who barely touched their tattered hats and grinned, before lifting on to each other's heads the trunks which were to be thus carried to the house after the carriage which bore the whites and upper servants altogether. This humbler kind did not say one word to their master or mistress, and only grinned in sympathy with the excitement of the young people, nor were they spoken to at all, so far as I observed.

I am here reminded that I may seem to have hitherto too much overlooked a certain view of Southern life, much delighted in by novelists and poets, and not usually neglected by travelers. I mean that which, in debates, is commonly alluded to when the terms, patriarchal, paternal, filial, tutellary and pupilage, are used, the two latter terms being less frequently heard of late years than in the early days of the republic.

The truth is, that I have made, as all travelers are inclined to make, the most I honestly could of every instance or indication of such a relation as these terms express, that I have seen. Anything of the kind is always interesting, and gratifying to read of and to write of, as it is to witness. Would I then have it inferred that Slavery has been too much honored in this respect? I must say that such is my conviction. . . .

The supposition of a master's occupying the position of a father toward his slaves and of the slaves accepting this relation, affectionately, faithfully and confidingly, is an improbable one. Imagine a household consisting of first a man and wife, second an ordinary family of sons and daughters, for whom the parents must have a special affection, and who must be favored and petted, as compared with—third, twenty to fifty additional sons and daughters, of all ages, the majority being adults, however, but all subject in all their movements, not to the influence and advice merely, but absolutely and abjectly, to the will, of their parents, not being able to eat or drink, or to dress, or to engage in any business, or to pursue any inclination of taste, or to marry, except with the approval of their father, not even after marriage to be any more independent than before. There is not one man among millions whose household under such circumstances would not be a pandemonium. The slaves are not their master's children; he is not affected in his government of them by the instinctive regard for their happiness which a parent might have.

DOCUMENT 3

Roger B. Taney, The Dred Scott Decision (1857)

On March 6, 1857, Chief Justice Roger B. Taney released his opinion for the 7–2 majority in *Scott* v. *Sandford*. The case originated from the claims of slaves Dred and Harriet Scott that they had acquired the right to be free because their master had resided with the former in Illinois, a free state, and with both of them on federal territory deemed free by an act of Congress. Rather than rule narrowly on the particulars of the case, the Taney Court issued a sweeping defense of slaveholders' rights and concluded that no African American could claim the rights of U.S. citizenship, even if free. The decision dealt a fatal blow to both established and proposed political compromises to the sectional conflict.

The question is simply this: can a negro whose ancestors were imported into this country and sold as slaves, become a member of the political community formed and brought into existence by the Constitution of the United States, and as such become entitled to all the rights, and privileges, and immunities, guaranteed by that instrument to the citizen. One of these rights is the privilege of suing in a court of the United States in the cases specified in the Constitution. . . .

The words "people of the United States" and "citizens" are synonymous terms, and mean the same thing. They both describe the political body who, according to our republican institutions, form the sovereignty, and who hold the power and conduct the government through their representatives. They are what we familiarly call the "sovereign people," and every citizen is one of this people, and a constituent member of this sovereignty. The question before us is, whether the class of persons de-

"HAIL COLUMBIA! HAPPY LAND!!!"

AUTHENTIC ACCOUNTS OF UNITED STATES'
SLAVERY.

' A good tree cannot bring forth evil fruit, neither can a corrupt tree brin
th good fruit. Wherefore by their fruits ye shall know them."

Republicans immediately denounced the Dred Scott decision, claiming that a pro-slavery power was dominating all branches of the federal government. For slaves, the decision offered little hope for future liberation. The broad findings of the Dred Scott decision declared that even free black people could not achieve full citizenship in the United States.

scribed in the plea of abatement compose a portion of this people, and are constituent members of this sovereignty. We think they are not, and that they are not included, and were not intended to be included, under the word "citizens" in the Constitution, and can, therefore, claim none of the rights and privileges which that instrument provides for an secures to citizens of the United States. On the contrary, they were at that time considered as a subordinate and inferior class of beings, who had been subjugated by the dominant race, and whether emancipated or not, yet remained subject to their authority, and had no rights or privileges but such as those who held the power and the government might choose to grant them. . . .

A perpetual and impassable barrier was intended to be erected between the white race and the one which they had reduced to slavery, and governed as subjects with absolute and despotic power, and which they then looked upon as so far below them in the scale of created beings, that intermarriages between white persons and negroes or mulattoes were regarded as unnatural and immoral, and punished as crimes, not only in the parties, but in the person who joined them in marriage. And no distinction in this respect was made between the free negro or mulatto and the slave, but this stigma, of the deepest degredation, was fixed upon the whole race. . . .

No one, we presume, supposed that any change in public opinion or feeling, in relation to this unfortunate race, in the civilized nations of Europe or in this country, should induce the court to give to the words of the Constitution a more liberal construction in their favor than they were intended to bear when the instrument was framed and adopted. Such an argument would be altogether inadmissible in any tribunal called out to interpret it. If any of its provisions are deemed unjust, there is a mode prescribed in the instrument itself by which it may be amended; but while it remains unaltered, it must be construed now as it was understood at the time of its adoption. It is not only the same in words, but the same in meaning, and delegates the same powers to the government, and reserves and secures the same rights and privileges to the citizen; and as long as it continues to exist in its present form, it speaks not only in the same words, but with the same meaning and intent with which it spoke when it came from the hands of its framers, and was voted on and adopted by the people of the United States. Any other rule of construction would abrogate the judicial character of this court, and make it the mere reflex of the popular opinion or passion of the day. This court was not created by the Constitution for such purposes. Higher and graver trusts have been confided to it, and it must not falter in the path of duty. . . .

But the power of Congress over the person or property of a citizen can never be a mere discretionary power under our Constitution and form of government. The powers of the government and the rights and privileges of the citizen are regulated and plainly defined by the Constitution itself. And when the territory becomes a part of the United States, the Federal Government enters into possession in the character impressed upon it by those who created it. It enters upon it with its powers over the citizen strictly defined, and limited by the Constitution, from which it derives its own existence, and by virtue of which alone it continues to exist and act as a government and sovereignty. It has no power of any kind beyond it; and it cannot, when it enters a territory of the United States, put off its character, and assume discretionary or despotic powers which the Constitution has denied to it. It cannot create for itself a new character separated from the citizens of the United States, and the duties it owes them under the provisions of the Constitution. The territory being a part of the United States, the government and the citizen both enter it under the authority of the Constitution, with their respective rights defined and marked out: and the Federal Government can exercise no power over his person or property, beyond what that instrument confers, nor lawfully deny any right which it has reserved. . . .

The powers over person and property of which we speak are not only not granted to Congress, but are in express terms denied, and they are forbidden to exercise them. And this prohibition is not confined to the States, but the words are general, and extend to the whole territory over which the Constitution gives it power to legislate, including those portions of it remaining under territorial government, as well as that covered by States. It is a total absence of power everywhere within the dominion of the United States, and places the citizens of a territory, so far as these rights are concerned, on the same footing with citizens of the States, and guards them as firmly and plainly against any inroads which the general government might attempt, under the plea of implied or incidental powers. And if Congress itself cannot do this—if it is beyond the

powers conferred on the Federal Government—it will be admitted, we presume, that it could not authorize a territorial government to exercise them. It could confer no power on any local government, established by its authority, to violate the provisions of the Constitution.

It seems, however, to be supposed, that there is a difference between property in a slave and other property, and that different rules may be applied to it in expounding the Constitution of the United States. And the laws and usages of nations, and the writings of eminent jurists upon the relation of master and slave and their mutual rights and duties, and the powers which governments may exercise over it, have been dwelt upon in the argument.

But in considering the question before us, it must be borne in mind that there is no law of nations standing between the people of the United States and their government and interfering with their relation to each other. The powers of the government and the rights of the citizen under it, are positive and practical regulations plainly written down. The people of the United States have delegated to it certain enumerated powers, and forbidden it to exercise others. It has no power over the person or property of a citizen but what the citizens of the United States have granted. And no laws or usages of other nations, or reasoning of statesmen or jurists upon the relations of master and slave, can enlarge the powers of the government, or take from the citizens the rights they have reserved. And if the Constitution recognizes the right of property of the master in a slave, and makes no distinction between that description of property and other property owned by a citizen, no tribunal, acting under the authority of the United States, whether it be legislative, executive, or judicial, has a right to draw such a distinction, or deny to it the benefit of the provisions and guarantees which have been provided for the protection of private property against the encroachments of the government.

DOCUMENT 4

Abraham Lincoln, Debate at Gatesburg, Illinois (1858)

A braham Lincoln had enjoyed only limited success as a lawyer and Whig politician during the 1840s and 1850s. But as the sectional crisis mounted, he hitched his fortunes to the new Republican Party, which combined free labor ideology, racism, and antislavery to forge a new coalition of Northern voters. In 1858, Lincoln ran against incumbent Senator Stephen A. Douglas for his seat. Douglas, a leading Democratic proponent of sectional compromise, and Lincoln traveled the state for a series of seven debates. In Galesburg, Illinois, for the fifth debate, Lincoln attempted to encourage fears that the Dred Scott decision constituted the first step toward legalizing slavery throughout the country. Though Lincoln lost this election, his performance propelled him to national prominence.

While we were at Freeport, in one of these joint discussions, I answered certain interrogatories which Judge Douglas had propounded to me, and then in turn propounded some to him, which he in a sort of way answered. The third one of these interrogatories I have with me, and wish now to make some comments upon it. It was in these words: "If the Supreme Court of the United States shall decide that States cannot exclude slavery from their limits, are you in favor of acquiescing in, adopting, and following such decision as a rule of political action?

To this interrogatory Judge Douglas made no answer in any just sense of the word. He contented himself with sneering at the thought that it was possible for the Supreme Court ever to make such a decision. He sneered at me for propounding the interrogatory. I had not propounded it without some reflection, and I wish now to address to this audience some remarks upon it.

In the second clause of the sixth article, I believe it is, of the Constitution of the United States, we find the following language: "This Constitution and the laws of the United States which shall be made in pursuance thereof; and all treaties made, or which shall be made, and the authority of the United States, shall be the supreme law of the land and the

judges in every State shall be bound thereby, anything in the Constitution or laws of any State to the contrary, notwithstanding."

The essence of the Dred Scott case is compressed into the sentence which I will now read: "Now, as we have already said in an earlier part of this opinion, upon a different point, the right of property in a slave is distinctly and expressly affirmed in the Constitution." I repeat it "The right of property in a slave is distinctly and expressly affirmed in the Constitution."

What is it to be "*affirmed*" in the Constitution? Made firm in the Constitution,—so made that it cannot be separated from the Constitution without breaking the Constitution; durable as the Constitution and part of the Constitution. Now, remembering the provision of the Constitution which I have read; affirming that that instrument is the supreme law of the land; that the Judges of every State shall be bound by it, any law or constitution of any State to the contrary notwithstanding that the right of property in a slave is affirmed in that Constitution, is made, formed into, and cannot be separated from it without breaking it; durable as the instrument; part of the instrument;—what follows as a short and even syllogistic argument from it? It think it follows, and I submit to the consideration of men capable of arguing, whether as I state it, in syllogistic form, the argument has any fault in it?

Nothing in the Constitution or laws of any State can destroy a right distinctly and expressly affirmed in the Constitution of the United States.

The right of property in a slave is distinctly and expressly affirmed in the Constitution of the United States.

Therefore, nothing in the Constitution or laws of any State can destroy the right of property in a slave.

I believe that no fault can be pointed out in that argument; assuming the truth of the premises, the conclusion, so far as I have capacity at all to understand it, follows inevitably. There is a fault in it as I think, but the fault is not in the reasoning: the falsehood in fact is a fault in the premises.

I believe that the right of property in a slave *is not* distinctly and expressly affirmed in the Constitution, and Judge Douglas thinks it *is*. I believe that the Supreme Court and the advocates of that decision may search in vain for the place in the Constitution where the right of property in a slave is distinctly and expressly affirmed. I say, therefore, that I think one of the premises is not true in fact. But it is true with Judge Douglas. It is true with the Supreme Court who pronounced it. They are estopped from denying it, and being estopped from denying it the conclusion follows that, the Constitution of the United States being the supreme law, no constitution or law can interfere with it. It being affirmed in the decision that the right of property in a slave is distinctly and expressly affirmed in the Constitution, the conclusion inevitably follows that no State law or constitution can destroy that right.

I then say to Judge Douglas and to all others, that I think it will take a better answer than a sneer to show that those who have said that the right of property in a slave is distinctly and expressly affirmed in the Constitution, are not prepared to show that no constitution or law can destroy that right. I say I believe it will take a far better argument than a mere sneer to show to the minds of intelligent men that whoever has so said, is not prepared, whenever public sentiment is so far advanced as to

justify it, to say the other. This is but an opinion, and the opinion of one very humble man; but it is my opinion that the Dred Scott decision, as it is, never would have been made in its present form if the party that made it had not been sustained previously by the elections. My own opinion is, that the new Dred Scott decision, deciding against the right of the people of the States to exclude slavery will never be made, if that party is not sustained by the elections. I believe, further, that it is just as sure to be made as to-morrow is to come, if that party shall be sustained.

I have said, upon a former occasion, and I repeat it now, that the course of argument that Judge Douglas makes use of upon this subject (I charge not his motives in this), is preparing the public mind for that new Dred Scott decision. . . .

In this I think I argue fairly (without questioning motives at all) that Judge Douglas is most ingeniously and powerfully preparing the public mind to take that decision when it comes; and not only so, but he is doing it in various other ways. In these general maxims about liberty, in his assertions that he "don't care whether slavery is voted up or voted down;" that "whoever wants slavery has a right to have it;" that "there is no inconsistency between free and slave institutions." In this he is also preparing (whether purposely or not) the way for making the institution of slavery national! I repeat again, for I wish no misunderstanding, that I do not charge that he means it so; but I call upon your minds to inquire, if you were going to get the best instrument you could, and then set it to work in the most ingenious way, to prepare the public mind for this movement, operating in the Free States, where there is now an abhorrence of the institution of slavery, could you find an instrument so capable of doing it as Judge Douglas, or one employed in so apt a way to do it? . . .

And I do think—I repeat, though I said it on a former occasion—that Judge Douglas and whoever, like him, teaches that the negro has no share, humble though it may be, in the Declaration of Independence, is going back to the era of our liberty and independence, and, so far as in him lies, muzzling the cannon that thunders its annual joyous return; that he is blowing out the moral rights around us, when he contends that whoever wants slaves has a right to hold them; that he is penetrating, so far as lies in his power, the human soul, and eradicating the light of reason and the love of liberty, when he is in every possible way preparing the public mind, by his vast influence, for making the institution of slavery perpetual and national. . . .

It is, therefore, as I think, a very important question for the consideration of the American people, whether the policy of bringing in additional territory, without considering at all how it will operate upon the safety of the Union in reference to this one great disturbing element in our national politics, shall be adopted as the policy of the country. You will bear in mind that it is to be acquired, according to the Judge's view, as fast as it is needed, and the indefinite part of this proposition is that we have only Judge Douglas and his class of men to decide how fast territory is needed. We have no clear and certain way of determining or demonstrating how fast territory is needed by the necessities of the country. Whoever wants to go out filibustering, then, thinks that more territory is needed. Whoever

wants wider slave-fields, feels sure that some additional territory is needed as slave-territory. Then it is as easy to show the necessity of additional slave-territory as it is to assert anything that is incapable of absolute demonstration. Whatever motive a man or a set of men may have for making annexation of property or territory it is very easy to assert, but much less easy to disprove, that it is necessary for the wants of the country.

And now it only remains for me to say that I think it is a very grave question for the people of this Union to consider, whether, in view of the fact that this slavery question has been the only one that has ever endangered our Republican institutions, the only one that has ever threatened or menaced a dissolution of the Union, that has ever disturbed us in such a way as to make us fear for the perpetuity of our liberty,—in view of these facts, I think it is an exceedingly interesting and important question for this people to consider whether we shall engage in the policy of acquiring additional territory, discarding altogether from our consideration, while obtaining new territory, the question how it may affect us in regard to this, the only endangering element to our liberties and national greatness. . . .

DOCUMENT 5

National Convention of Colored People, Report on Abolition (1847)

Most abolitionists, white and black, believed that intensive exposure and denunciation of slavery would make the South's position untenable. Northern blacks, those born in freedom, and those who ran away to freedom, formed a critical portion of the small Northern constituency for abolition. On their own as well as through participation in organizations led by whites such as William Lloyd Garrison, they advocated reform. Here the National Convention of Colored People's Committee on Abolition, which included runaway-slave-turned-abolitionist Frederick Douglass, expressed the importance of winning over public opinion through peaceful means.

❦ ❧

21st JULY.

In pursuance of a deed of trust executed to me by Walter B. Morris on the 2d day of June, 1840, and acknowledged and recorded the 5th day of September, 1840, I will on Thursday, the 21st day of July next, proceed to sell to the highest bidder, at the Sumner Mills, for purposes therein specified, six negroes, one man, two women and two children, *for cash.* Also 20 shares in the Gallatin Turnpike Company, Horses, Cows, and Cart, Beds and Bedding, Bedsteads, Beaureaus, Tables, Chairs, Carpets, Maps, Books, say 1500 volumes, with a great variety of furniture, &c. &c. mentioned in said deed of trust. All sums under five dollars, cash, over that sum, on a credit of twelve months; notes with approved security will be required.
April 18th, 1842.   GEO. A. WILLIE, *Trustee.*

☞I would take this occasion to say to my friends and the public generally, that I should be pleased to see them at the *Sumner Mills* on the day of sale.
Very respectfully,   WALTER B. MORRIS.

Slave auctions, like the one announced in this advertisement, became an embarrassment for many Americans. As frustrated abolitionists repeatedly learned, moral arguments against slavery made little impression on Southern planters whose economic prosperity depended on free labor.

The Committee appointed to draft a Report respecting the best means of abolishing Slavery and destroying Caste in the United States, beg leave most respectfully to Report: That they have had the important subjects referred to them, under consideration, and have carefully endeavored to examine all their points and bearings to the best of their ability; and from every view they have been able to take they have arrived at the conclusion that the best means of abolishing slavery is proclamation of truth, and that the best means of destroying caste is the mental, moral and industrial improvement of our people.

First, as respects Slavery, Your Committee find this monstrous crime, this stupendous iniquity, closely interwoven with all the great interests, institutions and organizations of the country; pervading and influencing every class and grade of society, securing their support, obtaining their approbation, and commanding their homage. Availing itself of the advantage which age gives to crime, it has perverted the judgment, blunted the moral sense, blasted the sympathies, and created in the great

mass,—the overwhelming majority of the people—a moral sentiment altogether favorable to its own character, and its own continuance. Press and pulpit are alike prostituted and made to serve the end of this infernal institution. The power of the government, and the sanctity of religion, church and state, are joined with the guilty oppressor against the oppressed—and the voice of this great nation is thundering in the ear of our enslaved fellow countrymen the terrible fiat, *you shall be slaves or die!* The slave is in the minority, a small minority. The oppressors are an overwhelming majority. The oppressed are three millions, their oppressors are seventeen millions. The one is weak, the other is strong; the one is without arms, without means of concert, and without government; the other possess every advantage in these respects; and the deadly aim of their million of musketry, and loud-mouthed cannon tells the down-trodden slave in unmistakable language, *he must be a slave or die.* In these circumstances, your committee are called upon to report as to the best means of abolishing slavery. And without pretending parties and factions, though did time permit, they would gladly do so, they beg at once to state their entire disapprobation of any plan of emancipation involving a resort to bloodshed. With the facts of our condition before us, it is impossible for us to contemplate any appeal to the slave to take vengence on his guilty master, but with the utmost reprobation. Your Committee regard any counsel of this sort as the perfection of folly, suicidal in the extreme, and abominably wicked. We should utterly frown down and wholly discountenance any attempt to lead our people to confide in brute force as a reformatory instrumentality. All argument put forth in favor of insurrection and bloodshed, however well intended, is either the result of an unpardonable impatience or an atheistic want of faith in the power of truth as a means of regenerating and reforming the world. Again we repeat, let us set our faces against all such absurd, unavailing, dangerous and mischievous ravings, emanating from what source they may. The voice of God and of common sense, equally point out a more excellent way, and that way is a faithful, earnest, and persevering enforcement of the great principles of justice and morality, religion and humanity. These are the only invincible and infallible means within our reach with which to overthrow this foul system of blood and ruin. Your Committee deem it susceptible of the clearest demonstration, that slavery exists in this country, because the people of this country WILL its existence. And they deem it equally clear, that no system or institution can exist for an hour against the earnestly-expressed WILL of the people. It were quite easy to bring to the support of the foregoing proposition powerful and conclusive illustrations from the history of reform in all ages, and especially in our own. But the palpable truths of the propositions, as well as the familiarity of the facts illustrating them, entirely obviate such a necessity.

Our age is an age of great discoveries; and one of the greatest is that which revealed that this world is to be ruled, shaped and guided by the *marvelous might of mind.* The human voice must supersede the roar of cannon. Truth alone is the legitimate antidote of falsehood. Liberty is always sufficient to grapple with tyranny. Free speech—free discussion—peaceful agitation,—the foolishness of preaching these, under God, will subvert this giant crime, and send it reeling to its grave, as if smitten by a voice from the throne of God. Slavery exists because it is popular. It will cease to exist when it is made unpopular. Whatever therefore tends to make Slavery unpopular tends to its destruction. This every Slaveholder knows full well, and hence his opposition to all discussion of the subject. It is an evidence of intense feeling of alarm, when John C. Calhoun calls upon the North to put down what he is pleased to term "this plundering agitation." Let us give the Slaveholder what he most dislikes. Let us expose his crimes and his foul abominations. He is reputable and must be made disreputable. He must be regarded as a moral lepor—slummed as a loathsome wretch—outlawed from Christian communion, and from social respectability—an enemy of God and man, to be execrated by the community till he shall repent of his foul crimes, and give proof of his sincerity by breaking every chain and letting the oppressed go free. Let us invoke the Press and appeal to the pulpit to deal out the righteous denunciations of heaven against oppression, fraud and wrong, and the desire of our hearts will soon be given us in the triumph of Liberty throughout all the land. . . .

DOCUMENT 6

Harriet Beecher Stowe, Uncle Tom's Cabin (1852)

For most Northerners even the most moderate abolitionist organizations appeared too radical. Those people who could not be reached through political agitation could be reached through literature. New Englander Harriet Beecher Stowe's story of the vagaries of life in the slave-holding South, her identification of good and evil characters, and her ability to play on Christian moral sentiments caused a sensation. Over 300,000 copies of the book sold within a year of its publication.

❧ ❧

Mr. Haley and Tom jogged onward in their wagon, each, for a time, absorbed in his own reflections. Now, the reflections of two men sitting side by side are a curious thing—seated on the same seat, having the same eyes, ears, hands, and organs of all sorts, and having pass before their eyes the same objects: it is wonderful what a variety we shall find in these same reflections.

As, for example, Mr. Haley: He thought first of Tom's length and breadth and height, and what he would sell for, if he was kept fat and in good case till he got him into market. He thought of how he should make out his gang; he thought of the respective market value of certain suppositious men and women and children who were to compose it, and other kindred topics of the business; then he thought of himself, and how humane he was, that whereas other men chained their "niggers" hand and foot both, he only put fetters on the feet, and left Tom the use of his hands, as long as he behaved well; and he sighed to think how ungrateful human nature was, so that there was even room to doubt whether Tom appreciated his mercies. He had been taken in so by "niggers" whom he had favored; but still he was astonished to consider how good-natured he yet remained!

As to Tom, he was thinking over some words of an unfashionable old book which kept running through his head again and again, as follows: "We have no continuing city, but we seek one to come; wherefore God Himself is not ashamed to be called our God; for He hath prepared for us a city." These words of an ancient volume, got up principally by "ignorant and unlearned men," have, through all time, kept up, somehow, a strange sort of power over the minds of poor, simple fellows like Tom. They stir up the soul from its depths, and rouse, as with trumpet-call, courage, energy, and enthusiasm where before was only the blackness of despair.

Mr. Haley pulled out of his pocket sundry newspapers, and began looking over their advertisements with absorbed interest. He was not a remarkably fluent reader, and was in the habit of reading in a sort of recitative, half-aloud, by way of calling in his ears to verify the deductions of his eyes. In this tone he slowly recited the following paragraph:—

"EXECUTORS' SALE—NEGROES!

"Agreeably to Order of Court, will be Sold, on Tuesday, February 20, before the Court-house door, in the town of Washington, Kentucky, the following Negroes:—Hagar, aged 60; John, aged 30; Ben, aged 21; Saul, aged 25; Albert, aged 14. Sold for the benefit of the creditors and heirs of the estate of Jesse Blutchford, Esq.

"SAMUEL MORRIS,
THOMAS FLINT,
Executors."

"This yer I must look at," said he to Tom, for want of somebody else to talk to. "Ye see, I am going to get up a prime gang to take down with ye, Tom; it'll make it sociable and pleasant like—good company will, ye know. We must drive right to Washington first and foremost, and then I'll clap you into jail while I does the business."

Tom received this agreeable intelligence quite meekly, simply wondering in his own heart how many of these doomed men had wives and children, and whether they would feel as he did about leaving them. It is to be confessed, too, that the naïve, off-hand information that he was to be thrown into jail by no means produced an agreeable impression on a poor fellow who had always prided himself on a strictly honest and upright course of life. However, the day wore on, and the evening saw Haley and Tom comfortably accommodated in Washington—the one in a tavern, the other in a jail.

About eleven o'clock the next day a mixed throng was gathered around the Court-house steps—smoking, chewing, spitting, swearing, and conversing, according to their respective tastes and turns, waiting for the auction to commence. The men and women to be sold sat in a group apart, talking in a low tone to each other. The woman who had been advertised by the name of Hagar was a regular African in feature and figure. She might have been sixty, but was older than that by hard work and disease, was partially blind and somewhat crippled with rheumatism. By her side stood her only remaining son, Albert, a bright-looking little fellow of fourteen years. The boy was the only survivor of a large family who had been successively sold away from her to a southern market. The mother held on to him with both her shaking hands, and eyed with intense trepidation everyone who walked up to examine him.

"Don't be fear'd, Aunt Hagar," said the oldest of the men; "I spoke to Mas'r Thomas 'bout it, and he thought he might manage to sell you in a lot both together."

"Dey needn't call me worn out yet," said she, lifting her shaking hands. "I can cook, yet, and scrub and scour—I'm wuth a buying, if I do come cheap; tell 'em dat ar—you *tell* 'em," she added, earnestly.

Haley here forced his way into the group, walked up to the first man, pulled his mouth open and looked in, felt of his teeth, made him stand and straighten himself, bend his back, and perform various evolutions, to show his muscles; and then passed on to the next, and put him through the same trial. Walking up last to the boy, he felt of his arms, straightened his hands and looked at his fingers, and made him jump to show his agility.

"He an't gwine to be sold widout me!" said the old woman, with passionate eagerness; "he and I goes in a lot together. I's rail strong yet, mas'r, and can do heaps o' work—heaps on't, mas'r."

"On plantation?" said Haley, with a contemptuous glance. "Likely story!" and, as if satisfied with his examination, he walked out and looked, and stood with his hands in his pockets, his cigar in his mouth, and his hat cocked on one side, ready for action.

What think of 'em?" said a man who had been following Haley's examination, as if to make up his own mind from it.

"Wal," said Haley, spitting, "I shall put in, I think, for the youngerly ones and the boy."

"They want to sell the boy and the old woman together," said the man.

"Find it a tight pull. Why, she's an old rack o'bones—not worth her salt!"

"You wouldn't, then?" said the man.

"Anybody'd be a fool 't would. She's half-blind, crooked with rheumatis, and foolish to boot."

"Some buys up these yer old critturs, and ses there's a sight more wear in 'em a body'd think," said the man, reflectively.

"No go 't all," said Haley; "wouldn't take her for a present—fact; I've *seen*, now."

"Wal, 'tis kinder pity, now, not to buy her with her son—her heart seems so sot on him, s'pose they fling her in cheap."

"Them that's got money to spend that ar way, it's all well enough. I shall bid off on that ar boy for a plantation hand; wouldn't be bothered with her, no way—not if they'd give her to me," said Haley.

"She'll take on desp't," said the man.

"Nat'lly, she will," said the trader, coolly.

The conversation was here interrupted by a busy hum in the audience; and the auctioneer, a short, bustling, important fellow, elbowed his way into the crowd. The old woman drew in her breath, and caught instinctively at her son.

"Keep close to yer mammy, Albert—close—dey'll put us up togeder," she said.

"Oh, mammy, I'm fear'd they won't," said the boy.

"Dey must, child; I can't live, no ways, if they don't," said the old creature, vehemently.

The stentorian tones of the auctioneer, calling out to clear the way, now announced that the sale was about to commence. A place was cleared, and the bidding began. The different men on the list were soon knocked off at prices which showed a pretty brisk demand in the market; two of them fell to Haley.

"Come, now, young un," said the auctioneer, giving the boy a touch with his hammer, "be up and show your springs, now."

"Put us to up togeder—togeder—do please, mas'r," said the old woman, holding fast to her boy.

"Be off," said the man, gruffly, pushing her away; "you come last. Now, darkey, spring"; and, with the word, he pushed the boy toward the block, while a deep, heavy groan rose behind him. The boy paused, and looked back; but there was no time to stay, and dashing the tears from his large, bright eyes, he was up in a moment.

His fine figure, alert limbs, and bright face raised

an instant competition, and half a dozen bids simultaneously met the ear of the auctioneer. Anxious, half-frightened, he looked from side to side, as he heard the clatter of contending bids—now here, now there—till the hammer fell. Haley had got him. He was pushed from the block towards his new master, but stopped one moment and looked back, when his poor old mother, trembling in every limb, held out her shaking hands towards him.

"Buy me too, mas'r; for de dear Lord's sake!—buy me—I shall die if you don't!"

"You'll die if I do, that's the kink of it," said Haley. "No!" And he turned on his heel.

The bidding for the poor old creature was summary. The man who had addressed Haley, and who seemed not destitute of compassion, bought her for a trifle, and the spectators began to disperse.

The poor victims of the sale, who had been brought up in one place together for years, gathered round the despairing old mother, whose agony was pitiful to see.

"Couldn't dey leave me one? Mas'r allers said I should have one—he did," she repeated over and over in heart-broken tones.

"Trust in the Lord, Aunt Hagar," said the oldest of the men, sorrowfully.

"What good will it do?" said she, sobbing passionately.

DOCUMENT 7

De Bow's Review, *"The Stability of the Union,"* (1850)

Southerners did not passively accept criticism, which increasingly rained down on their region from the North. Rather, they offered their own view of slavery as a "positive good" and began to suggest that their region might thrive just as well without the North. *De Bow's Review*, a New Orleans publication read throughout the South, trumpeted the South's virtues in many articles, including this one from 1850.

The South is now with its institutions and capabilities, possessed of that on which half the manufacturing and commercial interests of the world depends. It is the source whence the only means of employing and feeding at least 5,000,000 whites can be drawn, and without which, nearly $1,000,000,000 of active capital in ships and factory would be valued less. A country and institutions so important to the welfare of humanity at large, are not to be trifled with. This country forms one-half of our glorious Union, on terms agreed upon by those immortal men who separated from England, because they would no longer suffer the continuance of the African slave-trade; but, in its independent position, the South holds the welfare of other nations almost entirely within its keeping. The capital and laboring abilities of England are such as to afford the South an outlet for its staple, should it exclude all other customers. The result of such a movement, would be to force other countries to draw their goods from England only. On the other hand, the manufacturing progress of the North is such, that in a few years she may absorb the whole of the southern staple, and place herself at the head of the manufacturing interest for the supply of the world. To the South, it is comparatively of small importance, whether England or the North obtains this mastery. Between the North and England, it is a mortal duel; and yet, in the crisis of this struggle, there are to be found persons at the North so destitute of all moral sense and political acuteness as to attack, in violation of the sacred pledge of the constitution, those institutions which it guarantees, and which are so necessary to the interests of humanity.

The continued harmony of the United States, permitting the industry of each section to furnish materials for the enterprise of the others, the reciprocity of benefits and uninterrupted interchange of mutual productions, facilitated by continually increasing means of intercourse and accumulation of capital, are laying the foundation for an empire of which the world's history not only affords no example, but the magnitude of which the wildest dream of the most imaginative of the world's statesmen has failed to conceive. In this undisturbed progress, the condition of the black race is being elevated on the swelling tide of white progress. Inasmuch as that the first slaves imported were, under their new masters, vastly superior in condition to the nude cannibals by whom they were sold, only because avarice triumphed over appetite so is the condition of the slave of the present day far above that of his progenitor a few generations back. The black race, in its servitude to the whites, has undergone an improvement, which the same race, in its state of African freedom, has failed to manifest. By whatever degree, physically and morally, the blacks of the United States are superior to the nude cannibals of Africa, are they indebted to the white race for its active, though not disinterested agency. That process of improvement has not ceased, but is ever progressive in the train of white advancement. The huge lumber-car has no vitality of itself, but, attached to the resistless locomotive, moves forward with a vigor not its own. To cast off that race, in dependence on its own resources, is a singular manifestation of desire for its progress. As an indication of the progress in respect of freedom, which that race makes as it is

trained to endure it, we may take the numbers classified upon the continent, for three periods, according to the United States census:

	Slave States	Free States	
	Slaves		Free Blacks
1800,	857,095	61,441	73,100
1830,	2,005,475	182,070	137,525
1840,	2,486,226	215,568	172,509

In 1800 there were 36,946 slaves in what are now free States. The emancipation of these increased the free blacks in the free States; but the multiplication of the free blacks in the slave States is much more rapid, and is increasing on the proportion of slaves. Thus, the free blacks in those States, in forty years, reached 25 per cent of the original number of slaves—the emancipation being always 10 per cent of the increase. This has been greatly retarded by the abolition excitement. It is observable that the free blacks do not emigrate from the southern States. Their social position there is less onerous than the nominal freedom of the North. The increase of free blacks at the South, in forty years, was 250 per cent, and, at the North, 140 per cent. It is, undoubtedly, true, that the unconquerable repugnance of the North to permit the presence of blacks, if they can possibly be excluded, has, to a very great extent, checked emancipation. Thus, the constitution passed by Ohio on its organization as a State, with the black laws, passed by its Legislature, by preventing the ingress of slaves, greatly retarded emancipation. To suppose that the ordinance of 1787 stopped slave migration is a great mistake. It was the opposition of the white settlers to the presence of negroes that alone prevented it. Had any number of slaves been settled in Ohio, they would, ultimately, as in New York, have been emancipated, and would, by so much, have reduced the existing number of slaves. Thus, notwithstanding all the false sympathies of the North, the progress of emancipation at the South is quite as rapid as it should be, to avoid convulsions. It is more than probable, that, when the body of free blacks shall have become more considerable, they will supplant slaves as domestic servants, until slavery becomes, in those States, almost entirely predial. There is no comparison between the well-trained free black, subject to dismissal for misconduct as a domestic servant, and the slothful slave who has no fear of loss of place before his eyes. The free blacks must, necessarily, crowd out the slaves by a gradual and regular process, as the latter become more fitted for freedom. It is an inevitable law of political economy, that slavery must cease where trade is free and the population of freemen becomes more dense. This process is gradually and surely elevating the black race; and, to disturb it by any means, is at once to plunge this incapable race into hopeless barbarism, as complete as that which pervades Africa. An earnest desire for progress, political and social, for both races, as well on this continent as upon that of Europe, will find, in a firm adherence to the compromises of the constitution, the only sure mode of accomplishing that double end. To preserve the harmony of the several sections, by refraining from an attack upon that state of things which we may wish did not exist, but which we cannot remedy, is the only mode of ameliorating them. Those political schemers who seek for their own advancement amid the ruins of an empire, the desolation of a continent and the barbarizing of a race of men, will find, in the awakening intelligence of the people, the fiat of their own destruction.

DOCUMENT 8

Annie Young, Memoir of Slavery (1937)*

Whites on all sides claimed to speak on behalf of African Americans in bondage and to analyze their condition. In addition, some blacks who escaped North published their memoirs to encourage the abolitionist movement. But ordinary slaves who had little prospect of escape rarely, if ever, had the chance to render their opinions on what slavery was like. During the Great Depression of the 1930s, the federal government paid unemployed writers to record the memories of those who had lived through slavery. Though the memories of aging ex-slaves recorded by white strangers present their own difficulties for the historian, they make available unique insights. Here Annie Young of Oklahoma City recalls her childhood in Tennessee.

Annie Young

Age 86

Oklahoma City, Okla.

I was born in 1851, makes me 85 years old. I was born in Middle Tennessee, Summers County. My mother was put on a block and sold from me when I was a child. I don't remember my father real good. Sister Martha, Sister Sallie, nor Sister Jane wasn't sold. But my brother John was. My mother's name is Rachel Donnahue. We lived in a log hut. The white folks lived in a frame white building sitting in a big grove yard. Old master owned a big farm.

*"Annie Young, Memory of Slavery, 1937" from *The American Slave: A Composite Autobiography*, vol. 7, *Oklahoma and Mississippi Narratives* edited by George P. Radwick (Copyright © 1972 by Greenwood Publishing Group, Inc., Westport, CT.)

We ate molasses, bread and butter and milk in wooden bowls and crumbled our bread up in it. Old master had big smokehouses of meat. Dey ate chickens, possums and coons, and my old auntie would barbecue rabbits for de white folks. We ate ash cakes too.

I washed dishes, swept de yard, and kept de yard clean wid weed brush brooms. I never earned no money. All de slaves had gardens, and chickens too. My auntie, dey let her have chickens of her own and she raised chickens, and had a chicken house and garden down in de woods.

I remember in time of de War dey'd send me down in de woods to pick up chips and git wood. All de men had gone to de army. One morning and t'was cold dey sent me down in de woods and my hands got frostbitten. All de skin come off and dey had to tie my hands up in roasted turnips. Sallie she had gloves, and didn't get frostbitten. After my old master died, Master Donnahue was his name, his old son-in-law come to take over de plantation. He was mean, but my sister whipped him.

We had no nigger driver or overseer. We raised wheat, corn and vegetables, not much cotton, jest enough to spun de clothes out of.

At night when we'd go to our cabins we'd pick cotton from de seeds to make our clothes. Boys and girls alike wore dem long shirts slit up de side only to your necks. They'd have cornshuckings sometimes all night long. I see I didn't have no mother, no father, nobody to lead me, teach me or no one, and so jest lived with anybody [who] was good enough to let me stay and see what they did. They'd have log rollings, with all de whiskey dey could drink.

I remember going to church, de Methodist Church dey call it. We sing dis song and I sho did like it too:

> "I went down in de valley to pray,
> Studying dat good old way."

I been a Christian long before most of dese young niggers was born. My other favorites are:

> "Must Jesus bear This Cross Alone."

and

> "The Consecrated Cross I'll Bear 'til
> Death Shall Set Me Free,
> Yea, There's a Crown for Everyone,
> And There's a Crown for Me.

Lawd, there sho is.

One day a nigger killed one of his master's shoats and he catch and when he'd ask him, "What's that you got there?" The nigger said, "a sum." De master said, "Let me see." He looked and seen it was a shoat. nigger said, "Master it may be a shoat now, but it sho was a possum while when I put 'im in dis sack."

Dey didn't whip our folks much, but one day I saw a overseer on ther place. He staked a man down with two forked sticks 'cross his wrist led in de ground and beat him half to death with a hand saw 'til it drawed sters. Den he mopped his back wid vinegar, salt and pepper. Sometimes 'd drop dat hot rosin from pine knots on dose blisters.

When de Yanks come, business took place. I remember white folks was running and hiding, gitting everything dey could from de Yanks. Dey hid dey jewelry and fine dishes and such. Dose Yanks had on big boots. Dey's drive up, feed dey hosses from old Master's corn, catch dey chickens, and tell old Master's cook to cook 'em, and they'd shoot down old Master's hogs and skin 'em.

De Yanks used to make my nephew drunk, and have him sing (dis is kind of bad):

> "I'll be God O'Mighty
> God Dammed if I don't
> Kill a nigger,
> Oh Whooey boys! Oh Whooey!
> Oh Whooey boys! Oh Whooey!"

I don't remember never seeing no funerals. Jest-took 'em off and buried 'em. I remember dat old Master's son-in-law dat my sister whipped, he called hisself a doctor and he killed Aunt Clo. Give her some medicine but he didn't know what he was doing and killed her.

I married William Young and we had a pretty good wedding. Married in Crittington County

Arkansas. When I left Tennessee and went to Arkansas I followed some hands. You know after de War day immigrated niggers from one place to another. I owned a good farm in Arkansas. I came out here some 42 years ago.

I have three daughters. Mattie Brockins runs a rooming house in Kansas City. Jessie Cotton lives right up de street here. Osie Olla Anderson is working out in North town.

Well I think Abraham Lincoln is more than a type a man than Moses. I believe he is a square man, believe in union that every man has a right to be a free man regardless to color. He was a republican man. Don't know much 'bout Jeff Davis. . .

I can remember once my auntie's old Master tried to have her and she run off out in de woods and when he put those blood hounds or nigger hounds on her trail he catched her and hit her in de head wid something like de stick de police carry, and he knocked a hole in her head and she bled like a hog, and he made her have him. She told her mistress, and mistress told her to go ahead and be wid him 'cause he's gonna killa you. And he had dem two women and she had some chillun nearly white, and master and dey all worked in de fields side by side.

Study Questions

1. What interests united the North, the South, and the West? What divided these regions?

2. In what way did moral arguments and economic arguments about slavery overlap?

3. How big a role did racist sentiments play in shaping attitudes toward the sectional crisis?

4. Did blacks and whites interpret the issues before the nation in the same way?

5. Did these documents suggest an inevitable conflict between North and South? How might a compromise have been negotiated?

14

The Civil War

The Civil War (1861–1865) forced Americans of all regions, races, and classes to confront profoundly divisive issues that had festered for many decades. The breakdown by 1856 of the established two-party system, through which both Whigs and Democrats drew support from both North and South, symbolized the inability of the nation to deal effectively with sectional conflict. Spokesmen from each region suggested that opponents sought to impose their values, laws and political control over the other, especially with regard to the institution of slavery.

Abraham Lincoln, Republican nominee for president, won the White House by capturing virtually every northern electoral college vote and none from the South. Before Lincoln's March 1861 inauguration, seven slaveholding states in the Deep South seceded, forming the Confederate States of America. When Confederate troops seized Fort Sumter, a federal garrison in the harbor at Charleston, South Carolina, Lincoln requested that militias from Union states provide troops to subdue the southern rebellion. Four more southern states, including Virginia, joined the Confederacy in succeeding weeks. The Civil War, spanning four years and costing more than 600,000 lives, had begun.

Politicians, soldiers, and civilians in both the Union and the Confederacy not only had to contribute to the war effort—often with their lives—but also had to explain to themselves the meaning of this costly conflagration. The task severely taxed the abilities of leaders such as Lincoln and Confederate President Jefferson Davis, especially as the war, despite initial hopes of a brief conflict, required ever more manpower and material resources (Document 1). Lincoln, though enjoying the advantages of a larger population and much greater industrial capacity, faced the twin challenges of sustaining the offensive against former countrymen and of addressing the root cause of the conflict, the enslavement of African Americans (Document 2). To address the latter, he had to overcome white America's ingrained prejudices, as well as his own.

White northerners had sought not racial equality before the war but, rather, the geographic containment of an institution that threatened their own designs on western territory and their commitment to a wage-labor economy. Nonetheless, black slaves fled to Union areas in increasing numbers. Although eager for freedom and the opportunity to advance the cause of those still in bondage, northerners responded with uncertainty to their new allies (Document 3). In time, Lincoln came to appreciate the value—strategic and symbolic—of transforming the South's unfree laboring class into soldiers fighting against their former masters. On January 1, 1863, the president made the Emancipation Proclamation, which, with some caveats, put the Union on the side of freedom.

For the soldiers, black and white, northern and southern, the war brought trauma, tragedy, and triumph. Military camp life proved tedious at best and life-threatening at worst, as disease killed many thousands. The battlefield offered even more gruesome reminders of life's fragility. Whether fighting for personal glory, sectional defense, national unity, individual freedom, abstract liberty, or some mixture of these, the horrors of combat and the deprivations of army life strained the original commitment many ordinary people had made (Document 4). Black troops in particular, whether volunteers from northern states or fugitives from slavery, discovered that the struggle for genuine equality had only just been joined (Document 5).

The war also stimulated anxiety, guilt, and creativity among people who never saw the field of battle. In this "total war," the contest required the mobilization of productive and destructive resources on an unprecedented scale. New forms of organization aimed at the efficient deployment of war-related goods and services like munitions and medical care emerged during the course of the conflict (Document 6). In the South and contested border areas, families confronted hardships imposed by invading armies and a collapsing economy (Document 7). General William T. Sherman's sweep through the heart of the south epitomized the northern strategy of ultimately destroying the Confederacy's ability to sustain itself. On April 9, 1865, Confederate commander Robert E. Lee surrendered to Union General Ulysses S. Grant at Appomattox Courthouse in rural Virginia, signaling at once the death of a slave system and the birth of a new, powerful industrializing nation.

DOCUMENT 1

Jefferson Davis, Address to the Provisional Congress of the Confederate States of America (1861)

On April 29, 1861, President Jefferson Davis of the newly established Confederacy delivered a message to its Provisional Congress at Montgomery, Alabama. Davis outlined the sources of tension between North and South that had triggered secession. He argued on several different grounds that the South had been driven to extreme solutions by aggressive northerners, who seemed bent on destroying the U.S. Constitution as well as the slave-based economy.

❦   ❧

The declaration of war made against this Confederacy by Abraham Lincoln, the President of the United States, in his proclamation issued on the 15th day of the present month, rendered it necessary, in my judgment, that you should convene at the earliest practicable moment to devise the measures necessary for the defense of the country. The occasion is indeed an extraordinary one. It justifies me in a brief review of the relations heretofore existing between us and the States which now unite in warfare against us and in a succinct statement of the events which have resulted in this warfare, to the end that mankind may pass intelligent and impartial judgment on its motives and objects. During the war waged against Great Britain by her colonies on this continent a common danger impelled them to a close alliance and to the formation of a Confederation, by the terms of which the colonies, styling themselves States, entered "*severally* into a firm league of friendship with each other for their common defense, the security of their liberties, and their mutual and general welfare, binding themselves to assist each other against all force offered to or attacks made upon them, or any of them, on account of religion, sovereignty, trade, or any other pretense whatever." In order to guard against any misconstruction of their compact, the several States made explicit declaration in a distinct article—that "*each* State *retains its* sovereignty, freedom, and independence, and every power, jurisdiction, and right which is not by this Confederation *expressly delegated* to the United States in Congress assembled." . . .

Strange, indeed, must it appear to the impartial observer, but it is none the less true that all these carefully worded clauses proved unavailing to prevent the rise and growth in the Northern States of a political school which has persistently claimed that the government thus formed was not a compact *between* States, but was in effect a national government, set up *above* and *over* the States. An organization created by the States to secure the blessings of liberty and independence against *foreign* aggression, has been gradually perverted into a machine for their control in their *domestic* affairs. The *creature* has been exalted above its *creators*; the *principles* have been made subordinate to the *agent* appointed by themselves. The people of the Southern States, whose almost exclusive occupation was agriculture, early perceived a tendency in the Northern States to render the common government subservient to their own purposes by imposing burdens on commerce as a protection to their manufacturing and shipping interests. Long and angry controversies grew out of these attempts, often successful, to benefit one section of the country at the expense of the other. And the danger of disruption arising from this cause was enhanced by the fact that the Northern population was increasing, by immigration and other causes, in a greater ratio than the population of the South. By degrees, as the Northern States gained preponderance in the National Congress, self-interest taught their people to yield ready assent to any plausible advocacy of their right as a majority to govern the minority without control. They learned to listen with impatience of their will, and so utterly have the principles of the Constitution been corrupted in the Northern mind that, in the inaugural address delivered by President Lincoln in March last, he asserts as an axiom, which he plainly deems to be undeniable, that the theory of the Constitution requires that in all cases the majority shall govern; and in another memorable instance the same Chief Magistrate did not hesitate to liken the relations between a State and the United States to those which exist between a county and the State in which it is situated and by which it was created. This is the lamentable and fundamental error on which rests the policy that has culminated in his declaration of war against these Confederate States. In addition to the long-continued and deep-seated resentment felt by the Southern States at the persistent abuse of the powers they had delegated to the Congress, for the purpose of enriching the manufacturing and shipping classes of the North at the expense of the South, there has existed for nearly half a century another subject of discord, involving interests of such transcendent magnitude as at all times to create the apprehension in the minds of many devoted lovers of the Union that its permanence was impossible. When the several States delegated certain powers to the United States Congress, a large portion of the laboring population consisted of African slaves imported into the colonies by the mother country. In twelve out of the thirteen States negro slavery existed, and the right of property in slaves was protected by law. This property was recognized in the Constitution, and provision was made against its loss by the escape of the slave. The increase in the number of slaves by further importation from Africa was also secured by a clause forbidding Congress to prohibit the slave trade anterior to a certain date, and in no clause can there be found any delegation of power to the Congress authorizing it in any manner to legislate to the prejudice, detriment, or discouragement of the owners of that species of property, or excluding it from the protection of the Government.

The climate and soil of the Northern States soon proved unpropitious to the continuance of slave labor, whilst the converse was the case at the South. Under the unrestricted free intercourse between two sections, the Northern States consulted their own interests by selling their slaves to the South and prohibiting slavery within their limits. The South were willing purchasers of a property suitable to their wants, and paid the price of the acquisition without harboring a suspicion that their quiet possession was to be disturbed by those who were inhibited not only by want of constitutional authority, but by good faith as vendors, from disquieting a title emanating from themselves. As soon, however, as the Northern States that prohibited African slavery within their limits had reached a number sufficient to give their representation a controlling voice in the Congress, a persistent and organized system of hostile measures against the rights of the owners of slaves in the Southern States was inaugurated and gradually extended. A continuous series of measures was devised and prosecuted for the purpose of rendering insecure the tenure of property in slaves. Fanatical organizations, supplied with money by voluntary subscriptions, were assiduously engaged in exciting amongst the slaves a spirit of discontent and revolt; means were furnished for their escape

from their owners, and agents secretly employed to entice them to abscond; the constitutional provision for their rendition to their owners was first evaded, then openly denounced as a violation of conscientious obligation and religious duty; men were taught that it was a merit to elude, disobey, and violently oppose the execution of the laws enacted to secure the performance of the promise contained in the constitutional compact; owners of slaves were mobbed and even murdered in open day solely for applying to a magistrate for the arrest of a fugitive slave; the dogmas of these voluntary organizations soon obtained control of the Legislatures of many of the Northern States, and laws were passed providing for the punishment, by ruinous fines and long-continued imprisonment in jails and penitentiaries, of citizens of the Southern States who should dare to ask aid of the officers of the law for the recovery of their property. Emboldened by success, the theater of agitation and aggression against the clearly expressed constitutional rights of the Southern States was transferred to the Congress; Senators and Representatives were sent to the common councils of the nation, whose chief title to this distinction consisted in the display of a spirit of ultra fanaticism, and whose business was not "to promote the general welfare or insure domestic tranquility," but to awaken the bitterest hatred against the citizens of sister States by violent denunciation of their institutions; the transaction of public affairs was impeded by repeated efforts to usurp powers not delegated by the Constitution, for the purpose of impairing the security of property in slaves, and reducing those States which held slaves to a condition of inferiority. Finally a great party was organized for the purpose of obtaining the administration of the Government, with the avowed object of using its power for the total exclusion of the slave States from all participation in the benefits of the public domain acquired by all the States in common, whether by conquest or purchase; of surrounding them entirely by States in which slavery should be prohibited; of thus rendering the property in slaves so insecure as to be comparatively worthless, and thereby annihilating in effect property worth thousands of millions of dollars. This party, thus organized, succeeded in the month of November last in the election of its candidate for the Presidency of the United States.

D O C U M E N T   2

Abraham Lincoln, Second Inaugural Address (1865)

Lincoln also interpreted events, both historical and contemporary, in a light favorable to his cause. As the conflict entered its bloody endgame and as the future of slavery thrust itself into the nation's consciousness, the president redefined war aims in the broadest possible terms. Thus, in his Second Inaugural Address, delivered on March 4, 1865, Lincoln argued that underlying the prolonged conflict were the transcendent issues of slavery, freedom, and democracy.

Fellow-countrymen: At this second appearing to take the oath of the presidential office, there is less occasion for an extended address than there was at the first. Then a statement, somewhat in detail, of a course to be pursued, seemed fitting and proper. Now, at the expiration of four years, during which public declarations have been constantly called forth on every point and phase of the great contest which still absorbs the attention and engrosses the energies of the nation, little that is new could be presented. The progress of our arms, upon which all else chiefly depends, is as well known to the public as to myself; and it is, I trust, reasonably satisfactory and encouraging to all. With high hope for the future, no prediction in regard to it is ventured.

On the occasion corresponding to this four years ago, all thoughts were anxiously directed to an impending civil war. All dreaded it—all sought to avert it. While the inaugural address was being delivered from this place, devoted altogether to saving the Union without war, insurgent agents were in the city seeking to destroy it without war—seeking to dissolve the Union, and divide effects, by negoti-

ation. Both parties deprecated war; but one of them would make war rather than let the nation survive; and the other would accept war rather than let it perish. And the war came.

One-eighth of the whole population were colored slaves, not distributed generally over the Union, but localized in the Southern part of it. These slaves constituted a peculiar and powerful interest. All knew that this interest was, somehow, the cause of the war. To strengthen, perpetuate, and extend this interest was the object for which the insurgents would rend the Union, even by war; while the government claimed no right to do more than to restrict the territorial enlargement of it.

Neither party expected for the war the magnitude or the duration which it has already attained. Neither anticipated that the cause of the conflict might cease with, or even before, the conflict itself should cease. Each looked for an easier triumph, and a result less fundamental and astounding. Both read the same Bible, and pray to the same God; and each invokes his aid against the other. It may seem strange that any men should dare to ask a just God's assistance in wringing their bread from the sweat of other men's faces; but let us judge not, that we be not judged. The prayers of both could not be answered—that of neither has been answered fully.

The Almighty has his own purposes. "Woe into the world because of offenses! for it must needs be that offenses come; but woe to that man by whom the offense cometh." If we shall suppose that American slavery is one of those offenses which, in the providence of God, must needs come, but which, having continued through his appointed time, he now wills to remove, and that he gives to both North and South this terrible war, as the woe due to those by whom the offense came, shall we discern therein any departure from those divine attributes which the believers in a living God always ascribe to him? Fondly do we hope—fervently do we pray—that this mighty scourge of war may speedily pass away. Yet, if God wills that it continue until all the wealth piled by the bondman's two hundred and fifty years of unrequited toil shall be sunk, and until every drop of blood drawn with the lash shall be paid by another drawn with the sword, as was said three thousand years ago, so still it must be said, "The judgments of the Lord are true and righteous altogether."

With malice toward none; with charity for all; with firmness in the right, as God gives us to see the right, let us strive on to finish the work we are in; to bind up the nation's wounds; to care for him who shall have borne the battle, and for his widow, and his orphan—to do all which may achieve and cherish a just and lasting peace among ourselves, and will all nations.

DOCUMENT 3

Charles Harvey Brewster, Three Letters from the Civil War Front (1862)

One critical issue during the early phases of the war was what to do about slaves who escaped behind Union lines. They were seized as "contraband" by Union troops, but their status remained ambiguous before the North committed itself to eradicating slavery. Some Union officers exploited the opportunity to retain runaways as low-wage servants. In letters to his mother and sisters, Charles Harvey Brewster of Northampton, Massachusetts, represented the conflicting views stimulated by the presence of escaped slaves at an army post in 1862.

Thursday Morning.

I feel some better this morning. I had the Doctor last evening and he gave me something which carried off my headache. We had more marching orders yesterday in so far as to be ready to start at any moment, with 2 days rations and 100 rounds of Cartridges, and everybody thinks we shall go in less than a week. I don't know but I shall be discharged, as the whole Regiment is almost in a state of mutiny on the Nigger question. Capt Miller the pro slavery Captain of the Shelburne Falls Co undertook with Major Marsh to back him to drive all the Contraband out of camp, he came to me and I had quite a blow up with him. Major Marsh took the Regiment

NOW IN CAMP AT READVILLE!

54th REGIMENT!

MASS. VOLUNTEERS, composed of men of

AFRICAN DESCENT

Col. ROBERT G. SHAW.

☞ Colored Men, Rally 'Round the Flag of Freedom!

BOUNTY $100!

AT THE EXPIRATION OF THE TERM OF SERVICE.

Pay, $13 a Month!

Good Food & Clothing!

State Aid to Families!

RECRUITING OFFICE.

COR. CAMBRIDGE & NORTH RUSSELL STS.,

BOSTON.

Lieut. J. W. M. APPLETON, Recruiting Officer.

RWELL & CO., Steam Job Printers, No. 37 Congress Street, Boston.

Federal officials had blocked the enlistment attempts of African Americans in the early stages of the war. By the end of the war, however, some 44,000 African Americans had died in Union service.

off the camp to drill yesterday while they were gone Capt Miller searched the camp for niggers, but did not find any, this morning they are all here again, this morning placards were found posted around the camp threatening direful things if they persisted in driving them off, which is a most foolish thing, but the men did not come down here to oppress Niggers and they are not quite brutes yet, as some of their officers are. I have nothing to do with any of the trouble except that I refuse to order off my own servant, in this I am not alone, as Capt Walkly of the Westfield Co has done the same thing, the Officers are divided into two parties on the question, and most bitter and rancorous feelings have been excited

which will never be allayed. I do not know how it will all end but I should not be all surprised if they made a fuss about it and should prefer charges against me, Capt Parsons, Lieut Weatherill, the Adjutant, Capt Walkley, Capt Lombard, Lieut Shurtleff, + our one or two others hold the same opinion that I do in the matter. I should hate to have to leave now just as the Regiment is going into active service, but I never will be instrumental in returning a slave to his master in any way shape or manner, I'll die first. Major Marsh well knows that the slaves masters are waiting outside of camp ready to snap them up, and it is inhuman to drive them into their hands, if you could have seen strong men crying like children, at the very thought as I did yesterday you would not blame me for standing out about it nor can one blame the men for showing sympathy for them, for they are from Massachusetts and are entirely unused to such scenes, and cannot recognize this property in human flesh and blood.

You may wonder where the Col. is in all this and I do also, we have all offered to give our servants up if he gives the order, but nobody knows that he has given any such order, and he is off camp all the while, attending a Court Martial, and the whole thing seems to be the doing of Maj Marsh Lieut Col Decker and Capt Miller, the last has been threatening to have the men sent to the Tortugas for mutiny, and perhaps he can do it, but I doubt it. I must close now and send this to the office in order to get it off by this mornings mail. please write again as soon as you get this, as I do not know as we shall be in this camp to receive more than one more letter. Give my love to all. I shall write to Mattie some time to day With much love Your aff son

Charlie.

Dear Mattie

I received your most welcome letter accompanying the stockings, and also the pictures for which I cannot find words to express my thanks. I have to look at them fifty times a day. I am in camp alone to day as the Company is out on Grand Guard to day and as I went both of the last two times with them I managed to stay in this time. I have been slightly unwell for two or three days but have got pretty much over it now.

We have had another grand excitement over orders to march which we received last week. They were positive and we were to start at 3 o'clock in the morning but they were countermanded before 8 o'clock the same afternoon, and we are still here, but we are under standing orders to be ready at a moments notice, and to have 100 rounds of ammunition per man, and two days rations cooked all the time, and daily expecting orders to start, every man also is ordered to take an extra pair of shoes in his knapsack so it looks as if we were to have a long pull when we do move. Capt Lombard got a furlough the other day and started for home, and got as far as Washington where he got such information as convinced him that we should march in less than a week and he came back and gave it up. We were intended the other day to reinforce Gen Banks but the Rebels made no resistance to his advance and consequently we were not needed, and when it is proposed to send us next I am sure I cannot imagine.

We have had quite a row about giving up slaves and about the secessionists in this neighborhood and it threatened to be quite a serious affair for a time but things are quieter now. Capt Miller of Shelbourne Falls undertook to put all the Contrabands out of camp and myself and several other officers refused to give up our servants, at his order for we doubted his authority in the matter, as the Col had heretofor given us to understand that he was not opposed to our keeping them, and had appeared to be quite anti Slavery in his views, but he took the matter in hand and read the order for thier expulsion at the head of the Regt and pretended to consider it a mutiny and altogether got himself into a terrible rage about it, and went over to the pro Slavery side body and soul. so it seems that the prime object of our being in this country is to return niggers to thier masters. I don't think Massachusetts blood was ever quite so riled nor quite so humbled before, but we had to submit. I was mad enough to resign, if I had not thought it would please our slave catching brutes too much, we have a good many of that class among our officers, and I believe Major Marsh would go further to return a fugitive slave than he would to save the Union.

The stockings you sent were first rate. I have not put them on yet, but they look like just the thing I want

Dear Mother

I received your welcome letter to night and I think you must have received two from me before this time as I have written regularly though one of mine was delayed in consequence of your last (before this) having been sent by Captain and I was on Guard when I got it, and so I could not write in time to send it Monday morning. I expected you would be in fever when the news from here reached you but we have not gone yet, but we are expecting our orders every day. part of our division has already gone and we shall soon follow. we have had 2 Regiments of Regulars added to our Division, and they are the ones that have marched, but where they have gone to or where we are to go to nobody knows. You must not be alarmed at any reports that come from here as you cannot possibly hear any truth unless you have it from me, and you know we have got to go and take our part in the struggle. that's what we came for and we aught to be thankful that we did not have to meet the enemy while we were raw and undisciplined and not ready for battle. it is said that we are now about as well trained as well as can be for Volunteers and certainly we know everything that is in the book for Infantry tactics. The weather is getting warmer and the ground begins to settle and it seems as if the army must make an advance very soon if it ever does. We are as ready as we ever can be, and perfectly willing, and if God rules shall I truly believe render a good account of ourselves when the time comes. I am more concerned about the reports that will go home when the Army does move, and you cannot have even a shadow of truth to guide you and yet you will believe everything that comes. I could almost wish for your sakes that, all communication of every kind was cut off between here and the north.

We have not been paid off yet, and I don't know as we ever shall be again. The government has no money, and it takes three weeks just to sign enough paper money to pay 4 days expenses, and how they are ever going to catch up at that rate I am sure I do not know. . . .

DOCUMENT 4

John Dooley, Passages from a Journal (1863)

John Dooley recalled another side of the conflict in a private journal he maintained during the war and revised before his death in 1873. In this passage he discusses the anxious moments preceding Pickett's Charge, the Confederate Army's ill-conceived attempt to seize victory on the last day of the Battle of Gettysburg (July 1863). Rather than reflecting on national politics, he noted the hardships and horrors of the war around him, discovering that as much as he might wish to achieve glory, the desire to survive became his dominant motive force.

Unpleasantly for myself, I am today in command of the rear guard, whose duty it is to urge forward stragglers and to keep up in fact all who desert their ranks under any pretense whatever. This is at times a painful duty, for frequently it happens—especially when the Division is moving rapidly, as today—that many soldiers leave their ranks through necessity, and, weakened by diarrhoea, can scarcely with all their efforts rejoin the ranks. Others fall by the roadside either deadly sick or pretending to be so (and who can be sure that they are only pretending?); others are barefoot, and although they may have thrown away their shoes purposely so as to have an excuse for desertion and straggling, still their feet are bruised and even bleeding, and it is a hard thing to keep these men upon the move.

Many good persons during the war seem to have the idea that any man who wears the confederate uniform and hails from a confederate regiment must of necessity be the very essence of all that is truly brave and chivalrous; and they receive, as a general thing, all their accounts of battles and their knowledge of heroic deeds of war from men who, far from having performed the deeds of daring they so vividly describe, have never seen witnessed the noble exploits of their brave companions in arms. For the true soldier has no time to stop by the wayside and recount his brave deeds to persons whom he does not know, and then devour their *buttermilk,* apple butter, and chickens in payment for the beautiful and thrilling tales he has fabricated. But he keeps in his ranks, is found in his camp, in the charge and the retreat, and leaves to the straggling coward the grateful task of glorifying his actions, who at the same time adopts them and makes them his own.

Between five and six o'clock in the evening we come within sight of the town of Gettysburg, and are marched into a small copse of woods to the right of the road. Here we must bivouack for the night, for although orders from the front have been received urging our Division forward, still, owing to representations (as we understand) made by our General

(Pickett) regarding the jaded condition of his men, we are allowed a respite of a few hours, and our part in the action will not be executed until tomorrow.

The second day's fighting (the fiercest portion of which was the storming of Cemetery heights) is now at its height, and we can hear distinctly the roar of the cannon in our front and to the right of the town. It is a stubborn and bloody conflict and we are sure if we escape tonight, tomorrow we will have our full share.

July 3rd. Before the day was fully dawned we are on our way to occupy the position assigned to us for the conflict of the third day. As we turn from the main road to the right, Gen. Lee, or better known as Uncle Robert, silent and motionless, awaits our passing by, and anxiously does he gaze upon the only division of his army whose numbers have not been thinned by the terrible fires of Gettysburg. I must confess that the Genl's face does not look as bright as tho' he were certain of success. But yet it is impossible for us to be any otherwise than victorious and we press forward with beating hearts, hundreds of which will throb their last today.

How long we take to gain our position, what delays, what suspense! We are soon passing over the battlefield of yesterday, and the details of burying parties are digging graves to receive the freshly fallen comrades, and, in many instances, they have only the ghastly and mangled remnants of their gallant friends to deposit in these hastily dug pits. I pass very close to a headless body; the boy's head being torn off by a shell is lying around in bloody fragments on the ground. . . .

Now Genls. Lee, Longstreet, and Pickett are advising together and the work of the day is arranged. Soon we are ordered to ascend the rising slope and pull down a fence in our front, and this begins to look like work.

Farther to our right is posted a division of North Carolina troops who should have charged simultaneously or immediately following us, thus overlapping our flank (right) and preventing our force from being surrounded in that direction. Unfortunately, owing to bad management (I am sure not to want of

bravery) they were of no assistance to us in the charge; and, advancing either in the wrong direction or when too late, two thousand of them fell into the enemy's hands.

Again, orders come for us to lie down in line of battle; *that all the cannon* on our side will open at a given signal, will continue for an hour and upon their ceasing we are to charge straight ahead over the open field and *sweep from our path* any thing in the shape of a Yankee that attempts to oppose our progress. This order is transmitted from Regt. to Regt., from Brigade to Brigade, and we rest a long time awaiting the signal.

At last it sounds away to the right and the echoes have scarcely rebounded from the rocks of the mountain when the earth, mountains and sky seem to open and darken the air with smoke and death dealing missiles. Never will I forget those scenes and sounds. The earth seems unsteady beneath this furious cannonading, and the air might be said to be agitated by the wings of death. Over 400 guns nearly every minute being discharged!

We are immediately in rear of Genl. Dearing's batteries and receive nearly all the missiles intended for his gallant troops. In one of our Regts. alone the killed and wounded, even before going into the charge, amounted to 88 men; and men lay bleeding and gasping in the agonies of death all around, and we unable to help them in the least. Ever and anon some companion would raise his head disfigured and unrecognizable, streaming with blood, or would stretch his full length, his limbs quivering in the pangs of death. Orders were to lie as closely as possible to the ground, and *I like a good soldier* never got closer to the earth than on the present occasion.

The sun poured down his fiercest beams and added to our discomfort. Genl. Dearing was out in front with his flag waving defiance at the Yankees and now and then rushing forward to take the place of some unfortunate gunner stricken down at his post. The ammunition wagons fly back and forth bringing up fresh supplies of ammunition, and still the air is shaking from earth to sky with every missile of death fired from the cannon's mouth.

Around, above, beneath, and on all sides they schreech, sing, scream, whistle, roar, whirr, buzz, bang and whizz, and we are obliged to lie quietly tho' frightened out of our wits and unable to do any thing in our own defence or any injury to our enemies. . . .

Our artillery has now ceased to roar and the enemy have checked their fury, too. The time appointed for our charge is come.

I tell you, there is no romance in making one of these charges. You might think so from reading 'Charlies O'Malley,' that prodigy of valour, or in reading of any other gallant knight who would as little think of riding over *gunners and such like* as they would of eating a dozen oysters. But when you rise to your feet as we did today, I tell you the enthusiasm of ardent breasts in many cases *ain't there*, and instead of burning to avenge the insults of our country, families and altars and firesides, and the thought is most frequently, *Oh. if I could just come out of this charge safely how thankful would I be!*

DOCUMENT 5

The Christian Recorder *(1864)*

Nearly 200,000 African Americans, freed slaves as well as those living in the North, volunteered for service in the Union army. Although they played a critical role in ensuring a permanent end to slavery, such troops nonetheless suffered unequal treatment. In addition to serving under white officers in otherwise segregated units, African Americans received less pay than their white counterparts. In this May 1864 letter written by a free black volunteer from Ohio to the *Christian Recorder*, an African American newspaper published in Philadelphia, he expresses his anger not only with unequal treatment but with the dim prospects for genuine racial equality in the United States.

I am not willing to fight for anything less than the white man fights for. If the white man cannot support his family on seven dollars per month, I cannot support mine on the same amount.

And I am not willing to fight for this Government for money alone. Give me my rights, the rights that this Government owes me, the same rights that the white man has. I would be willing to fight three years for this Government without one cent of the mighty dollar. Then I would have something to fight for. Now I am fighting for the rights of the white man. White men have never given me the rights that they are bound to respect. God has not made one man better than another; therefore, one man's rights are no better than another's. They assert that, because a large proportion of our race is in bondage, we have a right to help free them. I want to know if it was not the white man that put them in bondage? How can they hold us responsible for their evils? And how can they expect that we

Private John Werth of the Richmond Howitzers Battalion. Two-thirds of the more than three million Civil War servicemen were under 23 years of age. These formal portraits were often taken just after enlistment and do not capture the horrific experience of battle.

Liberty is what I am struggling for; and what pulse does not beat high at the very mention of the name? Each of us has already discharged the duties devolving on us as men and as soldiers. The very fact of such a union on grounds so common and deeply interesting to all undoubtedly cannot always fail by the blessing of God, to exert a hallowed influence over society, well fitted to break up alike the extremes of aristocratic and social feeling, which too, often predominate in society, and to beget unity, love, brotherly kindness and charity.

Let liberty be duly observed, and its influence be extended from town to town, from city to city, from nation to nation. In short from sea to sea, and from pole to pole. But everything is to be feared in the future from the shackles now forging. As an individual case, I may fall, as I may stand; but I trust that I am in the right place with the multitude on my side. I pass light and darkness, seeing not the end, you believing that the unaswering eye of God and seen it in the unchanging light of eternity and that, His strong arm will bring me out into a large place. They say that it is only in the minor duties of our experience that our true character is shown. We may be courageous in the field, true and perfect in drill, watchful and trustworthy on guard; but, after all, this, we are by no means, cheerfully regarded for all the customs of camp life. Our merits are nowise measured or respected. I shall not take back anything that I have said, because, by so doing I should sanction the impieties of my opponents, who would thence take occasion to crush us with still more cruelty; yet, as I am a mere man and not God, I will defend myself after His example, who said: "If I have spoken evil, bear witness of the will." How much more should I, who am, but dust and ashes, and so press to error desire that every one should bring forward what he can against my doctrine. Therefore, most serene Republicans and you illustrious Democrats, and all who may hear this, I implore you, by the mercies of God, to prove to me, by the writings of the prophets and apostles, that I am in error. As soon as I shall be convinced, I will instantly retract my errors, and will myself be the first to seize my writings and commit them to the flames.

should do more to blot it out than they are willing to do themselves? If every slave in the United States were emancipated at once they would not be free yet. If the white man is not willing to respect my rights, I am not willing to respect his wrongs. Our rights have always been limited in the United States. It is true that, in some places, a colored man, if he can prove himself to be half white, can vote. Vote for whom? The white man. What good do such rights ever do us—to be compelled always to be voting for the white man, and never to be voted for? . . .

DOCUMENT 6

United States Sanitary Commission, Sketch of Its Purposes (1864)

Elite men and women in the North saw the war as an opportunity to donate time and money while maintaining social dominance. The most prominent example was the United States Sanitary Commission, which sought to ensure the orderly delivery of medical services and dissemination of information on hygiene. Such an endeavor met with mixed results, as disease claimed approximately twice as many deaths as did battle. Nonetheless, the Sanitary Commission—in the article, published in the *North American Review*—expressed the challenges that faced government and society in this new age of mass mobilization and mass production.

[I] in a national life like our own,—a democracy, where the people universally take part in political affairs,—the government has no option in the case. The popular affections and sympathies will force themselves into the administration of army and all other affairs in times of deep national awakening. The practical question was not, Is it best to allow the army to depend in any degree upon the care of the people as distinguished from the government? Considered on administrative grounds alone, that question, we have no doubt, should be answered negatively. But no such question existed in a pure and simple form. It was this question rather, How shall this rising tide of popular sympathy, expressed in the form of sanitary supplies, and offers of personal service and advice, be rendered least hurtful to the army system, and most useful to the soldiers themselves? How shall it be kept from injuring the order, efficiency, and zeal of the regular bureau, and at the same time be left to do its intended work of succor and sympathy,—to act as a steady expression of the people's watchful care of their army, and as a true helper and supplementer of what the government may find it possible or convenient to do from its own resources? It was this mixed question the Sanitary Commission found itself called to answer,

and its whole plan and working have been one steady reply to it. It could not be deemed wise, much less was it possible, to discourage and deaden the active sympathies of the people. They would follow their regiments to the field with home-comforts and provisions against wounds and sickness. The women would hurry to the hospitals and camps. For the first six months after the war began, the departments at Washington were fairly besieged by humane committees, masculine and feminine; business was interrupted, clogged, and snarled by the obtrusion of aid and comfort. Every regiment that went into the field had another regiment of anxious friends pushing into the camp to look after it, and supply its possible or real wants. State and local relief committees were named Legion; and it looked as if the Commissariat and Medical Departments were going to be swamped in popular ministrations. The beauty and glory of the affections which led to this self-sacrificing attendance and provision were not to be lost or dimmed by neglect. Nay, they were to be cherished with the utmost assiduity and the fullest sense of their national value.

On the other hand, the method, efficiency, and development of the governmental resources, the order and sway of the Medical Department, were not to be sacrificed or delayed by the allowance of an unregulated, superfluous, and sentimental beneficence. Scylla was to be shunned, and Charybdis not grazed. The people could not, let them try as hard as they would, do the government's work. They could neither build nor furnish nor work the hospitals. They could not even supply them with nurses; for men, as well as women, are absolutely necessary in that service, in military hospitals. On the other hand, a popular volunteer army could not live at all cut off from home sympathy, and from the demonstration of popular interest and watchfulness; nor could government fitly undertake certain services which the people were ready to render to the army, and which might, with extreme wisdom and pains, be permitted, and even encouraged, without injury to discipline and official responsibility.

Between these two important and indispensable interests, home feeling, and governmental responsibility and method, the Sanitary Commission steered its delicate and difficult way. It assigned to itself the task, requiring constant tact, of directing, without weakening or cooling, the warm and copious stream of popular beneficence toward the army. This owned its heat and fulness very much to its spontaneous and local character. Towns, cities, counties, States, were deeply interested in their own boys. To labor, night and day, for the very regiment that had rendezvoused in its square, or upon its common, to knit socks for feet that had crossed their own thresholds, and make garments to cover hearts that throbbed with their own blood, was not only easy for the people,—it was a necessity. And to send these by the hands of trusted townsmen, who should see these comforts put upon the very backs, or into the very mouths, they were designed for, was the most natural plan in the world, and seemingly the very best, as it certainly was the pleasantest. Why should not each State look after its own soldiers,— and each county, and each town, and each family? Certainly, this principle of local interest and personal affection could be depended on for longer and freer labors than any other. Was it safe to attempt to modify it, to mend it, to enlighten it, and to enlarge it? It was at least *necessary* to try to do this. Such a

spontaneous, local liberality, however productive of materials and supplies of comfort, was absolutely unfurnished, as a very short experience proved, with the means and facilities for conveying, delivering, and applying its resources to the army. While our soldiers were mustering at a few near points, and drilling and disciplining for the contest, it was comparatively easy to reach particular regiments through special delegations, and with special supplies. But, after a few months, the armies of the Union left these convenient centres, and a very few miles of mud road between a corps and its base soon showed local committees the immense difficulties of *private* and *special* transportation. Moreover, when sickness began to appear, and anxiety for the well and strong was concentrated upon the feeble and ailing, the people soon began to discover that a soldier, after all, belonged more to the army than to his own regiment, and was ultimately thrown more on the care of the federal government and the general staff than upon his own surgeon and immediate officers. Slowly the nation learned that new thing in the experience of this generation, what a *General Hospital* is, and what the course taken with a sick soldier must be. They discovered that in the suddenness and unexpected character of army movements, men were very soon put far beyond the reach of the knowledge and following of any local protectors; that regiments were liable to be thrown from North to South, from East to West; from Alexandria to Port Hudson and Vicksburg; from Newbern to Nashville and Chattanooga; and that their own sons and brothers, if they were to be followed and watched over at all, must be looked after by a national and ubiquitous body, which was with the army everywhere, at home at all points, and with ends and objects that recognized neither State nor county nor regiment, but saw only the United States or Union soldier, and ministered to him impartially according to his need, with absolute indifference as to where he hailed from. To explain this state of things at the earliest moment became the urgent duty of the Sanitary Commission. Naturally, but unfortunately, so many State and local associations were already at work, and represented in or near the great camps, that a swarm of angry and jealous rivals gathered about the plan of the Sanitary Commission, and have never ceased to sting its agents with disparaging reports. So kind and worthy were the intentions of those whom these associations represented, and in many cases so honorable and laborious the efforts of these agents, so natural their prejudices and jealousies, that, while strongly disapproving the principle involved in them as radically subversive of what they were laboring to popularize, the Sanitary Commission could not find the heart to oppose them. It therefore simply strove to make its own plan widely understood, and, by doing the work in hand in the only thorough and satisfactory manner possible, to win by the degrees the confidence of the more distant and interior communities. On the whole, the intelligence with which the people have understood and appreciated its method is worthy of all admiration; and the mingled sense

and magnanimity with which they have gradually substituted for their original motive the *federal* principle, which, though larger, nobler, and more patriotic, lacks personal incitement and local warmth and color, is a new proof of the capabilities of our people. . . .

[T]he wonder is, that, in spite of them, there should have been so prodigious a triumph of the Federal principle in the humane work of ministering to the army. Local, personal, and religious prejudices have all yielded, more or less slowly, but steadily, to the self-vindicating claims of the Sanitary Commission. . . .

This is chiefly due to the wonderful spirit of nationality that beats in the breasts of American women. They, even more than the men of the country, from their utter withdrawal from partisan strifes and local politics, have felt the assault upon the life of the nation in its true national import.

The African American 54th Regiment of Massachusetts led a heroic assault on Fort Wagner against an army with more than twice its number of men on July 18, 1863. This conflict shattered racist assumptions that African Americans could not master the art of war.

They are infinitely less *State-ish*, and more national in their pride and in their sympathies. They see the war in its broad, impersonal outlines; and while their particular and special affections are keener than men's, their general humanity and tender sensibility for unseen and distant sufferings is stronger and more constant. The women of the country, who are the actual creators, by the labor of their fingers, of the chief supplies and comforts needed by the soldiers, have been the first to understand, appreciate, and co-operate with the Sanitary Commission. . . .

DOCUMENT 7

Mary Boykin Chesnut, Passages from Her Diary (1861–1865)

Chesnut, a plantation mistress and wife of a prominent Confederate official, not only witnessed an actual battle but also commented painfully on the collapse of the traditional southern way of life. Diary entries spanning from April 1861, when she heard the shelling of Fort Sumter from Charleston, to January 1865, when General Sherman advanced through Georgia and South Carolina, trace the rise and fall of the Confederacy. The document captures Chesnut's anxious observation of her African American servants as well as the crippling effect of the war on southern manpower and the regional economy.

April 13th. [1861] Nobody has been hurt after all. How gay we were last night. Reaction after the dread of all the slaughter we thought those dreadful cannon were making. Not even a battery the worse for war. Fort Sumter has been on fire. Anderson has not yet silenced any of our guns. So the aides, still with swords and red sashes by way of uniform, tell us. But the sound of those guns makes regular meals impossible. None of us go to table. Tea-trays pervade the corridors going everywhere. Some of the anxious hearts lie on their beds and moan in solitary misery. Mrs. Wigfall and I solace ourselves with tea in my room. These women have all a satisfying faith. "God is on our side," they say. When we are shut in Mrs. Wigfall and I ask "Why?" "Of course, He hates the Yankees, we are told. You'll think that well of Him."

Not by one word or look can we detect any change in the demeanor of these negro servants. Lawrence sits at our door, sleepy and respectful, and profoundly indifferent. So are they all, but they carry it too far. You could not tell that they even heard the awful roar going on in the bay, though it has been dinning in their ears night and day. People talk before them as if they were chairs and tables. They make no sign. Are they stolidly stupid? or wiser than we are; silent and strong, biding their time? . . .

March 12th. [1862]—In the naval battle the other day we had twenty-five guns in all. The enemy had fifty-four in the Cumberland, forty-four in the St.

Lawrence, besides a fleet of gunboats, filled with rifled cannon. Why not? They can have as many as they please. "No pent-up Utica contracts their powers"; the whole boundless world being theirs to recruit in. Ours in only this one little spot of ground—the blockade, or stockade, which hems us in with only the sky open to us, and for all that, how tenderfooted and cautious they are as they draw near. . . .

[June 7, 1862] General Scott, on Southern soldiers, says, we have *élan*, courage, woodcraft, consummate horsemanship, endurance of pain equal to the Indians, but that we will not submit to discipline. We will not take care of things, or husband our resources. Where we are there is waste and destruction. If it could all be done by one wild, desperate dash, we would do it. But he does not think we can stand the long, blank months between the acts—the waiting! We can bear pain without a murmur, but we will not submit to be bored, etc.

Now, for the other side. Men of the North can wait; they can bear discipline; they can endure forever. Losses in battle are nothing to them. Their resources in men and materials of war are inexhaustible, and if they see fit they will fight to the bitter end. Here is a nice prospect for us—as comfortable as the old man's croak at Mulberry, "Bad times worse coming." . . .

I know how it feels to die. I have felt it again and again. For instance, some one calls out, "Albert Sidney Johnston is killed." My heart stands still. I feel no more. I am, for so many seconds, so many minutes, I know not how long, utterly without sensation of any kind—dead; and then, there is that great throb, that keen agony of physical pain, and the works are wound up again. The ticking of the clock begins, and I take up the burden of life once more. Some day it will stop too long, or my feeble heart will be too worn out to make that awakening jar, and all will be over. I do not think when the end comes that there will be any difference, except the miracle of the new wind-up throb. And now good news is just as exciting as bad. "Hurrah, Stonewall has saved us!" The pleasure is almost pain because of my way of feeling it. . . .

July 8th. [1862] Gunboat captured on the Santee. So much the worse for us. We do not want any more prisoners, and next time they will send a fleet of boats, if one will not do. The Governor sent me Mr. Chesnut's telegram with a note saying, "I regret the telegram does not come up to what we had hoped might be as to the entire destruction of McClellan's army. I think, however, the strength of the war with its ferocity may now be considered as broken."

Table-talk to-day: This war was undertaken by us to shake off the yoke of foreign invaders. So we consider our cause righteous. The Yankees, since the war has begun, have discovered it is to free the slaves that they are fighting. So their cause is noble. They also expect to make the war pay. Yankees do not undertake anything that does not pay. They think we belong to them. We have been good milk cows—milked by the tariff, or skimmed. We let them have all of our hard earnings. We bear the ban of slavery; they get the money. Cotton pays everybody who handles it, sells it, manufactures it, but rarely pays the man who grows it. Second hand the Yankees received the wages of slavery. They grew rich. We grew poor. The receiver is as bad as the thief. That applies to us, too, for we received the savages they stole from Africa and brought to us in their slave-ships. As with the Egyptians, so it shall be with us: if they let us go, it must be across a Red Sea—but one made red by blood. . . .

August 29th. [1864] I take my hospital duty in the morning. Most persons prefer afternoon, but I dislike to give up my pleasant evenings. So I get up at five o'clock and go down in my carriage all laden with provisions. Mrs. Fisher and old Mr. Bryan generally go with me. Provisions are commonly sent by people to Mrs. Fisher's. I am so glad to be a hospital nurse once more. I had excess excuses enough, but at heart I felt a coward and a skulker. I think I know how men feel who hire a substitute and shirk the fight. There must be no dodging of duty. It will not do now to send provisions and pay for nurses. Something inside of me kept calling out, "Go, you shabby creature; you can't bear to see what those fine fellows have to bear." . . .

I have excellent servants; no matter for their short-comings behind my back. They save me all thought as to household matters, and they are so kind, attentive, and quiet. They must know what is at hand if Sherman is not hindered from coming here—"Freedom! my masters!" But these sphinxes give no sign, unless it be increased diligence and absolute silence, as certain in their action and as noiseless as a law of nature, at any rate when we are in the house. . . .

Study Questions

1. What considerations motivated ordinary Americans to fight in the Civil War? Were the reasons the same for northerners and southerners? Blacks and whites?

2. Which documents provide the clearest understanding of the meaning of the war and its historical significance?

3. Did political leaders articulate what was on the minds of their wartime constituents?

4. Did the experiences of war cut across regional divisions?

5. What effect did slavery have on the course of the Civil War?

15

Reconstruction

The North's victory in the Civil War established the indivisibility of federal union and ensured the abolition of slavery. Yet the unconditional surrender of the rebellious southern states on the battlefield raised numerous questions for the nation's political leaders. Primary among these were how to reintegrate former Confederate states into the federal system and what position the millions of newly freed African Americans should occupy in society now that they were no longer slaves. Thus "Reconstruction," while focusing largely on the South, provoked national discussion of unprecedented scope (Document 1).

Abraham Lincoln, who successfully guided the Union through the war, only lived to implement the first tentative steps of reconstruction. Lincoln's assassination just a few days after the Confederacy surrendered at Appomattox elevated Vice President Andrew Johnson. Lincoln had selected Johnson, a Democratic senator from Tennessee—who at the time of his state's secession proclaimed staunch pro-Union sentiments—as his running mate in order to balance the 1864 presidential ticket. The rough-edged Johnson matched his contempt for wealthy white planters with his loathing of blacks. His temperament and his views on Reconstruction soon clashed with a Republican-dominated Congress wary of both the loyalty of southern whites and their intentions toward free blacks.

The Freedmen's Bureau oversaw Reconstruction in the South. A temporary and underfunded office of the War Department, the bureau nonetheless sought to reconcile the clashing needs of former slaves and former masters amid the physical devastation and social upheaval of the postwar landscape. Anticipating the transition to a free-wage economy, bureau agents and other northerners sought to introduce the values and customs of the market economy to the freed people (Document 2). Yet without a mandate to upset the traditional economic hierarchy, the bureau disappointed African American hopes of land reform, sparking protests of Bureau policies (Document 3). In an age of limited government and awkward race relations, condescending moral pronouncements and contradictory policies often substituted for effective action.

Yet African American ambitions and congressional concerns temporarily dove-tailed to construct a scaffolding for a more integrated political future. Blacks throughout the South participated in organizations demanding equal rights and drawing attention to the obstacles that whites placed in their way (Document 4).

The U.S. Congress, now thoroughly estranged from President Johnson, passed a series of civil rights laws and constitutional amendments (Document 5) to ensure the
full citizenship and voting rights of the freed people. Congress predicted the readmis-
sion of southern states to the Union on the ratification of these amendments.

For a time, a coalition of whites, consisting of former unionists as well as notorious "carpetbaggers" who had moved from the North to the South after the war, and
blacks governed the southern states. Only in one state, South Carolina, did African
Americans ever gain a majority of state legislative offices, but for the first time in
American history, blacks held office at all levels of government. Republican rule,
however, depended on the symbolic presence of the small number of federal troops
stationed in the South, the goodwill of national public opinion, and the enforcement
of federal laws to keep reactionary forces at bay.

Over time, the impact of each of these factors diminished. The foremost
sources of northern opinion, increasingly appalled by political malfeasance in their
own midst, seized on corruption and fiscal crises in southern Republican governments as evidence that the entire enterprise of Reconstruction and racial equality
had been illegitimate (Document 6). Meanwhile, the Ku Klux Klan mounted a bru-
tally effective campaign of terror against blacks, as well as Republican whites, making
political participation in the South increasingly hazardous (Document 7). White "redeemer" governments regained power throughout the South, rewriting recently revised state constitutions and passing laws to deny African Americans access to power
and deprive them of social services, such as education, essential to their economic
advancement (Document 8). The last federal troops withdrew from the South in
1877 as a part of a compromise in which the Congress ratified Republican Rutherford
B. Hayes's election as president with several electoral votes of disputable validity in
his column. When redeemers reclaimed the remaining Reconstruction governments,
prospects for African Americans fell into eclipse.

DOCUMENT 1

Carl Schurz, Report on the Condition of the South (1865)

The unprecedented emancipation of millions of slaves gave the federal government little time to savor the fruits of victory. In December 1865, President Andrew Johnson reluctantly presented Congress with Senator Carl Schurz's report on
conditions in five southern states. Schurz, a German immigrant and high-minded
Republican representing Missouri, stressed that a successful Reconstruction policy
must ensure the smooth transition to a free-labor economy.

❧   ❧

[W]e ought to keep in view, above all, the nature of the problem which is to be solved. As to what is commonly termed "reconstruction," it is not only the political machinery of the States and their constitutional relations to the general government, but the whole organism of southern society that must be reconstructed, or rather constructed anew, so as to bring it in harmony with the rest of American society. The difficulties of this task are not to be considered overcome when the people of the south take the oath of allegiance and elect governors and legislatures and members of Congress, and militia captains. That this would be done had become certain as soon as the surrenders of the southern armies had made further resistance impossible, and nothing in the world was left, even to the most uncompromising rebel, but to submit or to emigrate. It was also natural that they should avail themselves of every chance offered them to resume control of their home affairs and to regain their influence in the Union. But this can hardly be called the first step towards the solution of the true problem, and it is a fair question to ask, whether the hasty gratification of their desire to resume such control would not create new embarrassments.

The true nature of the difficulties of the situation is this: The general government of the republic has, by proclaiming the emancipation of the slaves, commenced a great social revolution in the south, but has, as yet, not completed it. Only the negative part of it is accomplished. The slaves are emancipated in point of form, but free labor has not yet been put in the place of slavery in point of fact. And now, in the midst of this critical period of transition, the power which originated the revolution is expected to turn over its whole future development to another power which from the beginning was hostile to it and has never yet entered into its spirit, leaving the class in whose favor it was made completely without power to protect itself and to take an influential part in that development. The history of the world will be searched in vain for a proceeding similar to this which did not lead either to a rapid and violent reaction, or to the most serious trouble and civil disorder. It cannot be said that the conduct of the south-

ern people since the close of the war has exhibited such extraordinary wisdom and self-abnegation as to make them an exception to the rule.

In my despatches from the south I repeatedly expressed the opinion that the people were not yet in a frame of mind to legislate calmly and understandingly upon the subject of free negro labor. And this I reported to be the opinion of some of our most prominent military commanders and other observing men. It is, indeed, difficult to imagine circumstances more unfavorable for the development of a calm and unprejudiced public opinion than those under which the southern people are at present laboring. The war has not only defeated their political aspirations, but it has broken up their whole social organization. When the rebellion was put down they found themselves not only conquered in a political and military sense, but economically ruined. The planters, who represented the wealth of the southern country, are partly laboring under the severest embarrassments, partly reduced to absolute poverty. Many who are stripped of all available means, and have nothing but their land, cross their arms in gloomy despondency, incapable of rising to a manly resolution. Others, who still possess means, are at a loss how to use them, as their old way of doing things is, by the abolition of slavery, rendered impracticable, at least where the military arm of the government has enforced emancipation. Others are still trying to go on in the old way, and that old way is in fact the only one they understand, and in which they have any confidence. Only a minority is trying to adopt the new order of things. A large number of the plantations, probably a considerable majority of the more valuable estates, is under heavy mortgages, and the owners know that, unless they retrieve their fortunes in a comparatively short space of time, their property will pass out of their hands. Almost all are, to some extent, embarrassed. The nervous anxiety which such a state of things produces extends also to those classes of society which, although not composed of planters, were always in close business connexion with the planting interest, and there was hardly a branch of commerce or industry in the south which was not directly or indirectly so connected. Besides, the southern soldiers, when returning from the war, did not, like the northern soldiers, find a prosperous community which merely waited for their arrival to give them remunerative employment. They found, many of them, their homesteads destroyed, their farms devastated, their families in distress; and those that were less unfortunate found, at all events, an impoverished and exhausted community which had but little to offer them. Thus a great many have been thrown upon the world to shift as best they can. They must do something honest or dishonest, and must do it soon, to make a living, and their prospects are, at present, not very bright. Thus that nervous anxiety to hastily repair broken fortunes, and to prevent still greater ruin and distress, embraces nearly all classes, and imprints upon all the movements of the social body a morbid character.

In which direction will these people be most apt to turn their eyes? Leaving the prejudice of race out of the question, from early youth they have been acquainted with but one system of labor, and with that one system they have been in the habit of identifying all their interests. They know of no way to help themselves but the one they are accustomed to. Another system of labor is presented to them, which, however, owing to circumstances which they do not appreciate, appears at first in an unpromising light. To try it they consider an experiment which they cannot afford to make while their wants are urgent. They have not reasoned calmly enough to convince themselves that the trial must be made. It is, indeed, not wonderful that, under such circumstances, they should study, not how to introduce and develop free labor, but how to avoid its introduction, and how to return as much and as quickly as possible to something like the old order of things. Nor is it wonderful that such studies should find an expression in their attempts at legislation. But the circumstance that this tendency is natural does not render it less dangerous and objectionable. The practical question presents itself: Is the immediate restoration of the late rebel States to absolute self-control so necessary that it must be done even at the risk of endangering one of the great results of the war, and of

This sketch, "Electioneering in the South," by W. L. Sheppard, displays the newfound freedom for African Americans to participate in politics after the passage of the Fifteenth Amendment in 1869. Though African Americans represented a majority in many former slave states, only a small number were elected to Congress.

bringing on in those States insurrection or anarchy, or would it not be better to postpone that restoration until such dangers are passed? If, as long as the change from slavery to free labor is known to the southern people only by its destructive results, these people must be expected to throw obstacles in its way, would it not seem necessary that the movement of social "reconstruction" be kept in the right channel by the hand of the power which originated the change, until that change can have disclosed some of its beneficial effects?

It is certain that every success of free negro labor will augment the number of its friends, and disarm some of the prejudices and assumptions of its opponents. I am convinced one good harvest made by unadulterated free labor in the south would have a far better effect than all the oaths that have been taken, and all the ordinances that have as yet been passed by southern conventions. But how can such a result be attained? The facts enumerated in this report, as well as the news we receive from the south from day to day, must make it evident to every unbiased observer that unadulterated free labor cannot be had at present, unless the national government holds its protective and controlling hand over it. It appears, also, that the more efficient this protection of free labor against all disturbing and reactionary influences, the sooner may such a satisfactory result be looked for. One reason why the southern people are so slow in accommodating themselves to the new order of things is, that they confidently expect soon to be permitted to regulate matters according to their own notions. Every concession made to them by the government has been taken as an encouragement to persevere in this hope, and, unfortunately for them, this hope is nourished by influences from other parts of the country. Hence their anxiety to have their State governments restored *at once*, to have the troops withdrawn, and the Freedmen's Bureau abolished, although a good many discerning men know well that, in view of the lawless spirit still prevailing, it would be far better for them to have the general order of society firmly maintained by the federal power until things have arrived at a final settlement. Had, from the beginning, the conviction been forced upon them that the adulteration of the new order of things by the admixture of elements belonging to the system of slavery would under no circumstances be permitted, a much larger number would have launched their energies into the new channel, and, seeing that they could do "no better," faithfully co-operated with the government. It is hope which fixes them in their perverse notions. That hope nourished or fully gratified, they will persevere in the same direction. That hope destroyed, a great many will, by the force of necessity, at once accommodate themselves to the logic of the change. If, therefore, the national government firmly and unequivocally announces its

policy not to give up the control of the free-labor reform until it is finally accomplished, the progress of that reform will undoubtedly be far more rapid and far less difficult than it will be if the attitude of the government is such as to permit contrary hopes to be indulged in.

The machinery by which the government has so far exercised its protection of the negro and of free labor in the south—the Freedmen's Bureau—is very unpopular in that part of the country, as every institution placed there as a barrier to reactionary aspirations would be. That abuses were committed with the management of freedmen's affairs; that some of the officers of the bureau were men of more enthusiasm than discretion, and in many cases went beyond their authority: all this is certainly true. But, while the southern people are always ready to expatiate upon the shortcomings of the Freedmen's Bureau, they are not so ready to recognize the services it has rendered. I feel warranted in saying that not half of the labor that has been done in the south this year, or will be done there next year, would have been or would be done but for the exertions of the Freedmen's Bureau. The confusion and disorder of the transition period would have been infinitely greater had not an agency interfered which possessed the confidence of the emancipated slaves; which could disabuse them of any extravagant notions and expectations and be trusted; which could administer to them good advice and be voluntarily obeyed. No other agency, except one placed there by the national government, could have wielded that moral power whose interposition was so necessary to prevent southern society from falling at once into the chaos of a general collision between its different elements. That the success achieved by the Freedmen's Bureau is as yet very incomplete cannot be disputed. A more perfect organization and a more carefully selected personnel may be desirable; but it is doubtful whether a more suitable machinery can be devised to secure to free labor in the south that protection against disturbing influences which the nature of the situation still imperatively demands.

DOCUMENT 2

Clinton B. Fisk, Plain Counsels for Freedmen *(1865)*

Fisk, chief of the Tennessee Freedman's Bureau, published a series of lectures advising emancipated African Americans on life after slavery. Fisk's lectures warned freed people not to entertain extravagant hopes about freedom. He condescendingly offered instead the eventual rewards of thrift and hard work, and urged the importance of knowing one's place.

I come to speak to you this evening about work; yes, work, good, honest, hard work. Do not turn away, and say you will not hear me,—that you know all about it, and that it is not a good subject for a lecture.

Listen! The very first verse of the Holy Bible tells us that God is a worker,—that in six days he made all this great world on which we dwell, and the sun and moon and stars.

All the holy angels in heaven are very busy. They go forth to do the will of the Great Being, and find their greatest bliss in action.

Good and great men are all hard workers. And do you know what it is that makes a free state so rich and strong? It is, above all things save God's blessing, *patient, honest work.*

There is nothing degrading in *free* labor,—nay, it is most honorable. Why, when God placed Adam and Eve in the garden of Eden, before either of them had ever done any wrong thing, and while they were as pure as the angels, he made gardeners of them. He required them to dress the garden and keep it nice and in good condition.

The blessed Saviour himself worked at the bench, at the carpenter's trade, until he was about thirty years of age.

And yet, some very silly people are above work, —are ashamed to have hard hands,—and do their best to get through the world without honest toil.

But this was not the case with Abraham Lincoln, the man who wrote the Proclamation of Emancipation. He used the hoe, the ax, and the maul, cleared ground, and fenced it with the rails he had split, and was ready to turn his hands to any honest work.

I know that it is quite natural that you should associate work with slavery, and freedom with idleness, because you have seen slaves working all their lives, and free people doing little or nothing. And I should not blame you if you should ask, "What have we gained by freedom, if we are to work, work, work!"

Now, let me explain. A slave works all his life for others. A free man works for himself,—that is, he gets pay for his labor; and if he saves what he earns and manages well, he can get on so well that he may spend the afternoon of his life in his own pleasant home, and never want for any thing. . . .

If you earn twelve dollars in a month, and spend thirteen, you are on the road to misery, for you will get into debt, deeper and deeper, until after awhile it will be a load you can not carry.

You should make it a rule, therefore, to spend less each month and each year than you make. If you do this, you will become well to do in the world.

A free man should always consider before he buys an article, whether he can afford it. He would like a new hat,—price five dollars,—but if he needs the five for other and more pressing uses, to make a payment, for example, for something he has bought, then he should deny himself the pleasure of the new hat, and brush up the old one. A new coat might be very desirable, but if its purchase would create a debt, better keep the old one in good repair as possible, and stick to it another season. It is much pleasanter to wear the old clothes than to have the constable chasing you in the new ones.

Many a poor man has been driven almost out of his wits by constables, who were pursuing him for the payment of debts made to gratify the vanity of his wife. She wanted a handsome breastpin, and begged him to buy it. He could not resist, and bought it with the proceeds of a week's hard toil, and, as a consequence, was obliged to go in debt for meat and bread. Then she wanted a fine dress; then this, and then that; and so he sank into debt, step by step, until he was ruined.

A wife can soon destroy her husband's good name, by urging him to buy her things she could do without, and for which he is unable to pay.

It is a good plan for a man and woman who are just setting out as you are to make a living, to balance their accounts—that is count up what they earn and what they spend, and see how they compare—a great many times in the year. It will not take them long to do it, and the task will be both pleasant and useful.

Resolve that you will, by the blessing of God, live within your means. This is one of the most important secrets of success. It may cost you a struggle, but stick to it resolutely, and the day will come when you will be able to purchase not only the necessaries, but the luxuries of life.

I am not counseling you to be mean and stingy,—by no means; but no man has a right to be liberal with another man's money and at another man's expense.

For the sake of your good name, do not make a splurge in society with jewelry and fine clothes which have not been paid for, and for which you will never be able to pay. That is almost as mean as theft.

"The borrower," says the Bible, "is servant to the lender," and, let me assure you, a creditor is a very hard master. Do not put your necks in his iron yoke.

I am acquainted with many white persons who commenced married life twenty-five years ago with as little as you have now, and who worked with their hands for less than is given to you, who are now owners of handsome houses and farms, and are in very easy circumstances. They made it a rule to spend less than they earned.

DOCUMENT 3

James C. Beecher, Report on Land Reform in the South Carolina Islands (1865, 1866)

Freed blacks, southern whites, and the federal government often harbored conflicting interpretations of the practical effects of emancipation. Former masters sought to regain plantations seized by slaves or distributed by Union officers and to gain access to the labor of their former slaves. The War Department cooperated in this land reclamation project, creating awkward confrontations. In this selection, Freedmen's Bureau officer James C. Beecher reports on black opposition to the return to white ownership of islands off the South Carolina coast promised to the ex-slaves by the Union's General Sherman.

❧ ❧

The controversial Reconstruction of the South after the Civil War was a difficult time for African Americans. Though given the right to voice political opinions for the first time, their voices often went unheeded. As southern whites regained control of political offices after Reconstruction, African Americans slowly lost much of their newfound political freedom.

November 29, 1865

Maj. Gen. R. Saxton
General:

I am to leave for Edisto Island in the morning. It seems that some of the planters whose lands have been restored were driven off by the freed people. Gen. Sickles immediately ordered that a company of white troops be sent there. Gen. Devens agreed with me that my troops were the ones to send if any and so I take a company with me.

I have apprehended trouble ever since the Govt determined to rescind the authority to occupy those lands. It is true that the War Dept. did not, in so many words, approve Gen. Sherman's order, but it certainly did *act* upon it, and there is an apparent bad faith in the matter which I am sure the freed people will feel. I cannot refrain from expressing grave fears of collisions on the island. The same difficulty is affecting the Combahee plantations. I hope to visit that section by Monday next.

James C. Beecher
National Archives

January 9, 1866

I . . . called the people together and carefully instructed them in their rights and duties. They said they had been assured by certain parties that Mr. Heyward [a local white planter] would be obliged to lease his land to them, and that they would not work for him at any price. They were perfectly good natured about it but firm. I then announced Mr. Heyward's offer:

That they were to retain their houses and gardens, with the privilege of raising hogs, poultry, etc. That he would pay for full hands, men $12, women $8 per month. They to find themselves—or he would pay $10 per month to men, $4 to women and ration them.

I am satisfied that no higher wages will be offered this year. Therefore I told the people that they could take it or leave it, and that if they declined to work the plantation the houses must be vacated. I proceeded to call the roll of all the able bodied men and women, each of whom responded "no." I then notified them that every house must be vacated on or before the 18th inst. I propose to remain and see everyone outside the plantation lines on that date.

Today I have pursued the same course on another large plantation, with the same results. Of course I anticipated this. It could not be otherwise considering the instructions which these people have received. I do not blame them in the slightest degree, and so long as they show no violence, shall treat them with all possible kindness. But it is better to stop the error they are laboring under, at once.

January 31, 1866

I am informed that on or about 12th inst a meeting was called on Wadmalaw Island to take measures to prevent white persons from visiting the island—that the Captain Commanding (very properly) forbade the proceeding, and notified the actors that in future no meetings could be held until notice of the same should be given him.

I am further informed that certain parties immediately proceeded to Charleston and returned with a document signed "By order Maj. Gen. Saxton" stating that the military authorities had nothing to do with them and they were at liberty to hold meetings when and where they pleased. This document was brought by three colored men calling themselves Commissioners from Edisto Island, attended by an escort of forty or fifty freedmen, and exhibited to the Officer. They then proceeded to Rockville, and held the meeting.

It is to be regretted that the Bureau should seem to bring the freed people in collision with the Military Police of the islands. Already in two instances the freed people have committed themselves seriously by acts of stupid violence and I have record of hurtful advice given by speakers at the meeting in question. I shall be exceedingly grieved to find myself in collision with the [Bureau] but being responsible for the military police of these islands cannot do otherwise than prevent disorder by any means in my power.

I respectfully request that instruction be sent to the same "Commissioners" to the effect that the order in question must be respected on Wadmalaw and Johns Island. Such instructions will prevent collision between the [freedmen] and the U.S. forces.

DOCUMENT 4

"Address from the Colored Citizens of Norfolk, Virginia, to the People of the United States" (1865)

African Americans quickly grasped the great divide separating formal emancipation from social and political equality. Organization and communication provided southern blacks with vehicles for advancing their cause. In this document "The Colored Citizens of Norfolk" assert the need for black activism and urge the "People of the United States" to defeat the opponents of freedom.

[We] believe our present position is by no means so well understood among the loyal masses of the country, otherwise there would be no delay in granting us the express relief which the nature of the case demands. It must not be forgotten that it is the general assumption, in the South, that the effects of the immortal Emancipation Proclamation of President Lincoln go no further than the emancipation of the Negroes then in slavery, and that it is only constructively even, that that Proclamation can be said, in any legal sense, to have abolished slavery, and even the late constitutional amendment, if duly ratified, can go no further; neither touch, nor can touch, the slave codes of the various southern States, and the laws respecting free people of color consequent therefrom, which, having been passed before the act of secession, are presumed to have lost none of their vitality, but exist, as a convenient engine for our oppression, until repealed by special acts of the State legislature. By these laws, in many of the southern

States, it is still a crime for colored men to learn or be taught to read, and their children are doomed to ignorance; there is no provision for insuring the legality of our marriages; we have no right to hold real estate; the public streets and the exercise of our ordinary occupations are forbidden us unless we can produce passes from our employers, or licenses from certain officials; in some States the whole free Negro population is legally liable to exile from the place of its birth, for no crime but that of color; we have no means of legally making or enforcing contracts of any description; we have no right to testify before the courts in any case in which a white man is one of the parties to the suit, we are taxed without representation, and, in short, so far as legal safeguards of our rights are concerned, we are defenceless before our enemies. While this is our position as regards our legal status, before the State laws, we are still more unfortunately situated as regards our late masters. The people of the North, owing to the greater interest excited by war, have heard little or nothing, for the past four years, of the blasphemous and horrible theories formerly propounded for the defence and glorification of human slavery, in the press, the pulpit and legislatures of the southern States; but, though they may have forgotten them, let them be assured that these doctrines have by no means faded from the minds of the people of the South; they cling to these delusions still, and only hug them closer for their recent defeat. Worse than all, they have returned to their homes, with all their old pride and contempt for the Negro transformed into bitter hate for the new-made freeman, who aspires for the suppression of their rebellion. That this charge is not unfounded, the manner in which it has been recently attempted to enforce the laws above referred to proves. In Richmond, during the three days sway of the rebel Mayor Mayo, over 800 colored people were arrested, simply for walking the streets without a pass; in the neighboring city of Portsmouth, a Mayor has just been elected, on the avowed platform that this is a white man's government, and our enemies have been heard to boast openly, that soon not a colored man shall be left in the city; in the greater number of counties in this State, county meetings have been held, at which resolutions have been adopted *deploring,* while accepting, the abolition of slavery, but going on to pledge the planters composing the meeting, to employ no Negroes save such as were formerly owned by themselves, without a written recommendation from their late employers, and threatening violence towards those who should do so, thereby keeping us in a state of serfdom, and preventing our free selection of our employers; they have also pledged themselves, in no event, to pay their late adult slaves more than $60 per year for their labor. In the future, out of which, with characteristic generosity, they have decided that we are to find clothes for ourselves and families, and pay our taxes and doctors' bills; in many of the more remote districts individual planters are to be found who still refuse to recognize their Negroes as free, forcibly retaining the wives and children of their late escaped slaves; cases have occurred, not far from Richmond itself, in which an attempt to leave the plantation has been punished by shooting to death; and finally, there are numbers of cases, known to ourselves, in the immediate vicinity of this city, in which a faithful performance, by colored men, of the duties or labor contracted for, has been met by a contemptuous and violent refusal of the stipulated compensation. These are facts, and yet the men doing these things are, in many cases, loud in their professions of attachment to the restored Union, while committing these outrages on the most faithful friends that Union can ever have. Even well known Union men have often been found among our oppressors; witness the action of the Tennessee legislature in imposing unheard of disabilities upon us, taking away from us, and giving to the County Courts, the right of disposing of our children, by apprenticing them to such occupations as the court, not their parents, may see fit to adopt for them, and in this very city, and under the protection of military law, some of our white friends who have nobly distinguished themselves by their efforts in our behalf, have been threatened with arrest by a Union Mayor of this city, for their advocacy of the cause of freedom.

Fellow citizens, the performance of a simple act

of justice on your part will reverse all this; we ask for no expensive aid from military forces, stationed throughout the South, overbearing State action, and rendering our government republican only in name; give us the suffrage, and you may rely upon us to secure justice for ourselves, and all Union men, and to keep the State forever in the Union.

While we urge you to this act of simple justice to ourselves, there are many reasons why you should concede us this right in your own interest. It cannot be that you contemplate with satisfaction a prolonged military occupation of the southern States, and yet, without the existence of a larger loyal constituency than, at present, exists in these States, a military occupation will be absolutely necessary, to protect the white Union men of the South, as well as ourselves, and if not absolutely to keep the States in the Union, it will be necessary to prevent treasonable legislation. . . .

You have not unreasonably complained of the operation of that clause of the Constitution which has hitherto permitted the slaveocracy of the South to wield the political influence which would be represented by a white population equal to three-fifths of the whole Negro population; but slavery is now abolished, and henceforth the representation will be in proportion to the enumeration of the whole population of the South, *including people of color,* and it is worth your consideration if it is desirable or politic that the fomentors of this rebellion against the Union, which has been crushed at the expense of so much blood and treasure, should find themselves, after defeat, more powerful than ever, their political influence enhanced by the additional voting power of the other two-fifths of the colored population, by which means four Southern votes will balance in the Congressional and Presidential elections at least seven Northern ones. The honor of your country should be dear to you, as it is, but is that honor advanced, in the eyes of the Christian world, when America alone, of all Christian nations, sustains an unjust distinction against four millions and a half of her most loyal people, on the senseless ground of a difference in color? You are anxious that the attention of every man, of every

State legislature, and of Congress, should be exclusively directed to redressing the injuries sustained by the country in the late contest; are these objects more likely to be effected amid the political distractions of an embarrassing Negro agitation? You are, above all, desirous that no future intestine wars should mar the prosperity and destroy the happiness of the country; will your perfect security from such evils be promoted by the existence of a colored population of four millions and a half, placed, by your enactments, outside the pale of the Constitution, discontented by oppression, with an army of 200,000 colored soldiers, whom you have drilled, disciplined, and armed, but whose attachment to the State you have failed to secure by refusing them citizenship? You are further anxious that your government should be an example to the world of true Republican institutions; but how can you avoid the charge of inconsistency if you leave one eighth of the population of the whole country without any political rights, while bestowing these rights on every immigrant who comes to these shores, perhaps from a despotism, under which he could never exercise the least political right, and had no means of forming any conception of their proper use? . . .

It is hardly necessary here to refute any of the slanders with which our enemies seek to prove our unfitness for the exercise of the right of suffrage. It is true, that many of our people are ignorant, but for *that* these very men are responsible, and decency should prevent *their* use of such an argument. But if our people are ignorant, no people were ever more orderly and obedient to the laws; and no people ever displayed greater earnestness in the acquisition of knowledge. Among no other people could such a revolution have taken place without scenes of license and bloodshed; but in this case, and we say it advisedly, full information of the facts will show that no single disturbance, however slight, has occurred which has not resulted from the unprovoked aggression of white people, and, if any one doubts how fast the ignorance, which has hitherto cursed our people, is disappearing, 'mid the light of freedom, let him visit the colored schools of this city and neighborhood, in which between two and three thousand pupils are being taught, while, in the evening, in colored schools may be seen, after the labors of the day, hundreds of our adult population from budding manhood to hoary age, toiling, with intensest eagerness, to acquire the invaluable arts of reading and writing, and the rudimentary branches of knowledge. One other objection only will we notice; it is that our people are lazy and idle; and, in support of this allegation, the objectors refer to the crowds of colored people subsisting on Government rations, and flocking into the towns. To the first statement we reply that we are poor, and that thousands of our young and able-bodied men, having been enlisted in the army to fight the battles of their country, it is but reasonable that that country should contribute something to the support of those whose natural protectors that country has taken away. With reference to the crowds collected round the military posts and in the cities, we say that though some may have come there under misapprehensions as to the nature of the freedom they have just received, yet this is not the case with the majority; the colored man knows that freedom means freedom to labor, and to enjoy its fruits, and in that respect evinces at least an equal appreciation of his new position with his late owners; if he is not to be found laboring for these late owners, it is because he cannot trust them, and feels safe, in his new-found freedom, nowhere out of the immediate presence of the national forces; if the planters want his labor (and they do) fair wages and fair treatment will not fail to secure it.

In conclusion, we wish to advise our colored brethren of the State and nation, that the settlement of this question is to a great extent dependent on them, and that supineness on their part will do as much to delay if not defeat the full recognition of their rights as the open opposition of avowed enemies. Then be up and active, and everywhere let associations be formed having for their object the agitation, discussion and enforcement of your claims to equality before the law, and equal rights of suffrage. Your opponents are active; be prepared, and organize to resist their efforts. We would further advise that all political associations of colored men, formed within the limits of the State of Virginia, should communicate the fact of their existence, with the names and post office addresses of their officers, to Joseph T. Wilson, Norfolk, Va., in order that communication and friendly cooperation may be kept up between the different organizations, and facilities afforded for common and united State action, should occasion require it.

DOCUMENT 5

The Fourteenth Amendment to the United States Constitution (1868)

The Fourteenth Amendment attempted to fortify the position of the former slaves against challenges to their full rights as citizens. As a condition of readmittance to the Union, Congress required southern states to ratify the amendment. Supreme Court decisions interpreting the amendment narrowly and the North's failure to oversee forcefully the implementation of its principles diluted the provision's impact, as well as the effect of other federal legislation.

❧   ❧

Amendment XIV

Section 1

All persons born or naturalized in the United States, and subject to the jurisdiction thereof, are citizens of the United States and of the State wherein they reside. No State shall make or enforce any law which shall abridge the privileges or immunities of citizens of the United States; nor shall any State deprive any person of life, liberty, or property, without due process of law; nor deny to any person within its jurisdiction the equal protection of the laws.

Section 2

Representatives shall be apportioned among the several States according to their respective numbers, counting the whole number of persons in each State, excluding Indians not taxed. But when the right to vote at any election for the choice of electors for President and Vice President of the United States, Representatives in Congress, the Executive and Judicial officers of a State, or the members of the Legislature thereof, is denied to any of the male inhabitants of such State, being twenty-one years of age, and citizens of the United States, or in any way abridged, except for participation in rebellion, or other crime, the basis of representation therein shall be reduced in the proportion which the number of such male citizens shall bear to the whole number of male citizens twenty-one years of age in such State.

Section 3

No person shall be a Senator or Representative in Congress, or elector of President and Vice President, or hold any office, civil or military, under the United States, or under any State, who, having previously taken an oath, as a member of Congress, or as an officer of the United States, or as a member of any State legislature, or as an executive or judicial officer of any State, to support the Constitution of the United States, shall have engaged in insurrection or rebellion against the same, or given aid or comfort to the enemies thereof. But Congress may by a vote of two-thirds of each House, remove such disability.

Section 4

The validity of the public debt of the United States, authorized by law, including debts incurred for payment for pensions and bounties for services in suppressing insurrection or rebellion, shall not be questioned. But neither the United States nor any State shall assume or pay any debt or obligation incurred in aid of insurrection or rebellion against the United States, or any claim for the loss or emancipation of any slave; but all such debts, obligations and claims shall be held illegal and void.

Section 5

The Congress shall have power to enforce, by appropriate legislation, the provisions of this article.

DOCUMENT 6

The Nation, "The State of the South" (1872)

Northern leaders grew increasingly uncertain about Reconstruction. Particularly alarming to some northerners was the fraud and graft perpetuated by various, mostly white, Reconstruction politicians. Singled out for particular criticism was a group known as carpetbaggers, whites who had moved south to capitalize on a devastated postwar economy. *The Nation*, a weekly political magazine founded in 1865 to voice reform-minded views on politics both North and South, captured the northern sense of frustration with the alleged course of events.

The indolent excuse for our failure to understand the condition of the South is that nobody can very accurately comprehend it who has not been there to see for himself. With regard to troubles of a social character, this excuse is valid; but there are some plain statistical facts recently brought to light and published which it is our duty to recognize and confront. We must acknowledge that the condition of the South from almost every point of view is extremely wretched. The property of the eleven States in 1860, exclusive of slaves, was valued at $2,728,825,006. At the end of the war their increased liabilities and loss, exclusive of slaves, was $1,272,900,390, nearly one-half the assessed value of their property at the beginning of the war. This, however, was only the State loss. Secretary Belknap fixes the rebel debt, on the 1st of April, 1865, at $2,345,297,823. This estimate would make the total loss of the rebellious States by the war $5,262,303,554. This sum, it will be seen, is about twice the assessed value of all Southern property in 1860, exclusive of slaves. Five-eighths of Southern property is gone, and the taxes upon the remainder are four times that upon the original property before the war. How much of the money wrung from this impoverished country is expended upon public improvements, it is difficult to tell; but it is likely that most of it, and certain that much of it, goes to feed the vulgar and rapacious rogues who rob and rule a people helpless and utterly exhausted.

With the exception of Virginia and Tennessee, the debts of all the States have been increased since the end of the war. The near neighborhood of those communities to the Ohio may have had some influence in driving rogues further south. The real reason, however, is the comparative fewness of the negroes. The debt of Alabama in 1866 was $5,000,000; under the rule of the enlightened and disinterested economists who have undertaken to repair her finances, that debt has been increased to $24,000,000. In North Carolina the new government was established in 1868. In 1860, the State debt was $14,000,000; in 1865, $20,000,000; in 1868, $24,000,000; and in 1871, $34,000,000. Thus the increase of debt since the war has been more than twice the increase during the war—which looks as if war were a cheaper and more prosperous condition than peace. At any rate, reconstruction seems to be morally a more disastrous process than rebellion. Guile is the strength of the weak, and the carpet-baggers have taught the Southern people to meet rogues with trickery. The Ku-klux Committee, commenting upon their dreadful poverty at the close of the war, says that manifestly they must have at once succumbed under their loss of $5,000,000,000 had it not been for the benefactions of the North. It states that the Freedmen's Bureau has spent $13,000,000 upon Southern sufferers of both colors. This does not seem a considerable sum when we think that the increased debt since the war in North Carolina has been $14,000,000. Certainly, our charities have done less good than our carpet-baggers have done damage. The theory, of course, is that something remains from the enormous sums raised by taxation, that they have been expended upon needed public improvements. In North Carolina, it was alleged, the large subsidies given to railroads would encourage immigration. There has been no immigration, however; the bonds have been sold at a disadvantage; some of the money has been stolen, and a few of the rogues have been indicted. It is impossible to say how much of the sums raised remain to the States. The carpet-baggers have had it pretty much their own way. If they chose to rob, there was nothing to prevent them. Give men a chance to be tyrants or scamps, and there is no fear that some will not be found who will avail themselves of it. Here in New York, where we have all the rascals and all the plunderers within a radius of five miles, we know how long we have been in bringing the Ring to bay. The carpet-baggers have an immense extent of country to rifle; they do not buy the legislatures, they constitute them; they enact their own registration acts and vote their own supplies. The persons they rob are not of that apathetic and well-to-do class too indifferent to go to the polls, but people who could not go if they would.

All accounts agree as to the widespread misery and penury. In Mississippi, a large planter testified that it took all his cotton for the year 1871 to pay his taxes. It is South Carolina, however, that enjoys the unenviable eminence of being the worst-robbed State of the whole eleven. In the single county of Kershaw, possessing a population of only 11,000, there were 3,600 tax-executions issued. The taxation during 1870, $2,365,047, was more than the whole taxation on double the property for five years before the war. In order to change the fiscal year, they proposed to double this, and, in 1871, to levy a tax of $4,730,094; whether this law was executed we do not know, but the fact remains that it was enacted. Peculation and corruption are as universal as poverty and distress. In 1860, South Carolina paid for offices and salaries, $123,800; in 1871, the State expended on these $581,640. In two years, $1,208,577 67 have been paid out, for which no vouchers are to be found in the Treasury. According to the minority report of the Ku-klux Committee, the disbursements exceed the appropriations by $170,683. This report, though spoiled by some rather low allusions to "ebony legislators," "men and brothers," etc., brings to light some amusing facts. Money voted with which to fit up committee-rooms has been expended on the private apartments of the colored members of the legislatures. Their rooms were furnished with Brussels carpets, sofas, mirrors, etc. About seventy-five imported porcelain spittoons, bought for the South Carolina State-House, likewise adorned their private apartments. This fact seemed to affect the democratic minority of the committee even more profoundly than the vast robberies and excessive taxations. They remark, with rugged, Spartan simplicity, that they themselves, in "the splendid capital of the nation," had never had anything but "an article of common, plain brown earthenware, of domestic manufacture." This striking disparity between fortune and desert does not excite in us any feeling of indignation against the negroes. Emerging from a long night of slavery and cruel bondage, who can grudge them their fantastic lease of liberty and luxury? Did not graver considerations check us, our humor would be to vote them State barbers and the most delightful of oriental baths. We suspect the truth to be that in the distribution of spoils the poor African gets the gilt and plush, the porcelain spittoons, the barbaric upholstery, while the astuter Caucasian clings to the soldier and more durable advantages. The negroes by themselves would be but little to be feared; yet, in the hands of the carpet-baggers, they have been the unwitting instruments of most of the harm that has been done. The swindlers could not have so got the control of things without the help of the negroes. They have made numerically the largest part of the conventions and legislatures in South Carolina. The Convention of 1868, which drew up a State constitution, was composed of 72 negroes and 49 white men. This convention made provision for a levy of $2,230,950 upon the State, which would necessitate taxation at the rate of 6 per cent; yet but 13 of the 72 negroes paid taxes. In the Legislature of 1869, there were twelve black and twenty white senators; eight of the twelve black senators paid no taxes. In the House, there were 86 black and 37 white members; 68 of the 86 black members paid no taxes. As things are at present, there seems to be no limit to the power of the carpet-baggers to plunder the South as they choose. The only ray of hope is in the passage of an act of universal amnesty. We have given the negro the ballot to protect him against his old master; we need now to give the white citizen the vote to protect him against the carpet-bagger.

Seven years have gone over us since the close of the war, and, instead of occupying this precious season with endeavors to re-establish prosperity and to sow the seeds of a peace which, in another generation, would ripen into good-will and forgetfulness, we have averted our eyes from the whole problem, refused to listen to the complaints of men whose hands we have tied, and have fallen back upon the lazy belief that in some way this great country is bound to go through. The unconscious syllogism working in the indolent Northern mind seems to be: "Things are no doubt very bad—how bad, we haven't the time or the inclination to ascertain. Examination of such unpleasant matters, if a duty at all, is a disagreeable one. After all, the rebels have made their own bed, and they must lie in it." Perhaps their sufferings are only the just punishment of their crimes; but at any rate, there can be no reason for giving over the criminals into the hands of the carpet-baggers. What services have these persons rendered the country that we should grant them the monopoly of robbing rebels? It would be better to levy tribute-money, and get some national advantage from the merciless exactions inflicted upon the Southern people. Let us make up our minds one way or the other—do we or do we not propose further to punish the rebel States for their rebellion? If we do, let us at once proceed to devise some intelligent means for that purpose. If we do not, let us make haste to protect society from the ravages of ignorance and rapacity, or give society the means to protect itself. We thought it worth four years of war to retain the Southern States in the Union, now we hardly deem it worth an act of Congress to preserve them.

DOCUMENT 7

Albion W. Tourgee, Letter on Ku Klux Klan Activities (1870)

Violence proved an effective weapon for whites seeking to curb black participation in politics and to unseat Republican rule in the South. The Ku Klux Klan, a secret organization with a diverse white membership, perpetrated brutal attacks throughout the South, intimidating blacks and whites alike from publicly voicing their opinions and asserting their rights. Albion Tourgee, a so-called carpetbagger who settled in North Carolina and served as a judge during Reconstruction, vividly describes the Klan's tactics in a letter to the *New York Tribune* in May 1870.

❦ ❦

Some of the Outrages—Letter from Judge Tourgee to Senator Abbott

Greensboro, N.C. May 24, 1870.

Gen. Jos. C. Abbott—My *Dear General:* It is my mournful duty to inform you that our friend John W. Stephens, State Senator from Caswell, is dead. He was foully murdered by the Ku-Klux in the Grand Jury room of the Court House on Saturday or Saturday night last. The circumstances attending his murder have not yet fully come to light there. So far as I can learn, I judge these to have been the circumstances: He was one of the Justices of the Peace in that township, and was accustomed to hold court in that room on Saturdays. It is evident that he was set upon by some one while holding this court, or immediately after its close, and disabled by a sudden attack, otherwise there would have been a very sharp resistance, as he was a man, and always went armed to the teeth. He was stabbed five or six times, and then hanged on a hook in the Grand Jury room, where he was found on Sunday morning. Another brave, honest Republican citizen has met his fate at the hands of these fiends. Warned of his danger, and fully cognizant of the terrible risk which surrounded him, he still manfully refused to quit the field. Against the advice of his friends, against the entreaties of his family, he constantly refused to leave those who had stood by him in the day of his disgrace and peril. He was accustomed to say that 3,000 poor, ignorant, colored Republican voters in that county had stood by him and elected him, at the risk of persecution and starvation, and that he had no idea of abandoning them to the Ku-Klux. He was determined to stay with them, and either put an end to these outrages, or die with the other victims of Rebel hate and national apathy: Nearly six months ago I declared my belief that before the election in August next the Ku-Klux would have killed more men in the State than there would be members to be elected to the Legislature. A good beginning has been made toward the fulfillment of this prophecy.

The following counties have already filled, or nearly so, their respective "quotas:" Jones County, quota full, excess 1; Orange County quota full; excess, 1. Caswell County quota full; excess, 2; Alamance County quota full; excess, 1. Chatham County quota nearly full. Or, to state the matter differently, there have been twelve murders in five counties of the district during the past eighteen months, by bands of disguised villains. In addition to this, from the best information I can derive, I am of the opinion that in this district alone there have been 1,000 outrages of a less serious nature perpetrated by the same masked fiends. Of course this estimate is not made from any absolute record, nor is it possible to ascertain with accuracy the entire number of beatings and other outrages which have been perpetrated. The uselessness, the utter futility of complaint from the lack of ability in the laws to punish is fully known to all. The danger of making such complaint is also well understood. It is therefore not unfrequently by accident that the outrage is found out, and unquestionably it is frequently absolutely concealed. Thus, a respectable, hard working white carpenter was working for a neighbor, when accidentally his shirt was torn, and disclosed his back scarred and beaten. The poor fellow begged for the sake of his wife and children that nothing might be said about it, as the Ku-Klux had threatened to kill him if he disclosed how he had been outraged. Hundreds of cases have come to my notice and that of my solicitor. . . .

Men and women come scarred, mangled, and bruised, and say: "The Ku-Klux came to my house last night and beat me almost to death, and my old woman right smart, and shot into the house, 'bust' the door down, and told me they would kill me if I made complaint;" and the bloody mangled forms attest the truth of their declarations. On being asked if any one knew any of the party it will be ascertained that there was no recognition, or only the most uncertain and doubtful one. In such cases as these nothing can be done by the court. We have not been accustomed to enter them on record. A man of the best standing in Chatham told me that

Members of the white supremacist Ku Klux Klan in typical regalia. The Klan was most active during elections, when members terrorized African Americans in an effort to keep them from voting.

he could count up 200 and upward in that county. In Alamance County, a citizen in conversation one evening enumerated upward of 50 cases which had occurred within his own knowledge, and in one section of the county. He gave it as his opinion that there had been 200 cases in that county. I have no idea that he exceeded the proper estimate. That was six months ago, and I am satisfied that another hundred would not cover the work done in that time.

These crimes have been of every character imaginable. Perhaps the most usual has been the drag-ging of men and women from their beds, and beating their naked bodies with hickory switches, or as witnesses in an examination the other day said, "sticks" between a "switch" and a "club." From 50 to 100 blows is the usual allowance, sometimes 200 and 300 blows are administered. Occasionally an instrument of torture is owned. Thus in one case two women, one 74 years old, were taken out, stripped naked, and beaten with a paddle, with several holes bored through it. The paddle was about 30 inches long, 3 or 4 inches wide, and $1/4$ of an inch thick, of oak. Their bodies were so bruised and beaten that they were sickening to behold. They were white women and of good character until the younger was seduced, and swore her child to its father. Previous to that and so far as others were concerned her character was good.

Again, there is sometimes a fiendish malignity and cunning displayed in the form and character of the outrages. For instance, a colored man was placed astride of a log, and an iron staple driven through his person into the log. In another case, after a band of them had in turn violated a young negro girl, she was forced into bed with a colored man, their bodies were bound together face to face, and the fire from the hearth piled upon them. The K. K. K. rode off and left them, with shouts of laughter. Of course the bed was soon in flames, and somehow they managed to crawl out, though terribly burned and scarred. The house was burned.

I could give other incidents of cruelty, such as hanging up a boy of nine years old until he was nearly dead, to make him tell where his father was hidden, and beating an old negress of 103 years old with garden pallings because she would not own that she was afraid of the Ku-Klux. But it is unnecessary to go into further detail. In this district I estimate their offenses as follows, in the past ten months: Twelve murders, 9 rapes, 11 arsons, 7 mutilations, ascertained and most of them on record. In some no identification could be made.

Four thousand or 5,000 houses have been broken open, and property or persons taken out. In all cases all arms are taken and destroyed. Seven hundred or

800 persons have been beaten or otherwise mal-treated. These of course are partly persons living in the houses which were broken into.

And yet the Government sleeps. The poor dis-armed nurses of the Republican party—those men by whose ballots the Republican party holds power—who took their lives in their hands when they cast their ballots for U.S. Grant and other offi-cials—all of us who happen to be beyond the pale of the Governmental regard—must be sacrificed, mur-dered, scourged, mangled, because some contempt-ible party scheme might be foiled by doing us jus-tice. I could stand it very well to fight for Uncle Sam, and was never known to refuse an invitation on such an occasion; but this lying down, tied hand and foot with the shackles of the law, to be killed by the very dregs of the rebellion, the scum of the earth, and not allowed either the consolation of fighting or the satisfaction that our "fall" will be noted by the Government, and protection given to others thereby, is somewhat too hard. I am ashamed of the nation that will let its citizens be slain by scores, and scourged by thousands, and offer no rem-edy or protection. I am ashamed of a State which has not sufficient strength to protect its own officers in the discharge of their duties, nor guarantee the safety of any man's domicile throughout its length and breadth. I am ashamed of a party which, with the reins of power in its hands, has not nerve or de-cision enough to arm its own adherents, or to pro-tect them from assassinations at the hands of their opponents. A General who in time of war would permit 2,000 or 3,000 of his men to be bushwhacked and destroyed by private treachery even in an en-emy's country without any one being punished for it would be worthy of universal execration, and would get it, too. How much more worthy of detestation is a Government which in time of peace will permit such wholesale slaughter of its citizens? It is simple cowardice, inertness, and wholesale demoralization. The wholesale slaughter of the war has dulled our Nation's sense of horror at the shedding of blood, and the habit of regarding the South as simply a lab-oratory, where every demagogue may carry on his reconstructionary experiments at will, and not as an integral party of the Nation itself, has led our Gov-ernment to shut its eyes to the atrocities of these times. Unless these evils are speedily remedied, I tell you, General, the Republican party has signed its death warrant. It is a party of cowards or idiots—I don't care which alternative is chosen. The remedy is in our hands, and we are afraid or too dull to bestir ourselves and use it.

But you will tell me that Congress is ready and willing to act if it only knew what to do. Like the old Irish woman it wrings its hands and cries, "O Lawk, O Lawk; if I only knew which way." And yet this same Congress has the control of the militia and can organize its own force in every county in the United States, and arm more or less of it. This same Congress has the undoubted right to guaran-tee and provide a republican government, and pro-tect every citizen in "life, liberty, and the pursuit of happiness," as well as the power conferred by the XVth Amendment. And yet we suffer and die in peace and murderers walk abroad with the blood yet fresh upon their garments, unharmed, unquestioned and unchecked. Fifty thousand dollars given to good detectives would secure, if well used, a com-plete knowledge of all this gigantic organization of murderers. In connection with an organized and armed militia, it would result in the apprehension of any number of these Thugs *en masque* and with blood on their hands. What then is the remedy? *First:* Let Congress give to the U. S. Courts, or to Courts of the States under its own laws, cognizance of this class of crimes, as crimes against the nation, and let it provide that this legislation be enforced. Why not, for instance, make going armed and masked or disguised, or masked or disguised in the night time, an act of insurrection or sedition? *Sec-ond:* Organize militia, National—State militia is a nuisance—and arm as many as may be necessary in each county to enforce its laws. *Third:* Put detec-tives at work to get hold of this whole organization. Its ultimate aim is unquestionably to revolutionize the Government. If we have not pluck enough for this, why then let us just offer our throats to the knife, emasculate ourselves, and be a nation of self-subjugated slaves at once.

And now, Abbott, I have but one thing to say to you. I have very little doubt that I shall be one of the next victims. My steps have been dogged for months, and only a good opportunity has been wanting to secure to me the fate which Stephens has just met, and I speak earnestly upon this matter. I feel that I have a right to do so, and a right to be heard as well, and with this conviction I say to you plainly that any member of Congress who, especially if from the South, does not support, advocate, and urge immediate, active, and thorough measures to put an end to these outrages, and make citizenship a privilege, is a coward, a traitor, or a fool. The time for action has come, and the man who has now only speeches to make over some Constitutional scarecrow, deserves to be damned.

DOCUMENT 8

James T. Rapier, Testimony Before U.S. Senate Regarding the Agricultural Labor Force in the South (1880)

As white southern Democrats reclaimed control in state after state, they enacted laws and constitutional provisions that attempted to ensure that blacks could never again compete for political power. State governments severely curtailed their ability to provide the social and educational services necessary for black upward mobility. "Redeemer" governments instead placed emphasis on creating a compliant agricultural labor force that would pose no threat to the wealthy whites who had regained their positions. In testimony given to a U.S. Senate Committee in 1880, James T. Rapier, an African American political leader and one-term congressman from Alabama during Reconstruction, described the results of this process among southern blacks.

A. Well, sir, there are several reasons why the colored people desire to emigrate from Alabama; one among them is the poverty of the South. On a large part of it a man cannot make a decent living. Another is their want of school privileges in the State: and there is a majority of the people who believe that they cannot any longer get justice in the courts; and another and the greatest reason is found in the local laws that we have, and which are very oppressive to that class of people in the black belt.

Q. State what some of them are.—A. First, we have only schools about three months in the year, and I suppose I need not say anything more on that head. In reference to the poverty of the soil, 33 to 40 per cent of the lands in Alabama is about all on which a man can make a living.

Q. Do you mean the parts that are subdued?—A. Yes, sir; the arable land. The average is one-third of a bale of cotton to the acre, not making three bales to the hand; and a hundred bushels of corn to the hand, on an average. Then take the price of cotton for the last two years; it has not netted more than $45 to $47.50 to the bale; and I suppose it would not be amiss for me to state something of the plans of working the land in Alabama.

Mr. Vance. It will be very proper.

The Witness. The general plan is that the landlord furnishes the land and the teams and feed for the teams and the implements, for which he draws one half of the crop. I remarked that the three bales of cotton and a hundred bushels of corn is about all that you can make to a hand. We allow in Alabama that much, for that is as much as a man can get out of it, and that is not enough to support his family, including himself and the feed of his family; $95 to $100 is as much as a hand can make, and that is not enough to feed any man in a Christian country. . . .

A. . . . Now, it is very clear that a man cannot live on such terms, and hence the conclusion of many of these people, that there is not a decent living for them in that State. They are like the white people, and their living no better. Numbers of them, probably not less than 20,000 whites, have left Alabama since the war and gone to Texas to better their condition, and the blacks are doing the same thing, and that is the whole there is of it. So far as the negroes are concerned now they have a high desire to submit their fate to their own keeping in another country. Now here is one of the laws which also affects us, to which I will call attention. It is found in the acts of Alabama for 1878–'79, page 63, act No. 57, section 1.

Section 1. *Be it enacted by the general assembly of Alabama,* That section 4369 of the Code be, and the same is hereby, amended so as to read as follows: Any person who shall buy, sell, receive, barter, or dispose of any cotton, corn, wheat, oats, pease, or potatoes after the hour of sunset and before the hour of sunrise of the next succeeding day, and any person who shall in any manner move, carry, convey, or transport, except within the limits of the farm or plantation on which it is raised or grown, any seed cotton between the hours of sunset and sunrise of the next succeeding day, shall be guilty of a misdemeanor, and, on conviction, shall be fined not less than ten nor more five hundred dollars, and may also be imprisoned in the county jail, or put to hard labor for the county, for not more than twelve months. But this section shall not effect the right of municipal corporations to establish and regulate under their charters public markets within their limits for the sale of commodities for culinary purposes, nor the right of any proprietor or owner of any plantation or premises to sell on such plantation or premises the necessary grain and provisions for the subsistence of man and beast for the night to traveling or transient persons, or for the use of agricultural laborers in his own employment on such plantation or premises: *Provided,* That the provisions of such section shall not apply to any person carrying seed cotton to a gin for the purpose of having the same ginned.

Now, the effect of this upon the labor of the South is this: A great many laborers work by the month, but all of them are under contract. If I live three miles from a store, and I must work from sunup to sundown, I cannot go where I can do my trading to the best advantage. A man is prevented, no matter whether his family is sick from sundown to sunrise, from going and selling anything that he has, as the landlord will not give them time between sunrise and sundown.

Q. What was the purpose of this law?—A. It was, as appears from the debates, to keep the negroes from going to stores and taking off seed cotton from the plantation. Certainly it was to have that effect, but it goes further and prevents a man from selling what he has raised and has a right to sell. If a man commits a crime he ought to be punished, but every man ought to have a right to dispose of his own property.

Q. Is there any particular limitation of time to which this law applies?—A. No, sir.

Q. It runs all the year round?—A. Yes, sir.

Q. After the division of the crops as well as before?—A. Yes, sir; it operates so that a man cannot sell his crop at all in many cases.

Q. Do you say that the landlord will not let him sell his crop or that he can prevent it?—A. I say he will not let him do it, because the landlord will not let him take two or three hours out of the time due him in the day to sell it, and the law prevents him from selling at night.

Q. You say the effect of it is not to let him sell his crop at all?—A. I do; for if a man agrees to work from sunup to sundown he is made to do it. I work them that way myself, and I believe all the rest do. . . .

Q. It shall not be lawful to buy or sell seed cotton?—A. Yes, sir.

Q. At any time?—A. Yes, sir; night or day.

Q. From nobody?—A. From nobody.

Q. White or black?—A. White or black; but you see it applies wholly to black counties.

Q. But there are some white people there, are there not?—A. Yes, sir; but I do not know many who raise seed cotton.

Q. I thought something, may be, was left out of that act?—A. No, sir; that is to say, the gist of the matter is this: I may raise as much cotton as I please in the seed, but I am prohibited by law from selling it to anybody but the landlord, who can buy it because he has advanced to me on the crop. One of the rules is this: I have people working for me to day, but I give them an outside patch. If a man makes outside 1,200 pounds of seed cotton, which is worth $2.50 per 100 pounds, he cannot sell it unless to me. I may say I will give him $1.50 per 100 pounds for it, and he will be forced to take it; but I cannot sell it again unless I have a merchantable bale, which is 500 pounds, or 450 pounds by the cotton congress.

Q. Then the effect of that law is to place all the seed cotton into the hands of the landlord?—A. Yes, sir.

Q. He is the only purchaser who is allowed by law to buy it?—A. Yes, sir; nobody else can buy it. . . .

Q. I thought the law said that grand larceny should consist of as much as $235 worth?—A. No, sir; you have not got it right yet. Two ears or a stalk of corn is a part of an outstanding crop, and any man who sells any part of an outstanding crop can be prosecuted and convicted of grand larceny. . . .

The Witness. The point is this: Under the laws of Alabama the probate judge, the clerk, and the sheriff have had the drawing of jurors, and have had since Alabama was admitted as a State; but this bill comes in and covers those counties where the Republicans are likely to have a majority, and where they would draw the jurors. The proper heading of the law might have been, "An act to keep negroes off the juries." I want to state that it is the general opinion of the colored people in Alabama, and I will say of some of the judges, that it is a difficult matter for a colored man to get justice when there is a case between him and a white man. I will cite one of those cases: There was a case in Montgomery in which Judge J. Q. Smith presided. It was a civil suit. A white man had a black man's crop attached, and he had lost it. The colored man sued him on the attachment bond, and employed Judge Gardiner to defend or prosecute it for him. Soon after the case was given to the jury they brought in a verdict for the defendant. Judge Gardiner moved for a new trial, on the ground that the verdict was not in accordance with the facts; and the judge said, "I have observed that where an issue is between a white and a black man before a jury the verdict is almost invariably against the black man. The grounds on which the judge said he would not grant a new trial would be because he thinks the next verdict would not be different from that rendered, and as I do not think there would be a different verdict, I decline to give the new trial."

Study Questions

1. Did various actors in Reconstruction address one another's concerns, or did they merely advance separate agendas?

2. How did competing perspectives and assumptions divide freed blacks from their presumed allies in the Freedman's Bureau?

3. What assumptions led northerners to believe first that Reconstruction might work and then that it could not succeed?

4. Why did blacks believe that northerners might endorse their efforts to assert their equality?

5. From whose perspective was Reconstruction a failure? From whose perspective could it be seen as a success? Did northern officials adequately comprehend the concerns of either blacks or whites in the South?

Acknowledgments

Selections not credited are in the public domain.

Chapter 1

Document 1: Cited in *Journals and Other Documents on the Life and Voyages of Christopher Columbus* translated and edited by Samuel Eliot Morrison (New York: The Limited Editions Club), 1963. *Document 3*: From *A Short Account of the Destruction of the Indies* by Bartolome de las Casas, translated by Nigel Griffin (Penguin Classics, 1992). Copyright © Nigel Griffin, 1992. *Document 4*: *The Long Journey to the Country of the Hurons* by Father Gabriel Sagard, edited by George M. Wrong, and trans. by H. H. Langton (Toronto: The Champlain Society), 1939. *Document 5*: *Travels and Explorations of the Jesuit Missionaries in New France, 1610–1791* edited by Reuben Gold Thwaites (Cleveland: The Burrows Brothers Company), MDCCCXCIX. *Document 6*: "Translation of the Cellere Codex" by Susan Tarrow cited in *The Voyages of Giovanni da Verrazzano, 1524–1528* by Lawrence C. Wroth (New Haven: Yale University Press), 1970.

Chapter 2

Document 1:*The Cabot Voyages and Bristol Discovery Under Henry VII* by James A. Williamson (Cambridge: The University Press), 1962, Published for the Hakluyt Society. *Document 3*: *The Roanoke Voyages: 1584–1590*, vol. I edited by David Beers Quinn (Hakluyt Society, 1955; reprinted by Kraus Reprint Limited), 1967. *Document 4*: *New-England's Plantation* by John Higginson (London: T. and R. Cotes), 1630. *Document 5*: First published by the New Hampshire Historical Society in *Collections*, vol. IV (1834). Reprinted in *The Founding of Massachusetts* edited by Edmund S. Morgan, and published by The Bobbs-Merrill Company, Inc. *Document 6*: Proceedings of the *Massachusetts Historical Society*, Second Series, vol. VIII, 1892–1894 (Boston: Published by the Society), MDCCCXCIV.

Chapter 3

Document 1: Cited in *Winthrop Papers: Volume II, 1623–1630* (The Massachusetts Historical Society), 1931. *Document 2*: *The New England Historical and Genealogical Register* for the year 1859, vol. XIII (Boston: Samuel G. Drake), 1859. *Document 3*: *The Laws and Liberties of Massachusetts* (Cambridge: Harvard University Press), 1929. Reprinted from the 1648 edition in the Henry E. Huntington Library. *Document 4*: *Records of the Governor and Company of the Massachusetts Bay in New England*, vol. I, 1628–1641 edited by Nathaniel B. Shurtleff, M.D. (Boston: The Press of William White), 1853. *Document 5*: Cited in *The History of the Colony and Province of Massachusetts-Bay* by Thomas Hutchinson (Cambridge: Harvard University Press), 1936. *Document 6*: *Winthrop's Journal: History of New England, 1630–1649*, vol. II edited by James Kendall

Hosmer, LLD (New York: Barnes & Noble, Inc.). *Document 7: Thomas Shepard's Record of Relations of Religious Experience, 1648–1649* by Mary Rhinelander McCarl. Cited in *The William and Mary Quarterly*, Third Series, vol. XLVIII, no. 3, July 1991. *Document 8: The Complete Works of Anne Bradstreet* edited by J. R. McElrath, Jr. and A. P. Robb (Boston: Twayne Publishers), 1981.

Chapter 4

Document 1: The Generall Historie of Virginia, New England & The Summer Isles, vol. I by Captaine John Smith (Glasgow: James MacLehose and Sons), MCMVII. *Document 2: Lawes Divine, Morall and Martiall*, etc. compiled by William Strachey, edited by David H. Flaherty (The University Press of Virginia), 1969. Reprinted from Peter Force, editor, *Tracts and Other Papers Relating Principally to the Colonies in North America* (4 vols.; Washington D.C., 1836–46), III, no. 2. *Document 3: The Records of the Virginia Company of London* edited by Susan Myra Kingsbury, vol. III (Washington D.C.: Government Printing Office), 1933. *Document 4*: Tracts and Other Papers, Relating Principally to the Orgin, Settlement, and Progress of the Collonies in North America from the Discovery of the Country to the Year 1776, vol. III. Collected by Peter Force (Gloucester, MA: Peter Smith), 1963. *Document 5: Proceedings of the Provincial Court of Maryland, 1658–1662* edited by Bernard Christian Steiner in *Archives of Maryland XLI* (Baltimore: Maryland Historical Society), 1922. Statutes at Large: A Collection of All the Laws of Virginia, from the first session of the legislature, in the year 1619, vol. II edited by William Waller Hening (New York: R. & W. & G. Bartow), 1823. *Document 6: The Records of the Virginia Company of London*, vol. IV edited by Susan Myra Kingsbury (Washington, D.C.: U. S. Government Printing Office), 1938. *Document 7: William and Mary College Quarterly*, vol. XI edited by Lyon G. Tyler (Richmond, VA: Whittet & Shepperson), 1903. *Document 8*: Cited in *The Old Dominion in the Seventeenth Century: A Documentary History of Virginia, 1606–1689* edited by Warren M. Billings (Chapel Hill: University of North Carolina Press), 1975.

Chapter 5

Document 1: Letters from America by William Eddis edited by Aubrey C. Land (Cambridge, MA: The Belknap Press of Harvard University Press), 1969. *Document 2: The Correspondence of the Three William Byrds of Westover, Virginia, 1684–1776*, edited by Marion Tinling, vol. II, published for the Virginia Historical Society (Charlottesville: The University Press of Virginia). *Document 4: Collections of the Nova Scotia Historical Society for the Year 1884*, vol. IV (Halifax, N.S.: Wm. Macnab, Printer), 1885. Cited in *A People's Army: Massachusetts Soldiers and Society in the Seven Years' War* by Fred Anderson (Chapel Hill: The University of North Carolina Press), 1984. *Document 5: Hamilton's Itinerarium: Being a Narrative of a Journey from Annapolis, Maryland through Delaware, Pennsylvania, New York, New Jersey, Connecticut, Rhode Island, Massachusetts and New Hampshire from May to September, 1744* by Doctor Alexander Hamilton, edited by Albert Bushnell Hart (Saint Louis, MO: William K. Bixby), MCMVII. *Document 6: The Papers of Benjamin Franklin*, vol. 2, January 1, 1735 through December 31, 1944 edited by Leonard W. Labaree (New Haven, CT: Yale University Press), 1960. *Document 7: The Danger of an Unconverted Ministry, Considered in a Sermon on Mark VI. 34* by Gilbert Tennent (2nd ed., Philadelphia, 1741; reprinted Boston, 1742). *Document 8: The Carolina Backcountry on the Eve of the Revolution: The Journal and Other Writings of Charles Woodmason, Anglican Itinerant,* edited by Richard J. Hooker (Chapel Hill: University of North Carolina Press), 1953. *Document 9: Notes and Documents: George Whitefield Comes to Middletown* by Leonard W. Labaree. *The William and Mary Quarterly,* Third Series, vol. VII, no. 4, October 1950.

Chapter 8

Document 2: Reprinted by permission of the publishers from *New Travels in the United States of America, 1788* by J. P. Brissot de Warville, edited by Durand Echeverria, translated by Mara Soceanu Vamos and Durand Echeverria (Cambridge, MA: The Belknap Press of Harvard University Press, Copyright © 1964 by the President and Fellows of Harvard College).

Chapter 13

Document 8: "Annie Young, Memory of Slavery, 1937" from The American Slave: A Composite Autobiography, vol. 7, *Oklahoma and Mississippi Narratives* edited by George P. Rawick (Copyright © 1972 by Greenwood Publishing Company). Reprinted with permission of Greenwood Publishing Group, Inc., Westport, CT.

Illustrations

Unless otherwise acknowledged, all photographs are the property of Scott, Foresman and Company. Page abbreviations are as follows: (T) top, (C)center, (B)bottom, (L)left, (R)right.

Page 5(R): Bayer Staatsbibliothek, Munich; *Page 6:* The British Library; *Page 29:* Society of Antiquaries, London; *Page 41(L):* Worcester Art Museum, Worcester, Massachusetts, Sarah C. Garver Fund; *Page 41(R):* Worcester Art Museum, Worcester, Massachusetts, Gift of Mr. and Mrs. Albert W. Rice; *Page 53:* Courtesy of The Newberry Library, Chicago; *Page 75:* Courtesy American Antiquarian Society; *Page 82:* From the Collection of the Newport Historical Society; *Page 87:* The Metropolitan Museum of Art, Gift of Edgar William and Bernice Chrysler Garbisch, 1963; *Page 89:* Copyright Yale University Art Gallery; *Page 111(L):* Library of Congress; *Page 111(R):* Lewis Walpole Library; *Page 112:* Library of Congress; *Page 134:* Courtesy American Antiquarian Society; *Page 141:* National Portrait Gallery, Smithsonian Institution; *Page 154:* Library of Congress; *Page 176:* New York Public Library, Astor, Lenox and Tilden Foundations; *Page 179:* The New-York Historical Society, New York City; *Page 189:* Rare Book Room/New York Public Library, Astor, Lenox and Tilden Foundations; *Page 196:* Missouri Historical Society; *Page 205:* The New-York Historical Society, New York City; *Page 211:* Courtesy of the Canal Society of New York State; *Page 226:* Baker Library, Harvard Business School; *Page 229:* Library of Congress; *Page 233:* Library of Congress; *Page 238:* The Cleveland Museum of Art; *Page 251:* Whaling Museum, New Bedford, Massachusetts; *Page 260:* National Portrait Gallery/Art Resource, New York; *Page 267: Harper's New Monthly Magazine,* 1871; *Page 271:* The Museum of the City of New York, Harry T. Peters Collection; *Page 275:* Library of Congress; *Page 277: Liberty Almanac* 1852; *Page 282:* Courtesy of Stanfield Wells; *Page 297:* Massachusetts Historical Society; *Page 302:* Courtesy The Museum of the Confederacy, Richmond, Va; *Page 305:* By permission of the Houghton Library, Harvard University; *Page 312:* July 25, 1868/Harper's Weekly; *Page 316:* July 25, 1868/Harper's Weekly; *Page 326:* Library of Congress.